AF361393

Inflectional Morphology in Harmonic Serialism

Inflectional Morphology
in
Harmonic Serialism

Gereon Müller

SHEFFIELD UK   BRISTOL CT

Published by Equinox Publishing Ltd.

UK: Office 415, The Workstation, 15 Paternoster Row, Sheffield, South Yorkshire
S1 2BX

USA: ISD, 70 Enterprise Drive, Bristol, CT 06010

www.equinoxpub.com

First published 2020

British Library Cataloguing-in-Publication Data

A catalogue record for this book is available from the British Library.
ISBN-13 978 1 78179 808 9 (hardback)
         978 1 78179 809 6 (ePDF)

Library of Congress Cataloging-in-Publication Data

Names: Müller, Gereon, 1964- author.
Title: Inflectional morphology in harmonic serialism / Gereon Müller.
Description: Sheffield, UK; Bristol, CT: Equinox Publishing Ltd, 2020. |
    Series: Advances in optimality theory | Includes bibliographical references and index.
    | Summary: "This book shows that harmonic serialism can be substantiated as a
    viable approach to inflectional morphology" – Provided by publisher.
Identifiers: LCCN 2019052579 (print) | LCCN 2019052580 (ebook) | ISBN 9781781798089
    (hardback) | ISBN 9781781798096 (ebook)
Subjects: LCSH: Grammar, Comparative and general–Inflection. | Grammar,
    Comparative and general–Morphology. | Optimality theory (Linguistics)
Classification: LCC P251 .M85 2020 (print) | LCC P251 (ebook) | DDC 415/.95–dc23
LC record available at https://lccn.loc.gov/2019052579
LC ebook record available at https://lccn.loc.gov/2019052580

Typeset by the author

Contents

Acknowledgements

The present study owes its existence to a sabbatical I got from Universität Leipzig for the summer term of 2018 (April 1–September 30). The main bulk of the book was written while I was a visiting scholar at the UCLA linguistics department in May–June, 2018, and I am grateful to everyone who made this stay in Los Angeles such a productive and pleasant experience. In particular, I would like to thank Anoop Mahajan and Tim Stowell for hosting me at the department; the motorists of this vast and beautiful city for not creating a single dangerous situation on my bike rides; Antje Zajonz, Jason Müller and Kirke Müller for long-distance and on-site support; and Bernhard Rohrbacher for everything else.

This work grew out of two seminars, one on harmonic serialism (summer term 2017) and one on recent developments in morphological theory (winter term 2017/2018, co-taught with Philipp Weisser). An early version of chapter 3 was presented at the workshop *The Word and the Morpheme* at Humboldt Universität Berlin ("Minimize Satisfaction", September 23, 2016); the main insight of section 3 of chapter 2 (viz., that a faithful transfer of analyses of affix order from standard parallel optimality theory to harmonic serialism automatically gives rise to movement in morphology) was presented at the workshop *Strata* at Universität Leipzig ("Prospects of Harmonic Serialism in Morphology", July 20, 2017); some of the material in chapter 4 was presented at the workshop *Shrinking Trees in Morphology* at Universität Leipzig ("Structure Removal in Disjunctive Blocking", April 27, 2018); and the analysis of non-local stem allomorphy in chapter 5 was presented at the workshop *Connecting Roots and Affixes* at Masarykova Univerzita, Brno ("Non-Local Stem Allomorphy by Morphological Movement in Harmonic Serialism", May 13, 2019). I am grateful to the seminar participants and the audiences of the talks for comments and discussion.

More specifically, I would like to acknowledge the contributions to this study made by members of the Institut für Linguistik at Universität Leipzig: Johanna Benz, Anna Bliß, Robert Fritzsche, Daniel Gleim, Fabian Heck, Greg Kobele, Maria Kouneli, Christine Marquardt, Andrew Murphy, Mariia

Privizentseva, Johannes Schneider, Barbara Stiebels, Sören Tebay, Jochen Trommer, Philipp Weisser, and Joanna Zaleska. It would be difficult for me to think of a better context for pursuing this kind of research. Finally, I would like to thank the anonymous reviewer for helpful comments, and Kay Coleman for excellent editorial assistance.

This monograph might not have come into being without Gerhild Zybatow, who let me teach a compact course on optimality-theoretic syntax at Universität Leipzig in 1998, and Gisela Zifonun, who encouraged me to study inflectional morphology at IDS Mannheim in 2000. I am grateful to both.

Chapter 1

Background

1. Proof of Concept

Harmonic serialism is a strictly derivational version of optimality theory
that relies on repeated optimization procedures based on typically small
(and necessarily finite) candidate sets. From the very beginning (see Prince
& Smolensky (1993; 2004)), it has been identified as a possible alternative
to standard parallel optimization:

> Much of the analysis given in this book will be in the parallel mode, and
> some of the results will absolutely require it. But it is important to keep
> in mind that the serial/parallel distinction pertains to *Gen* and not to the
> issue of harmonic evaluation *per se*. It is an empirical question [...] Many
> different theories [...] can be equally well accommodated in Gen, and the
> framework of Optimality Theory *per se* involves no commmitment to any
> set of such assumptions.
>
> Prince & Smolensky (2004, 95–96)

However, for quite a while, harmonic serialism was either neglected or explicitly rejected (see in particular McCarthy (2000) for the latter option).
Over the last decade, this situation has changed. Harmonic serialism has
become a vibrant research programme in phonology (see McCarthy (2008;
2010; 2016), McCarthy, Kimper & Mullin (2012), Kimper (2016), Pruitt
(2012), Torres-Tamarit (2016), Elfner (2016), Hauser & Hughto (2018),
and Marquardt (2018), among others). Similarly, work has been carried
out on harmonic serialism in syntax (see, e.g., Heck & Müller (2007; 2013;
2016), Lahne (2008; 2009b), Georgi (2012), Assmann, Georgi, Heck, Müller
& Weisser (2015), and Murphy (2017; 2018; 2019)). Here the model is often referred to as *extremely local optimization*, but the basic assumptions
are fully identical to those of harmonic serialism in phonology. Essentially,
harmonic serialism (extremely local optimization) in syntax is a version of
minimalist, phase-based syntax (see Chomsky (1995; 2001; 2014b)) that

explicitly incorporates optimization procedures (like Merge over Move; see Chomsky (2000), Hornstein (2009), Weisser (2015), among many others).[1] However, there is basically no work whatsoever yet on (inflectional) morphology in harmonic serialism.[2]

Against this background, the central goal of this monograph is a fairly modest one; it sets out to deliver a proof of concept: If both phonology and syntax are organized as envisaged under harmonic serialism, one expects an approach to morphology in terms of harmonic serialism to be possible as well, successfully covering roughly the same ground as other models like Distributed Morphology (see Halle & Marantz (1993)), Paradigm Function Morphology (see Stump (2001)), or Network Morphology (see Brown & Hippisley (2012)); and in this monograph I want to argue that this is indeed the case. In the course of doing so, it will become evident that an approach to inflectional morphology in terms of harmonic serialism offers new and (I believe) interesting perspectives on core phenomena in inflectional morphology, like affix order, extended exponence, disjunctive blocking, locality of allomorphy, and *ABA patterns. Perhaps the most striking property of the new approach is that, unlike virtually all established approaches recognizing a separate morphological component of the grammar, it will provide a principled approach to *movement* of morphological exponents in words.

2. Inflectional Morphology

Theoretical approaches to inflectional morphology may differ along a number of dimensions. In what follows, I will sketch some of these dimensions, and highlight the respective decisions taken for the approach in terms of harmonic serialism to be developed in this book.

Two fundamental dimensions have been identified by Stump (2001): First, an approach to inflectional morphology may be incremental or realizational. In an incremental analysis, inflectional exponents add morpho-syntactic features that would otherwise not be present on a word form. In contrast, in a realizational analysis, inflectional exponents do not add morpho-syntactic features; all pieces of morpho-syntactic information (as

---

[1] For alternative attempts to reconcile optimality theory and the minimalist program that do not rely on harmonic serialism, see Pesetsky (1998), Broekhuis & Dekkers (2000), Broekhuis (2000; 2006; 2008), Fanselow & Ćavar (2001), Heck & Müller (2000), Samek-Lodovici (2013), and Broekhuis & Woolford (2013), among others.

[2] Optimal construction grammar as developed in Caballero & Inkelas (2013) shares with harmonic serialism the concept of repeated optimization, but differs substantially from it in most other respects.

they are required for syntactic operations) are independently available, and the exponent just realizes them. Second, an approach may be lexical or inferential. In a lexical analysis, inflectional exponents are viewed as (possibly abstract) morphemes that exist independently, as separate objects in the mental lexicon, whereas in an inferential analysis, inflectional exponents do not have morpheme status and do not exist independently, as separate objects. As Stump notes, cross-classification of these binary dimensions yields four types of morphological theories: There are (i) lexical-incremental approaches (see Lieber (1992), or the Minimalist Morphology approach developed in Wunderlich (1996; 1997b;c), Stiebels (2000; 2002; 2006), and related work), (ii) lexical-realizational approaches like Distributed Morphology (see Halle & Marantz (1993; 1994), and many other contributions, too numerous to mention here), (iii) inferential-incremental approaches, which are hardly attested, and (iv) inferential-realizational approaches like the models adopted in Matthews (1991), Anderson (1992), and Aronoff (1994), Paradigm Function Morphology (see Stump (2001; 2016)), and Network Morphology (see Corbett & Fraser (1993), Brown & Hippisley (2012)). From this perspective, the approach to be developed in what follows qualifies as 'lexical-realizational', like Distributed Morphology: I assume that morphological exponents are stored as such in the mental lexicon, and they realize existing morpho-syntactic features in the course of morphological exponence.

Another dimension where morphological theories differ concerns the place of morphological operations in the grammar. Basically, there would seem to be four possibilities. First, inflectional morphology can be pre-syntactic (as, e.g., in Minimalist Morphology, or, more generally, lexicalist approaches to syntax, such as Di Sciullo & Williams (1987), Williams (1981; 1994), or Chomsky (1993)). Second, inflectional morphology can be post-syntactic (as in Distributed Morphology). Third, inflectional morphology can be independent of syntax, and work in parallel (as, e.g., in Paradigm Function Grammar). And fourth, inflectional morphology can take place in the syntax. I think it is fair to conclude that most of these last kinds of approaches suffer from not being able to accomodate the substantial evidence to the effect that there are clear differences between words and sentences, both with respect to the underlying mechanisms of structure-building and with respect to the ontology of the objects involved. To name just two very obvious fundamental differences: Nearly all current models of inflectional morphology envisage underspecification and competition resolution by specificity – concepts that do not seem to play a role in syntax; and inflection class features are prevalent in the morphological systems of the world's languages but, almost by definition, absent in syntax (in the sense that no syntactic rule ever refers to this information – the feature thus qualifies as 'morphomic'); see Aronoff (1994). However, this shortcoming does not necessarily arise in all approaches treating inflectional morphology as a part of syntax; e.g., in Bruening's (2017) Consolidated Morphology approach, inflectional exponence exclusively involves parts of the single syntactic tree below the X^0 level, and specific morphological operations and principles are taken to apply there.

The approach in terms of harmonic serialism laid out below is strictly pre-syntactic. For concreteness, I assume that there is a morphological component that follows the lexicon but precedes syntax, as in (1) (see Müller (2004; 2006a), Alexiadou & Müller (2008)).

(1)   *Components of grammar:*
        Lexicon → Morphology → Syntax → Phonological Form, Logical
        Form

Given an organization of the grammar as in Chomsky (2001), there already is a component between the lexicon and the syntax, viz., the numeration, which is a collection of lexical items taken from the lexicon before the syntactic derivation starts. Indeed, I would like to suggest that inflectional morphology takes place in this component.[3] Consequently, words enter the syntax fully inflected, with all morphological exponents already in place. The approach, then, basically conforms to the Strong Lexicalist Hypothesis (see Chomsky (1970; 1993), Halle (1973), Di Sciullo & Williams (1987)).[4]

---

[3] A level of grammar is standardly defined by the existence of constraints or rules that need to apply here but not (necessarily) elsewhere; see, e.g., Chomsky (1981; 1993), Riemsdijk & Williams (1981), and Sternefeld (1991). In Heck & Müller (2000) and Müller (2011a), it is argued that there are good reasons to adopt constraints on numerations, which then establishes the numeration as a proper level of grammar.

[4] Two caveats. First, throughout this book, I have very little to say about derivational morphology and its place in the grammar. On the one hand, it is conceivable (and would be perfectly compatible with the analyses of inflectional morphology in this book) that derivational morphology takes place in the syntax whereas inflectional morphology is pre-syntactic (see Alexiadou & Müller (2008) for such an approach); on such a view, a German nominative plural noun like, say, *Plan-ung-en* ('plan(n)-ing-s') would pre-syntactically involve two separate items: an inflected abstract noun [N *ung-en*] and a verb stem [V *plan*], which are then combined via head movement of V to N in the syntax. Alternatively, derivational morphology may also be pre-syntactic. Mostly for the sake of concreteness, this latter option will be presupposed in what follows (but it will in fact also be required in the brief foray into derivational morphology at the end of chapter 2, in section 3.7.). And second, whereas the pre-syntactic approach arguably offers the simplest possible harmonic serialist analyses of the phenomena under discussion in the

A final dimension worth addressing concerns the formal nature of the operations that are postulated for the morphological component. At one end of the scale are approaches like Distributed Morphology, which embraces a number of operations which have no counterpart in either syntax or phonology. For instance, vocabulary insertion, fission, fusion, local dislocation, and lowering are all structure-manipulating operations that do not exist anywhere outside morphology.[5] At the other end of the scale are approaches where it is assumed that all morphological operations should ideally be justified outside of morphology. I will assume the latter. In line with this, the approach to inflectional morphology to be developed here does not rely on specific substitution/insertion transformations applying to terminal nodes (as in Halle & Marantz (1993)), or entire subtrees (see Ackema & Neeleman (2003; 2004) and Caha (2013), among others), or spans (see Merchant (2015), Svenonius (2016), and Ermolaeva & Kobele (2019)); rather, morphological exponence is exclusively brought about by regular structure-building operations.

More specifically, I make the following assumptions about inflectional morphology in the numeration.

(2)   *Inflectional morphology in the numeration:*
    a.   For each basic stem (V, N, A, P, D, C, ...) α in the lexicon, there is a language-specific set of features that it can be characterized by (see Stump's (2001) concept of a set of well-formed morpho-syntactic properties).
    b.   A stem α is taken from the lexicon with its inherent features (e.g., inflection class and gender features). These features are always fully specified.
    c.   Non-inherent features are added in the numeration. These features are also always fully specified; they provide the context for underspecified inflection markers.[6]

---

present book, it is worth pointing out that it would for the most part also be possible to transfer the analyses given here to a post- or intra-syntactic approach.

[5] Incidentally, this does not necessarily hold for impoverishment, which deletes morphosyntactic features (see Bonet (1991) and Halle & Marantz (1993; 1994), among many others); see Keine (2010a) for evidence for this operation in syntax. Similarly, the even more radical deletion operation of obliteration (see Arregi & Nevins (2012)) arguably has a direct counterpart in syntax (see Müller (2017)). I will come back to this issue in chapter 4.

[6] Note that the assumptions (2-b) and (2-c) will later (in chapter 5) be modified to account for stem allomorphy.

  d.   Triggered by features on α, inflectional exponents β_1, β_2, γ_1, γ_2 ... are taken from the lexicon (where all β_i's compete for realizing a β-position in the ultimate word form).[7] All of an inflectional exponent's features are inherent; but they may often be underspecified.

  e. α successively combines with the optimal β_i, γ_j, ..., thereby ultimately producing the full word form.

  f.   This fully inflected word composed of stem and affixes is then transferred to the syntactic component. The syntactic component cannot see the internal structure of the word generated in the morphological component; but it can access all the morpho-syntactic features associated with the stem, and carry out Agree operations with them (see Chomsky (2001), Bruening (2017)).

The single most important aspect of this model is the successive combination of the stem with the optimal inflectional exponents for each position; this is where harmonic serialism comes into play.

3. Harmonic Serialism

3.1. *Basic Assumptions*

Standard parallel optimality-theoretic tenets are that the wellformedness of linguistic expressions in each grammatical component (phonology, morphology, syntax) is determined by constraints of a *H-Eval* (harmony evaluation) part of the grammar which are (i) violable, (ii) ranked and (iii) universal, with different constraint rankings accounting for cross-linguistic variation; see Prince & Smolensky (1993; 2004). Among the competing candidates of a given candidate set, one candidate emerges as *optimal* if there is no candidate with a better constraint profile; see (3).[8]

(3)   *Optimality:*
        A candidate C_i is optimal with respect to some constraint ranking $<\mathrm{Con}_1 \gg \mathrm{Con}_2 \gg \ldots \gg \mathrm{Con}_n>$ iff there is no other candidate C_j in the same candidate set that has a better *constraint profile*.

---

[7] This corresponds to a rule block in inferential-realizational approaches (cf. Anderson (1992), Stump (2001)), and to a functional morpheme in Distributed Morphology (cf. Halle & Marantz (1993)).

[8] Under certain conditions, more than one candidate may emerge as optimal in a candidate set; the definition in (3) reflects this possibility.

The concept of a better constraint profile can be defined as in (4).

(4)   *Constraint profile*:
       C_j has a better constraint profile than C_i if there is a constraint Con_k
       such that (a) and (b) hold:
       a. C_j satisfies Con_k better than C_i.
       b.   There is no constraint Con_l that is ranked higher than Con_k,
             and for which C_i and C_j differ.

Harmonic serialism maintains all these assumptions of standard parallel optimality theory. Where the two models diverge concerns the interaction of the *H-Eval* component based on (3) and (4) with the *Gen* (generator) component that creates the competing candidates. In standard parallel optimality theory, all generation operations precede a single step of harmony evaluation.[9] In contrast, in harmonic serialism, generation and harmony evaluation constantly alternate. More specifically, given an initial input representation, competing output candidates are generated that differ from the immediate input by application of at most one operation. After this, the optimal output is selected based on (3), (4). This output then forms the input for the next generation procedure, and so on. A property that inherently characterizes this approach is that optimal outputs will have to gradually improve the constraint profile. Once such gradual improvement is not possible anymore (i.e., where the optimal output is one that leaves the immediately preceding input unchanged), the derivation converges on a final output representation. Thus, the model looks as in (5).

(5)   *Harmonic serialism* (McCarthy (2008), Heck & Müller (2007)):
       a.   Given some input I_i, the candidate set $CS_i = \{O_{i1}, O_{i2}, \ldots O_{in}\}$
             is generated by applying at most *one operation* to I_i.
       b.   The output O_{ij} with the best constraint profile is selected as
             optimal.
       c. O_{ij} forms the input I_{ij} for the next generation step producing a
             new candidate set $CS_j = \{O_{ij1}, O_{ij2}, \ldots O_{ijn}\}$.

---

[9] A terminological clarification: Following McCarthy (2016) and many others, throughout this monograph the notion of *standard parallel optimality theory* refers to the approach adopted in Prince & Smolensky (1993; 2004). This should not be taken to imply that an approach along these lines would necessarily count as a/the "standard" approach in any of the relevant empirical subfields as such; while this would arguably be true for phonology (notwithstanding alternative optimality-theoretic models like output/output correspondence, and rule-based phonology), it is most emphatically not true for either morphology or syntax.

    d.   The output O_{ijk} with the best constraint profile is selected as optimal.

    e.   Candidate set generation stops (i.e., the derivation converges) when the output of an optimization procedure is identical to the input (i.e., when the constraint profile cannot be improved anymore).

As noted above, harmonic serialism has so far only been pursued in phonology and syntax. In what follows, I will therefore introduce the workings of this model based on analyses of phonological and syntactic phenomena. I will focus on two different aspects. First, many analyses given in standard parallel optimality theory can be transferred to harmonic serialist analyses without problems. Second, harmonic serialist analyses in some cases emerge as empirically superior since they permit reference to intermediate representations.

3.2. Transfer

3.2.1. Complex Onset Avoidance in Classical Arabic

Consider first a simple optimization procedure in phonology, with an analysis in standard parallel optimality theory as the starting point and a straightforward transfer to harmonic serialism (see McCarthy (2010)). In Classical Arabic, complex onsets are prohibited in optimal outputs; this is encoded by an undominated constraint *Complex-Onset. Consequently, if the input that is part of the mental lexicon starts with two consonants, an epenthetic vowel is inserted at the beginning, in violation of a lower-ranked Dep constraint. However, given that the requirement that syllables have onsets (Onset) also outranks Dep, an additional epenthetic glottal stop is also added to the optimal output form. A candidate that carries out vowel epenthesis between the two consonantal segments would do without the additional Dep violation; but this candidate is excluded by Contiguity. Other repair strategies like deletion of one of the two initial consonants are not an option because of a sufficiently highly ranked Max constraint that blocks deletion. The relevant constraints are given in (6).

(6)   a.   *Complex-Onset:
           Syllables do not have complex onsets.

    b.   Max:
           If material is present in the input, it is present in the output.

    c.   Contiguity:
           Segments that form a contiguous string in the input form a contiguous string in the output.

    d.   ONSET:
        Syllables have onsets.
    e.   DEP:
        If material is present in the output, it is present in the input.

In standard parallel optimality theory, the competition of outputs is resolved by a single optimization procedure based on the initial input, as in the tableau in (7).

(7)   *Double epenthesis in Classical Arabic* (standard parallel optimality theory):

I_1: /ʕal/ ('Do!')	*COMPLEX-ONSET	MAX	CONTIG	ONSET	DEP
O_{11}: ffal	*!				
O_{12}: fal		*!			
O_{13}: ifʕal				*!	*
☞O_{14}: ʔifʕal					**
O_{15}: fiʕal			*!		*

Next to the candidates shown here, a huge (in fact, without further restrictions, infinite) number of further candidates are generated (via additional epenthesis operations, or via modification of existing segments), all of which do not give rise to a better constraint profile.

    The harmonic serialist version of the account eventually yields the same optimal output but relies on a sequence of optimizations to produce it since each output can diverge from the (immediate) input by application of at most one operation only; given that O_{14} in (7) has two epenthesis operations, it is clear that it cannot be reached in one single step. All other things being equal, the first optimization procedure must get rid of the violation of the highest-ranked constraint incurred by the input, viz., that of *COMPLEX-ONSET; see (8).

(8)   *Double epenthesis in Classical Arabic* (harmonic serialism, step 1):

I_1: /ffal/	*COMPLEX-ONSET	MAX	CONTIG	ONSET	DEP
O_{11}: ffal	*!				
O_{12}: fal		*!			
☞O_{13}: ifʕal				*	*
O_{14}: fiʕal			*!		*

With O_{14} in (7) not being generable, O_{13} (which avoids a *COMPLEX-ONSET violation via i-epenthesis but now violates ONSET because there is no initial consonant) emerges as the optimal candidate in (8); as before, internal i-epenthesis is excluded by CONTIGUITY (see O_{14}). In the second step, a glottal stop is added so as to get rid of the Onset violation. This produces a new Dep violation, but this is unproblematic because of the low ranking of this constraint; see (9).[10]

(9)   *Double epenthesis in Classical Arabic* (harmonic serialism, step 2):

I₁₃: /ifʕal/	*Complex-Onset	Max	Contig	Onset	Dep
O₁₃₁: ifʕal				*!	
O₁₃₂: ffʕal	*!	*			
☞ O₁₃₃: ʔifʕal					*
O₁₃₄: ififʕal			*!	*	*

Finally, (10) shows that the constraint profile of O₁₃₃ is as good as it gets; if O₁₃₃ is used as the input for a further optimization procedure, the same output will be the winner. Thus, the derivation converges.

(10)   *Double epenthesis in Classical Arabic* (harmonic serialism, step 3):

I₁₃₃: /ʔifʕal/	*Complex-Onset	Max	Contig	Onset	Dep
☞ O₁₃₃₁: ʔifʕal					
O₁₃₃₂: ʔififʕal			*!		*
O₁₃₃₃: ʔifʕa		*!			
O₁₃₃₄: ifʕal		*!		*	
O₁₃₃₅: ʔifʕali					*!

Taking this case to be representative, it can be concluded that many phonological analyses couched in standard parallel optimality theory can be straightforwardly transferred to harmonic serialism. In the following subsection, I illustrate transferability for syntax.

3.2.2.   Do Support with Negation in English

The basic generalization about the occurrence of expletive *do* in negative environments in English as in (11-e) (and its concurrent absence in positive contexts) is that it instantiates a last resort (or repair) phenomenon; on this view, *do* support is possible only because the addition of negation creates severe problems for other items in the clause – in particular, for V and the subject DP. These problems are documented in (11-a-d); they are such that only *do* support (in violation of a Dep constraint) can solve them.

---

[10] Note that the original Dep violation triggered by i-epenthesis is gone in the outputs here if we assume (as I will throughout this book) that faithfulness violations are only determined with respect to the immediate input; earlier inputs are not accessible anymore at this point.

This hypothesis is implemented in standard parallel optimality theory in Grimshaw (1997, 381–393).

(11) a. *[NegP Not [VP Mary left]]
      b. *[NegP Mary₁ not [VP t₁ left]]
      c. *[TP Mary₁ [T –] [NegP not [VP t₁ left]]]
      d. *[TP Mary₁ [T left₂] [NegP not [VP t₁ t₂]]]
      e.   [TP Mary₁ [T did] [NegP not [VP t₁ leave]]]

The constraints that play a role in the analysis are given in (12).

(12) a. NO-LEX-MOV:
          Movement of lexical heads is prohibited (assign a * for every trace of a lexical head).
      b. CASE:
          The head of a DP chain must be in a case position (where a case position is part of a verbal projection).
      c. OB-HD:
          A projection has a (non-empty) head.
      d. SUBJ:
          The highest A-specifier of a sentence is filled by an argument.
      e. FULL-INT:
          Expletives must not be inserted (this blocks *do* support).
      f. STAY:
          Movement is prohibited (assign a * for every trace).

Note that FULL-INT (violated by *do* support), STAY (violated by movement), and NO-LEX-MOV (violated by movement of lexical V) can all be conceived of as DEP constraints, given that neither expletive verbs nor traces are part of the input.[11] The ranking suggested by Grimshaw (1997) is given in (13).

(13) NO-LEX-MOV ≫ CASE ≫ OB-HD ≫ SUBJ ≫ FULL-INT ≫ STAY

(14) illustrates the necessity of *do* support in this context. A basic assumption concerning the structure of the output candidates is that the size of clauses is variable, subject to optimization. A minimal clause is a

---

[11] As a matter of fact, it is not really clear what the input should be taken to be in standard parallel optimality-theoretic syntax. In Heck et al. (2002), it is argued that ultimately the concept of input should be fully dispensed with in optimality-theoretic syntax. As we will see, things are different with harmonic serialist approaches to syntax, though.

VP (which includes the external argument – which, of course, is then not strictly speaking external), but there may in principle be arbitrarily many additional extended projections on top of it. Negative *not*, by assumption, heads a separate Neg projection which must include the VP. In principle, one might therefore assume output O_{11} (= (11-a)) to be optimal in (14). However, given that NegP also has a potential A-specifier position, the subject DP is now not the highest A-specifier anymore, and a fatal violation of SUBJ results.

O_{12} (= (11-b)) tries to remedy this problem by moving the subject DP to SpecNeg. This gives rise to an unproblematic STAY violation; however, it also incurs a fatal violation of high-ranked CASE (because NegP hosting the head of the subject DP chain is not a verbal projection).

In O_{13} (= (11-c)), this problem is tackled by moving the subject DP even further, to a higher projection outside of NegP. However, this projection, according to Grimshaw's assumptions, is still not a verbal one (it does not have any independent features, qualifying as a purely positional category; see Stechow & Sternefeld (1988)); in addition, it brings about an additional OB-HD violation since the new projection does not have an overt head (plus a further irrelevant STAY violation). Thus, O_{13} is harmonically bounded by O_{12} (it cannot become optimal under any reranking of constraints; see Prince & Smolensky (1993; 2004)).

The obvious way to solve all these problems is a version of O_{13} where the empty head position of the top projection is filled by movement of V, as in O_{14} (= (11-d)): Now SUBJ is satisfied (the DP is in the highest A-position), CASE is satisfied (after V movement, it is part of a verbal projection), and OB-HD is satisfied as well (due to V movement). Thus, one might think that this is now the optimal candidate.

For contexts with auxiliary or modal verbs, this is indeed the case (cf. *Mary has not left, Mary will not leave*); however, V movement in O_{14} violates the highest-ranked constraint NO-LEX-MOV. Against this background, insertion of *do* in O_{15} (= (11-e)) emerges as the optimal solution; this candidate only violates FULL-INT (because of *do* support) and STAY (twice, because of successive-cyclic DP movement).[12]

---

[12] Yet another candidate must be excluded that base-generates the subject DP in its surface position and thus does without STAY violations. Such an output fatally violates a high-ranked (theta-related) constraint demanding base-generation of the subject close to the verb.

(14) *Negation and* do *support* (standard parallel optimality theory):

I_1: V, DP, Neg	No-Lex-Mvt	Case	Ob-Hd	Subj	Full-Int	Stay
O_{11}: [Neg [$_{VP}$ DP$_1$ V]]				*!		
O_{12}: [DP$_1$ Neg [$_{VP}$ t$_1$ V]]		*!				*
O_{13}: [DP$_1$ – [t$_1$ Neg [$_{VP}$ t$_1$ V]]]		*!	*			**
O_{14}: [DP$_1$ V$_2$ [t$_1$ Neg [$_{VP}$ t$_1$ t$_2$]]]	*!					***
☞ O_{15}: [DP$_1$ did$_2$ [t$_1$ Neg [$_{VP}$ t$_1$ V]]]					*	**

In contrast, consider the situation without negation; see (15).

(15) a. [$_{VP}$ Mary left]
    b. *[$_{TP}$ Mary$_1$ [$_T$ –] [$_{VP}$ t$_1$ left]]
    c. *[$_{TP}$ Mary$_1$ [$_T$ left$_2$] [$_{VP}$ t$_1$ t$_2$]]
    d. *[$_{TP}$ Mary$_1$ [$_T$ did] [$_{VP}$ t$_1$ leave]]

As illustrated in (16), *do* support is blocked here because the Full-Int violation incurred by inserting an expletive V does not lead to an improved constraint profile – in particular, Subj and Case can all be satisfied without adding additional projections for the subject DP since the VP can be assumed to be all that there is in the clause.

(16) *Absence of* do *support without negation* (standard parallel optimality theory):

I_1: V, DP	No-Lex-Mvt	Case	Ob-Hd	Subj	Full-Int	Stay
☞ O_{11}: [$_{VP}$ DP$_1$ V]						
O_{12}: [DP$_1$ – [$_{VP}$ t$_1$ V]]		*!	*			*
O_{13}: [DP$_1$ V$_2$ [$_{VP}$ t$_1$ t$_2$]]	*!					**
O_{14}: [DP$_1$ did$_2$ [$_{VP}$ t$_1$ V]]					*!	*

The question arises whether it is possible to faithfully transfer Grimshaw's standard parallel optimality-theoretic analysis to an analysis in terms of harmonic serialism. This is the case. In what follows, I will outline two possible reconstructions.

First Reconstruction   As a first step, note that there are a few other rankings than the one in (13) which are compatible with the evidence from English (this is explicitly acknowledged in Grimshaw (1997, 375)). Thus, suppose that the ranking is changed to (17), where Subj is promoted (it can easily be verified that this would not change anything in the parallel analysis just sketched).

(17) No-Lex-Mov ≫ Subj ≫ Case ≫ Ob-Hd ≫ Full-Int ≫ Stay

Furthermore, suppose that one of Grimshaw's assumptions is given up –
viz., the idea that clause size is inherently variable. For concreteness, assume that all clauses have to be minimally TPs, perhaps even CPs. This
can be implemented by postulating that a category T exists independently
in the lexicon, is selected in numerations, and subsequently needs to be
used in the derivation. This latter consequence follows if a high-ranked
(or undominated) constraint EXHAUST NUMERATION is adopted that ensures that eventually, all items that are initially placed in the numeration
(and then subjected to morphological realization; see above) are used in
the syntactic derivation.[13]

(18) EXHAUST NUMERATION (ExNUM):
      If an optimal syntactic output is identical to its input (= conver-
      gence), and the numeration is not yet empty, a new item from the nu-
      meration is selected and added to the current optimal output, forming
      an input set consisting of two items.

Finally, I will assume (following Heck & Müller (2007; 2013)) that basic
structure-building in harmonic serialism is brought about by designated
features [•X•] (for subcategorization and movement) that need to be discharged (and deleted) by Merge operations; the constraint that forces this
is the MERGE CONDITION in (19).

(19) MERGE CONDITION (MC):
      Structure-building features ([•X•]) participate in Merge.

With this in mind, consider now a faithful transfer of Grimshaw's analysis of *do* support in negative environments to harmonic serialism. The
initial numeration of (11-e) will contain four items: $V_{[•D•]}$, D(P) (*Mary*
– as noted in the last footnote, this is a simplification, given that DPs
can be of arbitrary complexity, and will ultimately call for a more general
concept of workspace supplementing the concept of numeration), $Neg_{[•V•]}$,

---

[13] Two remarks. First, ExNUM is clearly a constraint that is of a different kind than
standard constraints of the *H-Eval* system; in line with this, it seems likely that it always
has to be undominated in a language. One might therefore assume that it is in fact a
meta-constraint outside of *H-Eval*; I will come back to this question in chapter 3 and in
chapter 6, when discussing a core constraint for the morphological component (MINSAT)
that is similarly different from other constraints. Still, for reasons of perspicuity, I
include ExNUM in the optimality-theoretic competitions. And second, the system based
on ExNUM is somewhat simplified; ultimately, the more general concept of workspace
will be have to be postulated instead of (only) the numeration; see Heck & Müller (2007;
2013).

and $T_{[\bullet Neg \bullet]}$. The first step in the harmonic serialist analysis starts with selecting $V_{[\bullet D \bullet]}$; then DP is added in accordance with ExNum. The first step of structure-building then involves Merge of V and DP, as in (20).

(20) *Negation and* do *support* (harmonic serialism, step 1):

I_1: $V_{[\bullet D \bullet]}$, DP	Ex Num	MC	No-Lex-Mvt	Subj	Case	Ob-Hd	Full-Int	Stay
O_{11}: $V_{[\bullet D \bullet]}$, DP		*!						
☞ O_{12}: [vp DP V]								

The next step yields convergence (not indicated here), so $Neg_{[\bullet V \bullet]}$ is taken from the numeration and added to the input (if no selection from the numeration takes place, ExNum will be fatally violated); see (21).

(21) *Negation and* do *support* (harmonic serialism, step 2):

I_{12}: [vp DP V], $Neg_{[\bullet V \bullet]}$	Ex Num	MC	No-Lex-Mvt	Subj	Case	Ob-Hd	Full-Int	Stay
O_{121}: [vp DP V], $Neg_{[\bullet V \bullet]}$		*!						
☞ O_{122}: [NegP Neg [vp DP V]]				*				

As indicated, the optimal output creates a problem that was not present in the input: Due to Merge of Neg (triggered by higher-ranked MC), a temporary violation of lower-ranked Subj is now unavoidable. To get rid of the Subj violation, DP moves in the next step, thereby giving rise to violations of the lower-ranked Case and Stay constraints. Recall that the ranking of Subj and Case was irrelevant in Grimshaw's original parallel analysis; here it becomes important.[14]

(22) *Negation and* do *support* (harmonic serialism, step 3):

I_{122}: [NegP Neg [vp DP V]]	Ex Num	MC	No-Lex-Mvt	Subj	Case	Ob-Hd	Full-Int	Stay
O_{1221}: [NegP Neg [vp DP V]]				*!				
☞ O_{1222}: [NegP DP_1 [Neg [vp t_1 V]]]					*			*

The next step again yields convergence. Since $T_{[\bullet Neg \bullet]}$ is still part of the numeration, this means that ExNum will now spring into action and require addition of $T_{[\bullet Neg \bullet]}$ to the input. In the following step, $T_{[\bullet Neg \bullet]}$ is merged with NegP (due to MC), at the cost of a reintroduction of a Subj violation –

---

[14] Whereas MC can trigger movement in the same way that it triggers basic structure-building, via designated features, here the movement operation is repair-driven (i.e., not feature-driven, but triggered by a constraint); see Heck & Müller (2003)).

DP has earlier undergone movement, but as a consequence of the presence of T, it does not occupy the highest A-specifier anymore. In addition, the CASE violation is preserved. Furthermore, there now is a violation of OB-HD since T is empty.[15] This is illustrated in (23).

(23) *Negation and* do *support* (harmonic serialism, step 4):

I_{1222}: [$_{NegP}$ DP$_1$ [Neg [$_{VP}$ t$_1$ V]]], T$_{[\bullet Neg\bullet]}$	Ex Num	MC	No-Lex-Mvt	Subj	Case	Ob-Hd	Full-Int	Stay
O_{12221}: [$_{NegP}$ DP$_1$ [Neg [$_{VP}$ t$_1$ V]]], T$_{[\bullet Neg\bullet]}$		*!			*			
☞O_{12222}: [$_{TP}$ T [$_{NegP}$ DP$_1$ [Neg [$_{VP}$ t$_1$ V]]]]				*	*	*		

The constraint profile of O_{12222} is improved in the next optimization procedure by an additional movement step of DP$_1$. Given that T counts as a verbal projection (i.e., assuming that it is not a featureless positional category, like the respective functional projection in Grimshaw's original approach – which makes sense since T is now assumed to be part of the numeration), this gets rid of both the SUBJ and CASE violations, while preserving the OB-HD violation and introducing an irrelevant STAY violation. The alternative output that moves V to satisfy OB-HD violates not only SUBJ and CASE, but also high-ranked NO-LEX-MVT; and an alternative in terms of *do* insertion in T also pays for the satisfaction of OB-HD by fatal violations of SUBJ and CASE (plus a violation of FULL-INT).

(24) *Negation and* do *support* (harmonic serialism, step 5):

I_{12222}: [$_{TP}$ T [$_{NegP}$ DP$_1$ [Neg [$_{VP}$ t$_1$ V]]]]	Ex Num	MC	No-L Mvt	Subj	Case	Ob-Hd	Full-Int	Stay
O_{122221}: [$_{TP}$ T [$_{NegP}$ DP$_1$ [Neg [$_{VP}$ t$_1$ V]]]]				*!	*	*		
☞O_{122222}: [$_{TP}$ DP$_1$ [T [$_{NegP}$ t$_1$ [Neg [$_{VP}$ t$_1$ V]]]]]						*		*
O_{122223}: [$_{TP}$ V$_2$-T [$_{NegP}$ DP$_1$ [Neg [$_{VP}$ t$_1$ t$_2$]]]]			*!	*	*			*
O_{122224}: [$_{TP}$ do-T [$_{NegP}$ DP$_1$ [Neg [$_{VP}$ t$_1$ V]]]]				*!	*		*	

The current optimal output still has a violation of OB-HD that can in principle be removed in one of two ways: Either V is moved (thereby fatally violating NO-LEX-MVT), or *do* is inserted (which induces a violation of the lower-ranked FULL-INT). The latter strategy is optimal.

---

[15] Whether STAY continues to be violated or not depends on the exact interpretation of (12-f). In Grimshaw's original conception of STAY as a constraint on traces, the violation would be maintained; under an interpretation of STAY as a faithfulness constraint prohibiting scenarios where some item shows up in a different position in input and output, there is no STAY violation anymore if the movement trace is 'old'. I here follow the latter interpretation, though nothing depends on this in the present context.

(25) *Negation and* do *support* (harmonic serialism, step 6):

I_{122222}: $[_{TP}$ DP$_1$ [T $[_{NegP}$ t$_1$ [Neg $[_{VP}$ t$_1$ V]]]]]	Ex Num	MC	No-L Mvt	Subj	Case	Ob-Hd	Full-Int	Stay
$O_{1222221}$: $[_{TP}$ DP$_1$ [T $[_{NegP}$ t$_1$ [Neg $[_{VP}$ t$_1$ V]]]]]						*!		
$O_{1222222}$: $[_{TP}$ DP$_1$ [V$_2$-T $[_{NegP}$ t$_1$ [Neg $[_{VP}$ t$_1$ t$_2$]]]]]			*!					*
☞$O_{1222223}$: $[_{TP}$ DP$_1$ [do-T $[_{NegP}$ t$_1$ [Neg $[_{VP}$ t$_1$ V]]]]]							*	

Finally, since there is no way to further improve the constraint profile, and the numeration (by assumption) is empty, the optimization step taking $O_{1222223}$ as the input yields convergence.

So far, so good. However, at this point the question arises of how the absence of *do* support can be derived if there is no negation (hence, no NegP); see (15-a) vs. (15-d). As it stands, one might think that Ob-Hd would trigger realization of T by *do* in the same way in this environment. The underlying issue here is that I have assumed that T is always part of the numeration, and thus needs to show up eventually in the sentence, given ExNum. This problem can be solved if we distinguish between projections that are *activated* and projections that are not; for present purposes, a projection in the extended projection of V may count as activiated if its minimal domain (specifier or complement) contains material that is not part of the extended projection of V. Based on this assumption, Ob-Hd must be modified as in (26) (compare (12-c)).

(26) Ob-Hd:
      An activated projection has a (non-empty) head.

Similarly, Subj needs to be revised as in (27).

(27) Subj:
      The highest A-specifier of an activated verbal projection is filled by an argument.

Given (27), Ob-Hd triggers *do* support in T, and Subj triggers subject movement to SpecT, if negation is present (since TP is then activated); in contrast, the optimal output is an empty, inert TP dominating a VP including the subject in its base position if negation is not present. This closely corresponds to Grimshaw's assumptions about the structure of these kinds of clauses (the only difference being absence vs. inactivity of TP).[16]

Second Reconstruction Still, it can be noted that the first reconstruction departs from Grimshaw's (1997) original approach in two respects. First,

---

[16] The distinction between activity and inactivity also extends to the CP level, thereby capturing Grimshaw's approach to complementizer drop and *do* support in wh-questions.

as we have seen, the presence of T is obligatory throughout; and second, the constraint CASE, while fully compatible with the whole analysis, does not actually remove any output from the candidate set in the above optimization procedures. For these reasons, I briefly sketch an alternative reconstruction in harmonic serialism in what follows.

Thus, suppose that T is not in fact part of the initial numeration but can be added at any given point of the derivation if that does not lead to a worse constraint profile. Suppose further that the derivation has reached the optimal output O_{1222} in (22) (step 3), which violates CASE. In the next step, T is merged with NegP. This, of course, does not by itself lead to a CASE satisfaction, so it must minimally not deteriorate the constraint profile. To ensure this, the constraints that adding T would seem to violate – SUBJ and OB-HD – must be reformulated in such a way that they are in fact not violated at this stage; see (28).[17]

(28) a. SUBJ:
          If α is the highest A-specifier in the input, it must be filled by
          an argument in the output.
      b. OB-HD:
          If a projection is present in the input, it has a (non-empty) head
          in the output.

Given (28-ab), merging T with NegP is an option because the constraint profile does not get worse: SUBJ and OB-HD are not violated by the TP (without a specifier and without a non-empty head) in the output because TP was not present in the input. However, this does not yet suffice: It has to be ensured that adding T is in fact *obligatory* at this point. This can be derived from CASE if it is assumed that case can generally be assigned under m-command (i.e., either to a specifier, or under c-command; see below). On this view, adding T leads to a CASE satisfaction, and the competing output that does not add T is excluded by this constraint. For the next optimization step, SUBJ and OB-HD become relevant because TP is now present in the input. First, movement of the subject DP satisfies SUBJ; and finally, OB-HD triggers *do* support. If negation is not present, the initial problem with CASE will not arise, and adding a TP will be blocked (assuming that this violates some low-ranked constraint on structure-building).

Thus, irrespective of which of the two reconstructions is ultimately to be preferred, Grimshaw's original analysis based on standard parallel

---

[17] Markedness constraints of this type, which refer to both input and output, will indeed play a role later in the book, in chapters 4 and 6.

optimality theory has proven to be transferable to an approach in terms of harmonic serialism without changing the crucial insights behind her analysis (in particular, that the interaction of NO-LEX-MVT, SUBJ, CASE, and OB-HD forces *do* support). As in the case of phonology, closer scrutiny suggests that this result can be generalized: Most successful syntactic analyses developed in standard parallel optimality theory can be transferred to harmonic serialism without major problems, and without altering the gist of a proposal.

Of course, to show that harmonic serialism is at least a viable alternative to standard parallel optimality theory, empirical arguments are called for that support the former approach over the latter. I turn to two of these arguments (one for phonology, one for syntax) in the next subsection.

3.3. Intermediate Outputs

The two arguments in support of harmonic serialism to be discussed here take the same form; they show that the existence of an intermediate output representation is crucial to determine the optimal candidate.

3.3.1. Stress-Syncope Interaction in Macushi Carib

McCarthy (2008; 2010) argues that the interaction of stress assignment and vowel deletion in Macushi Carib favors an approach in terms of harmonic serialism. The empirical generalization underlying the system is straightforward: Stress assignment is predictable; foot formation takes place from left to right, and the feet are iambs. All the vowels that do not receive stress this way are then deleted. Data illustrating the pattern are given in (29).

(29)	Underlying	Stress	Syncope	Transl.
a.	piripi	(pirí)(pí)	(prí)(pí)	'spindle'
b.	wanamari	(waná)(marí)	(wná)(mrí)	'mirror'
c.	u-wanamari-rɨ	(uwá)(namá)(rirɨ)	(wá)(nmá)(rrɨ)	'my mirror'

The main constraints required to model this interaction of stress and syncope in McCarthy's analysis are given in (30).

(30) a.   PARSE-Σ:
          Syllables are parsed into metrical feet.

      b.   *V-PLACE_weak:
          Assign * to every vocalic place feature in the weak position of a
          foot.

    c.   FootForm=Iamb:[18]
        Feet are iambic.

    d.   Max:
        If material is present in the input, it is present in the output.

Independently of their ranking, some of the constraints are intrinsically ordered: *V-Place$_{weak}$ triggers deletion of unstressed vowels but is vacuously satisfied before feet are formed. On this basis, and given a ranking of the constraints that corresponds to the order in (30), a form like *(wná)(mrí)* in (29-b) is derived as follows. First, based on the initial input *wanamari*, the first two syllables are parsed into an iambic foot; see (31). Note that the restriction to (at most) one operation separating input and output implies that foot formation must take place in individual steps.[19]

(31) *Stress and syncope* (harmonic serialism, step 1):

I$_1$: wanamari	Parse-Σ	*V-Place$_{weak}$	FootForm=Iamb	Max
O$_{11}$: wanamari	***!*			
☞O$_{12}$: (waná)mari	**	*		
O$_{13}$: (wána)mari	**	*	*!	
O$_{14}$: wanmari	***!			*
O$_{15}$: wnamari	***!			*

In the second step, high-ranked Parse-Σ ensures that the remaining two syllables undergo foot formation; see (32); this comes at the price of a second violation of *V-Place$_{weak}$ (since there are now two vowels in weak positions of feet).

(32) *Stress and syncope* (harmonic serialism, step 2):

I$_{12}$: (waná)mari	Parse-Σ	*V-Place$_{weak}$	FootForm=Iamb	Max
O$_{121}$: (waná)mari	*!*			
☞O$_{122}$: (waná)(marí)		**		
O$_{123}$: (waná)(mári)		**	*!	
O$_{124}$: (wná)mari	*!*			*

---

[18] There is of course also a mirror image constraint FootForm=Trochee, which is lower-ranked in the language and not relevant here.

[19] That it is the first pair of syllables and not, say, the second one, that undergoes foot formation in the first step follows from an independent constraint Align(Foot,Word) that is not given here.

Next, O_{122} is used as the input for a further step of optimization; now the first vowel deletion triggered by *V-PLACE$_{weak}$ takes place; see (33). (As before, the one operation restriction implies that there is no candidate where all vowels in unstressed positions are deleted simultaneously.)

(33) *Stress and syncope* (harmonic serialism, step 3):

I_{122}: (waná)(marí)	PARSE-Σ	*V-PLACE$_{weak}$	FOOTFORM=IAMB	MAX
O_{1221}: (waná)(marí)		*!*		
☞O_{1222}: (wná)(marí)		*		*

In the following step, the second unstressed vowel undergoes deletion; again, the process is triggered by *V-PLACE$_{weak}$. This is shown in (34).

(34) *Stress and syncope* (harmonic serialism, step 4):

I_{1222}: (wná)(marí)	PARSE-Σ	*V-PLACE$_{weak}$	FOOTFORM=IAMB	MAX
O_{12221}: (wná)(marí)		*!		
☞O_{12222}: (wná)(mrí)				*

Finally, there is convergence: It is clear that any further operation applying to the optimal output of (34) will invariably lead to a worse constraint profile. (As one of many failed candidates, O_{122222} in (35) removes foot structure again.)

(35) *Stress and syncope* (harmonic serialism, step 5):

I_{12222}: (wná)(mrí)	PARSE-Σ	*V-PLACE$_{weak}$	FOOTFORM=IAMB	MAX
☞O_{122221}: (wná)(mrí)				
O_{122222}: wná(mrí)	*!			

Crucially, other things being equal, standard parallel optimality theory makes wrong predictions about possible winning candidates. Since reference to intermediate outputs is not possible in such an approach (because there are no such intermediate representations), the issue of iambic vs. trochaic foot formation does not arise, and vowel deletion could equally well affect the vowels which would be weak under trochaic foot formation because the system cannot distinguish the two options. This is shown in the tableau in (36); here (and in what follows), ☛ signals an output that is wrongly expected to be optimal.

(36) *Stress and syncope* (standard parallel optimality theory):

I_1: wanamari	PARSE-Σ	*V-PLACE$_{\text{weak}}$	FOOTFORM=IAMB	MAX
O_{11}: wanamari	*!***			
O_{12}: (wána)(mári)		*!*	**	
O_{13}: (waná)(marí)		*!*		
☛O_{14}: (wán)(már)				**
☞O_{15}: (wná)(mrí)				**

Thus, the problem with standard parallel optimality theory is that it over-generates; because relevant information borne by an intermediate representation is not available, nothing can decide between O_{14} and O_{15} in (36).[20]

3.3.2. SpecC Expletives in German

An argument for harmonic serialism (extremely local optimization) in syntax that takes a very similar form is developed in Heck & Müller (2013) on the basis of evidence from SpecC expletives in German. The first thing to note is that the phenomenon of expletive *es* ('it') pronouns in German verb-second clauses looks like a repair phenomenon: Declarative verb-second clauses with the finite verb in C need to have a specifier (SpecC); see (37-b) vs. (37-c). An expletive *es* can be merged if no other element shows up as SpecC to meet this requirement; see (37-a).

(37) a. Es   haben viele Leute   geschlafen
         EXPL have   many people$_{nom}$ slept
     b. Viele Leute   haben geschlafen
         many people$_{nom}$ have   slept
     c. *Haben viele Leute   geschlafen
         have   many people$_{nom}$ slept

However, in verb-final clauses (e.g., those headed by the C element *dass* ('that')), expletive insertion is blocked (both as SpecC and in some other, TP-internal, position); see (38).

(38) a. dass viele Leute   geschlafen haben
         that many people$_{nom}$ slept   have
     b. *dass es   viele Leute geschlafen haben
         that EXPL many people slept   have

---

[20] Closer inspection reveals that depending on some further assumptions, the parallel approach might in fact even face an undergeneration problem that would be even worse since O_{15} (and, irrelevantly, O_{14}) could not be predicted to be optimal anymore; see McCarthy (2008), Zimmermann (2017b).

    c. *es   dass viele Leute   geschlafen haben
       EXPL that many people$_{nom}$ slept   have

The optionality of the two strategies to have a SpecC in a verb-second clause (expletive insertion or movement of some TP-internal XP) is traced back in Müller (2000a, 48–49) to a (global) tie of the two constraints favouring the different options: The grammar of German permits two rankings; one ranking leads to expletive insertion, and the other ranking leads to movement.

Next, it turns out that there is a peculiar restriction on expletive insertion. As noted by Bierwisch (1961) (also cf. Erdmann (1886)), expletive insertion is incompatible with the occurrence of subject pronouns. This is shown by the data in (39-abc) (with expletive insertion and a nominative pronoun in the TP) vs. (39-def) (where the pronoun or something else moves to SpecC).

(39)   *Expletive/subject pronoun incompatibility:*
    a. *Es   habe   ich   geraucht
         EXPL have.1.SG I.1.SG.NOM smoked

    b. *Es   halft   ihr   der Frau
         EXPL helped.2.PL you.2.PL.NOM the woman.DAT

    c. *Es   hat er   geschlafen
         EXPL has he.3.SG.NOM slept

    d. Ich$_1$ habe   t$_1$ geraucht
         I.1.SG.NOM have.1.SG   smoked

    e. Der Frau$_2$ halft   ihr   t$_2$
         the woman.DAT helped.2.PL you.2.PL.NOM

    f.   Er$_1$ hat t$_1$ geschlafen
         he.3.SG.NOM has   slept

This state of affairs can be taken to suggest that expletive *es* and subject pronouns compete for something that is only present once. The analysis in Heck & Müller (2013) implements this idea; it relies on essentially the constraints in (40).

(40) a. MERGE CONDITION (MC, repeated here from (19)):
       Structure-building features ([•X•]) participate in Merge.
    b. AGREE CONDITION (AC):
       Probes ([*F*]) participate in Agree.

    c.   SPECIFIER-HEAD BIAS (SHB):
         Spec/head Agree is preferred to Agree under c-command.[21]

    d.   LAST RESORT (LR):
         Move of α and β follows Agree of α and β.

    e.   FULL-INT (FI, repeated here from (12-e)):
         Expletives must not be inserted.

First, the MERGE CONDITION has already been introduced above; it demands structure-building via Merge to take place in the presence of a designated [•F•] feature on the current head. In verb-second clauses in German, C has a category-neutral EPP (Extended Projection Principle; cf. Chomsky (1982)) feature [•X•] that requires filling of SpecC.

Next, the AGREE CONDITION, in contrast, requires probe features (see Chomsky (2001)) to participate in Agree operations; as a notational convention, probe features show up enclosed by asterisks here ([∗F∗]). Furthermore, suppose that a checking approach to Agree relations is adopted, rather than an approach in terms of valuation.[22] In Heck & Müller (2013), we follow Platzack (1987), Holmberg & Platzack (1995), and Chomsky (2008) in assuming that [ϕ]/[case] features on C are relevant for subject agreement and nominative assignment in German (rather than on T; also see Haider (1993) for evidence against this latter option). Taken together, the two assumptions about verb-second C in German imply that this head has a dual role: It has a [•X•] feature that triggers Merge, and [∗ϕ/case∗] features that trigger Agree.

Third, the SPECIFIER-HEAD BIAS ensures that if C can agree with either an XP in its specifier, or an XP that is included in its complement, the former option will be given preference.

Fourth, LAST RESORT (see Chomsky (1995)) states that moving some item requires an earlier Agree relation with the attracting head. This constraint can be satisfied with topicalization (i.e., movement of some XP to SpecC) only if the moved XP has undergone prior Agree with C.

---

[21] See Chomsky (1986; 1995), Koopman (2006), and Assmann, Georgi, Heck, Müller & Weisser (2015) for independent motivation. In Heck & Müller (2013) it is argued that the Specifier-Head Bias follows from Chomsky's (2001) more general Minimal Link Condition, given an appropriate concept of path length. These complications need not concern us here, though.

[22] This is a deviation from Heck & Müller (2013), where a valuation approach is adopted. The underlying rationale is to ensure compatibility with the pre-syntactic approach to inflectional morphology adopted in the present book.

Finally, FULL-INT has already been introduced above, in the course of discussing Grimshaw's (1997) approach to *do* support in negative environments. In the present context, FULL-INT blocks the insertion of an expletive pronoun *es* in SpecC; by assumption, expletives are never part of the numeration (see Hornstein (2001), among others).

The ranking of these constraints is given in (41). Note that in this analysis, it is the tie of the constraints MC and AC (signalled here by the symbol ∘, which can be resolved into the two orders AC ≫ MC and MC ≫ AC) that is responsible for the existence of two strategies for creating the specifier of verb-second clauses in German.[23]

(41)   SHB ≫ AC ∘ MC ≫ LR ≫ FI

Suppose that the derivation has reached a stage Σ where C has been merged with a TP containing DP_{ext}, with nothing waiting to be merged with C in the workspace. Then AC demands application of the operation $Agree(C,DP_{ext})$, and MC demands insertion of an expletive pronoun in SpecC, yielding $Merge(DP_{expl},C)$; thus, a conflict arises. This conflict is resolved by ranking AC and MC in one of the two possible ways, yielding a co-occurrence of expletive insertion and movement of DP_{ext} in a single language, in interaction with FI, LR, and SHB.

For concreteness, assume first that a ranking AC ≫ MC is chosen, and earlier optimization steps have resulted in stage Σ, as illustrated in (42).[24] Then the optimal step will be for C to carry out ϕ- and case-feature-based Agree with the closest available category; since there is no specifier of C yet, this will have to be the TP-internal subject; see O_{13}. Expletive insertion as in O_{12} is blocked at this point because, while satisfying MC, this could not directly satisfy Agree – here the restriction of competing outputs to differ from the input by at most one operation emerges as crucial. Note that since there are two probes on C, two violations of AC are registered if Agree does not take place. On the other hand, it can be assumed that

---

[23] As argued in Heck & Müller (2013), in other areas of German syntax there is actually evidence for a strict ranking of AC and MC (viz., as AC ≫ MC only). Ultimately, we take this to indicate that the two constraints should be relativized with respect to phasal domains, such that the tie in (41) only holds on the CP level: $AC_C ∘ MC_C$, but $AC_v ≫ MC_v$. Again, for present purposes we can disregard this complication.

[24] Here and in what follows, I abstract away from verb-second movement to C. This is also an operation triggered by a designated feature on C, but since it does not interact with the operations that we are currently interested in (viz., expletive insertion and XP movement), it can safely be ignored here.

AC can be satisfied by a single successful Agree operation for both probes, as in O_{13}. (But nothing would change if satisfaction of AC would have to be split up into two separate operations for two probes co-occuring on a single head.) Movement of the subject DP without prior Agree, as in O_{14}, also clearly emerges as a suboptimal operation since it fatally violates AC (plus, irrelevantly in the present context, LR). And finally, doing nothing is of course also not an option; see O_{11}.[25]

(42) *SpecC by movement* (harmonic serialism, step 1):

I_1: $\Sigma = [_{C'}\ C_{[*case*],[*pers*],\ldots,[\bullet X\bullet]}$ $\ldots DP_{[case],[pers],\ldots} \ldots\ ]$	SHB	AC	MC	LR	FI
O_{11}: $[_{C'}\ [_{C'}\ C_{[*case*],[*pers*],\ldots,[\bullet X\bullet]}$ $\ldots DP_{[case],[pers],[num],[gen]} \ldots\ ]]$		*!*	*		
O_{12}: $[_{CP}\ EXPL_{[pers]}\ [_{C'}\ C_{[*case*],[*pers*],\ldots}$ $\ldots DP_{[case],[pers],[num],[gen]} \ldots\ ]]$		*!*			*
☞O_{13}: $[_{C'}\ C_{[case]^1,[pers]^2,\ldots,[\bullet X\bullet]}$ $\ldots DP_{[case]^1,[pers]^2,\ldots} \ldots\ ]$			*		
O_{14}: $[_{CP}\ DP_{[case],[pers],\ldots}$ $[_{C'}\ C_{[*case*],[*pers*],\ldots} \ldots t_{DP} \ldots\ ]$		*!*		*	

The second step of CP optimization under the ranking AC $\gg$ MC consists of movement of DP_{ext} to SpecC, which satisfies the next-highest ranked constraint MC; see O_{132} in (43). In addition, O_{132} also satisfies LR because C has undergone Agree with the moved subject DP. Expletive insertion is blocked at this point by FI; see O_{133}. O_{131} fails to carry out any operation, which lets the MC violation persist.

(43) *SpecC by movement* (harmonic serialism, step 2):

I_{13}: $[_{C'}\ C_{[case]^1,[pers]^2,\ldots,[\bullet X\bullet]}$ $\ldots DP_{[case]^1,[pers]^2,\ldots} \ldots\ ]$	SHB	AC	MC	LR	FI
O_{131}: $[_{C'}\ [_{C'}\ C_{[case]^1,[pers]^2,\ldots,[\bullet X\bullet]}$ $\ldots DP_{[case]^1,[pers]^2,[num],[gen]} \ldots\ ]]$			*!		
☞O_{132}: $[_{CP}\ DP_{[case]^1,[pers]^2,\ldots}\ [_{C'}\ C_{[case]^1,[pers]^2,\ldots}$ $\ldots t_{DP} \ldots\ ]]$					
O_{133}: $[_{CP}\ EXPL_{[pers]}\ [_{C'}\ C_{[case]^1,[pers]^2,\ldots}$ $\ldots DP_{[case]^1,[pers]^2,[num],[gen]} \ldots\ ]]$					*!

---

[25] As a notational convention, checked probe features lose their asterisks; and successful Agree operations are indicated by co-superscripts.

Obviously, since all relevant constraints are now satisfied, the next step will lead to convergence.[26]

Consider now the reversed ranking MC $\gg$ AC. Starting again at stage Σ where a verb-second C has undergone Merge with a TP containing a subject DP, O_{11} (which does not carry out any operation) fails, as before. However, this time O_{13}, which carries out Agree with the subject DP, emerges as suboptimal because of a fatal MC violation, and the decision is passed on to the competition between O_{12} (with expletive insertion) and O_{14} (with movement of the subject DP). Given that O_{12} violates lowest-ranked FI but satisfies LR (since it does not involve movement), and satisfaction of MC by O_{14} implies satisfaction of FI but incurs a violation of the higher-ranked LR (since there is movement without prior Agree), expletive insertion in O_{12} is correctly predicted to be optimal.

(44) *SpecC by expletive insertion* (harmonic serialism, step 1):

I_1: $\Sigma = [_{C'}\ C_{[*case*],[*pers*],...,[\bullet X\bullet]}$ $...\ DP_{[case],[pers],...}\ ...\ ]$	SHB	MC	AC	LR	FI
O_{11}: $[_{C'}\ [_{C'}\ C_{[*case*],[*pers*],...,[\bullet X\bullet]}$ $...\ DP_{[case],[pers],[num],[gen]}\ ...\ ]]$		*!	**		
☞O_{12}: $[_{CP}\ EXPL_{[pers]}\ [_{C'}\ C_{[*case*],[*pers*],...}$ $...\ DP_{[case],[pers],[num],[gen]}\ ...\ ]]$			**		*
O_{13}: $[_{C'}\ C_{[case]^1,[pers]^2,...,[\bullet X\bullet]}$ $...\ DP_{[case]^1,[pers]^2,...}\ ...\ ]$		*!			
O_{14}: $[_{CP}\ DP_{[case],[pers],...}$ $[_{C'}\ C_{[*case*],[*pers*],...}\ ...\ t_{DP}\ ...\ ]$			**	*!	

In the next step, the optimal output will have to get rid of the input's AC violations; see (45). O_{121} is identical to the input and is therefore blocked, as before.[27] O_{122} carries out partial Agree with the expletive *es* in SpecC. Agree cannot be complete since the expletive bears a person feature, but it does not bear a case feature (or a number feature). Therefore, only the person probe of verb-second C is discharged. Despite this output's non-perfect satisfaction of AC, it is optimal at this stage: If C checks both

---

[26] An orthogonal question is how fronting of a non-subject XP to SpecC can be brought about under present assumptions, as it is required for (39-e), for example. Here the assumption is that designated information-structural features are involved, which show up as probes on C and require Agree operations with matching XPs prior to movement. Expletive insertion will never be a viable option in this kind of environment.

[27] It can be assumed that the FI violation goes away now since the expletive is already part of the input at this point.

probes with the subject DP, thereby improving the satisfaction of AC, a fatal violation of the highest-ranked constraint SHB will automatically occur because Agree with a specifier is given preference to Agree with an item contained in the complement; see O_{123}.

(45) *SpecC by expletive insertion* (harmonic serialism, step 2):

I_{12}: [CP EXPL$_{[pers]}$ [C′ C$_{[*case*],[*pers*]},$... ... DP$_{[case],[pers],}$... ...]	SHB	MC	AC	LR	FI
O_{121}: [CP EXPL$_{[pers]}$ [C′ C$_{[*case*],[*pers*]},$... ... DP$_{[case],[pers],[num],[gen]}$ ...]]			**!		
☞O_{122}: [CP EXPL$_{[pers]^2}$ [C′ C$_{[*case*],[pers]^2,}$... ... DP$_{[case],[pers],[num],[gen]}$ ...]]			*		
O_{123}: [CP EXPL$_{[pers]}$ [C′ C$_{[case]^1,[pers]]^2,}$... ... DP$_{[case]^1,[pers]^2,}$... ...]	*!				

A candidate that would simultaneously check C's person probe with the expletive and C's case probe with the subject DP in (45) cannot be generated in a single step; it is hard to see how this could be conceived of as a single operation of *Gen*. However, the optimal output in (45) can still be improved by checking C's case probe with the subject DP in a following optimization step; this is illustrated in (46).[28]

(46) *SpecC by expletive insertion* (harmonic serialism, step 3):

I_{122}: [CP EXPL$_{[pers]^2}$ [C′ C$_{[*case*],[pers]^2,}$... ... DP$_{[case],[pers],}$... ...]	SHB	MC	AC	LR	FI
O_{1221}: [CP EXPL$_{[pers]^2}$ [C′ C$_{[*case*],[pers]^2,}$... ... DP$_{[case],[pers],[num],[gen]}$ ...]]			*!		
☞O_{1222}: [CP EXPL$_{[pers]^2}$ [C′ C$_{[case]^1,[pers]^2,}$... ... DP$_{[case]^1,[pers],[num],[gen]}$ ...]]					

Finally, the last step leads to convergence. Given that pronouns (but not non-pronominal DPs) need checking of their person features to be legitimate, the incompatiblity of expletive *es* and subject pronouns is derived (see (39)): A subject pronoun cannot be spelled out in the context of an expletive because its [pers] feature has not been checked.

---

[28] Note that the same reasoning as with case features applies in the case of number features. The expletive pronoun *es* is not specified for number, so that C may carry out Agree with DP$_{ext}$ with respect to number after the expletive pronoun has been merged, and agreed with for person. This accounts for the wellformedness of sentences like (37-a).

Turning now to standard parallel optimality theory, it can be noted that ceteris paribus a wrong prediction is made, and for a similar reason as in the case of stress-syncope interaction in Macushi Carib addressed in the previous subsection: The parallel approach does not have access to an intermediate output representation where the expletive pronoun qualifies as optimal. The expletive *es* has a temporary advantage at the stage where moving the subject DP is blocked by LR, but the FI violation does eventually not pay off if the the whole derivation is considered. Therefore, it is wrongly predicted never to be able to show up. To see this, consider first the AC $\gg$ MC ranking, which also produces the correct result under standard parallel optimality theory; see (47).

(47) *SpecC by movement* (standard parallel optimality theory):

I_1: $C_{[*case*],[*pers*],...,[\bullet X\bullet]}$, T, V, $\quad$ ... $DP_{[case],[pers],...}$ ...]	SHB	AC	MC	LR	FI
O_{11}: $[_{CP}$ $C_{[*case*],[*pers*],...,[\bullet X\bullet]}$ $\quad$ ... $DP_{[case],[pers],[num],[gen]}$ ...]		*!*	*		
O_{12}: $[_{CP}$ $DP_{[case],[pers],[num],[gen]}$ ... $[_{C'}$ $C_{[*case*],[*pers*],...}$ $\quad$ ... t_{DP}]]		*!*		*	
O_{13}: $[_{CP}$ $C_{[case]^1,[pers]^2,...,[\bullet X\bullet]}$ $\quad$ ... $DP_{[case]^1,[pers]^2,[num],[gen]}$ ...]			*!		
☞O_{14}: $[_{CP}$ $DP_{[case]^1,[pers]^2,...}$ $[_{C'}$ $C_{[case]^1,[pers]^2,...}$ $\quad$ ... t_{DP} ...]]					
O_{15}: $[_{CP}$ $EXPL_{[pers]}$ $[_{C'}$ $C_{[case]^1,[pers]^2,...}$ $\quad$ ... $DP_{[case]^1,[pers]^2,[num],[gen]}$ ...]]					*!

The optimal candidate O_{14} satisfies all relevant constraints: The subject DP is in SpecC (satisfying MC); and in this position it can also respect AC, LR, as well as SHB and FI (the latter two constraints are satisfied vacuously). However, a wrong prediction arises under the ranking MC $\gg$ AC, which is supposed to derive the expletive strategy. Since the order of AC and MC satisfaction does not play a role in the parallel analysis (and both of these constraints can eventually be satisfied by an optimal output), it follows that O_{14} will again be the winner under this ranking, due to the intended winner's fatal FI violation and the fact that this implies harmonic bounding of O_{15} by O_{14}: Violating FI by inserting an expletive pronoun in SpecC can only pay off if a satisfaction of high-ranked MC would otherwise induce a violation of LR; but under parallel optimization, this does not have to be the case. This unwanted consequence is shown in (48) (where ☆ identifies the intended winner that does not emerge as optimal under a given ranking of constraints).

(48) *SpecC by expletive insertion* (standard parallel optimality theory):

I_1: $C_{[*case*],[*pers*],...,[\bullet X\bullet]}$, T, V, ... $DP_{[case],[pers],...}$ ...]	SHB	MC	AC	LR	FI
O_{11}: $[_{CP}$ $C_{[*case*],[*pers*],...,[\bullet X\bullet]}$ ... $DP_{[case],[pers],[num],[gen]}$ ...]		*!	**		
O_{12}: $[_{CP}$ $DP_{[case],[pers],[num],[gen]}$ ... $[_{C'}$ $C_{[*case*],[*pers*],...}$ ... t_{DP}]]			*!*	*	
O_{13}: $[_{CP}$ $C_{[case]^1,[pers]^2,...,[\bullet X\bullet]}$ ... $DP_{[case]^1,[pers]^2,[num],[gen]}$ ...]		*!			
☞O_{14}: $[_{CP}$ $DP_{[case]^1,[pers]^2,...}$ $[_{C'}$ $C_{[case]^1,[pers]^2,...}$ ... t_{DP} ...]]					
☆O_{15}: $[_{CP}$ $EXPL_{[pers]}$ $[_{C'}$ $C_{[case]^1,[pers]^2,...}$ ... $DP_{[case]^1,[pers]^2,[num],[gen]}$ ...]]					*!

To sum up this section: Not only is it the case that many convincing, simple analyses in phonology and syntax can be transferred from standard parallel optimality to harmonic serialism; there is also direct empirical evidence for harmonic serialism in phonology and syntax that comes from environments where it looks as though reference must be made to an intermediate output representation.

To these empirical considerations can be added a conceptual argument in favour of harmonic serialism: Whereas candidate sets in standard parallel optimality theory are typically not just huge but de facto infinite, candidate sets in harmonic serialism are by definition small and finite, due to the restriction on outputs to differ from inputs by at most one operation. To get a glimpse of this significant conceptual difference, it may be suggestive to just take into account the consequences of the numbering system for input and output candidates presupposed so far (and throughout this book; see (5)), where an optimal output O_{ij}, based on an input I_i, forms the input I_{ij} for the next generation step producing a new candidate set $\{O_{ij1}, O_{ij2}, ... O_{ijn}\}$: In harmonic serialism, only descendants of O_{ij} need to be subjected to optimization; however, in standard parallel optimality theory, all other continuations of O_i – e.g., O_{ik}, O_{il}, etc. – also need to be taken into account; and all of *their* possible continuations as well (not just one, as in harmonic serialism); and so on. All in all, these considerations would seem to suggest that an approach to both phonology and syntax in terms of harmonic serialism is viable, and that consequently an approach to morphology in terms of harmonic serialism is well worth pursuing.

4. Overview

The remainder of this monograph is organized as follows.

In chapter 2, I address disjunctive blocking and affix order. On the one hand, I show that an optimality-theoretic perspective offers new insights into these phenomena, and arguably represents a major advancement over non-optimality-theoretic approaches in these areas. And on the other hand, I illustrate how optimality-theoretic analyses of disjunctive blocking and affix order can be transferred to harmonic serialism. As it turns out, the reconstructions give rise to a simple concept of movement in morphology without any further assumptions.

Next, chapter 3 is concerned with extended (or multiple) exponence. I argue that the phenomenon poses a problem for standard optimality-theoretic (and other) approaches to inflectional morphology. However, extended exponence can be derived in harmonic serialism once a general constraint Minimize Satisfaction (MinSat) is adopted which slows down derivations, and which can be shown to be independently motivated in phonology (where it helps to derive counter-bleeding) and syntax (where it covers Merge over Move effects).

Chapter 4 then turns to a problem created by the introduction of MinSat: There is a tension between what this constraint demands (viz., selection of the least specific – minimally improving – candidate at any step), and what seems to be required for disjunctive blocking (viz., selection of the most specific – maximally improving – candidate). I argue that this paradox can be solved by adopting the idea that structure that is generated by elementary structure-building operations in the grammar can in principle be undone again at some later point by equally basic operations of structure removal. In executing this hypothesis, I also show how a language can employ extended exponence and disjunctive blocking in the same grammatical domain.

Whereas chapters 2–4 are mainly concerned with inflectional exponents, chapter 5 addresses cases of suppletion – more specifically, stem allomorphy that is regulated by morpho-syntactic features. I show how apparent cases of non-local stem allomorphy can straightforwardly be derived in a strictly local way, via movement in morphology; and I also show how the approach in terms of harmonic serialism makes a new approach to the *ABA generalization possible (one that does not rely on asymmetric feature sets, as they are standardly postulated in accounts of *ABA).

Finally, chapter 6 discusses some general consequences that the analyses developed in the present monograph have for optimality theory and harmonic serialism in general, and points to some areas for further research that suggest themselves against the background of the studies presented here (related, inter alia, to phenomena suggesting impoverishment or rules of referral, to cases of (generalized) deponency, and to paradigm gaps).

Chapter 2

From Optimality Theory to Harmonic Serialism

1. Introduction

The goal of this chapter is twofold. On the one hand, based on two separate morphological phenomena (disjunctive blocking and affix order), I argue that existing approaches developed on the basis of standard parallel optimality theory offer simple and elegant analyses of a type that cannot be provided in other frameworks (like Distributed Morphology or Paradigm Function Morphology). And on the other hand, I show that these analyses can faithfully be transferred to harmonic serialism. In one case (disjunctive blocking), the transfer will be pretty straightforward; but it will also be subject to a drastic, major modification later in the book (in chapter 4). In the other case, the transfer will automatically, without any further stipulation, give rise to a well-defined concept of movement in morphology that will subsequently play a huge role in the analysis of discontinuous extended exponence (in chapter 3) and in the analysis of (long-distance) allomorphy (in chapter 5).

The first thing to note is that there are a number of studies of inflectional morphology developed on the basis of standard parallel optimality theory which may look very different at first sight but actually converge on a number of core properties; cf., e.g., work like Grimshaw (2001), Trommer (2001; 2003; 2006a; 2008a), Wunderlich (1999; 2001a;b; 2004), Don & Blom (2006), Ortmann (2002; 2004), and Stiebels (2000; 2002; 2006)). One such piece of convergence concerns the role of underspecification in disjunctive blocking.[1]

---

[1] That said, there are also several optimality-theoretic approaches to inflectional morphology that do not exhibit this general convergence but qualify as somewhat more

2. Disjunctive Blocking

2.1. *Disjunctive Blocking in Classical Approaches*

Inflectional paradigms in the world's languages are full of syncretism (conceived of in a broad sense as an identity of form with morphological exponents for different syntactically defined contexts); and there is both whole-word syncretism and partial syncretism (which only affects parts of inflected words). In some cases, one may argue that a syncretism is just an instantiation of accidental homonymy.[2] However, in at least some cases, it is uncontroversial that the syncretism is systematic, and requires a principled explanation. Thus, the question arises of how systematic instances of syncretism can be derived in morphological theory.

For concreteness, consider the paradigm of determiner inflection (also known as 'pronominal inflection', and illustrated here for the determiner *dies* ('this')) in German, which also (with minimal changes) represents the paradigm of strong adjective inflection in German; see (1). There cannot be any reasonable doubt about the systematicity of some of the syncretisms here, e.g., as regards the /m/ in minimally different DAT.MASC.SG contexts and DAT.NEUT.SG contexts, or the /s/ in minimally different NOM.NEUT.SG contexts and ACC.NEUT.SG contexts, which instantiates an extremely old pattern of nominative/accusative identity with neuters that is active in nearly all Indo-European languages.[3]

---

idiosyncratic, in the sense that they pursue somewhat different agendas, employ a somewhat different technical machinery, and, more generally, do not necessarily present themselves as comprehensive approaches that are designed to compete with standard current theoretical approaches to inflectional morphology (like Distributed Morphology, Network Morphology, Paradigm Function Morphology, etc.). Work of this type includes Xu & Aronoff (2008), Xu (2007; 2011), and Müller (2011b); here the concept of underspecification that is prevalent in virtually all current morphological models is basically abandoned. It also includes Müller (2002; 2013c) and Carstairs-McCarthy (2008), where a radically amorphematic approach is adopted, in the sense that the assumption that morphological exponents (whether as lexical items or as inferential markings, in Stump's (2001) taxonomy) are paired with morpho-syntactic feature specifications is fully dispensed with.

[2] See, however, Müller (2007b) for a conceptual argument against this view.

[3] See Corbett & Fraser (1993) for a marginal exception with animate neuter nouns in Russian, though.

(1)   *Determiner inflection in German*:

dies	MASC.SG	NEUT.SG	FEM.SG	PL
NOM	dies-r	dies-s	dies-e	dies-e
ACC	dies-n	dies-s	dies-e	dies-e
DAT	dies-m	dies-m	dies-r	dies-n
GEN	dies-s	dies-s	dies-r	dies-r

The paradigm in (1) reveals that there are only five different exponents – /m/, /r/, /n/, /s/, and /e/ (= ə) – for twenty-four different paradigm cells – or, at least, sixteen different paradigm cells if one takes seriously the fact that German never distinguishes gender in the plural. The standard approach to account for such instances of syncretism goes back to Jakobson (1962a;b) and Bierwisch (1967), and relies on the concepts of (i) decomposition, (ii) underspecification, and (iii) competition resolution. The first step is that morpho-syntactic features capturing instantiations of grammatical categories (like, e.g., nominative as an instantiation of the grammatical category case) are *decomposed* into combinations of more primitive features (e.g., nominative = [–obl(ique),–gov(erned)]). Shared primitive features then define *natural classes* of instantiations of grammatical categories (like case, number, person, tense, gender, etc.); e.g., if accusative is is composed of the more primitive features [–obl,+gov], the shared feature [–obl] defines a natural class consisting of nominative and accusative. Next, *underspecification* of exponents with respect to these features makes reference to natural classes possible and thereby derives instances of syncretism – e.g., if neuter /s/ is underspecified as [–obl] rather than fully specified as [–obl,–gov] or [–obl,+gov], it represents the natural class of nominative and accusative, rather than just nominative, or just accusative.

Underspecification of exponents invariably gives rise to *competition*: More than one exponent typically fits into a given context, but in *disjunctive blocking* (or 'disjunctive ordering') environments like the one at hand, only one exponent from the set of competing exponents can actually be used, blocking all the other ones. The competition can in principle be resolved in different ways. Traditionally (see, e.g., Bierwisch (1967), Chomsky & Halle (1968)), the competition among underspecified items was resolved by simple extrinsic ordering. Such an approach has been generally replaced by postulating a constraint like the *Subset Principle* in (2) (see Halle (1997)); crucially, this constraint incorporates (a) a compatibility requirement and (b) a specificity requirement.[4]

---

[4] Alternatives with very similar effects (and also relying on both compatibility and specificity) go by the names of Specificity Condition, Elsewhere Principle, Blocking Principle,

(2)   *Subset Principle*:
A vocabulary item V is inserted into a functional morpheme M iff (a) and (b) hold:

    a.   *Compatibility*:
The morpho-syntactic features of V are a subset of the morpho-syntactic features of M.

    b.   *Specificity*:
V is the most specific vocabulary item that satisfies (a).

As concerns specificity, (at least) three concepts have been proposed in the literature: one that just counts sets of features (where the set with the greater cardinality is more specific), one that relies on subset/superset relations (such that α can be more specific than β only if it characterized by a superset of (relevant) morpho-syntactic features), and one based on feature hierarchies. It is this latter concept that I will presuppose here; see (3).[5]

(3)   *Specificity of vocabulary items*:
A vocabulary item V_i is more specific than a vocabulary item V_j iff there is a class of features $\mathbb{F}$ such that (a) and (b) hold.

    a. V_i bears more features belonging to $\mathbb{F}$ than V_j does.

    b.   There is no higher-ranked class of features $\mathbb{F}'$ such that V_i and V_j have a different number of features in $\mathbb{F}'$.

Thus, according to (3), an exponent that is characterized by a single higher-ranked feature will count as more specific than another exponent with several lower-ranked features.

On this basis, let us come back to the analysis of the paradigm of determiner inflection in German in (1). As it turns out, this is an extremely well-researched inflectional paradigm, for which underspecification-based analyses have been proposed in Bierwisch (1967), Blevins (1995),

---

Pāṇini's Principle, Proper Inclusion Principle, etc.; see Kiparsky (1973b), Di Sciullo & Williams (1987), Fanselow (1991), Anderson (1992), Lumsden (1992), Noyer (1992), Williams (1994), Williams (1997), Wiese (1999), Stump (2001), among many others. In nanosyntactic approaches based on overspecification rather than underspecification (see Caha (2009), Baunaz et al. (2018), and De Clercq & Vanden Wyngaerd (2018)), the Superset Principle also consists of these two separate requirements: compatibility and specificity.

[5] Note that this concept of specificity is structurally similar to the concept of optimality; see (3) and (4) from chapter 1.

Wunderlich (1997b), Wiese (1999), Trommer (2005), Opitz et al. (2013)), and elsewhere. The illustration here follows Wiese (1999).

Suppose that case and gender features are decomposed as in (4). Case feature decomposition directly follows Bierwisch (1967) – nominative and accusative form a natural class ([–obl]), as do dative and accusative ([+gov]), dative and genitive ([+obl]), and so on. As for gender feature composition, Wiese (1999) argues that the grammatical categories gender and number are merged, such that plural is characterized by the feature combination [–masc,–fem] (recall that there is no gender distinction in the plural in German), whereas the remaining three feature combinations capture masculine, neuter, and feminine genders in the singular. Thus, masculine and neuter form a natural class ([+masc]), feminine and plural form a natural class ([–masc]), etc.

(4) *Feature decomposition:*

  Case   *Gender/Number*

  NOM: [–obl,–gov] MASC: [+masc,–fem]

  ACC: [–obl,+gov] FEM: [–masc,+fem]

  DAT: [+obl,+gov] NEUT: [+masc,+fem]

  GEN: [+obl,–gov] PL: [–masc,–fem]

Against this background, Wiese (1999) proposes the system of underspecified morphological exponents in (5).[6,7]

(5) *Underspecified exponents:*

  a. /m/^{1} ↔ [+masc,+obl,+gov]   (DAT.MASC.SG./NEUT.SG.)

  b. /s/^{2} ↔ [+masc,+obl]   (GEN.MASC.SG./NEUT.SG.)

  c. /s/^{3} ↔ [+masc,+fem]   (NOM./ACC.NEUT.SG.)

  d. /n/^{4} ↔ [+masc,+gov]   (ACC.MASC.SG.)

  e. /r/^{5} ↔ [+masc]   (NOM.MASC.SG.)

  f. /r/^{6} ↔ [+obl,+fem]   (DAT./GEN.FEM.SG.)

---

[6] The notation here follows standard practice in Distributed Morphology: /m/ stands for the form of an exponent, and [+masc,+obl,+gov] for the (typically underspecified) morpho-syntactic features associated with it (the association is signalled by ↔). The information in brackets at the end of a line here does not belong to the exponent's intrinsic properties; rather, it just serves to indicate what contexts the exponents will ultimately end up in.

[7] Independent motivation for this assignment of features to exponents comes from iconicity: Heavier exponents (/m/, /s/) are characterized by more, and higher-ranked, features than lighter exponents (/n/, /r/), which in turn are less underspecified than the elsewhere (default) exponent /e/ (ə).

g. /n/^{7} ↔ [+obl,+gov]   (DAT.PL.)

h. /r/^{8} ↔ [+obl]   (GEN.PL.)

i. /e/^{9} ↔ [ ]   (NOM./ACC.FEM.SG./PL.)

The analysis envisages nine exponents, which leaves a few unresolved syncretisms (Wiese argues that there is independent evidence for this): There are two separate /n/ exponents, two /s/ exponents, and three /r/ exponents. (To properly distinguish different exponents with an identical form, I have added numbers as superscripts to the exponent list in (5).) Indeed, it turns out that without further assumptions extending the theoretical framework (like second-order features, as in Trommer (2005)), it is impossible to derive many more instances of syncretism by underspecification; eight exponents would seem to be the minimum number in standard approaches (see Opitz et al. (2013)).

The hierarchy of morpho-syntactic features presupposed by Wiese is given in (6).

(6) *Feature hierarchy:*

[+masc] > [+obl] > [+fem] > [+gov].

Given the concept of specificity in (3), this implies that exponents bearing [+masc] are always more specific than exponents without this feature; if [+masc] is not present among compatible exponents, then an exponent bearing [+obl] is more specific than one that does not; and so on. The resulting resolution of competition by specificity is shown in (7). Here, the set of exponents that meet the compatbility requirement in (2-a) is given for each context; and the (unique) exponent that also satisfies the specificity requirement in (2-b) is singled out by underlining.

(7) *Competition of exponents:*

dies	Masc.Sg.	Neut.Sg.	Fem.Sg.	Pl.
Nom	$\underline{r}^5$, e^9	$\underline{s}^3$, r^5, e^9	$\underline{e}^9$	$\underline{e}^9$
Acc	$\underline{n}^4$, r^5, e^9	$\underline{s}^3$, n^4, r^5, e^9	$\underline{e}^9$	$\underline{e}^9$
Dat	$\underline{m}^1$, s^2, n^4, r^5, n^7, r^8, e^9	$\underline{m}^1$, s^2, s^3, n^4, r^5, r^6, n^7, r^8, e^9	$\underline{r}^6$, n^7, r^8, e^9	$\underline{n}^7$, r^8, e^9
Gen	$\underline{s}^2$, r^5, r^8, e^9	$\underline{s}^2$, s^3, r^5, r^6, r^8, e^9	$\underline{r}^6$, r^8, e^9	$\underline{r}^8$, e^9

Note that, given Wiese's (1999) exponent entries, the feature hierarchy in (6) is crucial: For instance, the feature specifications of /r/^{6} and /n/^{7} are not in a subset relation; nor do they involve a different number of features. However, /r/^{6} is characterized by [+fem] whereas /n/^{7} is characterized by [+gov], and given that they both bear the feature [+obl], this ensures that /r/^{6} blocks /n/^{7} in DAT.FEM.SG. environments.

2.2. Disjunctive Blocking in Standard Parallel Optimality Theory

A main result of standard parallel optimality-theoretic approaches to inflectional morphology is that the two basic principles of morphological realization by underspecified exponents – viz., *compatibility* (see (2-a)) and *specificity* (see (2-b)) – do not have to be *stipulated* (as they are, e.g., in the Subset Principle in Distributed Morphology, or in Pāṇini's Principle in Paradigm Function Morphology) but *follow* from independently motivated faithfulness constraints (see, e.g., Grimshaw (2001), Trommer (2001), Wunderlich (2001a), Don & Blom (2006), Stiebels (2006), and Wolf (2008)):[8] If the input of morphological realization contains a (fully specified) set of morpho-syntactic features, and the output contains underspecified morphological exponents, it is clear that there will be faithfulness constraints for these features. In particular, it can be assumed that there will be IDENT constraints for morpho-syntactic features which militate against having different values of these features for input and output; and there will be MAX constraints which ensure that features of the input also show up in the output. IDENT thus derives the compatibility requirement of morphological exponence, and MAX derives the specificity requirement.[9]

---

[8] However, also cf. Xu (2007, 80) and Wunderlich (2004, 383), where constraints incorporating compatibility and specificity requirements are still postulated as primitives in optimality-theoretic analyses.

[9] What about DEP constraints? At first sight, one might think that they should play a major role in underspecification-based approaches since the scenario of features in the output which are not present in the input would seem to be exactly what the Subset Principle forbids. However, closer inspection reveals that this is in fact not the case: Abstracting away from the effects of impoverishment (see chapter 6), in applications of the Subset Principle in morphological exponence, it is usually a conflicting feature value that leads to a compatibility violation, not the presence of some different feature. As a matter of fact, Halle & Marantz (1994) explicitly assume that morphological exponents (vocabulary items, in Distributed Morphology terminology) may bring with them features that determine subsequent morphological realization: To wit, in their analysis of Spanish object clitics, morphological exponents for D are accompanied by inflection class features which would not otherwise be present (in this sense, the approach does in fact not qualify as purely realizational in Stump's (2001) sense), and which then trigger subsequent choice of the morphological exponent for the theme vowel position. Similarly, in his study of periphrastic verb constructions, Bonami (2015) suggests that morphological exponents can also be equipped with selectional features that are not independently in place, which then indirectly produce periphrastic verb forms by triggering further morphological exponence. In both cases, the additional morpho-syntactic features on the exponents are not assumed to give rise to compatibility violations. Furthermore, it can be noted that it has often been argued that morphological exponents can introduce features triggering non-trivial (in many cases, far-reaching) phonological modifications of stem material, again without violating compatibility (see Wolf (2008),

For concreteness, suppose that in the morphological component of the grammar, *Gen* brings about a realization of sets of fully specified features by morphological exponents. (I will be more specific about these issues when I transfer the standard parallel optimality-theoretic analysis to harmonic serialism below). The faithfulness constraints that play a role in an optimality-theoretic reconstruction of Wiese's (1999) analysis are given in (8).

(8) a. IDENT-F:
         Morpho-syntactic features of input and output cannot have
         different values.
     b. MAX(MASC):
         [masc] of the input is realized on an exponent in the output.
     c. MAX(OBL):
         [obl] of the input is realized on an exponent in the output.
     d. MAX(FEM):
         [fem] of the input is realized on an exponent in the output.
     e. MAX(GOV):
         [gov] of the input is realized on an exponent in the output.

The required ranking corresponds to the order in which the constraints show up in (8); see (9).

(9)   IDENT-F ≫ MAX(MASC) ≫ MAX(OBL) ≫ MAX(FEM) ≫ MAX(GOV)

It is evident that the ranking of MAX constraints required in the optimality-theoretic reconstruction of Wiese's analysis corresponds exactly to the feature hierarchy in (6).[10]

In what follows, I will go through three sample optimizations to show how the right exponents are chosen for each environment (i.e., for each

---

Trommer (2011), and Zimmermann (2017a), among others). For all these reasons, I will generally disregard the issue of DEP constraints in what follows. I will come back to this issue in section 2 of chapter 5, though, and argue there that DEP can become relevant for morphological realization in one specific context after all.

[10] Of course, this is one of the reasons why I have focussed on this particular analysis of the German determiner inflection paradigm (the other reasons being intrinsically linguistic, though; see in particular the remarks on iconicity in footnote 7 above). However, it should be noted that an optimality-theoretic reconstruction would work just as well for all the other underspecification-based analyses of the determiner inflection paradigm mentioned above (see page 36).

fully specified set of morpho-syntactic features). Consider dative masculine singular contexts first; see (10).

(10) *Dative masculine singular contexts* (standard parallel optimality theory):

I_1: *dies*, [+masc,−fem,+obl,+gov]	ID-F	MAX(MASC)	MAX(OBL)	MAX(FEM)	MAX(GOV)
☞ O_{11}: /m/^{1} ↔ [+masc,+obl,+gov]				*	
O_{12}: /s/^{2} ↔ [+masc,+obl]				*	*!
O_{13}: /s/^{3} ↔ [+masc,+fem]	*!		*		*
O_{14}: /n/^{4} ↔ [+masc,+gov]			*!	*	
O_{15}: /r/^{5} ↔ [+masc]			*!	*	*
O_{16}: /r/^{6} ↔ [+obl,+fem]	*!	*			*
O_{17}: /n/^{7} ↔ [+obl,+gov]		*!		*	
O_{18}: /r/^{8} ↔ [+obl]		*!		*	*
O_{19}: /e/^{9} ↔ [ ]		*!	*	*	*

Two outputs introduce conflicting feature values and are thus directly filtered out by IDENT-F (O_{13} = /s/^{3}, with [+fem] rather than [−fem], as required by the fully specified environment, and O_{16} = /r/^{6}, which has the same problem). More generally, note that an output that violates IDENT-F (i.e., compatibility) can never be optimal as long as there is an elsewhere marker in the system (O_{19}, in the case at hand), which cannot violate IDENT-F by definition. All the other exponents satisfy IDENT-F (i.e., they meet the compatbility requirement of the Subset Principle). Next, O_{17}, O_{18}, and O_{19} fatally violate MAX(MASC) because they do not realize [±masc]. O_{14} and O_{15} are successfully blocked by MAX(OBL) since here the exponents do not bear a [±obl] feature. Thus, the decision comes down to a choice between O_{11} and O_{12}, both of which satisfy the three highest-ranked faithfulness constraints; they also both violate MAX(FEM) since they do not realize [±fem]. In the end, the lowest-ranked constraint MAX(GOV) decides the competition, selecting O_{11} as the optimal output.

Dative masculine singular contexts qualify as an environment where several exponents satisfy compatibility (IDENT), and specificity (MAX) is crucial. The opposite situation occurs with nominative feminine singular contexts, as in (11).

(11) *Nominative feminine singular contexts* (standard parallel optimality theory):

I_1: [−masc,+fem,−obl,−gov]	ID-F	MAX(MASC)	MAX(OBL)	MAX(FEM)	MAX(GOV)
O_{11}: /m/^{1} ↔ [+masc,+obl,+gov]	*!**			*	
O_{12}: /s/^{2} ↔ [+masc,+obl]	*!*			*	*
O_{13}: /s/^{3} ↔ [+masc,+fem]	*!		*		*
O_{14}: /n/^{4} ↔ [+masc,+gov]	*!*		*	*	
O_{15}: /r/^{5} ↔ [+masc]	*!		*	*	*
O_{16}: /r/^{6} ↔ [+obl,+fem]	*!	*			*
O_{17}: /n/^{7} ↔ [+obl,+gov]	*!*	*		*	
O_{18}: /r/^{8} ↔ [+obl]	*!	*		*	*
☞O_{19}: /e/^{9} ↔ [ ]		*	*	*	*

In (11), all exponents have conflicting feature values, thereby giving rise to fatal IDENT-F violations, except for the elsewhere marker, O_{19}. Consequently, /e/^{9} emerges as optimal here, despite the fact that it violates all four MAX constraints.

As a final illustration of how the German determiner inflection paradigm is derived by IDENT and MAX constraints in an optimality-theoretic approach, the tableau in (12) addresses accusative neuter singular contexts.

(12) *Accusative neuter singular contexts* (standard parallel optimality theory):

I_1: [+masc,+fem,−obl,+gov]	ID-F	MAX(MASC)	MAX(OBL)	MAX(FEM)	MAX(GOV)
O_{11}: /m/^{1} ↔ [+masc,+obl,+gov]	*!			*	
O_{12}: /s/^{2} ↔ [+masc,+obl]	*!			*	*
☞O_{13}: /s/^{3} ↔ [+masc,+fem]			*		*
O_{14}: /n/^{4} ↔ [+masc,+gov]			*	*!	
O_{15}: /r/^{5} ↔ [+masc]			*	*!	*
O_{16}: /r/^{6} ↔ [+obl,+fem]	*!	*			*
O_{17}: /n/^{7} ↔ [+obl,+gov]	*!	*		*	
O_{18}: /r/^{8} ↔ [+obl]	*!	*		*	*
O_{19}: /e/^{9} ↔ [ ]		*!	*	*	*

Here, O_{11}, O_{12}, O_{16}, O_{17}, and O_{18} incur fatal violations of IDENT-F (because of a [+obl] specification that is incompatible with the feature [−obl] of the fully specified input specification). The elsewhere exponent O_{19} fatally violates MAX(MASC). O_{13}, O_{14}, and O_{15} all violate MAX(OBL). O_{14} and O_{15} do not satisfy MAX(FEM). This leaves O_{13} as the sole winner, despite violations of both MAX(OBL) and MAX(GOV).[11]

---

[11] Based on analyses developed within Distributed Morphology, Hein (2008) and Driemel (2018) argue that two (or more) exponents can in principle be selected for a given morpho-syntactic environment if they qualify as equally specific (and satisfy

At this point, a question may arise concerning the ranking of IDENT and MAX constraints in inflectional morphology. Clearly, free reranking would threaten to undermine a successful transfer of non-optimality-theoretic analyses because highly specific exponents (maximizing MAX satisfaction) could emerge as optimal even if they violate compatibility (i.e., IDENT) by having conflicting feature values. One might argue that the option of incompatible feature specifications on optimal exponents might actually not be an unattractive consequence since it could be used to model scenarios where concepts like impoverishment (in Distributed Morphology) or rules of referral (e.g., in Paradigm Function Morphology, or Network Morphology) have been proposed. However, I will not adopt this view here (see chapter 6 for some pertinent remarks, though). As a first step towards a solution of this problem, it can be noted that it is by no means always the case in optimality theory that constraints are freely rerankable. For instance, a constraint X&Y derived by local conjunction (see Smolensky (1995; 2006)) of the constraints X and Y inherently outranks X and Y. As regards the case at hand, for the time being I will simply assume that higher-level faithfulness constraints (like MAX constraints on features) always have to be outranked by lower-level faithfulness constraints (like IDENT constraints on feature values) in morphology. Note that this stipulation is not actually categorially different from the analogous stipulation needed in non-optimality-theoretic approaches relying on special compatibility and specificity constraints: These approaches also need to assume the same ranking of compatibility and specificity so as to ensure that the most specific morphological exponent is chosen only among those that are compatible with a given fully specified feature matrix.

Before I next turn to the question of how disjunctive blocking can be implemented in harmonic serialism, let me briefly introduce two further studies from the literature, viz., Grimshaw (2001) on Italian object clitics, and Stiebels (2006) on agent focus markers in Mayan languages. The goal here is to show that the optimality-theoretic account just sketched can indeed be generalized. In line with this goal, I will focus on what I take to be the core of the analyses throughout, sometimes tacitly adjusting minor (and sometimes also not-so-minor) differences concerning the overall

---

compatibility). The same situation may arise under the present optimality-theoretic approach in terms of faithfulness constraints, assuming two (or more) outputs to have identical constraint profiles (with respect to the relevant morpho-syntactic features – by definition, their form will vary, and their phonological constraint profile can thus not be identical for principled reasons).

organization of the morphological component of the grammar, the underlying feature ontologies, the constraint names, etc.

2.3. Further Case Studies

2.3.1. Italian Object Clitics

Grimshaw (2001) sets out to derive the system of Italian object clitics by combining underspecification with an optimality-theoretic approach based on faithfulness constraints. The paradigm that is to be derived looks as in (13).

(13) *Italian clitics*:

	1.SG	2.SG	3.SG	1.PL	2.PL	3.PL
ACC	mi	ti	lo/la	ci	vi	li/le
DAT	mi	ti	gli/le	ci	vi	–
ACC-REF	mi	ti	si	ci	vi	si
DAT-REF	mi	ti	si	ci	vi	si

Evidently, there is a lot of syncretism that needs to be accounted for. In Grimshaw's (2001) analysis, some of the morphological exponents are fully specified (see (14-a)); but others are underspecified with respect to the morpho-syntactic grammatical categories gender, case, person, number, and reflexivity (see (14-b)).[12]

(14) *Fully specified and underspecified lexical entries*:

    a. (i)   /lo/ $\leftrightarrow$ [−refl,−1,−2,−pl,+masc,−obl,+gov]   (him/it)

        (ii) /la/ $\leftrightarrow$ [−refl,−1,−2,−pl,+fem,−obl,+gov]   (her/it)

        (iii) /li/ $\leftrightarrow$ [−refl,−1,−2,+pl,+masc,−obl,+gov]   (them (masc))

        (iv) /le/^{1} $\leftrightarrow$ [−refl,−1,−2,+pl,+fem,−obl,+gov]   (them (fem))

        (v) /gli/ $\leftrightarrow$ [−refl,−1,−2,+pl,+masc,+obl,+gov] (to them (masc))

        (vi) /le/^{2} $\leftrightarrow$ [−refl,−1,−2,+pl,+fem,+obl,+gov] (to them (fem))

    b. (i)   /mi/ $\leftrightarrow$ [+1,−2,−pl]   ((to) me(self))

        (ii) /ti/ $\leftrightarrow$ [−1,+2,−pl]   ((to) you(self))

        (iii) /ci/ $\leftrightarrow$ [+1,−2,+pl]   ((to) us(self))

---

[12] Here I assume that first, second, and third person are rendered as [+1,−2], [−1,+2], and [−1,−2], respectively, and that accusative and dative have the fine structure [−obl,+gov], [+obl,−gov], as before. This is solely to maximize homogeneity throughout the present monograph; there is no need to invoke natural classes of either instantiations of person or instantiations of case in Grimshaw's analysis. – That said, instead of the absence of case specifications of the exponents in (14-b), a decomposition of case would make it possible to specify these exponents as [+gov], and thereby minimize violations of MAX(CASE) in these outputs.

$$\text{(iv)} \quad /\text{vi}/ \leftrightarrow [-1,+2,+\text{pl}] \qquad\qquad ((\text{to}) \text{ you(self)})$$
$$\text{(v)} \quad /\text{si}/ \leftrightarrow [+\text{refl}] \qquad\qquad ((\text{to}) \text{ self})$$

The faithfulness constraints that play a role in the analysis are IDENT-F, MAX(PERS), MAX(REFL), MAX(NUM), MAX(GEN), and MAX(CASE), and they are ranked in this order. The competitions are trivial in the case of the fully specified morphological exponents in (14-a) showing up in non-reflexive environments since these exponents satisfy all the constraints, given the respective input specifications. Underspecification and competition become relevant in reflexive environments, though.[13] As an example, consider first the case of a second person plural reflexive accusative input, as in (15). Here we can basically disregard all the [−refl]-marked exponents in (14-a); as shown exemplarily here for /li/ (O_{13}), they will invariably induce fatal IDENT-F violations in a [+refl] context. The crucial competition is between the "proper" reflexive exponent /si/ (O_{11}) and the person-marked exponents /vi/ (O_{12}) and /ti/ (O_{14}). O_{14} is blocked by O_{12} due to an IDENT-F violation (a singular specification in a plural context); and since MAX(PERS) outranks MAX(REFL), O_{12} also successfully blocks the reflexive clitic of output O_{11} in this environment.

(15) *First and second person reflexive inputs* (standard parallel optimality theory):

I_1: [+refl,−1,+2,+pl,+masc,−obl,+gov]	IDENT-F	MAX PERS	MAX REFL	MAX NUM	MAX GEN	MAX CASE
O_{11}: /si/ ↔ [+refl]		*!		*	*	*
☞O_{12}: /vi/ ↔ [−1,+2,+pl]			*		*	*
O_{13}: /li/ ↔ [−refl,−1,−2,+pl,+masc,−obl,+gov]	*!*					
O_{14}: /ti/ ↔ [−1,+2,−pl]	*!		*		*	*

However, the situation is different in third person reflexive contexts; the input in (16) differs minimally from the one in (15) in that the person specification is [−1,−2] rather than [−1,+2]. All the exponents in (14-a) have a conflicting value for [±refl] giving rise to a fatal IDENT-F violation, and all the exponents in (14-b) have a conflicting value for [±1] or [±2], which also produces a fatal IDENT-F violation, except for the radically underspecified reflexive exponent /si/ in O_{11}, which therefore emerges as optimal.

---

[13] Interestingly, in his concise reconstruction of Grimshaw's analysis, McCarthy (2002, 81) does not invoke underspecification. Here, syncretism is assumed to be derivable from neutralization of input differences in the feature system, but the analysis is not carried out in detail.

46   Chapter 2. From Optimality Theory to Harmonic Serialism

(16)   *Third person reflexive inputs* (standard parallel optimality theory):

I₁: [+refl,−1,−2,+pl,+masc,−obl,+gov]	IDENT-F	MAX PERS	MAX REFL	MAX NUM	MAX GEN	MAX CASE
☞ O₁₁: /si/ ↔ [+refl]		*		*	*	*
O₁₂: /vi/ ↔ [−1,+2,+pl]	*!		*		*	*
O₁₃: /li/ ↔ [−refl,−1,−2,+pl,+masc,−obl,+gov]	*!					
O₁₄: /ti/ ↔ [−1,+2,−pl]	*!*		*		*	*

2.3.2.   *Agent Focus Markers in Mayan*

Mayan languages are head-marking languages in the sense that the core arguments are encoded by case markers on the verb. In many of these languages, movement of a DP that acts as the external argument of a transitive verb and is identified by an ergative exponent on the verb is impossible; and some of these languages in turn have the option of making such DP movement possible after all if a so-called agent focus marker shows up on the verb instead of the expected ergative marker. The pattern is illustrated here on the basis of data involving wh-movement from Q'anjobal (see Coon (2010a;b)). (17-a) shows that the expected ergative marker on V (ERG) leads to ungrammaticality if the external argument DP is wh-moved; in contrast, (17-b) illustrates that the presence of the agent focus marker on V (AF) makes such extraction possible.

(17)   a.   *Maktxel max-ach   s-laq'-a' ?
            who   ASP-2.SG.ABS 3.SG.ERG-hug-TV
            'Who hugged you?'
       b.   Maktxel max-ach   laq'-on i?
            who   ASP-2.SG.ABS hug-AF-ITV
            'Who hugged you?'

The agent focus marker is inherently restricted to this kind of extraction environment. If an external argument DP does not undergo movement, or if what is moved is another kind of DP, the agent focus marker is blocked. This is shown for Tzotzil in (18-a) (no movement of the external argument DP) and (18-b) (movement of an internal argument DP); see Aissen (1999a).

(18)   a.   *I-kolta-on   tzeb li   Xun-e
            COMPL-help-AF girl the Juan-ENC
            'Juan helped the girl.'
       b. ?*A   li Xun-e,   I-kolta-o   li   tzeb-e
            FOC the Juan-ENC COMPL-help-AF the girl-ENC
            'The girl helped JUAN.'

Whereas many analyses of Mayan agent focus address the phenomenon from a syntactic perspective, Stiebels (2006) argues that it is ultimately due to disjunctive blocking in morphology, which is implemented in a standard parallel optimality-theoretic approach. In her analysis, the ergative exponent in Mayan languages is (unsurprisingly) an expression of an ergative case feature; but the agent focus exponent (more surprisingly) serves both to express ergative case *and* the information-structural feature (focus, in her analysis) that is involved in (A-bar) movement. For this reason, agent focus is blocked in environments where there is no movement of an external argument DP that is syntactically encoded by an ergative feature because of a violation of compatibility; but it emerges as optimal in environments where an external argument DP undergoes focus-driven movement (which includes wh-movement): Here agent focus marking successfully blocks the pure ergative case feature because it is more specific.

There are three core faithfulness constraints that play a role in Stiebels's (2006) analysis of agent focus. The first one is MAX(ERG), which demands a realization of an ergative case feature in the input. For present purposes, and to maintain compatibility with the decomposition of case features introduced above, it can be assumed that the ergative case feature of an ergative system of argument encoding is identical to the accusative case feature of accusative encoding systems: [–obl,+gov]; on this view, it is independently ensured by syntactic constraints that this case feature identifies an external argument of a transitive verb, rather than an internal argument of a transitive verb (see Murasugi (1992) and Assmann, Georgi, Heck, Müller & Weisser (2015), among others).[14] Next, there is a faithfulness constraint MAX(FOCUS), which requires a realization of the information-structural focus feature on the verb (that also gives rise to DP movement). And third, there is a constraint MAX(ϕ), according to which ϕ-features must be expressed. This is possible with the ergative exponent but not with the agent focus exponent (i.e., whereas agent focus marking implies full syntactic transitivity, with respect to agreement the verb behaves as if it were intransitive); however, the constraint is lowest-ranked, and thus does not decide the outcome. Adding, as before, a general IDENT-F requirement,

---

[14] In Stiebels' original analysis, a dependent case approach is adopted (see Marantz (1991), Wunderlich (1997a), McFadden (2004), Preminger (2014), and Baker (2015), among many others), and the feature identifying the ergative is assumed to be [+lr] ("there is a lower argument"). Nothing hinges on the exact nature of the ergative case feature in the present context.

we arrive at the competition in (19) in contexts where there is a V that registers focus movement of an external argument DP.[15]

(19)   *Agent focus marking in movement contexts* (standard parallel optimality theory):

I_1: [–obl,+gov]^1,[–1,–2,–pl]^1,[+foc]^1	IDENT-F	MAX ERG	MAX FOC	MAX ϕ
O_{11}: V-3.SG.ERG $\leftrightarrow$ [–obl,+gov],[–1,–2,–pl]			*!	
☞ O_{12}: V-AF $\leftrightarrow$ [–obl,+gov],[+foc]				*
O_{13}: V		*!	*	*

In contrast, if the input does not contain a [+foc] feature identifying the external argument DP of V (but, e.g., a [–foc] feature identifying all non-focussed, or backgrounded, material of a clause), the optimal output will be one with the ergative exponent; the agent focus exponent here fatally violates the compatibility requirement for morphological realization that is derivable from a high-ranked IDENT-F.[16]

(20)   *Ergative marking without movement* (standard parallel optimality theory):

I_1: [–obl,+gov]^1,[–1,–2,–pl]^1,[–foc]^1	IDENT-F	MAX ERG	MAX FOC	MAX ϕ
☞ O_{11}: V-3.SG.ERG $\leftrightarrow$ [–obl,+gov],[–1,–2,–pl]			*	
O_{12}: V-AF $\leftrightarrow$ [–obl,+gov],[+foc]	*!			*
O_{13}: V		*!	*	*

To sum up, an interesting consequence of this approach is that there is not actually much wrong with moving a DP argument encoded by the ergative in Mayan languages; it just so happens that using an agent focus exponent gives rise to an even better constraint profile since an agent focus marker realizes ergative case as well as the movement-related information-structural focus feature.

More generally, then, against the background of the case studies just addressed (German determiner inflection, Italian object clitics, and Mayan

---

[15] Identical superscripts in the input are supposed to indicate that the case, ϕ and focus features single out the same argument DP. In the outputs, I abstract away from linearization of the exponents.

[16] It does not matter for the eventual outcome whether the ergative case marker is assumed to realize [–foc] or not; I postulate here that it does not.

agent focus markers), I would like to contend that optimality-theoretic approaches to disjunctive blocking can be viewed as successful. In the following subsection, I address the issue of how these analyses can be transferred to an approach to morphology that relies on harmonic serialism.

2.4. *Disjunctive Blocking in Harmonic Serialism*

Standard parallel optimality-theoretic analyses of disjunctive blocking of the type just discussed can be transferred to harmonic serialism without problems; the reason is that in disjunctive blocking, there is only one operation to begin with, viz., selection of the most faitfhul morphological exponent. Still, in the course of showing how such a transfer can proceed, some basic assumptions underlying the present approach can be introduced. As noted in chapter 1, I assume that inflectional morphology applies pre-syntactically, in the numeration. First, for each basic stem belonging to some syntactic category (i.e., possibly complex stem that has not been subject to inflection) α in the lexicon, a (language-specific) matrix of fully specified morpho-syntax features is generated in the numeration that comprises both inherent features of the stem (like inflection class) and non-inherent features that are added in the numeration (like, e.g., person and number with Vs, or case and number with Ns). This provides the fully specified context for morphological exponence. Second, I assume that all the competing exponents β_1, β_2, ..., β_n that are involved in morphological realization relying on disjunctive blocking are initially part of a *morphological array* (see Kager (1996), Mascaró (1996)). Simplifying a bit, suppose that morphological exponents β_1, β_2, ..., β_n belong to the same morphological array if they share a category feature that is subcategorized for by the stem α, and that in turn characterizes the array. In cases where there is more than one affix eventually showing up with a stem, the stem will be equipped with more than one subcategorization feature, and these features will target different morphological arrays with a matching feature.[17] What then happens in structure-building morphological exponence is that the stem α successively combines with the morphological arrays, picking the optimal morphological exponent contained in each array. What are these subcategorization features for morphological arrays? I suggest that, exactly as in the syntax (see chapter 1), there are designated structure-building features [•X•] associated with stems (either inherently or, more likely, added in the numeration) whose discharge (and deletion) is brought

---

[17] These assumptions will undergo some slight modification in the following chapter.

about by the MERGE CONDITION (MC), which is repeated here from (19) of chapter 1 in (21).

(21)　MERGE CONDITION (MC):
　　　Structure-building features ([•X•]) participate in Merge.

Consider an abstract example. Suppose that a (fully specified) stem α has come to be equipped with two subcategorization features [•β•] and [•γ•] in the numeration; this then gives rise to an input for morphological realization including the stem α, the morphological array γ, and the morphological array β. Clearly, β and γ need to be ordered.[18] Suppose that the empirical evidence suggests that β is closer to the stem than γ. Then, the STRICT CYCLE CONDITION in (22), as an elementary and inviolable constraint on incremental structure-building in grammar (i.e., belonging to *Gen* under present assumptions), requires the operation of selection of the optimal exponent β_i in β *before* the stem combines with the optimal exponent γ_j in γ.

(22)　STRICT CYCLE CONDITION (SCC; Chomsky (1973)):
　　　Within the current domain δ, an operation may not target a position
　　　that is included within another domain ϵ that is dominated by δ.

This can be achieved in various ways. One possibility would be to assume that α's morphological structure-building features [•β•] and [•γ•] are ordered as part of a list, and some feature can only be visibile for the grammar if it has reached the top of the list (due to prior deletion of higher features); see Heck & Müller (2013; 2016) for this concept in syntax. Under this approach, a problem with the STRICT CYCLE CONDITION can never arise. An alternative possibility is to derive the order of combination of α with β and γ by designated ranked subconstraints of the *H-Eval* component (e.g., $\mathrm{MC}_\beta \gg \mathrm{MC}_\gamma$). In both approaches, it would in principle be possible to implement substantive universals concerning the hierarchy of inflectional exponents (e.g., by recourse to a general functional sequence of categories (see Starke (2001)). I will adopt the latter kind of approach in what follows. As before, the constraint profile gradually improves, and the morphological derivation terminates when there is convergence (identity of input and output).

---

[18] As remarked in chapter 1 (see (2-d)), β and γ ultimately have a role that is similar to functional morphemes into which insertion takes place in Distributed Morphology, and to rule blocks in models like Paradigm Function Morphology or Network Morphology.

With these assumptions in place, let me go back to disjunctive blocking in German determiner inflection. Since this example only involves the combination of a D stem with a single morphological exponent, it turns out that the transfer of the standard parallel optimality-theoretic analysis to harmonic serialism is not particularly challenging. Consider first the choice of the optimal exponent in dative masculine singular contexts (see (10) above). By assumption, the input in inflectional morphology in harmonic serialism contains the stem with its fully specified set of morpho-syntactic features – in the case at hand, this includes a structure-building feature [•X•] identifying the members of the morphological array from which the selection takes place.[19] In German determiner inflection, this is a fusional case/number/gender category that I will simply refer to as K; so D is equipped with a [•K•] feature that it needs to discharge, given MC, with some K exponent from the morphological array characterized by this feature. Thus the morphological array K is also part of the input; the exponents that are members of this morphological array have exactly the same specifications as before; see (5). Given that D does not have any other structure-building feature, nothing else shows up in the input. Against this background, (23) shows how O_{11} emerges as optimal: It discharges D's [•K•] feature (like other outputs based on all the other members of the K array would have done), it does not violate IDENT-F (compatibility), and it best satisfies the ranked MAX constraints (specificity).[20]

---

[19] At this point, it should be pointed out that the MC-based approach is actually not so different from orthodox faithfulness-based approaches employing PARSE (see Prince & Smolensky (2004)) or MAX (see McCarthy & Prince (1995)) constraints. In fact, in the present context, MC(X) on a stem requires X to show up on the inflectional exponent of the derived word in the same way that PARSE(X) or MAX(X) does; in this sense the MERGE CONDITION can be viewed as a faithfulness constraint. The main difference between MC and MAX is that, under present assumptions, MC targets a feature that defines a morphological array, and not just any feature of a morphological exponent included in such an array.

[20] As a notational convention, for space reasons I have not included the feature specifications of the individual morphological exponents here. Instead, the satisfaction of a MAX constraint by an exponent is signalled by underlining the respective feature in the fully specified matrix associated with the stem. Similarly, the (fatal) violation of IDENT-F is indicated by a superscript ^{i}.

(23) *Dative masculine singular contexts* (harmonic serialism, step 1):

I_1: $[_D$ dies]: $[\bullet K\bullet]$, $[+m,-f,+o,+g]$, $\{[_K e^9], [_K r^8], [_K n^7], [_K r^6], [_K r^5], [_K n^4], [_K s^3], [_K s^2], [_K m^1]\}$	MC	ID-F	MAXM	MAXO	MAXF	MAXG
☞O_{11}: $D[\underline{+m},-f,\underline{+o},+g]$-$m^1$					*	
O_{12}: $D[\underline{+m},-f,\underline{+o},+g]$-$s^2$					*	*!
O_{13}: $D[\underline{+m},\underline{-f^i},+o,+g]$-$s^3$		*!		*		*
O_{14}: $D[\underline{+m},-f,+o,\underline{+g}]$-$n^4$				*!	*	
O_{15}: $D[\underline{+m},-f,+o,+g]$-$r^5$				*!	*	*
O_{16}: $D[+m,\underline{-f^i},\underline{+o},+g]$-$r^6$		*!	*			*
O_{17}: $D[+m,-f,\underline{+o},+g]$-$n^7$			*!		*	
O_{18}: $D[+m,-f,\underline{+o},+g]$-$r^8$			*!		*	*
O_{19}: $D[+m,-f,+o,+g]$-e^9			*!	*	*	*
O_{20}: $D[+m,-f,+o,+g]_{[\bullet K\bullet]}$	*!		*	*	*	*

As before, O_{13} and O_{15} fatally violate IDENT-F. O_{17}, O_{18}, and O_{19} are removed from the competition by MAX(MASC). O_{14} and O_{15} are excluded by MAX(OBL). And O_{12} is finally blocked by O_{11} via MAX(GOV). The only thing that is new here is that there is now also an additional candidate O_{20} (which, however, would strictly speaking also already have been present in the earlier standard parallel optimality-theoretic analysis). O_{20} neglects to carry out any inflection and therefore fatally violates MC: The stem's $[\bullet K\bullet]$ feature cannot be discharged.

At this point, two further assumptions about the morphological array can be specified. First, if an allomorph is taken out of the morphological array, the morphological array's cardinality is irrevocably reduced by one. This is reflected in the input for the second optimization step leading to convergence in (24). And second, since the task is to implement disjunctive blocking, it can for now be assumed that it is a property of *Gen* that the only way to effect morphological exponence is by discharging a structure-building feature.[21] This implies that the derivation need not consider at this point whether the constraint profile could be further improved by selecting another exponent in addition, which might then help to get rid of the remaining MAX(FEM) violation. Also, it seems clear that a deletion of the exponent cannot possibly improve the candidate's constraint profile; again, for present purposes we can assume that such a deletion is not

---

[21] As we will see in chapter 3, there is good reason to give up this stipulation so as to account for cases of extended exponence, and this will then have massive repercussions for the analysis of disjunctive blocking, which will give rise to a revision of the present system in chapter 4.

available.[22] Consequently, the optimization step leading to convergence in (24) is completely trivial.

(24) *Dative masculine singular contexts* (harmonic serialism, step 2):

I_{11}: $[_D$ dies$]$: $[\underline{+m},-f,\underline{+o},\underline{+g}]$, $\{[_K e^9], [_K r^8], [_K n^7], [_K r^6], [_K r^5], [_K n^4], [_K s^3], [_K s^2]\}$	MC	ID-F	MaxM	MaxO	MaxF	MaxG
☞O_{111}: D$[\underline{+m},-f,\underline{+o},+g]$-m^1					*	

The optimization procedures work exactly the same way in the other cases of disjunctive blocking in German determiner inflection; and other standard parallel optimality-theoretic analyses of disjunctive blocking like the ones developed in Grimshaw (2001) and Stiebels (2006) can be transferred to harmonic serialism with similar ease. Also, it should be clear how scenarios are accounted for where there is more than one slot (i.e., more than one morphological array).

Before moving on to the topic of affix order, a remark is due concerning the scope of the IDENT and MAX constraints adopted so far. In principle, the morpho-syntactic features for which correspondence relations mediated by IDENT and MAX (and possibly DEP) constraints (see McCarthy & Prince (1995)) are present show up in several different places: First, there is a fully specified feature matrix associated with the stem in the input; second, the same stem also has these features in the output; third, the individual morphological exponents that are part of a morphological array bear (typically underspecified) features in the input; and fourth, these exponents also bear the features in the output, when they are part of a word generated by *Gen*. It is clear that for the modelling of disjunctive blocking, the relevant correspondence relation is one between features on the stem and features on the inflectional exponent that it is merged with; and these can be read off the respective output representations. But what about the other relations? Can there be unfaithful mappings from the morpho-syntactic features of the input stem to the morpho-syntactic features of the output stem? And can there be unfaithful mappings from the morpho-syntactic features of the input markers included in a morphological array to the individual output markers that have combined with a stem? What is more, given an approach based on harmonic serialism, can there be unfaithful mappings between outputs that again serve as inputs for further optimizations, and the new outputs? For the time being, I will abstract away from this issue,

---

[22] And again, it will turn out in chapter 4 that there is reason to revise this assumption.

and simply pretend that the answer is negative in all these scenarios; however, I will come back to this issue in chapter 6.

3. Affix Order

3.1. Introduction

As argued by Trommer (2001; 2008a), an optimality-theoretic approach to the order of morphological exponents is potentially interesting because it permits both an account of general tendencies of affix order in the languages of the world, and the systematic integration of interfering factors that blur an otherwise simple picture in this domain. Non-optimality-theoretic approaches to inflectional morphology have usually very little to say about these issues. For instance, in Distributed Morphology, affix order is basically regulated by the sequence of functional heads (into which vocabulary insertion takes place) after all the syntactic (head) movement operations have applied; and any deviation from this sequence is then handled by ad hoc operations without deeper motivation. Among these are, e.g., fusion and fission operations in Halle & Marantz (1993), lowering and local dislocation in Embick & Noyer (2001; 2007), metathesis in Arregi & Nevins (2012), and, finally, individual assignments of morphological exponents to prefix or suffix status that may override the placing that would be required on the basis of where the respective functional head is located in the syntax (see Noyer (1992), Frampton (2002)); etc.

Given this state of affairs, in what follows, I first sketch a version of the standard parallel optimality-theoretic account of affix order developed in Trommer (2001; 2008a), based on data involving person and number marking in Wardaman. I then illustrate how the analysis can be transferred to harmonic serialism. After that, I go through a second example: First, I introduce Trommer's analysis of person and number marking in Island Kiwai. And after that, I show that the analysis can be transferred to harmonic serialism without problems.[23]

The analyses based on harmonic serialism can be shown to be extensionally equivalent for the available data; however, ceteris paribus the harmonic serialist approach systematically predicts the existence of movement in morphology, and thus the availability of intermediate stages that may give rise

---

[23] As before, to ensure compatibility with the rest of the material in this book, simplify exposition, and make the eventual transfer of the analysis more transparent, I focus on (what I perceive as) the core of Trommer's analyses throughout, and I adjust and modify (sometimes tacitly) his assumptions about the organization of the grammar, the formulations of constraints, and so on.

to opacity effects (in the sense of Kiparsky (1973a)), as with movement
in syntax in general. Finally, at the end of the chapter, I argue that the
harmonic serialist approach can shed new light on some recalcitrant phenomena involving discontinuous exponents (or circumfixes), and I provide
independent evidence for movement in morphology based on phonological
reflexes in positions occupied by exponents at an earlier stage.

3.2. *Affix Order in Standard Parallel Optimality Theory: Wardaman*

The first case study is on person and number marking on the verb in
Wardaman, a Non-Pama-Nyungan language from Northern Australia; the
data come from Merlan (1994). Trommer's (2008a) analysis relies on two
kinds of constraints. First, there are constraints ensuring that the verb
stem combines with separate person and number exponents. In Trommer's
system, these constraints are referred to as PARSEPERS and PARSENUM.
This translates to MAX(PERS) and MAX(NUM) under present assumptions.

(25) a.   MAX(PERS):
           [pers] of the input is realized on an exponent in the output.
      b.   MAX(NUM):
           [num] of the input is realized on an exponent in the output.

Second, there are four constraints determining the position of the affixes
introduced via (25-ab). The first two – L⇐PERS and NUM⇒R – encode
the cross-linguistically valid tendency that person exponents tend to show
up to the left in a word, whereas number exponents tend to show up to the
right; cf. (26-ab).[24] The third constraint, COHERENCE(D), is at the heart
of the analysis; it ensures that agreement exponents that encode the same
argument (which is indicated by co-indexation) stay as close together in
the final word as possible; see (26-c). Finally, Trommer assumes that there
is a constraint REFLECT which, however, turns out to be irrelevant for the

---

[24] This is not quite coextensional with saying the the former want to be prefixes and
the latter suffixes, given that the constraints are gradient: A violation is counted for
each affix that intervenes between the affix that is subject to the constraint, and the
left (person) or right (number) edge of the word; so a person suffix showing up closer
to the root violates the constraint less severely than a person suffix showing up in
the right periphery of a word. (See Grimshaw (2006) and Steddy & Samek-Lodovici
(2011) for the same conclusion with respect to alignment constraints in the syntax.) In
addition, it is worth pointing out that Trommer (2001, 301) postulates that mirror image
alignment constraints pulling person exponents to the right edge, and number exponents
to the left edge, do not exist. Also note that I have minimally changed the wording of
these alignment constraints, mainly to ensure compatibility with later chapters of this
monograph.

analyses to be discussed here, and is added at this point only for the sake of completeness; see (26-d).[25]

(26) a. L⇐PERS:
          A morphological exponent realizing person is aligned with the left edge of a word.
      b. NUM⇒R:
          A morphological exponent realizing number is aligned with the right edge of a word.
      c. COHERENCE (D) (COH):
          Count a constraint violation for each morphological exponent V containing index i which is immediately preceded in domain D by another morphological exponent V′ containing index j such that $i \neq j$.
      d. REFLECT (REFL):
          Realize at least one of the set of co-indexed agreement exponents in its unmarked position in a language.
          (The unmarked position for person and number exponents is to the right of T in Wardaman.)

From these constraints it follows that if person and number corresponding to some argument DP in the syntax are realized by separate exponents on the verb, they may both be prefixes, or both suffixes, or one is a prefix and one is a suffix, but the person exponent will always precede the

____

[25] Trommer's original version of REFLECT requires morphological exponents to show up in the positions where a functional morpheme is provided for them in the syntax. Here is the original definition of REFLECT in Trommer (2001).

(i)   REFLECT (REFL, original version):
       An affix realizing an agreement category A should reflect the position of its host H by
       a.   being right-adjacent to an affix realizing H, or by
       b.   occupying the position of H, if H is not realized in this position.

A background assumption made by Trommer (2001; 2008a) is that morphological realization is actualy post-syntactic vocabulary insertion into functional morphemes, exactly as in Distributed Morphology (accordingly, his approach as a whole is dubbed Distributed Optimality). However, given the first three constraints in (26), it is clear that morphological exponents may also end up in other positions as a result of optimization, which begs the question whether vocaubary *insertion* can be maintained as a coherent concept in such an approach. (Also see the remarks on Noyer (1992) and Frampton (2002) above.)

number exponent. The list of underspecified person and number exponents in Wardaman that Trommer assumes on this basis is given in (27).[26]

(27) *Underspecified exponents*:

    a.   /nu/ $\leftrightarrow$ [+2,+pl]
    b.   /ŋa/ $\leftrightarrow$ [+1]
    c.   /wu/ $\leftrightarrow$ [+3]/[+pl]
    d.   /yi/ $\leftrightarrow$ [−3]
    e.   /rr/ $\leftrightarrow$ [+pl]

A ranking of the constraints that derives the data from Wardaman is given in (28).

(28) *Ranking*:

MAX(NUM) $\gg$ MAX(PERS) $\gg$ L$\Leftarrow$PERS $\gg$ COH $\gg$ NUM$\Rightarrow$R $\gg$ REFL

The competition for third person plural argument encoding environments is shown in (29).

(29) *Third person plural argument encoding* (standard parallel optimality theory):

I_1: V_1 T_2 [+3+pl]$_3$	MAX(NUM)	MAX(PERS)	L$\Leftarrow$PERS	COH	NUM$\Rightarrow$R	REFL
☞O_{11}: wu:[+3]$_3$-rr:[+pl]$_3$-V_1-T_2				**	**	*
O_{12}: wu:[+3]$_3$-V_2-rr:[+pl]$_3$-T_2				***!	*	*
O_{13}: wu:[+3]$_3$-V_2-T_2-rr:[+pl]$_3$				***!		
O_{14}: V_2-T_2-wu:[+3]$_3$-rr:[+pl]$_3$			*!*	**		
O_{15}: V_2-T_2-rr:[+pl]$_3$-wu:[+3]$_3$			*!**	**	*	
O_{16}: rr:[+pl]$_3$-wu:[+3]$_3$-V_1-T_2			*!	**	***	*

The only way to satisfy the two highest-ranked constraints MAX(NUM) and MAX(PERS) (given a compatibility requirement as it can be implemented via a high-ranked IDENT-F) is to combine the V-T complex with both /wu/ and /rr/. As for the position in which these two exponents show up, L$\Leftarrow$PERS is ranked highest and forces the person exponent /wu/ to be at the left periphery, as a prefix, as in O_{11}, O_{12}, and O_{13}. Conversely, NUM$\Rightarrow$R requires the number exponent /rr/ to be at the right periphery, as in O_{13} and O_{14}. However, this latter constraint is outranked by COH,

---

[26] The exponent /wu/ in (27-c) has a contextual feature as part of its specification, which strictly speaking makes this an instance of extended exponence; and essentially the same goes for the exponent /nu/. For the time being, I will abstract away from this complication. See the next chapter on how to deal with extended exponence.

which demands that the two exponents (that encode the same argument DP) stay as close together as possible. Consequently, /rr/ is not realized as a suffix, but shows up as a prefix, next to /wu/; thus, O_{11} emerges as optimal.[27]

Note that while maintaining adjacency, a reversal of the order of the person and number exponents, as in O_{16}, is harmonically bounded by the winner: This candidate does not improve the behaviour with respect to any constraints but, on the contrary, adds unmotivated violations of $L{\Leftarrow}$PERS (since /wu/ is not at the left edge anymore) and NUM${\Rightarrow}$R (since /rr/ is even further to the left than it has to be to bring about adjacency in O_{11}). Also note that REFL, which is violated by all outputs where none of the two exponents in question shows up to the right of T, does not play a role in this competition.

As observed by Trommer (2008a), the system also makes plausible predictions from the point of view of factorial typology. First, an order Per_3-Num_3-V_1-T_2 results whenever COH and $L{\Leftarrow}$PERS outrank NUM${\Rightarrow}$R, as in (28).[28] Second, a serialization V_1-T_2-Per_3-Num_3 results if COH outranks REFL, which outranks all the other constraints (here REFL does indeed become relevant). Third, if COH is ranked below $L{\Leftarrow}$PERS and NUM${\Rightarrow}$R, this gives rise to the order Per_3-V_1-T_2-Num_3. Fourth, the system predicts an order V_1-Per_3-T_2-Num_4 if REFL outranks COH, which in turn outranks $L{\Leftarrow}$PERS and NUM${\Rightarrow}$R. Finally, low-ranked MAX(PERS) (or MAXNUM) and high-ranked COH lead to non-realization of person (or number) exponents.

Let me now show how the analysis can be transferred to harmonic serialism.

------

[27] COHERENCE is formulated in an indirect way in Trommer (2008a) (and in (26-c)), so that it will invariably be violated if there is more than one exponent (with a different index) in a word. Crucially, thus, COH violations can only be minimized by putting two exponents with the same index into an adjacent position; they cannot be avoided completely.

[28] At this point, one may note that the actual hierarchy assumed by Trommer (2008a) has the ranking of the two highest constraints – COH and $L{\Leftarrow}$PERS – reversed. I have chosen the alternative ranking here that makes exactly the same predictions in his analysis because it gives rise to a more interesting derivation in the reconstruction of the analysis in harmonic serialism.

3.3. *Affix Order in Harmonic Serialism: Wardaman*

3.3.1. *A First Implementation*

Recall first from the implementation of disjunctive blocking on page 52 that I have provisionally assumed that the only way to realize a morphological exponent from a morphological array is by virtue of a structure-building feature [•F•] that characterizes the morphological array. This assumption will be given up in the next chapter, but suppose for now that it holds. It can then be postulated that there are two separate morphological arrays for person and number in Wardaman verb inflection, one defined by [•Num•] and one defined by [•Pers•]. Suppose further (basically following Trommer's reasoning) that of the exponents in (27), the first four (including /wu/) are person markers whereas the last one (i.e., /rr/) is a number marker. The two morphological arrays are given in (30).[29]

(30) *Morphological arrays for Wardaman person and number inflection:*

    a.   Person:
        $\{[_\text{Pers} \text{ /nu/} \leftrightarrow [+2,+\text{pl}]], [_\text{Pers} \text{ /ŋa/} \leftrightarrow [+1]],$
        $[_\text{Pers} \text{ /wu/} \leftrightarrow [+3]/[+\text{pl}]], [_\text{Pers} \text{ /yi/} \leftrightarrow [-3]]\}$

    b.   Number:
        $\{[_\text{Num} \text{ /rr/} \leftrightarrow [+\text{pl}]]\}$

In line with this, the constraints MAX(NUM) and MAX(PERS) are now replaced with MERGE CONDITION(NUM) and MERGE CONDITION(PERS), respectively. These constraints affect the grammatical categories postulated here (Pers and Num); and there are additional IDENT-F and MAX constraints for the different instantiations of these grammatical categories (like [+3] and [+pl], according to Trommer's assumptions).

(31) a.   MERGE CONDITION(NUM) (MC(NUM)):
          [•Num•]) participates in Merge.
     b.   MERGE CONDITION(PERS) (MC(PERS)):
          [•Pers•]) participates in Merge.
     c.   IDENT-F:
          Morpho-syntactic features of input and output cannot have different values.

---

[29] Why is it that /nu/ is a person marker rather than a number marker, or both? And what about /wu/? As noted, these questions, related to the presence of extended exponence in the system, will be resolved in a systematic way in the next chapter. However, it is worth noting that the assumptions introduced there will not affect the core mechanics of the analysis developed below.

    d.   MAX(3):
        [3] of the input is realized on an exponent in the output.
    e.   MAX(PL):
        [pl] of the input is realized on an exponent in the output.

In contrast to what has been the case with the harmonic serialist reconstruction of disjunctive blocking, this time a faithful transfer of the analysis will not lead to a system of optimization that is virtually indistinguishable from the standard parallel optimality-theoretic approach. The reason is that this time, there are indeed several non-trivial optimization steps, with repeated optimization gradually improving the constraint profile. In particular, it will become clear that the implementation of Trommer's COHERENCE-based approach to affix order in harmonic serialism automatically predicts a change of position for one of the affixes – i.e., a systematically defined and constrained movement operation in the morphological component of the grammar. The underlying reason is that COHERENCE is a constraint that is trivially satisfied (or, given Trommer's formulation, that is trivially *best* satisfied) as long as only one morphological exponent β is present in the structure encoding a DP argument; so, a constraint that inherently determines β-placement will decide on the position of β at this point. However, subsequently, another exponent γ will be merged that cross-references the same DP argument, and this means that COHERENCE becomes active, and may then force a change of β's position if sufficiently highly ranked.

To turn to a concrete example, let us look again at environments in which a third person plural argument needs to be encoded.[30] The first step in (32) ensures exponence of number: Due to a high-ranked MC(NUM), all outputs that do not merge an exponent from the morphological array Num are immediately filtered out. This includes O_{11} (which does not carry out any morphological structure-building), O_{12} (where an exponent is taken from the Pers morphological array that satisfies IDENT and MAX(3)), O_{13} (where an exponent is taken from the Pers morphological array that violates both IDENT and MAX(3), which implies harmonic bounding of the candidate by O_{12}), O_{14} (where an exponent is taken from the Pers morphological array that satisfies IDENT and MAX(3) but shows up in the wrong position, given L⇐PERS), and O_{15} (where an exponent is taken from the Pers morphological array that violates both IDENT and MAX(3), *and* shows

---

[30] To simplify things, I assume here that V_1 has already been merged with T_2. Also, since no candidate can ever satisfy MAX(1), MAX(2) without violating IDENT-F in this context (given the marker inventory), these constraints are not listed here.

up in the wrong position). Thus, the competition boils down to a choice between O_{16} and O_{17}. Both these outputs merge the plural marker /rr/ from the morphological array Num, thereby satisfying highest-ranked MC(NUM) and violating MC(PERS) – but this latter violation is unavoidable, given that *Gen* can only carry out one operation before optimization takes place. O_{16} places the number marker in a right-peripheral position; O_{17} places it in a left-peripheral position. Since COHERENCE is not yet active and cannot discriminate between the two options (because there is only one exponent with index 3, and the two violations of COHERENCE incurred by T_2 and V_1 in O_{17} exactly match the two violations of COHERENCE incurred by /rr/$_3$ and T_2 in O_{16}), NUM$\Rightarrow$R decides the competition in favour of O_{16}.

(32) *Third person plural argument encoding* (harmonic serialism, step 1):

I_1: V_1-T_2:[•Num•], [•Pers•], $[-1,-2,+3,+pl]_3$, {[Pers /nu/], [Pers /ŋa/], [Pers /wu/], [Pers /yi/]}, {[Num /rr/]},	MC (NUM)	MC (PERS)	ID F	MAX 3	MAX PL	L⇐ PERS	COH	NUM ⇒R	REFL
O_{11}: V_1-T_2:[•Num•], [•Pers•]	*!	*		*	*		*		
O_{12}: wu:$[+3]_3$-V_1-T_2:[•Num•]	*!				*		**		*
O_{13}: ŋa:$[+1]_3$-V_1-T_2:[•Num•]	*!		*	*	*		**		*
O_{14}: V_1-T_2-wu:$[+3]_3$:[•Num•]	*!				*	**	**		
O_{15}: V_1-T_2-ŋa:$[+1]_3$:[•Num•]	*!		*	*	*	**	**		
☞O_{16}: V_1-T_2-rr:$[+pl]_3$:[•Pers•]		*		*			**		
O_{17}: rr:$[+pl]_3$-V_1-T_2:[•Pers•]		*		*			**	*!*	*

In the next step, O_{16} is used as the input for further optimization; /rr/ has been deleted from the Num morphological array, which has now become irrelevant (since [•Num•] is gone from the stem). Now MC(PERS) forces selection of an item from the Pers array; cf. O_{161}. The person marker /wu/ is merged from the Pers morphological array, and it is placed in the leftmost position in the word, because of L⇐PERS, as in O_{162} in (33). If /wu/ shows up in a rightmost position, adjacent to the number exponent, a fatal violation of L⇐PERS occurs; see O_{164}. As before, selecting an unfaithful exponent like /ŋa/ instead of /wu/, as in O_{163}, gives rise to fatal IDENT-F and MAX(3) violations; and putting it into the wrong position, as in O_{165}, violates L⇐PERS in addition.

62   Chapter 2. From Optimality Theory to Harmonic Serialism

(33) *Third person plural argument encoding* (harmonic serialism, step 2):

I_{16}: V_1-T_2-rr:$[+pl]_3$:$[\bullet Pers\bullet]$, $[-1,-2,+3,+pl]_3$, $\{[_{Pers}$ /nu/], $[_{Pers}$ /ŋa/], $[_{Pers}$ /wu/], $[_{Pers}$ /yi/]\}, $\{-\}$	MC (NUM)	MC (PERS)	ID F	MAX 3	MAX PL	L⇐ PERS	COH	NUM ⇒R	REFL
O_{161}: V_1-T_2-rr:$[+pl]_3$:$[\bullet Pers\bullet]$		*!		*			**		
☞ O_{162}: wu:$[+3]_3$-V_1-T_2-rr:$[+pl]_3$							***		*
O_{163}: ŋa:$[+1]_3$-V_1-T_2-rr:$[+pl]_3$			*!	*			***		*
O_{164}: V_1-T_2-rr:$[+pl]_3$-wu:$[+3]_3$						*!**	**		
O_{165}: V_1-T_2-rr:$[+pl]_3$-ŋa:$[+1]_3$			*!	*			***	**	

Note, however, that the optimal output O_{162} in (33) has added a COHERENCE violation that was not present in the input – the exponents of number and person that encode one and the same argument DP are now both in the positions where they would be required by NUM⇒R and L⇐PERS, respectively, but this means that they are not adjacent. Since COHERENCE outranks NUM⇒R, the derivation now strives to get rid of the additional COHERENCE violation by *moving* the number exponent in the next step. A first possible implementation of this is shown in (34).

(34) *Third person plural argument encoding* (harmonic serialism, step 3):

I_{162}: wu:$[+3]_3$-V_1-T_2-rr:$[+pl]_3$, $[-1,-2,+3,+pl]_3$, $\{[_{Pers}$ /nu/], $[_{Pers}$ /ŋa/], $[_{Pers}$ /yi/]\}, $\{-\}$	MC (NUM)	MC (PERS)	ID F	MAX 3	MAX PL	L⇐ PERS	COH	NUM ⇒R	REFL
O_{1621}: wu:$[+3]_3$-V_1-T_2-rr:$[+pl]_3$							*!**		*
O_{1622}: V_1-T_2-rr:$[+pl]_3$-wu:$[+3]_3$						*!**	**		
O_{1623}: rr:$[+pl]_3$-wu:$[+3]_3$-V_1-T_2						*!	**	***	*
☞ O_{1624}: wu:$[+3]_3$-rr:$[+pl]_3$-V_1-T_2							**	**	*

O_{1621} leaves the input intact, thereby producing a fatal COHERENCE violation. O_{1622} moves the person exponent to the right; this improves the candidate's behaviour towards COHERENCE, but does so at the cost of maximizing violations of the high-ranked constraint L⇐PERS. O_{1623}, in contrast, moves the number marker to the left. Again, a third violation of COHERENCE is avoided, but since the person marker is now not at the left edge anymore, this still gives rise to a L⇐PERS violation, which is fatal in the case at hand because L⇐PERS is ranked higher than COHERENCE. Finally, O_{1624} moves the number marker to a position directly following the person marker. As shown in (34), O_{1624} then emerges as the optimal output, giving rise to convergence in the next step.

Or does it? The movement step carried out by O_{1624} is of exactly the same type as movement steps in the syntax that involve tucking in (i.e., movement to a lower specifier in the presence of a higher specifier; see

Richards (2001) and Branigan (2013), among many others). Depending on its exact formulation, such movement may or may not violate the STRICT CYCLE CONDITION.[31] Given the definition adopted here (see (22) above), it needs to be clarified exactly what counts as a cyclic "domain" in morphology for a given operation. This issue may perhaps be resolved in favour of a status of O_{1624} as an optimal output. Still, it might be worthwhile to see if there is an alternative way to ultimately end up with the sequence wu:$[+3]_3$-rr:$[+pl]_3$-V_1-T_2 in Wardaman by movement of the number marker that is compatible with the strictest possible interpretation of the STRICT CYCLE CONDITION (basically, Chomsky's (1995) Extension Condition).

3.3.2. A Second Implementation

Intuitively, a derivation of optimizations that is compatible with the STRICT CYCLE CONDITION in its most radical form will have O_{1623} in (34) as the optimal candidate since it minimizes COHERENCE violations by moving the number marker to the front of the person marker. However, this is at variance with L⇐PERS. A lower ranking of L⇐PERS would solve the problem at this point, but such a ranking would ceteris paribus not place the person marker at the left edge to begin with: In the prior step in (33), O_{162} (with the person marker at the left edge) would be blocked in favour of O_{164} (with the person marker at the right edge, so as to maximize satisfaction of COHERENCE). Thus it looks as though there is a ranking dilemma.

This dilemma can be solved, though, by incorporating a standard means in optimality theory to model cumulative effects, viz., *local conjunction.* Local conjunction goes back to Smolensky (1995; 2006); it has been crucially invoked in many analyses in phonology (see, e.g., Alderete (1997), Itô & Mester (1998), Kager (1999, 392–400), and Łubowicz (2005), among many others), in syntax (see Legendre et al. (1998; 2006), Fischer (2001)), and in approaches to the morphology/syntax interface (see Aissen (1999b; 2003), Keine & Müller (2011), and Müller & Thomas (2017)).[32] Thus, suppose that L⇐PERS undergoes *reflexive* local conjunction (see Smolensky (1995; 2006) for this general option), such that the local conjunction of L⇐PERS with itself, L⇐PERS^2 (i.e., L⇐PERS&L⇐PERS), is violated if there are two violations of this constraint (in the same local domain), but not yet if there is only one violation of it. By definition, L⇐PERS^2

---

[31] Also see Heck (2018) for an argument against tucking in in syntax.

[32] Also, in Müller (2020), I argue that local conjunction is empirically preferable to harmonic grammar when it comes to modelling cumulative effects in morphology and syntax.

must outrank $L{\Leftarrow}$PERS, the basic constraint from which it is derived.[33] Given these assumptions, a partial ranking as in (35) makes the right predictions: COHERENCE must be violable by exponent placement if $L{\Leftarrow}$PERS would otherwise be violated twice (or more often), but cannot be violated by exponent placement if otherwise only one violation of $L{\Leftarrow}$PERS would result.

(35) $L{\Leftarrow}$PERS^2 $\gg$ COHERENCE $\gg$ $L{\Leftarrow}$PERS

With this in mind, consider again the individual optimization procedures for person and number marking in Wardaman third person plural contexts.

In the first step, nothing changes. COHERENCE and $L{\Leftarrow}$PERS are not yet relevant because the highest-ranked constraint demands a number exponent; see (36).

(36) *Third person plural argument encoding* (harmonic serialism alternative, step 1):

I_1: V_1-T_2:[•Num•], [•Pers•], $[-1,-2,+3,+pl]_3$, {[Pers /nu/], [Pers /ŋa/], [Pers /wu/], [Pers /yi/]}, {[Num /rr/]}	MC (NUM)	MC (PERS)	ID F	MAX 3	MAX PL	L⇐ PERS^2	COH	L⇐ PERS	NUM ⇒R	REFL
O_{11}: V_1-T_2:[•Num•], [•Pers•]	*!	*		*	*		*			
O_{12}: wu:$[+3]_3$-V_1-T_2:[•Num•]	*!				*		**			*
O_{13}: ŋa:$[+1]_3$-V_1-T_2:[•Num•]	*!		*	*	*		**			*
O_{14}: V_1-T_2-wu:$[+3]_3$:[•Num•]	*!				*	*	**	**		
O_{15}: V_1-T_2-ŋa:$[+1]_3$:[•Num•]	*!		*	*	*	*	**	**		*
☞O_{16}: V_1-T_2-rr:$[+pl]_3$:[•Pers•]		*		*			**			
O_{17}: rr:$[+pl]_3$-V_1-T_2:[•Pers•]		*		*			**		*!*	*

In the next step, the person exponent is merged at the left edge because an improved behaviour towards COHERENCE would give rise to a fatal violation of the higher-ranked constraint $L{\Leftarrow}$PERS^2 derived by reflexive local conjunction; see O_{162} vs. O_{164}.

---

(37) *Third person plural argument encoding* (harmonic serialism
alternative, step 2):

I_{16}: V_1-T_2-rr:$[+pl]_3$:$[\bullet Pers\bullet]$, $[-1,-2,+3,+pl]_3$, {$[_{Pers}$ /nu/], $[_{Pers}$ /ŋa/], $[_{Pers}$ /wu/], $[_{Pers}$ /yi/]}, { – }	MC (NUM)	MC (PERS)	ID F	MAX 3	MAX PL	L⇐ PERS²	COH	L⇐ PERS	NUM ⇒R	REFL
O_{161}: V_1-T_2-rr:$[+pl]_3$:$[\bullet Pers\bullet]$		*!		*			**			
☞O_{162}: wu:$[+3]_3$-V_1-T_2-rr:$[+pl]_3$							***			*
O_{163}: ŋa:$[+1]_3$-V_1-T_2-rr:$[+pl]_3$			*!	*			***			*
O_{164}: V_1-T_2-rr:$[+pl]_3$-wu:$[+3]_3$						*!	**	***		
O_{165}: V_1-T_2-rr:$[+pl]_3$-ŋa:$[+1]_3$			*!	*		*	**	***		

In the third step, O_{1623} – the candidate that moves the number exponent
to the left edge, in front of the person exponent – can now emerge as optimal if we assume that the tucking-in candidate O_{1624} cannot be produced
by *Gen* because of the STRICT CYCLE CONDITION: In order to minimize
COHERENCE violations, O_{1623} introduces a new violation of L⇐PERS (because it removes the person marker from the left edge by one position); but
crucially O_{1623} does *not* violate the higher-ranked constraint L⇐PERS².
This implements the intuition that minimal violations of the left-edge requirement for person markers can be tolerated in the derivation whereas
stronger violations of this requirement cannot be.

(38) *Third person plural argument encoding* (harmonic serialism
alternative, step 3):

I_{162}: wu:$[+3]_3$-V_1-T_2-rr:$[+pl]_3$ $[-1,-2,+3,+pl]_3$, {$[_{Pers}$ /nu/], $[_{Pers}$ /ŋa/], $[_{Pers}$ /yi/]}, { – }	MC (NUM)	MC (PERS)	ID F	MAX 3	MAX PL	L⇐ PERS²	COH	L⇐ PERS	NUM ⇒R	REFL
O_{1621}: wu:$[+3]_3$-V_1-T_2-rr:$[+pl]_3$							*!**			*
O_{1622}: V_1-T_2-rr:$[+pl]_3$-wu:$[+3]_3$						*!	**	***		
☞O_{1623}: rr:$[+pl]_3$-wu:$[+3]_3$-V_1-T_2							**	*	***	*

Of course, there is now still room for improvement: At this point, the person
marker can also undergo movement – an extremely local, metathesis-like
movement step that changes the order of person and number exponents
while maintaining adjacency (and thus preserving the maximal satisfaction
of COHERENCE). (39) shows how O_{16233} leads to further improvement of
the constraint profile, by satisfying L⇐PERS and, in doing so, reducing the
violations of the lower-ranked NUM⇒R constraint.

(39) *Third person plural argument encoding* (harmonic serialism alternative, step 4):

I_{1623}: rr:$[+pl]_3$-wu:$[+3]_3$-V_1-T_2, $[-1,-2,+3,+pl]_3$, {$[$Pers$/$nu$/]$, $[$Pers$/$ŋa$/]$, $[$Pers$/$yi$/]$}, { $-$ }	MC (NUM)	MC (PERS)	ID F	MAX 3	MAX PL	L⇐ PERS²	COH	L⇐ PERS	NUM ⇒R	REFL
O_{16231}: rr:$[+pl]_3$-wu:$[+3]_3$-V_1-T_2							**	*!	***	*
O_{16232}: wu:$[+3]_3$-V_1-T_2-rr:$[+pl]_3$							*!**			*
☞O_{16233}: wu:$[+3]_3$-rr:$[+pl]_3$-V_1-T_2							**		**	*

At this point, no further improvement is possible; the derivation converges in the next step.

To sum up, I have presented two harmonic serialist approaches to COH-driven person/number marking in Wardaman, one that requires tucking-in and makes it necessary to adopt a slightly more liberal version of the STRICT CYCLE CONDITION, and one that embraces the concept of (reflexive) local conjunction. Importantly, both analyses predict movement of morphological exponents, without any further assumptions.[34] For the remainder of the book, I adopt the strictest version of strict cyclicity.

The final optimal output candidates are identical in the parallel and the (two) serial approaches. Still, the question arises whether the analysis in terms of harmonic serialism can in principle make different predictions from the standard parallel optimality-theoretic analysis. Basically, we should expect that it can: In the serial analysis, there is an intermediate stage where the number exponent is in a right-peripheral (i.e., its canonical) position, next to T. One might therefore expect that opacity effects can be found with these kinds of data: The number exponent rr_3 can locally interact with, say, T_2 under adjacency (e.g., triggering or blocking other processes with T_2), which could never be detected by simply inspecting the final output structure. For Wardaman, I am not aware of any such operations empirically distinguishing between the two approaches; but I will come back to this general issue of empirical differences between parallel and serial optimization in inflectional morphology. Before doing so, I will present another case study in the next subsection: Trommer's (2001) analysis of person and number marking in Island Kiwai.

---

[34] Trommer (2008a) also discusses the case of person and number marking in Udmurt, which can be viewed as the mirror image of the situation in Wardaman: Here COHERENCE forces a right-peripheral position of person markers (in violation of L⇐PERS), so as to ensure adjacency to the number marker (whose placement corresponds to what is required by NUM⇒R). Given the approach(es) to Wardaman developed here, the reconstruction of Trommer's analysis of Udmurt in terms of harmonic grammar is entirely straightforward, with the positions of L⇐PERS and NUM⇒R swapped in the ranking.

3.4.   Affix Order in Standard Parallel Optimality Theory: Island Kiwai

Island Kiwai is a Trans-Fly language from Papua New Guinea. Grammatical descriptions of person and number marking are given in Ray (1931) and Wurm (1975); from a theoretical point of view, the system has been studied by Julien (2002) and Trommer (2001; 2008a), who develops a standard parallel optimality-theoretic analysis. The relevant paradigm of verb inflection in Island Kiwai is given in (40); following Trommer (2008a), I will focus on the two forms enclosed by boxes, viz., first person dual marking in present and indefinite future tenses.

(40)   *Verbal paradigm:*

	Pres	NearPast	DefPast	ImmedFut	IndefFut	RemFut
1s	n-V	n-V	n-V	n-V-ri	ni-do-V-ri	ni-mi-V-ri
1d	n-V-duru-do	n-V-do	n-V-ru-do	ni-do-V-ri	ni-du-do-V-ri	ni-mi-du-do-V-ri
1t	n-V-bi-duru-mo	n-V-bi-mo	n-V-bi-ru-mo	ni-bi-mo-V-ri	ni-bi-du-mo-V-ri	ni-mi-bi-du-mo-V-ri
1p	n-V-duru-mo	n-V-mo	n-V-ru-mo	ni-mo-V-ri	nidu-mo-V-ri	ni-mi-du-mo-V-ri
2/3s	r-V	w-V	g-V	w-V-ri	wi-do-V-ri	ri-mi-V-ri
2/3d	r-V-duru-do	w-V-do	g-V-ru-do	wi-do-V-ri	wi-du-do-V-ri	ri-mi-du-do-V-ri
2/3t	r-V-bi-duru-mo	w-V-bi-mo	g-V-bi-ru-mo	wi-bi-mo-V-ri	wi-bi-du-mo-V-ri	ri-mi-bi-du-mo-V-ri
2/3p	r-V-duru-mo	w-V-mo	g-V-ru-mo	wi-mo-V-ri	wi-du-mo-V-ri	ri-mi-du-mo-V-ri

The present tense marker is *duru*, the indefinite future tense markers are *du* and *ri*. Person and number exponents are given in (41).

(41)   *Person and number exponents:*

   a.   /n(i)/ $\leftrightarrow$ [+1]
   b.   /r/ $\leftrightarrow$ [−1]/_[pres]
   c.   /g/ $\leftrightarrow$ [−1]/_[def.past]
   d.   /w(i)/ $\leftrightarrow$ [−1]
   e.   /Ø/ $\leftrightarrow$ [+sg]
   f.   /do/ $\leftrightarrow$ [−sg,−pl]
   g.   /mo/ $\leftrightarrow$ [+pl]
   h.   /bi/ $\leftrightarrow$ [trial]

The relevant observation is that the position of number exponents depends on tense: While person exponents are prefixes throughout, number exponents are suffixes in non-future tenses, and prefixes in future tenses.[35] Trommer accounts for the variable position of the number marker by assuming that it is due to the REFLECT constraint. By assumption, the positions in which REFLECT wants to realize number markers (provided

---

[35] In the words of Ray (1931, 48): "In present and past tenses the suffix showing the number of agents forms the final of the verb complex. In future tenses the sign of number immediately precedes the verb-base."

by the syntax) vary depending on which tense is present: In present tense environments, the dual marker in first person dual contexts shows up to the right of the present tense suffix; in indefinite future tense environments, the dual marker shows up to the right of the first tense marker. This is shown by the tableaux in (42) and (43).

(42) *First person dual, present tense* (standard parallel optimality theory):

I_1: V_1 [$_{T_2}$ present], [+1,–2,–sg,–pl]$_3$	L⇐PERS	REFL	NUM⇒R
☞O_{11}: n_3-V_1-$duru_2$-do_3			
O_{12}: n_3-do_3-V_1-$duru_2$		*!	**
O_{13}: V_1-$duru_2$-n_3-do_3	*!*		
O_{14}: do_3-V_1-$duru_2$-n_3	*!**		***

(43) *First person dual, indefinite future tense* (standard parallel optimality theory):

I_1: V_1 [$_{T_2}$ indef.fut], [+1,–2,–sg,–pl]$_3$	L⇐PERS	REFL	NUM⇒R
☞O_{11}: ni_4-du_3-do_4-V_1-ri_2			**
O_{12}: ni_4-do_4-du_3-V_1-ri_2		*!	***
O_{13}: du_3-ni_4-do_4-V_1-ri_2	*!		**
O_{14}: ni_4-du_3-V_1-ri_2-do_4		*!	

This analysis works well, but it requires a number of further assumptions. For instance, as noted by Trommer (2001), there must be an additional "blocking constraint" that ensures that there is "only one affix allowed to the right of Tense", and that must be restricted to future contexts. Moreover, it is not totally clear why it is the first tense exponent and not the second one that determines the position favoured by REFLECT, especially in view of the fact that it is the second exponent – *ri* – that signals proper future tense, and the first exponent – *du* – provides additional aspectual information only ("indefinite action", in Ray's (1931) words). Finally, it is worth pointing out that COHERENCE is irrelevant in this analysis (i.e., must be ranked very low) even though the effect visible in indefinite future tense environments could in principle also be viewed as an attempt to minimize the distance between the the person and number exponents. For these reasons, I will in fact deviate from the general strategy pursued in this chapter and not come up with a maximally faithful transfer of the analysis to harmonic serialism (although it should be clear that this task would not pose any particular challenges). Rather, I will present a reanalysis that (a) acknowledges COHERENCE-driven movement of the number marker in indefinite future tense environments, and (b) offers a new perspective on the presence of the two tense markers that is also made possible by the option of having movement in morphology.[36]

3.5.   Affix Order in Harmonic Serialism: Island Kiwai

As before, there will have to be MERGE CONDITION constraints ensuring that the exponents are merged with the verb stem. I assume that there are three such constraints: MC(TENSE), MC(NUM), and MC(PERS); suppose they are ranked in this order.

(44) a.   MERGE CONDITION(TENSE) (MC(TENSE)):
           [•Tense•] participates in Merge.
      b.   MERGE CONDITION(NUM) (MC(NUM)):
           [•Num•] participates in Merge.
      c.   MERGE CONDITION(PERS) (MC(PERS)):
           [•Pers•] participates in Merge.

This leaves three slots for what looks like four exponents in indefinite future environments. Indeed, I would like to suggest that the two future exponents actually start out as one complex tense exponent characterized by the features [–def,+fut]; this corresponds to the intuition that we are dealing with one discontinuous ('circumfix') future marker here. Thus, the basic exponents in the three morphological arrays that play a role in the analysis of first person dual present and indefinite future contexts look as in (45).

(45) a.   Pers: {/n(i)/↔[+1,–2], ... }
      b.   Num: {/do/↔[–sg,–pl], ... }
      c.   Tense: {/duru/↔[–past,–fut], /du/↔[–def]-/ri/↔[+fut], ... }

Note that in this way the very similar shapes of the continuous present tense exponent and the discontinuous indefinite future exponent do not come as a surprise; as a matter of fact, the only relevant difference between the two exponents is that one is stable in morphology whereas the other can (and, as we will see, must) disintegrate in morphology.

Next, there need to be IDENT and MAX constraints that guarantee choice of the most specific underspecified exponent among the set of exponents in a morphological array (Tense, Num, Pers) that are compatible with the matrix of fully specified morpho-syntactic features associated with V; but I will abstract away from these constraints in what follows because

---

[36] I hasten to add that the analysis is somewhat tentative and exploratory.

of space considerations (plus, their presence will not contribute anything new). Further constraints are L⇐Pers (plus the reflexive local conjunction L⇐Pers², Num⇒R, and T⇒R. All of this is more or less exactly as before. In addition, the analysis relies on a Coherence constraint restricted to future contexts; following the reasoning in Aissen (2003), I assume that this can be achieved by local conjunction: Coh&*Fut is violated if Coh is violated in a future environment. This complex constraint is needed to ensure that Coherence-driven movement of the number exponent from a suffix position to a prefix position happens only in future contexts, not in present or past contexts. What is more, it will turn out that as with L⇐Pers, an additional version Coh²&*Fut is required that is derived by local conjunction (first reflexive local conjunction of Coh, then non-reflexive local conjunction with *Fut). And finally, just as Coherence is a trigger for number exponent movement, there has to be a trigger for movement of the /du/ part of the complex /du/-/ri/ indefinite future exponent; I assume that this role is played by a constraint Def⇒Num.[37] These constraints are listed in (46); the ranking corresponds to the order of presentation (and all these constraints can be assumed to be ranked below the MC constraints that trigger exponence in the first place).[38]

(46)　a.　L⇐Pers²:

　　　　　A person exponent is separated from the left edge of a word by at most one other exponent.

　　b.　Coh²&*Fut:

　　　　　Two exponents that correspond to the same DP argument are separated by at most one intervening exponent in future tense environments.

　　c.　Def⇒Num:

　　　　　A [−def] tense exponent precedes a number exponent.

　　d.　L⇐Pers:

　　　　　A person exponent is separated from the left edge of a word by no other exponent.

---

[37] Def⇒Num is a precedence constraint that is reminiscent of bigram constraints in the sense of Ryan (2010); however, in contrast to bigram constraints, this constraint does not require Num to *immediately* follow Def; it is satisfied as long as Num follows Def. Such precedence constraints are also pervasive in optimality-theoretic studies of syntactic word order variation; see, e.g., Müller (2000a) for an early overview.

[38] I have slightly altered Trommer's original definitions for these constraints. For the most part, this should not have any relevant consequences, except for, perhaps, Coherence, where the new version is arguably somewhat more transparent.

  e.   COH&*FUT:
       Two exponents that correspond to the same DP argument are
       not separated by an intervening exponent in future tense envi-
       ronments.

  f.   NUM⇒R:
       A number exponent is separated from the right edge of a word
       by no other exponent.

  g.   T⇒R:
       A tense exponent is separated from the right edge of a word by
       no other exponent.

  h.   COH:
       Two exponents that correspond to the same DP argument are
       not separated by an intervening exponent.

On this basis, consider now first the competition in first person dual present
tense environments. At the start of the derivation, the tense exponent
/duru/$_2$ is merged in order to satisfy the highest-ranked constraint MC(T);
and it is placed in the position required by T⇒R; see (47).[39]

(47)   *First person dual, present tense* (harmonic serialism, step 1):

I_1: V_1:[•T•], [•Num•], [•Pers•], [+1,−2,−sg,−pl,−fut,+def], {[Pers /ni/$_4$], ... }, {[Num /do/$_4$], ...}, {[$_T$ /duru/$_2$], [$_T$ /du/$_3$-/ri/$_2$], ... }	MC (T)	MC (NUM)	MC (PERS)	L⇐ PERS²	COH² &*FUT	DEF⇒ NUM	L⇐ PERS	COH &*FUT	NUM ⇒R	T ⇒R	COH
O_{11}: V_1: [•T•], [•Num•], [•Pers•]	*!	*	*								
☞O_{12}: V_1-duru$_2$: [•Num•], [•Pers•]		*	*								
O_{13}: V_1-do$_4$: [•T•], [•Pers•]	*!		*								
O_{14}: do$_4$-V_1: [•T•], [•Pers•]	*!		*						*		
O_{15}: ni$_4$-V_1: [•T•], [•Num•]	*!	*									
O_{16}: V_1-ni$_4$: [•T•], [•Num•]	*!	*					*				
O_{17}: duru$_2$-V_1: [•Num•], [•Pers•]		*	*							*!	

In the next step, the number exponent /do/ is merged at the right edge,
which satisfies MC(NUM); see (48).

---

[39] Throughout this analysis, I adopt the strongest version of the STRICT CYCLE CONDI-
TION, according to which all structure-building (including movement) will have to take
place at the edges.

(48) *First person dual, present tense* (harmonic serialism, step 2):

I_{12}: V_1-duru$_2$: [•Num•], [•Pers•], [+1,−2,−sg,−pl,−fut,+def], {[Pers /ni/$_4$], … }, {[Num /do/$_4$], …}, {[T /du/$_3$-/ri/$_2$], … }	MC (T)	MC (Num)	MC (Pers)	L⇐ Pers^2	Coh^2 &*Fut	Def ⇒Num	L⇐ Pers	Coh &*Fut	Num ⇒R	T ⇒R	Coh
O_{121}: V_1-duru$_2$: [•Num•]		*!	*								
☞ O_{122}: V_1-duru$_2$-do$_4$: [•Pers•]			*							*	
O_{123}: do$_4$-V_1-duru$_2$: [•Pers•]			*						*!*		
O_{124}: ni$_4$-V_1-duru$_2$: [•Num•]		*!									
O_{125}: V_1-duru$_2$-ni$_4$: [•Num•]		*!		*			*			*	

This gives rise to an unavoidable violation of T⇒R because /duru/ is now not at the right edge anymore.

Finally, the person exponent is merged as a prefix; see (49).

(49) *First person dual, present tense* (harmonic serialism, step 3):

I_{122}: V_1-duru$_2$-do$_4$: [•Pers•] [+1,−2,−sg,−pl,−fut,+def], {[Pers /ni/$_4$], … }, {…}, {[T /du/$_3$-/ri/$_2$], … }	MC (T)	MC (Num)	MC (Pers)	L⇐ Pers^2	Coh^2 &*Fut	Def ⇒Num	L⇐ Pers	Coh &*Fut	Num ⇒R	T ⇒R	Coh
O_{1221}: V_1-duru$_2$-do$_4$: [•Pers•]			*!							*	
☞ O_{1222}: ni$_4$-V_1-duru$_2$-do$_4$										*	**
O_{1223}: V_1-duru$_2$-do$_4$-ni$_4$				*!				*		*	

The optimal output has two violations of Coherence (since /do/ and /ni/ encode the same DP argument but are separated by the T exponent /duru/ and by the verb stem), but this is unavoidable; given the ranking Num⇒R ≫ Coherence in non-future contexts in Island Kiwai, this violation will have to be preserved in an optimal candidate. Thus, the following step leads to convergence.

Let us turn now to the slightly more interesting case of first person dual exponence in indefinite future tense environments. As we will see, there are two "primary" movement operations involved (of the definite future exponent and of the number exponent), plus two "secondary" movement operations that are indirectly triggered by the application of the primary movement operations, and serve to restore the original left-peripheral position of the person exponent. In the first step, as before, the tense exponent is merged; however, this time the exponent is a complex item consisting of a [−def] part and a [+fut] part.

(50) *First person dual, indefinite future tense* (harmonic serialism, step 1):

I_1: V_1:[•T•], [•Num•], [•Pers•], [+1,–2,–sg,–pl,+fut,–def], {[Pers /ni$_4$/, …]}, {[Num /do$_4$/, …]}, {[T /duru$_2$], [T /du$_3$-/ri$_2$], … }	MC (T)	MC (Num)	MC (Pers)	L⇐ Pers^2	Coh^2 &*Fut	Def ⇒Num	L⇐ Pers	Coh &*Fut	Num ⇒R	T ⇒R	Coh
O_{11}: V_1: [•T•], [•Num•], [•Pers•]	*!	*	*								
☞ O_{12}: V_1-[du$_3$-ri$_2$]: [•Num•], [•Pers•]		*	*								
O_{13}: V_1-do$_4$: [•T•], [•Pers•]	*!		*								
O_{14}: do$_4$-V_1: [•T•], [•Pers•]	*!		*						*		
O_{15}: ni$_4$-V_1: [•T•], [•Num•]	*!	*									
O_{16}: V_1-ni$_4$: [•T•], [•Num•]	*!	*					*				
O_{17}: [du$_3$-ri$_2$]-V_1: [•Num•], [•Pers•]		*	*							*!	

In general, the derivation is nearly identical to that of present tense contexts at these early stages; (51) shows how the optimal number exponent is chosen, and why it is placed at the right edge.

(51) *First person dual, indefinite future tense* (harmonic serialism, step 2):

I_{12}: V_1-[du$_3$-ri$_2$]: [•Num•], [•Pers•], [+1,–2,–sg,–pl,+fut,–def], {[Pers /ni$_4$/, …]}, {[Num /do$_4$/, …]}, {[T /duru$_2$/, …]}	MC (T)	MC (Num)	MC (Pers)	L⇐ Pers^2	Coh^2 &*Fut	Def ⇒Num	L⇐ Pers	Coh &*Fut	Num ⇒R	T ⇒R	Coh
O_{121}: V_1-[du$_3$-ri$_2$]: [•Num•], [•Pers•]		*!	*								
☞ O_{122}: V_1-[du$_3$-ri$_2$]-do$_4$: [•Pers•]			*							*	
O_{123}: do$_4$-V_1-[du$_3$-ri$_2$]: [•Pers•]			*						*!**		
O_{124}: ni$_4$-V_1-[du$_3$-ri$_2$]: [•Num•]		*!									
O_{125}: V_1-[du$_3$-ri$_2$]-ni$_4$: [•Num•]		*!		*			***			*	

As before, in the third step the person exponent is introduced as a prefix; see (52). However, this time the optimal candidate, O_{1222}, does not merely incur violations of the lowest-ranked constraints T⇒R and Coh, as before; rather, Coh&*Fut and, more importantly, Coh^2&*Fut are now also violated. These violations are temporarily tolerable, though, because placing the person exponent at the right edge, as in O_{1223}, would give rise to an even more severe violation of L⇐Pers^2, and given the Strict Cycle Condition, there is no third option for placing the person marker at this point.

(52) *First person dual, indefinite future tense* (harmonic serialism, step 3):

I_{122}: V_1-[du$_3$-ri$_2$]-do$_4$: [•Pers•] [+1,–2,–sg,–pl,+fut,–def], {[Pers /ni$_4$/, …]}, {…}, {[T /duru$_2$], … }	MC (T)	MC (Num)	MC (Pers)	L⇐ Pers^2	Coh^2 &*Fut	Def ⇒Num	L⇐ Pers	Coh &*Fut	Num ⇒R	T ⇒R	Coh
O_{1221}: V_1-[du$_3$-ri$_2$]-do$_4$: [•Pers•]			*!							*	
☞ O_{1222}: ni$_4$-V_1-[du$_3$-ri$_2$]-do$_4$					*			*		*	***
O_{1223}: V_1-[du$_3$-ri$_2$]-do$_4$-ni$_4$				*!*			****		*	*	

Thus, the next step does not lead to convergence this time. Instead, the violation of Coh^2&*Fut is removed by moving the number exponent to the front, as shown in (53). This violates not only $\text{Num}{\Rightarrow}\text{R}$ (as in the case of Wardaman), but also the higher-ranked constraints $\text{Def}{\Rightarrow}\text{Num}$ (because /du/$_3$ in T does not precede the number exponent /do/$_4$ anymore) and $\text{L}{\Leftarrow}\text{Pers}$ (because the person marker /ni/$_4$ is not left-peripheral anymore). Still, output O_{12222} is the optimal solution at this point: If the person marker moves to the right, as in O_{12223}, a violation of the even higher-ranked constraint $\text{L}{\Leftarrow}\text{Pers}^2$ will result. Moving one of the two constituents of the complex T exponent to the left, as in O_{12224} and O_{12225}, will not produce a better constraint profile either because this does not satisfy $\text{Coh}^2\&{*}\text{Fut}$, which is thus identified as the trigger for movement at this point. Evidently, the same goes for movement of either T exponent to the right.[40]

(53)   *First person dual, indefinite future tense* (harmonic serialism, step 4):

I_{1222}: ni$_4$-V$_1$-[du$_3$-ri$_2$]-do$_4$: [+1,–2,–sg,–pl,+fut,–def], {…}, {…}, {[$_\text{T}$ /duru/$_2$], … }	MC (T)	MC (Num)	MC (Pers)	L⇐ Pers^2	Coh^2 &*Fut	Def ⇒Num	L⇐ Pers	Coh &*Fut	Num ⇒R	T ⇒R	Coh
O_{12221}: ni$_4$-V$_1$-[du$_3$-ri$_2$]-do$_4$					*!			*		*	*
☞O_{12222}: do$_4$-ni$_4$-V$_1$-[du$_3$-ri$_2$]						*	*		****		
O_{12223}: V$_1$-[du$_3$-ri$_2$]-do$_4$-ni$_4$				*!*			****		*	**	
O_{12224}: du$_3$-ni$_4$-V$_1$-[ri$_2$]-do$_4$					*!		*	*		*	*
O_{12225}: [ri$_2$]-ni$_4$-V$_1$-[du$_3$]-do$_4$					*!		*	*	****		*

As shown in (54), the following step involves a "secondary" movement operation in order to restore the person exponent at the left edge of the word; this operation is triggered by $\text{L}{\Leftarrow}\text{Pers}$. Note that movement of the indefinite future exponent is again not an option at this stage even though this would satisfy the constraint $\text{Def}{\Rightarrow}\text{Num}$, which is ranked higher than $\text{L}{\Leftarrow}\text{Pers}$. The reason is that this would give rise to a violation of $\text{L}{\Leftarrow}\text{Pers}^2$, with both the number exponent and the indefinite future exponent separating the person exponent from the left edge.

---

[40] What about moving the complex T constituent as a whole? I assume that this is simply not an option for Gen; i.e., the complex T can be merged as a single item, but once it has entered the structure, only its subconstituents can be targeted by movement. (Note that this is also in line with how gradient violations of alignment constraints have been determined so far; e.g., /do/$_4$ in O_{123} violates $\text{Num}{\Rightarrow}\text{R}$ *three times* (not *twice*)). As a matter of fact, if the complex T item could move as a single unit, leftward movement would be excluded without problems because it would give rise to a fatal violation of $\text{L}{\Leftarrow}\text{Per}^2$, with the person exponent /ni/ separated from the left edge of the word by two exponents (/du/ and ri/); but rightward movement would wrongly be expected to result in optimality because /ni/$_4$ and /do/$_4$ would be sufficiently close to avoid a violation of $\text{Coh}^2\&{*}\text{Fut}$ (as in the case of competing O_{12222}). The output would incur a violation of $\text{Def}{\Rightarrow}\text{Num}$ (as does O_{12222}), but would satisfy $\text{L}{\Leftarrow}\text{Pers}$ (which O_{12222} violates).

(54) *First person dual, indefinite future tense* (harmonic serialism, step 5):

I_{12222}: do_4-ni_4-V_1-[du_3-ri_2]: [+1,–2,–sg,–pl,+fut,–def], {...}, {...}, {[$_T$ /duru/$_2$], ... }	MC (T)	MC (Num)	MC (Pers)	L⇐ Pers²	Coh² &*Fut	Def ⇒Num	L⇐ Pers	Coh &*Fut	Num ⇒R	T ⇒R	Coh
O_{122221}: do_4-ni_4-V_1-[du_3-ri_2]						*	*!		****		
☞O_{122222}: ni_4-do_4-V_1-[du_3-ri_2]						*			***		
O_{122223}: du_3-do_4-ni_4-V_1-[ri_2]				*!			**		***		

At this point, the indefinite future marker /du/$_3$ can finally undergo movement to the left edge, triggered by Def⇒Num; carrying out this operation reintroduces a violation of lower-ranked L⇐Pers (as with number movement at the earlier stage) but respects higher-ranked L⇐Pers². This is shown in the tableau in (55).

(55) *First person dual, indefinite future tense* (harmonic serialism, step 6):

I_{122222}: ni_4-do_4-V_1-[du_3-ri_2]: [+1,–2,–sg,–pl,+fut,–def], {...}, {...}, {[$_T$ /duru/$_2$], ... }	MC (T)	MC (Num)	MC (Pers)	L⇐ Pers²	Coh² &*Fut	Def ⇒Num	L⇐ Pers	Coh &*Fut	Num ⇒R	T ⇒R	Coh
$O_{1222221}$: ni_4-do_4-V_1-[du_3-ri_2]						*!			***		
☞$O_{1222222}$: du_3-ni_4-do_4-V_1-[ri_2]							*		**		

Finally, the person exponent /ni/$_4$ is required to participate in yet another "secondary" movement operation to the left edge, so as to get rid of the L⇐Pers violation. The resulting optimal output representation violates Coh&*Fut (and Coh) (and it continues to violate Num⇒R), but crucially it respects higher-ranked Coh²&*Fut – there is only one exponent intervening between the person exponent at the left edge and the number exponent in its derived position preceding V.

(56) *First person dual, indefinite future tense* (harmonic serialism, step 7):

$I_{1222222}$: du_3-ni_4-do_4-V_1-[ri_2]: [+1,–2,–sg,–pl,+fut,–def], {...}, {...}, {[$_T$ /duru/$_2$], ... }	MC (T)	MC (Num)	MC (Pers)	L⇐ Per²	Coh² &*Fut	Def ⇒Num	L⇐ Per	Coh &*Fut	Num ⇒R	T ⇒R	Coh
$O_{12222221}$: du_3-ni_4-do_4-V_1-[ri_2]							*!		**		
☞$O_{12222222}$: ni_4-du_3-do_4-V_1-[ri_2]								*	**		*

At this point, no further improvement is possible; the next optimization procedure yields convergence.

To sum up, it has turned out that the fairly complex internal structure of verbs in first person dual indefinite future environments in Island Kiwai can be derived in a fully systematic way, given the option of movement operations in morphology. In the present analysis, Coherence constraints can automatically trigger movement of an exponent from its base position, and the same goes for DEF⇒NUM. Furthermore, given the strongest version of the STRICT CYCLE CONDITION, such movement operations always have to target edges of words, and this means that a constraint like L⇐PERS may subsequently give rise to secondary movement operations that restore the original order of exponents. It is worth emphasizing that none of the constraints that trigger movement in this approach are designed to do just that: These constraints hold, and are active, independently of movement; they govern the basic placement of exponents in exactly the same way (and recall that these kinds of constraints were originally adopted in a system where there is no movement in morphology). I would like to contend that in this respect, the present approach emerges as radically different from (and, in my view, conceptually superior to) Distributed Morphology approaches where movement-like operations have sometimes been stipulated for the morphological component (see Halle & Marantz (1993), Embick & Noyer (2001; 2007), Embick (2010), and Arregi & Nevins (2012), among others).

Note finally that movement in morphology of the type we have just encountered can have three different types of effects: It can restore the original placement of exponents (this is what L⇐PERS did); it can bring two exponents together that were initially separated (this is what COHERENCE did); and it can split up a complex exponent into what on the surface looks like a discontinuous exponent (this is what DEF⇒NUM did). It is this latter effect that I want to turn to in the next subsection of this chapter.

3.6. Discontinuous Exponence

3.6.1. Introduction

The phenomenon of discontinuous exponence involves scenarios where two phonologically separate morphological pieces occur discontinuously (i.e., are interrupted by one or more other morphological exponents) even though there is no evidence for assigning them different functions, because the two pieces strictly co-occur to express a given instantiation of a grammatical function. In Harris's (1945) words:

> In Yokuts, whenever *na'aş* occurs, a verb with the suffix *-al* occurs with it; and whenever the verb-suffix *-al* occurs, *na'aş* occurs nearby. Together, they indicate uncertainty of the action; it would presumably be impossible to give the descriptive meaning of each one of them, since they never occur separately.
>
> Harris (1945, 122)

Discontinuous exponents of this type pose a problem for standard lexical approaches to morphological realization because it is a priori unclear how an item that is one element in the mental lexicon can be distributed over two positions in the word. In contrast, inferential approaches can formulate rules of exponence that, e.g., simply add two morphological items to the left and to the right of a given stem, as it can be the rule that introduces them, rather than the pieces of additional structure directly, that is associated with (possibly underspecified) morpho-syntactic features (see, e.g., Stump (2001)). However, it seems to me that even in inferential approaches that can technically account for the phenomenon, the very existence of such discontinuous marking remains deeply mysterious. While I would not claim that the option of movement in the morphological component of grammar solves this problem, it can at least be noted that it offers a reasonably simple implementation of discontinuous exponence. Ultimately, the solution is very similar to what has been argued for comparable cases in syntax, like, e.g., separable prefixes of verbs in German. Suppose that separable prefixes are base-generated as parts of complex verbs in the morphological component (see, e.g., Johnson (1991), Stiebels (1996)). Then it is clear that a separation of the two items can be brought about by movement of the verb, e.g., to a verb-second position in German; see (57-a) (where no verb movement takes place in the presence of a lexical complementizer) vs. (57-b) (where the P item *auf* ('up') is stranded under verb-second movement).

(57) a. $[_{CP}$ $[_C$ dass] sie gestern   auf-stand]
                  that   she yesterday up-stood

      b. $[_{CP}$ Gestern $[_{C'}$ $[_V$ stand]-C sie $[_V$ $[_P$ auf] t_V]]]
                 yesterday   stood   she   up

In the previous subsection, I have already addressed one possible instance of discontinuous exponence, viz., the case of the indefinite future marker in Island Kiwai (recall (45)). However, in that case, it was in fact straightforwardly possible to assign separate specifications to the indivual items making up the complex exponent. In this subsection, I will consider two cases of discontinuous exponents where this does not seem to suggest itself as straightforwardly.

3.6.2. *Verb Inflection in Wambon*

Consider the following paradigms for verb inflection in present tense and past tense contexts in the Trans-New Guinea language Wambon (as described by De Vries & De Vries-Wiersma (1992); also see Cysouw (2003)

and Müller (2008) on the exponence of person in this language and its
consequences for natural classes).[41]

(58) *Verb inflection in Wambon*:

en/ande ('eat')	PRES	PAST
1.SG	en-kende-ep	ande-t-ep-mbo
2.SG	en-ke-Ø	ande-t-Ø-mbo
3.SG	en-ke-Ø	ande-t-Ø-mbo
1.PL	en-kende-eva	ande-t-eva-mbo
2.PL	en-kende-e	ande-t-e-mbo
3.PL	en-kende-e	ande-t-e-mbo

This suggests the following underspecified exponents for person/number
and tense:

(59) a. *Person/number exponents*:
          (i)   /ep/ ↔ [+1,–2]
          (ii)   /Ø$_{[sub]}$/ ↔ [–1]
          (iii) /eva/ ↔ [+1,–2,+pl]
          (iv)   /e/ ↔ [–1,+pl]
      b. *Tense exponents*:
          (i)   /kende/ ↔ [–past]
          (ii)   /t-mbo/ ↔ [+past]

As for the person/number exponents, second and third person contexts exhibit syncretism in singular and in plural environments; this is reflected
here by assigning the exponents in question (/ep/, /e/) underspecified
person information ([–1]). The exponent /Ø/ in (59) is special in that,
although it is zero itself, it gives rise to subtractive morphology: It re-
duces the preceding exponent to maximally a single CV structure. As
for the tense exponents, /kende/ is the regular exponent for present tense
contexts (which is reduced to *ke* by Ø$_{[sub]}$ in second and third person singular contexts); and /t-mbo/ is the past tense exponent that is realized
discontinuously (with only *t* showing up in the position that is subject to
shortening by Ø$_{[sub]}$, which does not apply here because *t* already meets
the CV maximality requirement). From a purely synchronic point of view,

---

[41] Note that there is stem allomorphy: *en* is the present tense stem, *ande* is the past
tense stem. I will not address the issue of how to derive stem allomorphy here; but I will
return to stem allomorphy in chapter 5. Also, there are certain phonological operations
altering the forms depicted here (e.g., hiatus resolution) that I abstract away from.

/t-mbo/ satisfies Harris's (1945) criteria for discontinuous exponence: The two items strictly co-occur, and assigning them different non-empty feature specifications would seem to be an arbitrary decision. Rather, I would like to suggest that in /t-mbo/, the morpho-syntactic feature [+past] is really only present on the /t/ part (which shows up in the canonical position for tense markers); and the /mbo/ part is actually a feature-less appendix to it, as in (60).

(60) /t/↔[+past]-/mbo/

Most of the constraints needed to account for the paradigm in (58) in terms of a harmonic serialist analysis are already in place. There need to be constraints that trigger Merge operations applying with tense and with person/number exponents; I will refer to these as MC(T) and MC(AGR). As before, there must be constraints that determine the position of the exponents: T⇒R, AGR⇒R; for the latter constraint, it will be important that it also shows up in a version derived by reflexive local conjunction, i.e., as AGR⇒R^2.[42] Furthermore, there need to be IDENT and MAX constraints deriving, respectively, the compatibility and specificity requirements for morphological realization; the MAX constraints can for present purposes be assumed to be MAX(1), MAX(2), MAX(PL), and MAX(PAST). Only one new constraint is required that triggers movement of the feature-less appendix exponent of the past tense marker; see (61).

(61) ZERO⇒R:
      An exponent without morpho-syntactic features is separated from
      the right edge of a word by no other exponent.

Suppose that the ranking of the relevant constraints in Wambon looks as in (62).

(62) MC(T) ≫ MC(AGR) ≫ AGR⇒R^2 ≫ ZERO⇒R ≫ AGR⇒R ≫ T⇒R
      ≫ IDENT-F ≫ MAX(1) ≫ MAX(2) ≫ MAX(PL) ≫ MAX(PAST)

With this in mind, consider first the derivation of an inflected verb in a first person singular present tense environment. Based on the complex input specification given in (63), in the first step the optimal output merges the tense marker /kende/ as a suffix.

---

[42] Alternatively, the role of AGR⇒R^2 in the analysis could be taken over by a general constraint L⇐V demanding that the V stem is word-initial (i.e., that no prefixes can occur); see below.

(63) *First person singular, present tense* (harmonic serialism, step 1):

I_1: V_1:[•T•], [•Agr•]; [+1,−2,−pl,−past]; {[$_T$/kende/]$_2$, [$_T$/t/]$_2$-/-mbo/}; {[$_{Agr}$/ep/]$_3$, [$_{Agr}$/Ø$_{[sub]}$/]$_3$, [$_{Agr}$/eva/]$_3$, [$_{Agr}$/e/]$_3$}	MC (T)	MC (AGR)	AGR⇒R^2	ZERO⇒R	AGR⇒R	T⇒R	ID F	MAX (1)	MAX (2)	MAX (PL)	MAX (PAST)
O_{11}: V_1: [•T•], [•Agr•]	*!	*						*	*	*	*
O_{12}: kende$_2$-V_1: [•Agr•]		*				*!		*	*	*	
☞O_{13}: V_1-kende$_2$: [•Agr•]		*						*	*	*	
O_{14}: V_1-t_2-mbo: [•Agr•]		*					*!	*	*	*	
O_{15}: t_2-mbo-V_1: [•Agr•]		*				*!	*	*	*	*	
O_{16}: V_1-ep$_3$: [•T•]	*!									*	*
O_{17}: ep$_3$-V_1: [•T•]	*!				*					*	*
O_{18}: V_1-Ø$_{[sub]3}$: [•T•]	*!						*		*	*	*
...	*!										

In the following step, the most specific compatible exponent from the AGR morphological array is merged; see (64).

(64) *First person singular, present tense* (harmonic serialism, step 2):

I_{13}: V_1-kende$_2$: [•Agr•]; [+1,−2,−pl,−past]; {[$_T$/t/]$_2$-/-mbo/}; {[$_{Agr}$/ep/]$_3$, [$_{Agr}$/Ø$_{[sub]}$/]$_3$, [$_{Agr}$/eva/]$_3$, [$_{Agr}$/e/]$_3$}	MC (T)	MC (AGR)	AGR⇒R^2	ZERO⇒R	AGR⇒R	T⇒R	ID F	MAX (1)	MAX (2)	MAX (PL)	MAX (PAST)
O_{131}: V_1-kende$_2$: [•Agr•]		*!									
☞O_{132}: V_1-kende$_2$-ep$_3$						*				*	
O_{133}: ep$_3$-V_1-kende$_2$				*!	*					*	
O_{134}: V_1-kende$_2$-Ø$_{[sub]3}$						*	*!		*	*	
O_{135}: Ø$_{[sub]3}$-V_1-kende$_2$				*!	*		*		*	*	
O_{136}: V_1-kende$_2$-eva$_3$						*	*!				
...				(*!)	(*)		(*!)				

The next step is the final one: It leads to convergence.

Consider now the minimally different first person singular past tense scenarios. The first step differs insofar as the tense exponent /t-mbo/ will now be chosen instead of /kende/.

(65) *First person singular, past tense* (harmonic serialism, step 1):

I_1: V_1:[•T•], [•Agr•]; [+1,−2,−pl,+past]; {[$_T$/kende/]$_2$, [$_T$/t/]$_2$-/-mbo/}; {[$_{Agr}$/ep/]$_3$, [$_{Agr}$/Ø$_{[sub]}$/]$_3$, [$_{Agr}$/eva/]$_3$, [$_{Agr}$/e/]$_3$}	MC (T)	MC (AGR)	AGR⇒R^2	ZERO⇒R	AGR⇒R	T⇒R	ID F	MAX (1)	MAX (2)	MAX (PL)	MAX (PAST)
O_{11}: V_1: [•T•], [•Agr•]	*!	*						*	*	*	*
O_{12}: t_2-mbo-V_1: [•Agr•]		*		*!		*		*	*	*	
☞O_{13}: V_1-t_2-mbo: [•Agr•]		*						*	*	*	
O_{14}: V_1-kende$_2$: [•Agr•]		*					*!	*	*	*	
O_{15}: kende$_2$-V_1: [•Agr•]		*				*!	*	*	*	*	
O_{16}: V_1-ep$_3$: [•T•]	*!									*	*
O_{17}: ep$_3$-V_1: [•T•]	*!				*					*	*
O_{18}: V_1-Ø$_{[sub]3}$: [•T•]	*!						*		*	*	*
...	*!										

In the next step, the optimal AGR exponent is selected; as before, this is /ep/. However, as shown in (66), this means that ZERO⇒R is now violated in the optimal output. Here the reflexive local conjunction AGR⇒R^2 is important. This constraint ensures that O_{133} is filtered out; it thus lets

O_{132} win: In O_{133}, the person/number marker $/ep/_3$ taken from the morphological array Agr is separated from the right edge of the word by more than one intervening exponent, so $\text{AGR} \Rightarrow R^2$ is invariably violated.[43]

(66) *First person singular, past tense* (harmonic serialism, step 2):

I_{13}: V_1-t_2-mbo: [•Agr•] [+1,–2,–pl,+past], {[$_T$ /kende/]$_2$, [$_T$ /t/]$_2$-/-mbo/}, {[$_{Agr}$ /ep/]$_3$, [$_{Agr}$ /Ø$_{[sub]}$/]$_3$, [$_{Agr}$ /eva/]$_3$, [$_{Agr}$ /e/]$_3$}	MC (T)	MC (AGR)	AGR $\Rightarrow R^2$	ZERO $\Rightarrow R$	AGR $\Rightarrow R$	T $\Rightarrow R$	ID F	MAX (1)	MAX (2)	MAX (PL)	MAX (PAST)
O_{131}: V_1-t_2-mbo: [•Agr•]		*!						*	*	*	
☞O_{132}: V_1-t_2-mbo-ep$_3$				*		**				*	
O_{133}: ep$_3$-V_1-t_2-mbo			*!		*					*	
...			(*!)		(*)	(*!)					

Next, movement of the feature-less appendix /mbo/ of the tense marker /t/ to the right edge position takes place, triggered by $\text{ZERO} \Rightarrow R$; see (67). Such rightward movement in the morphological component violates lower-ranked $\text{AGR} \Rightarrow R$, but importantly, it does not violate higher-ranked $\text{AGR} \Rightarrow R^2$ (because only one intervening exponent separates the person/number marker from the right edge).

(67) *First person singular, past tense* (harmonic serialism, step 3):

I_{132}: V_1-t_2-mbo-ep [+1,–2,–pl,+past], {[$_T$ /kende/]$_2$, [$_T$ /t/]$_2$-/-mbo/}, {[$_{Agr}$ /ep/]$_3$, [$_{Agr}$ /Ø$_{[sub]}$/]$_3$, [$_{Agr}$ /eva/]$_3$, [$_{Agr}$ /e/]$_3$}	MC (T)	MC (AGR)	AGR $\Rightarrow R^2$	ZERO $\Rightarrow R$	AGR $\Rightarrow R$	T $\Rightarrow R$	ID F	MAX (1)	MAX (2)	MAX (PL)	MAX (PAST)
O_{1321}: V_1-t_2-mbo-ep$_3$				*!		**				*	
☞O_{1322}: V_1-t_2-ep$_3$-mbo					*	**				*	
O_{1323}: mbo-V_1-t_2-ep$_3$				*!**		*				*	

The final step leads to convergence.

3.6.3. Past Participles in German

The exponents in past participle formation in German lend themselves to the same kind of analysis. With verbs of the weak inflection class, this participle is typically formed by adding -*et* as a suffix to the verb stem and prefixing *ge-*. With verbs of the strong inflection class (with Ablaut-governed stem alternations), it is derived by using -*en* as a suffix to the verb stem, and also adding the prefix *ge-* to it; see (68-ab).

---

[43] Note that it is possible to dispense with local conjunction in this analysis if another reason can be found why leftward placement of the AGR exponent is suboptimal. As indicated in footnote 42, an obvious alternative producing the same outcome would be a constraint L⇐V against realizing an Agr item (or, for that matter, anything else) as a prefix in Wambon verb inflection. Like $\text{AGR} \Rightarrow R^2$, L⇐V would not be violable by optimal outputs.

(68) a.   ge-arbeit-et
           PART-work-PART
      b.   ge-fund-en
           PART-find-PART

Research on the morphological structure of these participles has not produced unequivocal results. Helbig & Buscha (1981, 87), e.g., assume that
the -*et* and -*en* exponents are primary, and *ge-* is simply an addition showing up with some verbs. In contrast, Eisenberg (2000b, 28 & 194) and
Meibauer (2002, 32) explicitly refer to *ge- -et* and *ge- -en* as circumfixes,
which makes these items instances of discontinuous exponence. From the
present perspective, a harmonic serialist approach in terms of movement in
morphology suggests itself. Thus, suppose that non-finite V, like finite V,
combines with a member of the morphological array T; and suppose that
the features for past participles are [–fin,+past].[44] The T morphological
array can then include the exponents /et/↔[–fin,+past,–strong]$_2$-/ge/ and
/en/↔[–fin,+past,+strong]$_2$-/ge/, for weak and strong V stems, respectively. Here *ge* is not associated with any feature specification; it is simply
an appendix to *et/en*.

   The constraints that are needed to produce the correct output forms
are MC(T), T⇒R, and L⇐ZERO, which I assume to be an alternative
option, on an equal footing with ZERO⇒R. In addition, there is an IDENT-
F requirement deriving compatibility, and there are MAX constraints for the
individual morpho-syntactic features involved: MAX(FIN), MAX(PAST).[45]
Consider now the derivation of the form *ge-arbeit-et* in (68-a). In the first
step, V_1 merges with the optimal exponent from the morphological array
T; see (69).

---

[44] See, e.g., Wiese (2008). It is clear that the feature [±past] as it is used here cannot
directly correspond to the semantic concept of past tense since past participles in German
are not just used in perfect tense environments (where [+past] can be interpreted as such)
but also in passive environments (which are neutral with respect to tense, and where
present or future tense can also show up).

[45] For reasons that will become clear in the following chapter, suppose for present purposes that there are no MAX constraints for inflection class (strong vs. weak, in the case
at hand); here specificity does not play a role, only compatibility does.

(69) *Past participle formation, weak verbs* (harmonic serialism, step 1):

I_1: $[_{V_1}$ arbeit $]$:$[\bullet T\bullet]$ $[-$fin,$+$past,$-$strong$]$, $\{[_{T_2}$ /et/$\leftrightarrow[-$fin,$+$past,$-$strong$]_2$-/ge/ $]$, $[_{T_2}$ /en/$\leftrightarrow[-$fin,$+$past,$+$strong$]_2$-/ge/ $]$, ...$\}$,	MC (T)	T $\Rightarrow$R	L$\Leftarrow$ Zero	Id F	Max (fin)	Max (past)
O_{11}: $[_{V_1}$ arbeit $]$: $[\bullet T\bullet]$	*!				*	*
☞O_{12}: $[_{V_1}$ arbeit $]$-$[_{T_2}$ et-ge $]$			*			
O_{12}: $[_{T_2}$ et-ge $]$-$[_{V_1}$ arbeit $]$		*!	*			
O_{13}: $[_{V_1}$ arbeit $]$-$[_{T_2}$ en-ge $]$			*	*!		
O_{14}: $[_{T_2}$ en-ge $]$-$[_{V_1}$ arbeit $]$		*!	*	*		

The optimal output O_{12} has a violation of L$\Leftarrow$Zero; this is addressed by moving the feature-less exponent *ge* to the left edge in the next step; cf. (70).

(70) *Past participle formation, weak verbs* (harmonic serialism, step 2):

I_{12}: $[_{V_1}$ arbeit $]$-$[_{T_2}$ /et/-/ge/ $]$ $[-$fin,$+$past,$-$strong$]$, $\{[_{T_2}$ /en/$\leftrightarrow[-$fin,$+$past,$+$strong$]_2$-/ge/ $]$, ...$\}$,	MC (T)	T $\Rightarrow$R	L$\Leftarrow$ Zero	Id F	Max (fin)	Max (past)
O_{121}: $[_{V_1}$ arbeit $]$-$[_{T_2}$ et-ge $]$			*!			
☞O_{122}: ge-$[_{V_1}$ arbeit $]$-$[_{T_2}$ et $]$						

Since the optimal output of this optimization procedure violates no relevant constraints, it is clear that the next step will be the final one and yields convergence.

Thus, the movement-based analysis of discontinuous exponence made possible in harmonic serialism resolves the dilemma posed by past participle formation in German: There is both evidence for assigning *ge – et* the status of a discrete entity in the grammar (viz., unity of function, and the difficulty of assigning non-arbitrary feature specifications to the individual parts), and evidence against it (viz., the discontinuous linearization). Postulating a derivational account where the item in question is a constituent at the beginning of the derivation but not at the end corresponds fully to the classical transformational strategy of resolving similar dilemmas in syntax: The displacement property of natural languages provides the solution.

Needless to say, there is a lot more that would eventually have to be said about past participle formation in German. As shown by the data in (71), *ge* cannot show up with all verbs.

(71)   a.   (*ge)-bestell-t,   (*ge)-offenbar-t,   (*ge)-erzähl-t
                PART-order-PART   PART-reveal-PART   PART-narrate-PART

    b.   (*ge)-zerriss-en,   (*ge)-erfund-en,   (*ge)-entgang-en
        PART-shred-PART   PART-invent-PART   PART-escape-PART

    c.   (*ge)-akzeptier-t,   (*ge)-prophezei-t
        PART-accept-PART   PART-predict-PART

The correct generalization underlying the restrictions on *ge*-placement in
(71) is that the verb stems here are not trochees (see Geilfuß-Wolfgang
(1998) and references cited there): The weak verbs in (71-a) all have iden-
tifiable (inseparable) prefixes that are unstressed and lead to an iambic
or anapaestic metrical structure of the (extended) verb stem; the same
goes for the strong verbs in (71-b). Finally, the non-complex stems in
(71-c) instantiate loan verbs that also instantiate anapaests. As argued by
Geilfuß-Wolfgang (1998), these morphophonological restrictions ultimately
also support an optimality-theoretic approach; I assume that these issues
can be dealt with in a separate morphophonological component that is independent of, and follows, the proper morphological component that I am
concerned with here.

Furthermore, *ge does* show up again if the prefix is a separable one
(e.g., if it gets stranded by verb-second movement; see above); and in this
context, it follows the separable prefix.

(72) ab-ge-trenn-t,   ab-ge-lauf-en,   vor-ge-mach-t
      off-PART-split-PART off-PART-run-PART fore-PART-make-PART

Given the analysis just developed, the obvious way to proceed here might
be to assume that the verbs in question are equipped with an additional
structure-building feature [•P•] for the separable prefix, which is merged
after the item from the T array and directly placed in the first position
by virtue of a linearization constraint that is ranked higher than L⇐ZERO,
thereby leading to a minimal violation of the latter constraint in the optimal
output. However, since the focus of the present discussion has been on
the question of how to derive discontinuous exponence, rather than on a
comprehensive investigation of past participles in German, I will not dwell
on these issues any longer here.

3.7. *Reflexes of Movement in Derivational Morphology*

In the preceding sections, I have presented evidence for movement in inflectional morphology, and there will be further evidence for this option in the
chapters below. All of this evidence is morphology-internal, though. By
analogy to how movement is motivated in syntax, one might also expect
there to be an additional type of independent evidence for movement steps
in morphology based on reflexes in other domains of grammar; see, e.g.,

Fox (2000) and Nissenbaum (2000) on semantic reconstruction to intermediate positions in syntax, and McCloskey (1979), Clements et al. (1983), Urk (2015), and Georgi (2017), among many others, on morphological or phonological reflexes of movement. And in fact, the study of affix order in Bantu languages in Hyman (1994; 2002; 2003) simultaneously provides very direct semantic and phonological evidence for postulating movement in morphology.

The only complication consists in the fact that Hyman is concerned not with inflectional morphology, but rather with derivational morphology, more specifically, with causative and applicative exponents. However, as far as semantics is concerned, it is clear that, given the assumptions made about inflectional morphology in the present monograph, there can be no evidence from inflectional morphology, for the simple reason that the morphological exponents attached to the stem do not bring with them any kind of information that would not independently be there already – the system is strictly realizational. Therefore, the question of whether some order Σ–ρ–ω or some alternative order Σ–ω–ρ (with Σ the stem, and ρ and ω two inflectional exponents as suffixes) is unexpected from the point of view of semantic interpretation is not a meaningful one in inflectional morphology under present assumptions.

With this qualification, consider Hyman's arguments to the effect that some derivational affixes in Bantu languages do not overtly show up in positions in which they are semantically and phonologically interpreted.

In Lomongo, a root can be causativized by adding the causative suffix /i̧/ to it; this is a productive and semantically fully transparent operation; see (73).

(73) a.   bómb ('keep') → bómb-i̧ ('make/let keep')
      b.   kók ('suffice') → kók-i̧ ('make suffice')

These outputs can then be further enriched by an applicative suffix /el/ (with /el/ realized as [ej] before i̧). Semantically, the applicative morpheme introduces an argument for the complex causativized verb (not for the basic root), so it is interpreted outside of the complex verb formed in (73). However, as illustrated in (74), the order of causative and applicative is at variance with what one would expect if the applicative exponent has to attach at the edge of the word generated so far.

(74) a.   bómb-i̧ ('make/let keep') → bómb-ej-i̧ ('make keep for/at')
      b.   kók-i̧ ('make suffice') → kók-ej-i̧ ('make suffice for/at')

In view of this, Hyman (2002) supposes that the data should be analyzed in such a way that an initial sequence Σ–ρ, where ρ is the first affix to combine with the stem Σ and is thus adjacent to it at some point of the derivation, is subsequently interrupted by a special process of counter-cyclic "interfixing" of ω, yielding Σ–ω–ρ, which is an opaque form since ω is the affix attached later, and a minimal unit required for semantic interpretation is Σ–ρ, not Σ-ω.

In the same way, the combination of initial causativization and applicative formation in Bantu languages can have phonological effects that can only be explained if a surface order Σ–ω–ρ masks a previously established minimal structure Σ–ρ. Thus, Hyman observes that there is a regular phonological operation of frication in Bemba where causative /i̧/ changes labials like /p/ or /b/ to [f], and /t/, /d/, /l/, /k/, and other consonants exhibiting tongue-involvement to [s]; see (75).

(75) a.   leep ('be long') $\rightarrow$ leef-i̧ ('lengthen')
      b.   fiit ('be dark') $\rightarrow$ fiis-i̧ ('darken')
      c.   lil ('cry') $\rightarrow$ lis-i̧ ('make cry')

Importantly, frication persists if applicative formation of the causativized verbs takes place, even though the context for this phonological operation to apply is evidently not present in the surface representation; see (76).

(76) a.   leef-i̧ ('lengthen') $\rightarrow$ leef-es-i̧ ('lengthen for/at')
      b.   fiis-i̧ ('darken') $\rightarrow$ fiis-is-i̧ ('darken for/at')
      c.   lis-i̧ ('make cry') $\rightarrow$ lis-is-i̧ ('make cry for/at')

In addition to opaque frication of the final root consonant, there is transparent frication of the applicative morpheme in the forms in (76). Hyman's (2002) account in terms of interfixation extends to this phonological effect: First, the verb root is combined with the causative morpheme, feeding immediate phonological frication of the final root consonant under adjacency; and subsequently, the applicative morpheme is interfixed counter-cyclically, feeding frication of the final consonant of the applicative exponent and counter-bleeding frication of the final consonant of the root.

I assume that an approach based on interfixing is to be avoided if possible because it inherently violates the STRICT CYCLE CONDITION. However, it can be noted that a simple approach suggests itself for both the semantic and phonological instances of opacity with affix order in Bantu languages in the present approach based on harmonic serialism. In these cases, when there is semantic or phonological evidence for an original Σ–ρ unit even though the surface shows a sequence Σ–ω–ρ, this is due to the fact that ω

is first attached outside of Σ–ρ, and ρ is finally moved around it, as shown in (77).

(77) a. Σ–ρ
    b. Σ–ρ–ω
    c. Σ–ω–ρ

In what follows, let me briefly sketch how this movement effect can be implemented. To simplify exposition, let us assume that, in the case at hand, the V root can optionally bear two features for structure-building, viz., [•Caus•] and [•Appl•], and that there are two MCs sensitive to these features, viz., MC(CAUS) and MC(APPL); the two constraints are ranked in this order, which gives rise to a semantically transparent derivation.[46] Against this background, the data follow if one assumes that (i) both the applicative and the causative morpheme need to be right-aligned; (ii) the respective requirement for causative markers outranks the respective requirement for applicative markers; and (iii) realizing the applicative morpheme as a prefix is never an option, e.g., because of a high-ranked constraint $\text{APPL}{\Rightarrow}\text{R}^2$ that is the reflexive local conjunction of $\text{APPL}{\Rightarrow}\text{R}$; see (78).[47]

(78) $\text{APPL}{\Rightarrow}\text{R}^2 \gg \text{CAUS}{\Rightarrow}\text{R} \gg \text{APPL}{\Rightarrow}\text{R}$

As we will see, this is sufficient to trigger movement of causative morphemes in the presence of applicative formation without further ado. In particular, there is no need to identify a separate trigger for the movement operation. The constraint that forces movement is the constraint that requires right-alignment; everything else is done automatically by the basic harmonic serialist setting.

The first optimization step underlying the generation of a surface form like *leef-es-i* ('lengthen for/at') in Bemba is illustrated in (79).

---

[46] This is a gross simplification. Eventually, the order of causativization and applicative formation should not have to be stipulated by a given ranking of constraints, but should follow from the way compositional interpretation takes place. This, in turn, would seem to presuppose a strictly incremental (rather than realizational) approach to derivational morphology. However, for present purposes, all that is needed is some means ensuring that causativization and applicative formation both take place; and that causativization precedes applicative formation. The two MCs adopted here may suffice for this purpose.

[47] Alternatively, as noted above for Wambon verb inflection, a constraint $\text{L}{\Leftarrow}\text{V}$ with the same ranking would yield the same consequence.

(79) *Causative and applicative* (harmonic serialism, step 1):

I_0: [$_V$ leep], [•Caus•], [•Appl•] [$_{Caus}$ ị], [$_{Appl}$ el]	MC CAUS	MC APPL	APPL $\Rightarrow R^2$	CAUS $\Rightarrow R$	APPL $\Rightarrow R$
O_1: [$_V$ leep], [•Caus•], [•Appl•]	*!	*			
O_2: [$_V$ leep]-[$_{Appl}$ el], [•Caus•]	*!				
☞O_3: [$_V$ leep]-[$_{Caus}$ ị], [•Appl•]		*			
O_4: [$_{Appl}$ el]-[$_V$ leep], [•Caus•]	*!				*
O_5: [$_{Caus}$ ị]-[$_V$ leep], [•Appl•]		*		*!	

In (79), the causative morpheme /ị/ is first combined with the verb root /leep/ so as to satisfy highest-ranked MC(CAUS) (see O_3 vs. O_2, where the applicative morpheme is concatenated first, and vs. O_1, which does not carry out any operation); and /ị/ must show up as a suffix rather than as a prefix because of CAUS⇒R (see O_3 vs. O_5). Next, the applicative morpheme is attached; see (80).

(80) *Causative and applicative* (harmonic serialism, step 2):

I_3: [$_V$ leep]-[$_{Caus}$ ị], [•Appl•] [$_{Appl}$ el]	MC CAUS	MC APPL	APPL $\Rightarrow R^2$	CAUS $\Rightarrow R$	APPL $\Rightarrow R$
O_{31}: [$_V$ leep]-[$_{Caus}$ ị], [•Appl•]		*!			
☞O_{32}: [$_V$ leep]-[$_{Caus}$ ị]-[$_{Appl}$ el]				*	
O_{33}: [$_{Appl}$ el]-[$_V$ leep]-[$_{Caus}$ ị]			*!		*

The optimal output is O_{32}, where the applicative morpheme /el/ shows up as a suffix, in minimal violation of CAUS⇒R, because realizing it as a prefix, as in O_{33}, is never an option in the language. (In the present analysis, this is implemented via APPL⇒R^2, which is violated if /el/ left-attaches to the stem; but see footnote 47.)

Suppose now that as soon as all Merge operations triggered by MCs have applied, and all initial morphological arrays are exhausted, a first morphological cycle (or phase) is completed, and phonological operations can take place. This implies that once O_{32} has emerged as the optimal output of the competition in (80), phonological processes like frication apply if their contextual specification is met, and root-final /p/ is accordingly realized as [f]. After completion of the first phonological cycle, the output is fed back into the morphological component, and subjected to further optimization. In the case at hand, such optimization is clearly possible. A violation of CAUS⇒R, which was not tolerable in the first optimization step, has become temporarily optimal in (80). However, the derivation of course tries to do without this violation, and consequently, rightward morphological movement of the causative morpheme /i̧/ is carried out in the next step; see (81).

(81) *Causative and applicative* (harmonic serialism, step 3):

I$_{32}$: [$_V$ leef]-[$_{Caus}$ i̧]-[$_{Appl}$ el]	MC Caus	MC Appl	Appl ⇒R^2	Caus ⇒R	Appl ⇒R
O$_{321}$: [$_V$ leef]-[$_{Caus}$ i̧]-[$_{Appl}$ el]				*!	
O$_{322}$: [$_{Appl}$ el]-[$_V$ leef]-[$_{Caus}$ i̧]			*!		*
☞O$_{323}$: [$_V$ leef]-[$_{Appl}$ el]-[$_{Caus}$ i̧]					*
O$_{324}$: [$_{Caus}$ i̧]-[$_V$ leef]-[$_{Appl}$ el]				*!*	

If movement of /i̧/ takes place to the right, this gives rise to a violation of lowest-ranked Appl⇒R, but this is as good as it can get because the alternative way of satisfying higher-ranked Caus⇒R – viz., to move /el/ to the left – fatally violates Appl⇒R^2 (or whatever ensures that prefixation is not an option here). It is clear that at this point the morphological derivation yields convergence. The optimal output is then subject to a second (and final) phonological cycle. In the surface representation, frication is triggered again by /i̧/, this time affecting the final consonant of the adjacent applicative morpheme and realizing it as [s], thereby producing *leef-es-i̧*. However, the context for /i̧/ affecting the final stem consonant is not present anymore; the output form is thus opaque, instantiating counterbleeding.

To sum up, with the proviso that an extension of the harmonic serialist approach from inflectional morphology to derivational morphological is possible and plausible, Hyman's data (and, essentially, analysis) of the order and form of roots, causative morphemes and applicative morphemes can be viewed as strong independent evidence for semantic and phonological reflexes of movement. It would thus seem to corroborate the present approach to movement in morphology.

3.8. *Reflexes of Movement in Inflectional Morphology*

The question arises whether similar phonological reflexes of movement can also be found with inflectional morphology, even if semantic considerations determining the order of Merge operations are irrelevant here. As shown in Gleim, Müller, Privizentseva & Tebay (2019), this is indeed the case: Phonological operations like de-spirantization in Barwar Aramaic (see Khan (2008)), Saussurean accent shift in Lithuanian (see Kushnir (2018)), *ni*-insertion in Quechua (see Myler (2013)), *ruki* rule application in Sanskrit (see Kiparsky (1982b)), and vowel harmony in Kazakh (see Bowman & Lokshin (2014)) can all be triggered by morphological exponents that are not adjacent to the affected material in the surface representation. For these kinds of phenomena, there have standardly only been two kinds of explanations – either in terms of non-local phonological operations, or by resort to counter-cyclic morphological operations like interfixation. In contrast, the present approach in terms of morphological movement induced by alignment constraints in harmonic serialism accounts for these data without further ado. Let me illustrate this here for the first of the processes just mentioned, viz., de-spirantization in Barwar Aramaic (see Gleim et al. (2019) for more comprehensive discussion and analyses of all the phenomena).

De-spirantization in Barwar Aramaic is normally a strictly local process that (optionally) changes dental fricatives into stops before coronal /n/ and /l/; thus, /ð/, /θ/ can be realized as [d], [t] in this context. Interestingly, however, it looks as though a morphological exponent with an initial /l/, like the 3.SG.MASC subject marker /le/, can trigger de-spirantization of a stem-final /ð/, as in /tˠr⟨i⟩ð/ ('chase.away⟨PAST⟩'), even if the tense/aspect-related morphological exponent /wa/ ('REMOTE') intervenes, i.e., in an apparently non-local context. Thus, an underlying form such as /tˠr⟨i⟩ðwale/ ('chase.away⟨PAST⟩-REMOTE-3.SG.SBJ') can be realized as [tˠr⟨i⟩dwale].

The analysis in Gleim et al. (2019) is similar to the one given for Bemba above. First, there are two MCs: MC_{Agr} is responsible for merging the ϕ exponent /le/ with the stem, and a lower-ranked $MC_{Adv:T}$ is responsible for merging the temporal adverb exponent /wa/. For both exponent types, there is an alignment constraint demanding an occurrence at the right edge of the word: AGR⇒R, ADV:T⇒R, with the former outranking the latter. Thus, the internal order of the two constraint pairs is identical as far as the objects that they hold for is concerned – this is the ranking that can give rise to movement. Finally, there is a higher-ranked alignment constraint ensuring that none of the exponents can show up as a prefix. It is assumed that this constraint is the general requirement L⇐V (alternatively, this role could be played by a constraint ADV:T⇒R^2 based on reflexive local conjunction, as in some of the earlier analyses in this chapter).

Given these assumptions, the first optimization step for the eventual output [tˠr⟨i⟩dwale] looks as in (82): The exponent from the Agr morphological array that best matches faithfulness constraints (which are not shown here) – /le/ – is merged with the verb stem, as a suffix (because of AGR⇒R); see O_{12}.

(82) *De-spirantization in Barwar Aramaic* (harmonic serialism, step 1):

I_1: [$_V$ t^{ɣ}r⟨i⟩ð]: [•Agr•], [•Adv:T•], [3], [SG], [MASC] [PAST], {[$_{Agr}$ /le/↔[3.SG.MASC]], ... }, {[$_{Adv:T}$ /wa/↔[REMOTE]], ... }	MC$_{Agr}$	MC$_{Adv:T}$	L⇐V	AGR⇒R	ADV:T⇒R
O_{11}: [$_V$ t^{ɣ}r⟨i⟩ð]: [•Agr•], [•Adv:T•]	*!	*			
☞O_{12}: [$_V$ [$_V$ t^{ɣ}r⟨i⟩ð]-le]: [•Adv:T•]		*			
O_{13}: [$_V$ [$_V$ t^{ɣ}r⟨i⟩ð]-wa]: [•Agr•]	*!				
O_{14}: [$_V$ le-[$_V$ t^{ɣ}r⟨i⟩ð]]: [•Adv:T•]		*	*!	*	
O_{15}: [$_V$ wa-[$_V$ t^{ɣ}r⟨i⟩ð]]: [•Agr•]	*!		*		*

Next, the remaining MC$_{Adv:T}$ that must be violated by O_{12} is satisfied by merging /wa/. This exponent is added at the right edge, as in O_{122}, even though this incurs a violation of AGR⇒R. If /wa/ is merged as a prefix, higher-ranked L⇐V will be fatally violated; cf. O_{123}. Not merging /wa/ leads to a worse constraint profile (see O_{121}), and merging /wa/ counter-cyclically between the V stem and the Agr exponent is not an option from the beginning, due to the STRICT CYCLE CONDITION restricting *Gen*.

(83) *De-spirantization in Barwar Aramaic* (harmonic serialism, step 2):

I_{12}: [$_V$ [$_V$ t^{ɣ}r⟨i⟩ð]-le]: [•Adv:T•], [3], [SG], [MASC] [PAST], { ... }, {[$_{Adv:T}$ /wa/↔[REMOTE]], ... }	MC$_{Agr}$	MC$_{Adv:T}$	L⇐V	AGR⇒R	ADV:T⇒R
O_{121}: [$_V$ [$_V$ t^{ɣ}r⟨i⟩ð]-le]: [•Adv:T•]		*!			
☞O_{122}: [$_V$ [$_V$ [$_V$ t^{ɣ}r⟨i⟩ð]-le]-wa]				*	
O_{123}: [$_V$ wa-[$_V$ [$_V$ t^{ɣ}r⟨i⟩ð]-le]]			*!		**

Now V has discharged its structure-building features, and exhausted the morphological arrays. Hence, by assumption, a morphological cycle is completed, and phonological operations can be triggered. Thus, de-spirantization applies to O_{122} under adjacency, and /t^{ɣ}r⟨i⟩ð-le-wa/ becomes /t^{ɣ}r⟨i⟩d-le-wa/. After this, the morphological derivation continues. As illustrated in (84), at this point, the constraint profile can and must be further improved by carrying out morphological movement of /le/ to the right edge: O_{1222} trades in the violation of higher-ranked AGR⇒R incurred by O_{1221}, which leaves the input intact, for a violation of lower-ranked Adv:T⇒R.

(84) *De-spirantization in Barwar Aramaic* (harmonic serialism, step 3):

I_{122}: [v [v [v tʸr⟨i⟩d]-le]-wa] [3], [SG], [MASC] [PAST], { ... }, { ... }	MC$_{Agr}$	MC$_{Adv:T}$	L⇐V	Agr⇒R	Adv:T⇒R
O_{1221}: [v [v [v tʸr⟨i⟩d]-le]-wa]				*!	
☞O_{1222}: [v [v [v [v tʸr⟨i⟩d]]-wa]-le]					*
O_{1223}: [v wa-[v [v tʸr⟨i⟩d]-le]]			*!		**
O_{1224}: [v le-[v [v tʸr⟨i⟩d]]-wa]			*!	**	

The next step yields convergence, and a second phonological cycle can start. However, this comes too late to prevent de-spirantization: Again, morphological movement counter-bleeds de-spirantization.

Chapter 3

Extended Exponence

1. Introduction

The main claim of this chapter is that the phenomenon of extended exponence in morphology provides an empirical domain in which an approach in terms of harmonic serialism suggests itself. At the heart of the analysis is a new constraint called MINIMIZE SATISFACTION (MINSAT) which ensures that it is not just the typical scenario that repeated optimizations in harmonic serialism improve the constraint profile in a gradual manner; serial optimization actually *has to* proceed very slowly. The constraint will be shown to be active outside morphology, both in phonology (where it derives counter-bleeding) and in syntax (where it derives Merge over Move effects).

I will proceed as follows. Section 2 introduces extended exponence, and points out the problems this phenomenon raises for standard parallel optimality-theoretic (and other) approaches to morphology. Section 3 argues for MINSAT in phonology; section 4 does the same for syntax. In section 5, then, I show how MINSAT derives extended exponence; and I argue that this approach is empirically and conceptually superior to an alternative approach in terms of stratal optimality. Finally, section 6 concludes.

2. Extended Exponence

2.1. Introduction

The concept of extended (or multiple) exponence as an issue in theoretical approaches to morphology goes back to Matthews (1972; 1974). Extended exponence refers to cases of morphological realization where a single morpho-syntactic property seems to be expressed by more than one exponent. Matthews' original focus was on phenomena like verb inflection in

Greek, English, and German, where in many cases the classification as extended exponence might legitimately be called into doubt. The reason is that here, it may be the case that one (or more) of the two (or more) items α, β participating in what looks like extended exponence might better be analyzed as a non-segmental marking that is just a realization of a feature associated with a single exponent α (so that β does not exist independently). Arguably, this is the case with, e.g., the co-occurrence of segmental plural marking and umlaut in certain German nouns (cf. *Buch* ('book') vs. *Büch-er* ('books'), where both umlaut and *er* signal plural); see, e.g., Wiese (1996) for an analysis that relies on an abstract ('floating') feature associated with the single plural exponent. Similar conclusions may be drawn in the case of deverbal noun formation in Kujamaat Jóola discussed in Aronoff & Fudeman (2005, 154), where a class marker change is accompanied by vowel tensing.

Another possibility is that two items α, β participating in what looks like extended exponence might preferably be viewed as an underlyingly single complex item giving rise to discontinuous exponence on the surface (as with past participles like *ge-arbeit-et* in German; see the previous chapter).

Most of the phenomena instantiating extended exponence that I will look at in this chapter concern argument encoding and person/number marking. More specifically, I will be concerned with extended exponence of number with case-marking on nouns in German and in Archi; with extended exponence of person with case-marking on nouns in Timucua, and with verbal agreement morphology in Sierra Popoluca. In addition, I will also address extended exponence of negation with verb inflection in Swahili.[1]

2.2. *Extended Exponence of Number in German*

It is a very basic observation that with some inflection classes, plural can be marked twice on nouns in dative (DAT) contexts in German (see Eisenberg (2000b) and Wiese (2000), among others). Thus, in (1-a), the plural exponent *er* is followed by a dative exponent *n* that is itself also specified for plural. This can be seen by inspecting (1-b): In singular contexts, the dative *n* is impossible, which shows that *n* has a conflicting feature specification here; instead the dative singular context either remains without an overt exponent on the noun, or uses the somewhat archaic exponent *e*; see (1-c). The same is shown for another noun inflection class in (1-def): In plural contexts, dative *n* can accompany a plural marker *e*. In singular

---

[1] The presentation of the empirical evidence loosely follows Müller (2007a); however, as we will see, the analysis given in this chapter will be radically different.

contexts, it cannot occur, which shows that n bears the feature [+pl]. Finally, an archaic exponent e can optionally show up in this environment.[2]

(1) a. Kind-er-n
         child-PL-DAT.PL

     b. *Kind-n
         child.SG-DAT.PL

     c. Kind-(e)
         child.SG-DAT

     d. Tisch-e-n
         table-PL-DAT.PL

     e. *Tisch-n
         table.SG-DAT.PL

     f. Tisch-(e)
         table.SG-DAT

2.3. Extended Exponence of Number in Archi

The same phenomenon exists in the Daghestanian language Archi (see, e.g., Kibrik (1991; 2003), Mel'čuk (1999), and Plank (1999)). Archi exhibits an ergative-absolutive (ERG-ABS) pattern of argument encoding. For a stem like *gel* ('cup'), the ERG plural is created by adding the plural marker *um* and the ERG plural marker *čaj* (in that order); for a stem like *qIin* ('bridge'), the ERG plural is derived by adding the plural marker *or* and, again, the ERG plural marker *čaj*; see (2-ad). As before, it is clear that *čaj* must be involved in extended exponence: It is a marker of both case (ERG) and number (plural). This is evidenced by the fact that this marker cannot be used in the singular, where the case markers *li, i* are used for marking ERG instead; cf. (2-be) vs. (2-cf).

(2) a. gel-um-čaj
         cup-PL-ERG.PL

     b. gel-li
         cup.SG-ERG

     c. *gel-čaj
         cup.SG-ERG.PL

     d. qIinn-or-čaj
         bridge-PL-ERG.PL

---

[2] See Regel et al. (2019) for independent neurophysiological evidence for the morphological segmentation given here, and against treating a sequence like *ern* in dative plural contexts, as in (1-a), as a single exponent.

    e.   qIonn-i
        bridge.SG-ERG

    f.   *qIonn-čaj
        bridge.SG-ERG.PL

2.4. *Extended Exponence of Case and Person in Timucua*

A similar phenomenon can be found in the domain of verb inflection in Timucua, an extinct language isolate from Florida (see Mithun (1999, 520); the discussion here is based on Granberry (1990)). Arguments are encoded by head-marking, i.e., case-sensitive agreement morphology on the verb; the pattern is a nominative-accusative one (NOM-ACC). Here and in what follows, CASE is supposed to cover both regular case marking and argument encoding by agreement.[3] Timucua verbs have a complex morphological structure, with various prefix and suffix exponents. As for the prefix markers, the internal argument of a transitive verb is encoded by an 'object', i.e., ACC, prefix. Other primary arguments, including the external argument of a transitive verb, are encoded by a 'subject', i.e., NOM, prefix. A NOM prefix precedes a ACC prefix in transitive contexts; the two markers occupy positions no. 1 and 2 in the template identified by Granberry. These prefixes encode person (but not number) in addition to case: First, there are two 1.NOM markers *ho-* and *ni-*, which "occur with approximately equal frequency" (see Granberry (1990, 86)). Second, there is a 2.NOM marker *ci-*. And third, there is a zero 3.NOM marker Ø-. Many more types of affixes show up on the inflected Timucua verb, but they are all suffixes. Among these are number markers indicating plural (in 7th position in Granberry's template). Crucially, these plural markers also indicate case (NOM) and person (local vs. 3) information; thus they qualify as combined PERS.NUMBER.NOM markers (not too unlike typical subject agreement markers in Indo-European languages like German or Icelandic). These markers are *-bo* (for 1./2.PL.NOM arguments) and *-ma* (for 3.PL.NOM arguments). The data in (3) illustrate the resulting instances of extended exponence of the grammatical category person in the Timucua verb; person exponents are underlined here.

(3)   a.   <u>ho</u>-ini-ta-la
           1.NOM-be-ASP-LOC
           'I am.'

---

[3] Note that this does not imply that the two operations are mirror images of one another; see Bobaljik (2015) and references cited there.

    b.   ni-huba-so-si-bo-te-la
        1.NOM-love-TR-REC-1/2.NOM.PL-ASP-LOC
        'We love each other.'

    c.   ci-huba-so-te-le
        2.NOM-love-TR-ASP-LOC
        'You$_{sg}$ love (someone).'

    d.   ci-huba-so-bo-te-le
        2.NOM-love-TR-1/2.NOM.PL-ASP-LOC
        'You$_{pl}$ love (someone).'

    e.   ano Ø-hewa-na-no
        man 3.NOM-speak-ASP-LOC
        'The man is speaking.'

    f.   Ø-ini-ma-bi-la
        3.NOM-be-3.NOM.PL-ASP-LOC
        'They are just now.'

(3-ace) involve singular subjects (1., 2., 3. person), with a prefix encoding person and case. More interestingly in the present context, (3-bdf) are corresponding examples with plural subjects (1., 2., 3. person) that exhibit extended exponence of case and person marking in Timucua.[4]

2.5. *Extended Exponence of Person in Sierra Popoluca*

Another, slighly less obvious (but ultimately no less clear), case of extended exponence of person arises with argument encoding in Sierra Popoluca, a Mixe-Zoque language spoken in Mexico. Sierra Popoluca employs a head-marking system of argument encoding that follows an ergative-absolutive pattern (ERG-ABS) (see Elson (1960a, 29–30), Elson (1960b, 207–208), Elson & Pickett (1964) and Marlett (1986)). The examples in (4) illustrate how argument encoding is registered on the verb by means of an ABS exponent in intransitive contexts.

(4)   a.   A-nɨk-pa
         1.ABS-go-INC
         'I am going.'

     b.   A-pɨːšiñ
         1.ABS-man
         'I am a man.'

---

[4] Other markers in (3) that are not directly relevant and can be ignored for present purposes include ASP (aspect exponents, here encoding durative or bounded action), LOC/TENSE (exponents representing proximate vs. distant time), TR (transitivity exponents), and REC (exponents of reciprocity); also note that *te/ta, le/la* are variants.

    c.   Ta-hoːy-pa
          1.INCL.ABS-take.a.walk-INC
          'You and I take a walk.'

Argument encoding in transitive contexts (with the presence of an ERG exponent in addition to an ABS exponent) is shown in (5).

(5)   a.   A-Ø-koʔc-pa
           1.ABS-3.ERG-hit-INC
           'He hits me.'
    b.   Ø-Aŋ-koʔc-pa
           3.ABS-1.ERG-hit-INC
           'I hit him.'
    c.   Ø-Taŋ-koʔc-pa
           3.ABS-1.INCL.ERG-hit-INC
           'You and I hit him.'

From these data, the order of Sierra Popoluca verbal affixes in (6) can be derived.

(6)   PERS.ABS – PERS.ERG – V – NUM – PASS – ASP

Let us ignore number, passive, and aspect markers here, and focus exclusively on the exponents for ABS and ERG case features. At first sight, it would seem that the inventory of exponents for argument encoding in Sierra Popoluca looks as in (7).

(7)

	ABS	ERG
1.	a	an
1.INCL	ta	tan
2.	mi	iñ
3.	Ø	i

	ABS ← ERG
1 → 2	man
2 → 1	an

However, as already noted by Elson (1960a;b), taking the exponents in (7) to be primitive makes it impossible to capture the various partial syncretisms that are evident here. For instance, the apparent portmanteau marker in transitive contexts encoding 1.ERG and 2.ABS arguments would clearly seem to be decomposable into separate exponents *m(i)* (for 2.ABS) and *an* (for 1.ERG). Similarly, the distribution of *a* and *i* (for [+1] vs. [−1] environments) would seem to be non-accidental; and so on. For these reasons, following Elson's ideas, a subanalysis of the exponents in (7) is carried out in Müller (2006b). According to this analysis, the individual exponents for argument encoding in Sierra Popolocua have the size of segments.

An indispensable assumption for subanalyzing the exponents in (7) so as
to capture partial syncretism is that person features are decomposed into
more abstract features $[\pm 1],[\pm 2]$, whose cross-classification yields the four
instanations of the grammatical category person in (8); underspecification
with respect to this information captures natural classes of persons.[5]

(8)   a. $[+1,-2]$ = 1. pers.
        b. $[-1,+2]$ = 2. pers.
        c. $[-1,-2]$ = 3. pers.
        d. $[+1,+2]$ = 1. pers. incl.

As argued in Müller (2006b), the simplest analysis (that accounts for all
instances of syncretism) will have to postulate that there is an exponent /a/
in the system which is specified as $[+1]$ – it shows up in both 1. person (i.e.,
$[+1,-2]$) and 1. person inclusive ($[+1,+2]$) contexts. In addition, there has
to be a separate exponent /t/ which is associated with the features $[+1,+2]$
– it is confined to 1. person inclusive contexts. This, however, entails that
there is extended exponence of $[+1]$ in Sierra Popoluca argument encoding.

2.6.   Extended Exponence of Negation in Swahili

As a final example, consider marking of negation on verbs in Swahili (see
Stump (2001)). In positive past tense environments, there is a past tense
exponent *li*. In negative past tense environments, there is a negative exponent *ha* at the beginning of the word. In addition, a special past exponent
ku shows up in the regular slot for tense exponents that also indicates the
fact that the sentence is negated; cf. the 1. person plural contexts in (9-ab).

(9)   a.   tu-li-taka   (positive)
             1.PL-PAST-want
             'We wanted'
        b.   ha-tu-ku-taka   (negative)
             NEG-1.PL-NEG.PAST-want
             'We did not want'

Thus, negation is realized by two exponents in (9-b). In contrast, there is
no such extended exponence in negated future tense contexts in Swahili;
cf. (10-ab).

---

[5] See, e.g., Frampton (2002). Also see chapter 2, where a decomposition along these
lines has been presupposed throughout, and has actively been used to account for non-
first-person syncretism in Island Kiwai and in Wambon via having exponents refer to
non-first environments as a natural class.

(10) a.   tu-ta-taka   (positive)
           1.PL-FUT-want
           'We will want'

      b.   ha-tu-ta-taka   (negative)
           NEG-1.PL-FUT-want
           'We will not want'

The pattern of extended exponence in Swahili differs from the other patterns of extended exponence discussed thus far in one interesting respect: The exponent that, in addition to 'primarily' realizing some instantiation of a grammatical category α, gratuitously indicates a realization of a grammatical category β even though there is also a 'primary' exponent of β, would seem to be closer to the stem; we will see that this poses a particular challenge for theoretical analyses.

2.7.   Interim Conclusion

To sum up so far, extended exponence exists in the argument encoding systems of German, Archi, Timucua, and Sierra Popoluca, and with verb inflection in negated sentences in Swahili. More generally, it is probably uncontroversial to conclude that the phenomenon is widespread in the languages of the world.[6]

At this point, the question arises of how current theories of morphology deal with extended exponence. To address this issue, it is helpful to slightly broaden the perspective on what extended exponence can look like. Caballero & Harris (2012) have proposed a taxonomy of extended exponence that identifies three distinct types. First, two exponents are said to instantiate *partially superfluous multiple exponence* if the feature specifications associated with them are in a proper subset relation. This has been the case in all the examples discussed here: Exponent α is characterized by the features $[F_1, F_2]$, and exponent β is characterized only by $[F_1]$. Second, two exponents give rise to what Caballero & Harris (2012) call *overlapping multiple exponence* when they share some morpho-syntactic feature, but the whole specifications of morpho-syntactic features are not in a subset relation. In this scenario, exponent α bears the features $[F_1, F_2]$, and exponent β realizes $[F_1, F_3]$. Third and finally, Caballero and Harris envisage the possibility of *fully superfluous multiple exponence*: Exponents α and β have identical feature specifications. In what follows, I will disregard

---

[6] Also recall footnote 26 in chapter 2 (and marker entries in (27) of that chapter) on person and number marking in Wardaman, where the systems makes use of two exponents /wu/ (realizing [+3] and [+pl]) and /rr/ (realizing just [+pl]).

the third possibility right from the start.[7] That leaves partially superfluous extended exponence and overlapping extended exponence as the only options.

The first thing to note is that extended exponence of both types is fully expected to show up all over the place in inferential-realizational approaches (see, e.g., Matthews (1972), Anderson (1992), Aronoff (1994), Stump (2001), and Brown & Hippisley (2012)). Here there are no direct associations of rule blocks with subsets of the fully specified feature matrix that defines a paradigm cell (or syntactic context) and gets realized by morphological exponence; rather, each rule block has access to the full feature specification. Consequently, in principle it is predicted to be possible that each feature contained in the fully specified matrix is accessed by every rule block. In practice, though, this never seems to happen: If one looks at the individual analyses developed in these studies, it is typically the case that each rule block is primarily focussed on a certain subset of the full matrix. To give a simple example: In the analysis of Bulgarian verb inflection developed in Stump (2001), there are four rule blocks, each of which can realize all of the relevant features for which verbs can be specified in the language. However, as a matter of fact, rule block A deals with stem selection; rule blocks B and C centre around tense exponents; and rule block D is mainly concerned with the realization of number and person exponents. This is a clear pattern that can be read off both the data and, even more so, Stump's (2001) analysis; but the generalizations cannot be expressed in the theory: Basically, the tendency of certain positions to realize certain grammatical categories necessarily has to be left unexplained.

---

[7] Caballero & Harris (2012) give an example from Nahuatl that is supposed to exhibit fully superfluous multiple exponence but this may well be misanalyzed. It is claimed that there can be two causative suffixes in some cases, viz., *l* and *tia*, that correspond to only one instance of causativization; however, there is no evidence for the independent availability of *l* as a causative marker, and synchronically the *l*-version might simply be an optional part of the causative exponent *tia*. (Thanks to Barbara Stiebels for discussion of this issue.) In the same vein, it can be noted that the cases of discontinuous exponence discussed in chapter 2 (cf. /t-mbo/ in Wambon, /et-ge/ in German), where I have proposed that one part is entirely feature-less and undergoes movement to the edge, could pre-theoretically also be viewed as instances of fully superfluous multiple exponence. From this perspective, this type of seemingly multiple exponence would actually always be reduced to single exponence, accompanied by movement in cases of non-adjacency. (Thanks to Mariia Privizentseva for pointing this out.) At this point, I will have to leave open whether such a reanalysis might qualify as a viable approach for all relevant cases (see, e.g., Kouneli (2019) on the challenge posed by multiple number marking in Kipsigis).

Let me next turn to lexical approaches. Here extended exponence is prima facie unexpected throughout. Interestingly, it turns out that both lexical-incremental and lexical-realizational approaches need to incorporate the concept of secondary, contextual features on exponents to accomodate extended exponence. On the one hand, in lexical-incremental approaches like the one developed in Wunderlich (1996), the reason is that all morpho-syntactic features of a word are introduced by the morphological exponents themselves, and there is an explicit ban in this kind of system on morphological exponents that do not contribute anything new (which is implemented via a designated Monotonicity requirement). Thus, the only scenario in which extended exponence (both of the overlapping and partially superfluous variety) can arise at all is one where the second exponent primarily contributes another feature than the one contributed by the first exponent (which is closer to the stem); furthermore, since the second exponent cannot contribute some feature that is already in place, a different type of feature – a contextual feature – must be postulated that is exempt from the requirement to add something new to the word; see Stiebels (2015).

On the other hand, in the lexical-realizational approach of Distributed Morphology (see Halle & Marantz (1993)), contextual features are needed to account for extended exponence for the following reason: Morphological realization is brought about by insertion transformations that place inflectional exponents in functional heads; these functional heads bear the fully specified features realized by exponence. For insertion of an exponent α bearing the feature $[F_1]$ into a given functional morpheme Γ, there are therefore two cases to consider. First, the functional morpheme Γ may itself not be equipped with $[F_1]$ because this feature belongs to some other functional morpheme, and gets realized there by some other morphological exponent. Then, given that α bears $[F_1]$, it is obviously necessary for α to bear $[F_1]$ as a *contextual* feature (it does not satisfy compatibility in Γ alone). Second, suppose that Γ does bear $[F_1]$. Then α may be inserted, and realize $[F_1]$ in Γ as a primary, regular feature; but in order to derive disjunctive blocking in Γ, it has to be ensured that insertion can only take place once per functional morpheme; so a problem arises, and extended exponence cannot be modelled in this second version. These conclusions hold for both partially superfluous and overlapping versions of extended exponence.[8] It should be noted at this point that there are versions of

---

[8] As a matter of fact, in principle Distributed Morphology can also handle fully superfluous extended exponence via contextual features. Suppose that some morphological exponent $\beta \leftrightarrow [F_1]$ has realized feature $[F_1]$ in functional morpheme Γ'. Then, in the

Distributed Morphology that envisage multiple insertion of exponents into a single functional morpheme (as a consequence of one version of the operation of fission); see Noyer (1992), Trommer (1999), Frampton (2002), Georgi (2008), and Opitz (2008), among others. However, in these approaches it must be assumed that a morphological exponent *discharges* the features that it realizes in a functional morpheme (otherwise disjunctive blocking effects could never be modelled), and only the remaining features in the functional morpheme are accessible for further insertion. This concept therefore necessitates contextual features for the modelling of extended exponence in exactly the same way as the original Distributed Morphology approach. In addition, in this approach it may often be the case that contextual features of an exponent α have already been discharged by an earlier insertion operation β, thereby requiring the continued presence of discharged features and thus ultimately demanding a concept of discharge that goes beyond the simplest possibility, viz., deletion, and relies on some form of diacritic (such that the feature in question is accessible as a contextual feature but not anymore as a primary feature).

I take it that the widespread use of contextual features is far from innocuous. There are at least four kinds of problems associated with the concept. First, there is the problem of *ambiguity*. As shown by Stump (2001, 162–163), there are many cases where one and the same inflection marker must act as a primary exponent of a morpho-syntactic property in one context, and as a secondary exponent of the same morpho-syntactic property in another context; for instance, this holds for the negation marker *ha* in the Swahili examples discussed above (see (9-b) vs. (10-b)). Second, given that this ambiguity is an option in principle, a *learnability* problem arises: In the absence of independently motivated restrictions that would favour one of the two alternatives, it is not clear how it can be decided in the course of language acquisition whether some feature is associated with a morphological exponent as a primary or as a secondary (contextual) property. Third, it is notoriously unclear whether (and if so, to what extent) contextual features count for *specificity*.[9] And fourth, there is a *locality* issue: How far away can a contextual feature of α be from the locus of

---

absence of any compatible more specific exponent, $\alpha \leftrightarrow [-]/{}_{[\mathrm{F}_1]}$ can be inserted into Γ as an elsewhere marker radically underspecified with respect to primary features. Technically, this may not qualify as a true instance of fully superfluous extended exponence, but empirically there is no discernible difference between a featureless exponent that requires the feature $[\mathrm{F}_1]$ and an exponent associated with $[\mathrm{F}_1]$.

[9] See Arregi & Nevins (2012) and Hanink (2018) for suggestions, though.

morphological exponence of α?[10] I conclude from these considerations that there is every reason to dispense with the concept of contextual features, if at all possible.

In Müller (2007a), it is argued (against the background of a standard Distributed Morphology approach) that reference to secondary (contextual, discharged) features can be dispensed with if post-syntactic *enrichment rules* are postulated that copy features before morphological realization takes place, and that act as the counterpart of *impoverishment rules*. However, whatever the merits of this proposal otherwise may be, it can be noted that an enrichment approach is compatible with the existence of multiple exponents with an identical feature specification, i.e., with fully superfluous extended exponence. However, abstracting away from cases of *form replication* (i.e., multiple occurrence of the same exponents), as in cases of (total) reduplication, this does not seem to occur (see above). (And I am not aware of any theory of reduplication that would treat the phenomenon as separate realization of identical morpho-syntactic features.) Furthermore, as pointed out by Harris (2009), the phenomenon of exuberant exponence in a language like Batsbi, where not just two, but several markers are involved in extended exponence, sheds doubt on a concept like enrichment because the operation would have to apply post-syntactically exactly n times if there will eventually be n exponents that are in need of its application.

Let me finally turn to standard parallel optimality-theoretic approaches. Note first that existing optimality-theoretic approaches to inflectional morphology typically embrace the concept of contextual features in the modelling of extended exponence; cf. Grimshaw (2001), Wunderlich (2001a; 2004), Don & Blom (2006), and Trommer (2001; 2003; 2006a), among others. Thus, here the same considerations apply as in the case of non-optimality-theoretic approaches making use of this concept.

However, it is instructive to look at what standard parallel optimality-theoretic approaches unadorned by contextual features predict with respect to extended exponence. It turns out that they do not face any particular problem with respect to overlapping extended exponence. The reason is that if an exponent α is associated with the features $[F_1, F_2]$, and an exponent β is associated with the features $[F_1, F_3]$, the presence of both markers can easily be enforced by sufficiently highly ranked constraints MAX-F_2 and MAX-F_3, which can only both be satisfied if both markers are present in

---

[10] This question has given rise to much recent research on contextually determined allomorphy. I focus on this issue in chapter 5.

the output form and which must both outrank a general constraint against structure-building which we can for present purposes identify as *Struc ('*Structure'; see Aissen (2003)), as in (11).[11]

(11)   *Struc ('*Structure'):
       Adding exponents is prohibited.

In contrast, the situation is very different with partially superfluous extended exponence. Here a simple standard parallel optimality-theoretic approach will straightforwardly exclude this option. To see this, consider the simplified tableau for extended exponence of number in German nouns, as it was discussed in section 2.2. above (see (1)).[12]

(12)   *Extended exponence as a problem* (standard parallel optimality
       theory):

I_1: /[$_N$ Kind:[+pl,+obl,+gov]]/	Id-F	MaxNum	MaxCase	*Struc
☛O_{11}: Kind[+pl,+obl,+gov]-n[+pl,+obl,+gov]				*
O_{12}: Kind[+pl,+obl,+gov]-er[+pl]			*!*	*
O_{13}: Kind[+pl,+obl,+gov]-e[+gov,+obl]		*!		*
☆O_{14}: Kind[+pl,+obl,+gov]-er[+pl]-n[+pl,+obl,+gov]				**!

O_{14} is the intended winner (with realization of both /er/ as a plural marker and /n/ as a dative plural marker). However, O_{14} can never emerge as optimal because O_{11} (with just the dative plural marker) satisfies all faithfulness constraints equally well but manages to avoid an (additional) violation of *Struc (or whatever ultimately the price is that comes with each indivual structure-building operation): Clearly, partially superfluous extended exponence *is* superfluous extended exponence from the perspective of standard parallel optimality theory because the output that has extended exponence is harmonically bounded by the output that does not.

Basically, the situation is not per se different in an approach in terms of harmonic serialism. It can easily be verified that in a harmonic serialist version of (12), O_{11} would immediately emerge as optimal, blocking O_{12} and never permitting O_{14} to arise in the first place (because of the confinement to only one operation separating input and output).

---

[11] This may be a place-holder for whatever makes adding more structure costly, e.g., alignment constraints; cf. Grimshaw (2006).

[12] MaxNum and MaxCase are abbreviations for Max(pl) and Max(obl), Max(gov), respectively. As before (see chapter 1), a candidate that is wrongly predicted to be the winner by a given *H-Eval* operation is identified by ☛; and an intended winner that is not in fact classified as optimal by the constraints is singled out by the symbol ☆.

Against this background, the central claim of this chapter is that this fatal consequence with respect to partially superfluous extended exponence can be avoided if an approach in terms of harmonic serialism is pursued that incorporates a constraint MinSat ('Minimize Satisfaction'). MinSat ensures that each new optimization step leads to as few new constraint satisfactions as possible, and thereby slows down derivations; for this reason, postulating it in a standard parallel optimality-theoretic approach could never have the desired effect. MinSat can be defined as in (13).

(13) MinSat (Minimize Satisfaction):
     Assign * to an output O_i iff (a) and (b) hold.

    a. O_i has x new constraint satisfactions ($0 \leq x \leq n$).
    b.   There is an output O_j ($j \neq i$) in the same candidate set such that
        (i) O_j has y new constraint satisfactions ($0 \leq y \leq n$); and
        (ii) $0 < y < x$.

A *new constraint satisfaction* is a constraint satisfaction that is present in the output but not in the input. Thus, an output O_i is blocked by an output O_j via MinSat if O_j has fewer new constraint satisfactions than O_i but does improve the constraint profile by having at least one new constraint satisfaction. An output without a new constraint satisfaction cannot block another output via MinSat.

Postulating this constraint immediately raises a number of important questions. First, is there independent evidence for it? Second, unlike other constraints in optimality theory, MinSat is transderivational (one has to look at the properties of other outputs to decide whether a given output satisfies or violates it); what does this imply for possible interactions of this constraint with others in the H-Eval system of the grammar? Third, how does this constraint actually make it possible to derive extended exponence in an approach to morphology based on harmonic serialism? And fourth, to what extent is the evidence presented in the previous two chapters compatible with such a constraint (in particular, as regards disjunctive blocking in morphology)? I will address these questions in turn, beginning with independent motivation for MinSat which comes from phonology and syntax.

3. Minimize Satisfaction in Phonology: Counter-Bleeding

3.1. The Problem

Traditional wisdom has it that opacity effects like counter-bleeding and counter-feeding (see Kiparsky (1973a), and Chomsky (1975, 25–26), among many others) a priori pose a problem for non-derivational (representational, declarative) approaches to grammar but not for derivational approaches. In counter-bleeding scenarios, a rule A that would destroy the context in which rule B can apply (i.e., that would bleed B) applies too late to actually do so. As a consequence, the surface representation is opaque because it is not really clear why B could apply, given that A has applied; thus, an apparent case of overgeneration results. Conversely, in counter-feeding scenarios, a rule A that would create the context in which rule B can apply (i.e., that would feed B) comes too late to do so. As a consequence, the surface representation is also opaque because it is not really clear why B could not apply, given that A has applied; therefore, we end up with what at first sight looks like a case of undergeneration. In classical derivational, rule-based approaches (in phonology, morphology, and syntax) where grammatical operations are brought about by rule application, deriving opacity effects of this type is entirely straightforward. In contrast, in non-derivational approaches that only look at an output structure and, crucially, not at the derivational steps that have created it, opacity effects are a challenge, typically demanding much more abstract representations massively enriched by non-overt material whose main purpose is to make reference to information possible that would come for free if intermediate stages of the derivation were accessible – traces, copies, *pros*, PROs and other empty elements in syntax (see, e.g., Wasow (1972), Chomsky (1977; 1981; 1982; 1995), Fiengo (1977)), and various kinds of non-overt items in phonology (see, e.g., Goldrick (2000), Bye (2001), Oostendorp (2006; 2007), and Trommer (2011; 2015a) for proposals that share this general property).

Given this state of affairs, it may initially come as a surprise that harmonic serialism, despite being inherently derivational, also has difficulty accounting for counter-bleeding and counter-feeding (see McCarthy (2007)). Ultimately, the reason is that operations in harmonic serialism are not instantiations of primitive rules but are triggered indirectly, by the need to satisfy violable constraints. This implies, on the one hand, that if one operation can satisfy two constraints simultaneously, it may be given preference, which makes it impossible to derive counter-bleeding. On the other hand, constraints can never be switched off, so even low-ranked constraints will in principle have the chance to induce an operation, even if this operation then takes late in the derivation; this makes it difficult to derive counter-feeding.

The counter-bleeding problem for harmonic serialism in phonology is the one that I would like to focus on here. It is illustrated in McCarthy (2007, 37–38; 69–70) on the basis of the interaction of vowel deletion and palatalization in Bedouin Arabic.

The core empirical observation is that Bedouin Arabic has an operation of i deletion before a CV sequence and an operation that brings about
palatalization of a velar in front of an i; but words like [ħaːkʲmiːn] exhibit palatalization of k even though there is no i around in the surface
representation that could trigger it (because it was subject to i-deletion).
In a classical rule-based approach, this can be derived without further assumptions, simply by ordering the deletion and palatalization rules as in
(14).[13]

(14)   *Counter-bleeding in Bedouin Arabic:*

UR	/ħaːkimiːn/
Palatalization	ħaːkʲimiːn
Vowel deletion	ħaːkʲmiːn
Surface form	[ħaːkʲmiːn]

The following (simplified) constraints suggest themselves for a reconstruction of this effect in harmonic serialism (or, more generally, optimality
theory).

(15)   a. *iCV   (triggers i deletion)
       b. *ki (triggers palatalization of a velar in front of i)
       c. MAX   (blocks deletion of i).
       d. ID(back)   (blocks palatalization of k).

Suppose that *iCV and *ki outrank the counteracting faithfulness constraints, so that both deletion and palatalization can apply in principle.
To imitate the order of operations in (14), *ki can further be assumed
to outrank *iCV – thus, the constraint triggering palatalization is ranked
higher than the constraint triggering deletion. However, as the tableau in
(16) shows, in the very first step the optimal output is not O_{12} (which
preserves the i and carries out palatalization) but O_{11} (which removes the
i and thereby satisfies not only *iCV but also *ki).[14]

---

[13] UR stands for underlying representation, as provided by the lexicon.

[14] Note that an output like ħaːkʲmiːn cannot be reached by applying a single operation;
apart from that, its MAX operation would be identical to the one incurred by O_{11}, but
its additional ID(back) violation would render it suboptimal in any event.

(16) *Counter-bleeding in Bedouin Arabic* (harmonic serialism, step 1):

I_1: /ħaːkim-iːn/	$*ki$	$*i$CV	MAX	ID(back)
☞ O_{11}: ħaːkmiːn			*	
☆ O_{12}: ħaːkʲimiːn		*!		*
O_{13}: ħaːkimiːn	*!	*		

Unfortunately, this is basically all that has to happen; the following step fatally leads to convergence; see (17).

(17) *Counter-bleeding in Bedouin Arabic* (harmonic serialism, step 2):

I_{11}: /ħaːkmiːn/	$*ki$	$*i$CV	MAX	ID(back)
☞ O_{111}: ħaːkmiːn				
O_{112}: ħaːkimiːn	*!	*		
☆ O_{113}: ħaːkʲmiːn				*!

The underlying rationale is the following: In a rule-based account, an early application of the palatalization rule gives rise to immediate palatalization. In a harmonic serialism account, a high ranking of the constraint $*ki$ that normally triggers palatalization does in fact not give rise to immediate palatalization: Constraints trigger operations only indirectly, and fail to do so if they can also be satisfied by other operations, triggered by different constraints – like vowel deletion triggered by $*i$CV, in the case at hand.

Of course, reranking the constraints does not help. If MAX dominates $*i$CV, there will be an intermediate optimal output in which palatalization has applied and the vowel i has remained intact; see (18).

(18) *Counter-bleeding in Bedouin Arabic* (reranking, harmonic serialism, step 1):

I_1: /ħaːkim-iːn/	$*ki$	MAX	$*i$CV	ID(back)
O_{11}: ħaːkmiːn		*!		
☞ O_{12}: ħaːkʲimiːn			*	*
O_{13}: ħaːkimiːn	*!		*	

At first glance, this may look like the correct intermediate winner. However, i deletion will now simply never be permitted in the language; see (19).

(19) *Counter-bleeding in Bedouin Arabic* (reranking, harmonic serialism, step 2):

I_{12}: /ħaːkʲim-iːn/	$*ki$	MAX	$*i$CV	ID(back)
☆ O_{121}: ħaːkʲmiːn		*!		
☞ O_{122}: ħaːkʲimiːn			*	
O_{123}: ħaːkimiːn	*!		*	

Thus, a dilemma arises: A high ranking of Max (more specifically, domination of *iCV) is needed in step 1 so as to ensure that the the intended intermediate representation with palatalization is optimal; but afterwards, it becomes fatal because i deletion is permanently blocked. (More generally, i deletion is now wrongly predicted to be blocked throughout, i.e., also in transparent contexts.) This problem could only be solved if reranking between optimization procedures were an option – which it is not in harmonic serialism.[15,16]

Similarly, as shown by McCarthy (2007), harmonic serialism encounters problems with deriving counter-feeding. Again, this can be shown on the basis of Bedouin Arabic; in addition to the operation of i deletion we have already encountered, there is an operation of vowel raising which raises a to i. However, an i that is derived in such a way cannot in turn undergo deletion; this is an instance of standard chain-shift effects. (20) shows how a classical rule-based approach can account for counter-feeding by ordering vowel deletion before vowel raising.

(20) *Counter-feeding in Bedouin Arabic*:

UR	/dafaʕ/
Vowel deletion	–
Vowel raising	difaʕ
Surface form	[difaʕ]

The constraints that are needed in the analysis are given in (21) (again, following McCarthy, simplified forms of the actual markedness constraints involved in the competition are postulated here).

---

[15] The situation is different if a *stratal optimality-theoretic* approach is adopted that envisages reranking between strata (see Kiparsky (1982a; 2000), Bermúdez-Otero (2008; 2011), Trommer (2011; 2015a)).

[16] McCarthy's (2007) solution to this problem does not rely on harmonic serialism but on a theory that enriches classical optimality theory with the concept of *candidate chains* (OT-CC): The central assumption here is that the competing candidates are candidate chains that are generated by a special version of harmonic serialism. Candidate chains are essentially restricted derivations: Each derivational stage must differ from its predecessor by incurring a violation of a basic faithfulness constraint (so-called LUM, 'localized unfaithful mapping'), and by improving the overall constraint profile. On this basis, Prec(edence)(A,B) constraints demand that a violation of faithfulness constraint B in a candidate is accompanied by an earlier violation of a faithfulness constraint A. In the case at hand, Prec(Id(back),Max) states that a violation of Max incurred by i deletion *follows* a violation of Id(back) incurred by palatalization. The constraint, if ranked sufficiently high, selects the opaque candidate as the optimal one. Thus, core aspects of derivations in rule-based approaches are imitated.

(21) a. $*a$CV   (triggers raising of a to i)
      b. $*i$CV   (triggers i deletion)
      c. MAX   (blocks deletion of i (and of a))
      d. MAX-A   (blocks deletion of a)
      e. ID(low)   (blocks raising of a to i)

To trigger i deletion, $*i$CV must dominate MAX. The segment a is not deleted (but raised), so $*a$CV must dominate ID(low) but be dominated by MAX-A. (22) shows how an output becomes optimal in the first optimization step that carries out raising.

(22) *Counter-feeding in Bedouin Arabic* (harmonic serialism, step 1):

I_1: /dafaʕ/	MAX-A	$*a$CV	$*i$CV	MAX	ID(low)
☞O_{11}: difaʕ			*		*
O_{12}: dfaʕ	*!			*	
O_{13}: dafaʕ		*!			

This may at first sight look like the correct result but it is not: The problem is that whereas a lower ranking for $*i$CV implies that this markedness constraint becomes active later in the derivation, it does not mean that this constraint is switched off. Therefore, in the next step, vowel deletion applies, yielding a transparent rather than opaque winner. This is a fatal result since the following step invariably leads to convergence.

(23) *Counter-feeding in Bedouin Arabic* (harmonic serialism, step 2):

I_{11}: /difaʕ/	MAX-A	$*a$CV	$*i$CV	MAX	ID(low)
☆O_{111}: difaʕ			*		
☞O_{112}: dfaʕ				*	
O_{113}: dafaʕ		*!			*

It can easily be verified that a reranking of $*a$CV and $*i$CV would not help. Under a ranking $*i$CV $\gg$ $*a$CV, raising of a to i can never be brought about.

More generally, over the last decade, the issue of deriving opacity effects in harmonic serialism has been addressed, but it seems fair to conclude that general solutions of the problems with counter-bleeding and counter-feeding are so far outstanding.[17]

---

[17] See, e.g., McCarthy (2016), Torres-Tamarit (2016), and Elfner (2016). As regards counter-bleeding, Torres-Tamarit (2016) argues that counter-bleeding of compensatory lengthening by deletion of a mora-bearing coda follows in harmonic serialism if the following two assumptions are made: First, moras can be inserted in the course of the derivation (with C segments that are subsequently deleted or move away, as in so-called

3.2. A Minimize Satisfaction Approach to Counter-Bleeding in Phonology

I would like to suggest that otherwise recalcitrant cases of counter-bleeding in phonology can be derived by invoking the MinSat constraint in (24) (repeated here from (13)). MinSat ensures that serial optimization proceeds one step after the other, by giving preference to operations that are homogeneous in the sense that they satisfy (non-trivially) only one constraint.[18]

(24) MinSat (Minimize Satisfaction):
Assign * to an output O_i iff

   a. O_i has x new constraint satisfactions ($0 \leq x \leq n$).

   b.   There is an output O_j ($j \neq i$) in the same candidate set such that

      (i) O_j has y new constraint satisfactions ($0 \leq y \leq n$); and

      (ii) $0 < y < x$.

Let us look again at the case of counter-bleeding of palatalization by vowel deletion in Bedouin Arabic. Suppose that MinSat is undominated among the constraints relevant for these operations; everything else is exactly as before.

(25) *Counter-bleeding in Bedouin Arabic* (MinSat version, harmonic serialism, step 1):

I_1: /ħaːkim-iːn/	MinSat	*ki	*iCV	Max	Id(back)
☞O_{11}: ħaːkʲimiːn			*		*
O_{12}: ħaːkimiːn		*!	*		
O_{13}: ħaːkmiːn	*!			*	

'double flop' scenarios). And second, deletion must be viewed as a process that is composed of two basic *Gen* operations: On the one hand, there is debuccalization (i.e., deletion of the place feature, accompanied by generation of H); on the other hand, there is root note deletion (with deletion of H). As far as counter-feeding is concerned, Elfner (2016) suggests that counter-feeding of stress assignment by epenthesis in languages like Dakota can be accounted for in harmonic serialism if stress assignment counts as one *Gen* operation, whereas stress displacement necessarily involves two *Gen* operations (viz., foot deletion and foot assignment). On this view, there can be no local improvement of the constraint profile by application of the first operation, and since there is no look-ahead, the stress remains where it was before epenthesis took place. Both these approaches would seem to work well for the phenomena they set out to account for, but it seems clear that none of them can be generalized to cover all relevant cases of phonological opacity.

[18] Insofar as it enforces a general *gradualness* property, this approach in terms of MinSat is arguably conceptually related to McCarthy's (2007) OT-CC approach in terms of localized unfaithful mappings.

Output O_{13} ($ħa:kmi:n$) is the dangerous transparent candidate that emerged as optimal in McCarthy's (2007) original approach in terms of harmonic serialism. It is now excluded in step 1 in (25) due to a fatal MinSat violation: This output satisfies two markedness constraints in one go that are violated by the input (viz., both *ki and *iCV). In contrast, by carrying out palatalization, O_{11} only satisfies one markedness constraint violated by the input (viz., *ki), and is thus preferred by MinSat. Note that O_{12}, which leaves the input unchanged, therefore obviously does not satisfy any markedness constraint that is violated by input; still, given clause (24-b-ii) in the definition of MinSat, it is clear that this output cannot block the intended winner O_{11}: O_{12} has fewer new constraint satisfactions than O_{11}, but not more new constraints satisfactions than 0.

While vowel deletion was kept from applying in the first step by MinSat, the constraint permits the operation to take place in the following step. This is shown in (26).

(26) *Counter-bleeding in Bedouin Arabic* (MinSat version, harmonic serialism, step 2):

I_{11}: /ħa:k^{j}im-i:n/	MinSat	*ki	*iCV	Max	ID(back)
O_{111}: ħa:k^{j}imi:n			*!		
☞O_{112}: ħa:k^{j}mi:n				*	

Vowel deletion in O_{112} in (26) leads to one new constraint satisfaction (viz., of *iCV), but this is compatible with MinSat because the only alternative candidate, O_{111}, does not produce any new constraint satisfaction. Therefore, the presence of O_{111} cannot trigger a MinSat violation for O_{112}. In the next step, convergence is reached.

A question that arises at this point is how it can be ensured that the transparent rather than the opaque candidate might win the optimality-theoretic competition; this option evidently exists in the languages of the world. For now, the answer is straightforward:[19] MinSat must be ranked below *iCV. As shown in the tableaux in (27) and (28), a low ranking of MinSat ceteris paribus produces bleeding. In the first step, output O_{13} emerges as optimal; here vowel deletion applies, thereby satisfying two markedness constraints that were violated by the input in one fell swoop.

---

[19] As we will see, it will not be quite so straightforward anymore once we consider the role of MinSat in syntax and morphology.

(27) *Bleeding* (MinSat version, harmonic serialism, step 1):

I₁: /ħaːkim-iːn/	*ki	*iCV	MinSat	Max	Id(back)
O₁₁: ħaːkʲimiːn		*!			*
O₁₂: ħaːkimiːn	*!	*			
☞O₁₃: ħaːkmiːn			*	*	

The next step yields convergence; see (28).

(28) *Bleeding* (MinSat version, harmonic serialism, step 2):

I₁₃: /ħaːkmiːn/	*ki	*iCV	MinSat	Max	Id(back)
O₁₃₁: ħaːkʲmiːn					*!
O₁₃₂: ħaːkimiːn	*!	*			
☞O₁₃₃: ħaːkmiːn					

I would like to contend that this approach to counter-bleeding in Bedouin Arabic can be generalized to other cases of counter-bleeding in phonology. Consider, e.g., the opaque interaction of epenthesis and ʔ deletion outside of onsets in Tiberian Hebrew (see McCarthy (1999)): In a classical rule-based approach, ordering epenthesis before ʔ deletion yields the opaque derivation *deš?* → *deše?* → *deše* ('grass'). In a standard parallel optimality-theoretic analysis focussing on output constraints, it is a priori unclear why epenthesis can take place here, given that the constraints that trigger epenthesis (viz., a ban on complex codas) and ʔ deletion (viz., a ban on final ʔs) can all be satisfied by just carrying out deletion. In contrast, in a harmonic serialist approach incorporating high-ranked MinSat, epenthesis will be preferred in the first step since it (non-trivially) minimizes new constraint satisfactions, and subsequently deletion will apply, yielding the correct output form.

The same goes for other examples involving counter-bleeding, such as the interaction of vowel assimilation and syncope in Tunica (see Kenstowicz & Kisseberth (1979)): *náši-ʔáki* → *náši-ʔɛ́ki* → *náš-ʔɛ́ki*. Syncope does not bleed vowel assimilation here in the first step because it would satisfy both markedness constraints triggering these two operations in one go; therefore vowel assimilation takes place first, in accordance with MinSat, and syncope applies subsequently, again in accordance with MinSat, eventually producing the opaque output in which vowel assimilation seems to be unmotivated.

As a final case, let me mention the interaction of l-w-shift and dental stop deletion in Ukrainian – yet another textbook example of counter-bleeding (see Kenstowicz & Kisseberth (1979)): *klad-l* → *kla-l* → *kla-w*. Here, l-w-shift would remove the context for dental stop deletion to apply but cannot actually do so because it applies too late. And again, this is exactly what is predicted under (a high-ranked) MinSat: The transparent candidate is blocked as an optimal output in the first step because it does not minimize the new satisfaction of markedness constraints.

All that said, it seems that the MinSat approach to counter-bleeding in harmonic serialism has nothing insightful to say about cases of counter-feeding. Here the problem for an approach in terms of harmonic serialism was not that too many new constraint satisfactions are brought about too early in the derivation, but rather that a MinSat-compatible derivation continues, further improving the constraint profile, after the intended output has been reached. However, it is worth noting that this instance of opacity is known to pose fewer problems for non-rule-based approaches to begin with (see McCarthy (2007)), and alternative accounts are readily available under present assumptions.[20]

4. Minimize Satisfaction in Syntax: Merge over Move

4.1. *Merge over Move*

Turning to the role of MinSat in syntax next, the goal of the present section is to illustrate that it derives the general constraint MERGE OVER MOVE proposed in Chomsky (2000). Following Frampton & Gutmann (1999), MERGE OVER MOVE can be defined as in (29).

(29) MERGE OVER MOVE:
      Suppose that the derivation has reached stage Σ_n, and Σ_{n+1} is a legitimate instance of Merge, and Σ'_{n+1} is a legitimate instance of Move. Then, Σ_{n+1} is to be preferred over Σ'_{n+1}.

While postulating such a constraint is far from uncontroversial, it can be observed that substantial evidence for MERGE OVER MOVE has been accumulated over the years; see Frampton & Gutmann (1999), Hornstein (2001; 2009), Castillo, Drury & Grohmann (2009), Boeckx, Hornstein & Nunes (2010), Drummond (2011), Witkoś (2013), Weisser (2015), and Popp & Tebay (2019), among many others. In what follows, I will illustrate the workings of MERGE OVER MOVE in syntax on the basis of three phenomena: expletive constructions in English, control into adjuncts, and asymmetric coordination.

---

[20] Interestingly, however, Driemel & Stojković (2017) observe that MinSat *can* derive cases of counter-feeding if a standard parallel optimality-theoretic approach is adopted.

4.2. Expletive Constructions in English

The original evidence for MERGE OVER MOVE in Chomsky (2000) comes
from expletive constructions in English. Given that all T heads in English
have an EPP property that requires them to have a specifier, the question
arises why the specifier of the infinitival T in (30) needs to be filled by a
trace of a moved expletive pronoun *there*, as in (30-a), and cannot be filled
by a moved associate DP (here, *someone*), as in (30-b).

(30) a. There$_1$ seems [$_\text{TP}$ t$_1$ to be [$_\text{PP}$ someone$_2$ in the room]]
      b. *There$_1$ seems [$_\text{TP}$ someone$_2$ to be [$_\text{PP}$ t$_2$ in the room]]

Chomsky (2000) argues that this is due to MERGE OVER MOVE. The relevant stage of the derivation is where T has been merged with the infinitival
complement, yielding a complex T$'$ category as the input for the next operation. This stage is depicted in (31-a). Two further continuations are now
conceivable which may satisfy infinitival T's EPP property: An expletive
there can be merged from the numeration, as in (31-b$_1$), or the subject
DP *someone* can be moved from its base position in the predicative PP,
as in (31-b$_2$). The former operation is an instance of Merge, the latter is
an instance of Move, and other things being equal, MERGE OVER MOVE
correctly predicts only the former option to be able to apply at this point.

(31) a.   [$_{\text{T}'}$ to be [$_\text{PP}$ someone$_2$ in the room]] $\rightarrow$
      b$_1$. [$_\text{TP}$ there [$_{\text{T}'}$ to be [$_\text{PP}$ someone$_2$ in the room]]]   (Merge)
      b$_2$. *[$_\text{TP}$ someone$_2$ [$_{\text{T}'}$ to be [$_\text{PP}$ t$_2$ in the room]]]   (Move)

Continuations of this derivation can then only take (31-b$_1$) as the input,
eventually giving rise to (30-a). (30-b) can never be generated because
it would require a continuation of (31-b$_2$) to be an option.[21] Note that
subsequent movement of *there* in (30-a) is not blocked by MERGE OVER
MOVE because there is no alternative option anymore to merge from the
numeration (more precisely, the workspace) of the derivation. For the same
reason, MERGE OVER MOVE does not block regular subject movement in
raising constructions – as in (32-b), which ultimately produces (32-a) – if
there is no expletive present in the numeration to begin with.

(32) a.   Someone$_2$ seems [$_\text{TP}$ t$'_2$ to be t$_2$ in the room]

---

[21] If *someone* were to move to the position of the trace of the expletive in a later step
of the derivation, this would fatally violate the STRICT CYCLE CONDITION; see (22) of
chapter 2.

    b.   [$_{\text{TP}}$ someone$_2$ to be t$_2$ in the room]

There is much more to be said about this analysis. Ultimately, it requires a number of additional assumptions and has many further repercussions (among other things, it has given rise to the first, theory-internal, argument for the existence of phases). However, also in view of the fact that it is unclear to what extent Chomsky's (2000) approach can be said to be widely adopted in investigations of expletives in English, this brief illustration may suffice for the time being.

4.3. Control into Adjuncts

Another argument for a constraint like MERGE OVER MOVE comes from control; it goes back to Hornstein (2001) and can be found in various shapes in work like Hornstein (2009) and Boeckx, Hornstein & Nunes (2010)). In a nutshell, MERGE OVER MOVE, in conjunction with the Movement Theory of Control (MTC) and the hypothesis that sideward movement is available, predicts that objects cannot control into adjuncts, whereas subjects can. This restriction for object control in English is illustrated in (33).

(33)   John$_1$ saw Mary$_2$ [before PRO$_{1,*2}$ leaving the party]

Whereas normally (i.e., with control into complement clauses), object control is the unmarked strategy, in (33) it is only the subject *John*, and not the object *Mary*, that can effect control of the embedded non-overt subject of the infinitival clause. Hornstein's analysis of the prohibition against object control in an adjunct clause works as follows. First, given the movement theory of control, PRO in (33) is actually the trace of a moved DP. Suppose now that *Mary* shows up in the adjunct clause as a subject; this is a precondition for any attempt at deriving (33) with object control. At the relevant point in the derivation, there are two workspaces: *[before Mary leaving the party]* is in the first one, and *saw* is in the second one; *John$_1$* is still in the numeration. Now, for object control, *Mary$_2$* would have to sideward-move out of the adjunct and attach to the main verb *saw*; but given MERGE OVER MOVE, the preferred option will be to merge *John$_1$* from the numeration at this point, followed later by movement of *Mary$_2$* to matrix subject position. In other words: Any attempt at creating object control will invariably lead to subject control. Again, there are further issues that need to be clarified (e.g., how this effect can be avoided in cases of object control into complement clauses by invoking minimality, as in (34); or how subject control into complement clauses becomes possible with verbs like *promise*), but for now we may abstract away from these complications since they involve questions that are orthogonal to my present concerns.

(34)   John$_1$ persuaded Mary$_2$ [PRO$_{*1,2}$ to leave]

4.4.   Asymmetric Coordination

As a third and final application of the constraint MERGE OVER MOVE to be discussed here, I will focus on Weisser's (2015) analysis of extraction from conjuncts in asymmetric coordinations ("medial clauses") in languages like Choctaw and English. The relevant evidence in English comes from left-subordinating *and*-constructions with a conditional interpretation, which have been argued to qualify as a problem for standard approaches to grammatical theory in Culicover & Jackendoff (2007).

(35)   (You drink) one more can of beer and I'm leaving

The important observation here is that the construction permits asymmetric extraction from only one conjunct; either the left one (which is irrelevant in the present context) or the right one. Examples illustrating this apparent, selective violation of the COORDINATE STRUCTURE CONSTRAINT (cf. Ross (1967)) in English are given in (36-ab); (36-c) is a control example illustrating that the COORDINATE STRUCTURE CONSTRAINT holds outside of the construction at hand (as signalled, inter alia, by the absence of a conditional interpretation).

(36)   a.   ?This is the loot Op$_1$ that [you just identify t$_1$] and [we arrest the thief on the spot]

      b.   ?This is the thief Op$_2$ that [you just identify the loot] and [we arrest t$_2$ on the spot]

      c.   *This is the thief OP$_2$ that [you have identified the loot] and [we have arrested t$_2$ on the spot]

A similar effect shows up in Choctaw clause-chaining constructions (see Broadwell (1997)). Consider the case of well-formed extraction from the second conjunct in the clause-chaining construction (with a switch reference marker DS ('different subject')), in apparent violation of the COORDINATE STRUCTURE CONSTRAINT, in (37-a) vs. ill-formed extraction from the second conjunct with regular, symmetric coordination in (37-b).

(37)   a.   Katah-oosh$_1$ John-at   taloowa-nah t$_1$ hilhah ?
            who-FOC.NOM John-NOM sings-DS   dance
            'Who$_1$ did John$_2$ sing and t$_1$ dance?'

      b.   *Katah-oosh$_1$ John-at   toloowa-tok anoti t$_1$ hilhah-tok ?
            who-FOC.NOM John-NOM sing-PAST   and   dance-PAST
            'Who$_1$ did John$_2$ sing and t$_1$ dance?'

Weisser's (2015) analysis for English and Choctaw (and many other languages instantiating this kind of asymmetric coordination and clause chains) looks as follows. First, the construction involves two TPs: TP_1 and TP_2. Second, initially, TP_1 is a part of TP_2 (this is what underlies the asymmetric nature of the coordination). Third, TP_2 is first merged with &:*and*. And fourth, TP_1 undergoes movement out of TP_2 to Spec&. Thus, the structure of English left-subordinating *and*-constructions looks as in (38).

(38) $[_{\&P}$ TP_1 $[_{\&'}$ & $[_{TP_2}$ T $[_{vP}$ t_1 $[_{vP}$ ... $]]]]]$

The question that arises is why extraction from TP_2 in (36-b) and (37-a) is possible, given the validity of the COORDINATE STRUCTURE CONSTRAINT, which is formulated in (39).

(39) COORDINATE STRUCTURE CONSTRAINT (CSC; based on Ross (1967)):
      In a coordinate structure $[_{\&P}$ A $[_{\&'}$ & B $]]$, no conjunct may be moved, nor may any element contained in a conjunct be moved out of that conjunct.

Weisser (2015) argues that (36-b) and (37-a) do not violate (39) upon closer inspection, even though it may look like they do if one only considers the final output configuration. First note that the COORDINATE STRUCTURE CONSTRAINT in (39) is a derivational constraint; it prohibits extraction from conjuncts but not, say, a trace in a conjunct with an antecedent outside of it. Now, crucially, movement from TP_2 (first to an intermediate phase edge, viz. Spec&P) can precede movement of TP_1 to Spec&; but this means such an extraction happens at a stage of the derivation when there is no coordinate structure yet in the sense of (39).

Thus, the option of deriving asymmetric coordination by moving a conjunct from a base position in another conjunct creates a loophole for extraction from a conjunct in accordance with the COORDINATE STRUCTURE CONSTRAINT. Of course, the question then immediately arises why this option is not available for regular, symmetric coordination (as in (36-c) and (37-b)), given that there should also be a stage of the derivation where the second conjunct has merged with &, and the first conjunct is not yet present. Weisser's answer is that for symmetric coordination, such a derivation is blocked by MERGE OVER MOVE: Whereas it is two Move operations to Spec& that interact in (36-b) and (37-a) (and MERGE OVER MOVE is neutral as regards their order), in (36-c) and (37-b) there is a step in the derivation where a decision has to be taken whether the next step is Move (i.e., extraction from the second conjunct to an intermediate phase edge Spec&) or Merge (i.e., introduction of the first conjunct by merging it as

Spec&); and in this latter scenario, MERGE OVER MOVE requires the latter operation to take place first, thereby creating a full coordination structure and blocking extraction from the second (or, for that matter, first) conjunct via the COORDINATE STRUCTURE CONSTRAINT.

4.5.   A Minimize Satisfaction Approach to Merge over Move in Syntax

Chomsky (2000; 2001; 2005; 2008) has argued that there is a deeper reason why Merge is ceteris paribus preferred to Move. Essentially, he suggests that this follows from an economy principle according to which more general rules apply before less general rules. As for Merge, he assumes that it is a primitive operation; but Move is viewed as a more complex operation, consisting of Merge and Agree (plus, irrelevantly in the present context, Pied Piping). Consequently, Merge emerges as the more general operation, and Move as the less general one. Here is the original reasoning:[22]

> Plainly Move is more complex than its subcomponents Merge and Agree, or even the combination of the two, since it involves the extra step of determining P(F) (generalized 'pied-piping'). Good design conditions would lead us to expect that simpler operations are preferred to more complex ones, so that Merge or Agree (or their combination) preempts Move.   Chomsky (2000, 101)

This directly lends itself to an account in terms of MINSAT: Given that Merge is a single (primitive) *Gen* operation satisfying *one* constraint that triggers it, whereas Move counts as a (complex) single *Gen* operation satisfying *two* constraints that trigger it, MINSAT will always favour Merge over Move, other things being equal. MINSAT is repeated here once more for convenience.

(40)   MINSAT (MINIMIZE SATISFACTION):
       Assign * to an output O_i iff

       a. O_i has x new constraint satisfactions ($0 \leq x \leq n$).
       b.   There is an output O_j ($j \neq i$) in the same candidate set such
            that
            (i) O_j has y new constraint satisfactions ($0 \leq y \leq n$); and
            (ii) $0 < y < x$.

---

[22] More recently, Chomsky (2013; 2014a) has considered the possibility that there might be reason to expect the reverse order of Merge and Move: On this view, Move should be simpler than Merge "since it requires vastly less search" because external Merge "must access the workspace of already generated objects and the lexicon". I will not follow this alternative reasoning here; also see Hornstein (2014a) (particularly footnote 5) for critical remarks.

The constraints triggering Merge and Move, respectively, can be assumed to
be those in (41-ab): Merge is triggered by [•X•] features (via the MERGE
CONDITION (MC)), which is repeated here from (19) in chapter 1 (also
cf. (21) in chapter 2). Move, however, is triggered by co-occurring [•X•]
structure-building features (via the MERGE CONDITION) *and* [∗F∗] probe
features that trigger Agree (via the AGREE CONDITION (AC)); the latter is
repeated here from (40-b) in chapter 1.[23] In addition, a general constraint
NO TAMPERING (NOTAMP) can be postulated that counteracts MC and
AC but is violable in favour of MC and AC in relevant scenarios: NOTAMP
in (41-c) is violated both by Merge (since structure is added) and by Agree
(this is obvious if feature valuation is adopted but can also be assumed to
hold under a checking approach as it was postulated in chapter 1, given
that Agree establishes a link that was not present before the operation; cf.
footnote 22 of chapter 1).[24]

(41) a.   MERGE CONDITION (MC):
           Structure-building features ([•X•]) participate in Merge.
      b.   AGREE CONDITION (AC):
           Probes ([∗F∗]) participate in Agree.
      c.   NO TAMPERING (NOTAMP):
           Linguistic expressions are not modified in the course of the
           derivation.

As before, [•X•] and an [∗F∗] are discharged by the operations that they
induce, and they disappear (or are rendered inactive) as a consequence.
To see how a high-ranked MINSAT derives MERGE OVER MOVE effects
under these assumptions (and thus makes this latter principle superfluous),
consider the following derivation in terms of harmonic serialism. Suppose
that the derivation has reached a stage where a single head Y that triggers
both Merge (because of a feature [•X•]) and Move (because of combined
features [•X•]+[∗F∗]) has been merged with a WP containing a category α
that is designed to undergo movement to SpecY, and there is still a category
β in the numeration (or, more properly, the workspace) that is waiting to

---

[23] Note that Heck & Müller's (2013) analysis of SpecC expletives reported in chapter 1
(which is based on the constraints in (40) of that chapter) is but a notational variant of
the present implementation, as concerns the interaction of Merge and Move.

[24] Recall that I have argued for a relativization of MC to specific features in morphology
in chapter 2; from this perspective, MC (41-a) is a harmless simplification (as may be
AC).

be merged with Y as SpecY.[25] As shown in tableau (42), MinSat requires Merge to take place first, as in O_{12}; O_{13} is filtered out as suboptimal because it leads to a satisfaction of more constraints that are violated by the input than O_{12} does.

(42) *Merge over Move via MinSat* (harmonic serialism, step 1):

I_1: $[_{Y'}$ $Y_{[\bullet X\bullet]\,+\,[*F*]}$ $[_{WP}$ ... α ... $]$, β	MinSat	MC	AC	NoTamp
O_{11}: $[_{Y'}$ $Y_{[\bullet X\bullet]\,+\,[*F*]}$ $[_{WP}$ ... α ... $]$ $]$		**!	*	
☞O_{12}: $[_{Y'}$ β $[_{Y'}$ $Y_{[\bullet X\bullet]\,+\,[*F*]}$ $[_{WP}$ ... α ... $]]]$		*	*	*
O_{13}: $[_{Y'}$ α $[_{Y'}$ $Y_{[\bullet X\bullet]}$ $[_{WP}$ ... t_α ... $]]]$	*!	*		**

In the following step, the two remaining features $[\bullet X\bullet]+[*F*]$ on Y are discharged by carrying out movement; see O_{122} in (43). However, O_{122} does not violate MinSat despite satisfying two constraints that are violated in I_{12} (MC and AC, each of them once) because it still is the candidate with the least non-zero number of new constraint satisfactions; output O_{121}, which leaves the input intact, cannot block O_{122} via MinSat since it has no new constraint satisfaction (see (40)).

(43) *Merge over Move via MinSat* (harmonic serialism, step 2):

I_{12}: $[_{Y'}$ β $[_{Y'}$ $Y_{[\bullet X\bullet]\,+\,[*F*]}$ $[_{WP}$ ... α ... $]]]$	MinSat	MC	AC	NoTamp
O_{121}: $[_{Y'}$ β $[_{Y'}$ $Y_{[\bullet X\bullet]\,+\,[*F*]}$ $[_{WP}$ ... α ... $]]]$		*!	*	
☞O_{122}: $[_{YP}$ α $[_{Y'}$ β $[_{Y'}$ Y $[_{WP}$ ... t_α ... $]]]]$				**

Finally, the last step leads to convergence (so that the derivation may move on to the next cycle, via ExNum; see (18) of chapter 1).

(44) *Merge over Move via MinSat* (harmonic serialism, step 3):

I_{122}: $[_{YP}$ α $[_{Y'}$ β $[_{Y'}$ Y $[_{WP}$ ... t_α ... $]]]]$ $[_{WP}$ ... α ... $]]]$	MinSat	MC	AC	NoTamp
☞O_{1221}: $[_{YP}$ α $[_{Y'}$ β $[_{Y'}$ Y $[_{WP}$ ... t_α ... $]]]]$				

---

[25] This presupposes that it is indeed one and the *same* head triggering both Merge and Move, and it is the order of the operations that needs to be decided, not the question of whether an operation can apply at all. This is the scenario that corresponds to the case of control into adjuncts (assuming that intermediate movement steps target every phrase edge, i.e., also the VP projection in which objects are merged), and to the case of asymmetric coordination. It requires some additional assumptions to be extendable to Chomsky's account of expletive insertion in English, where the head in question has only *one* feature triggering satisfaction of the EPP property. I will not undertake the task of providing and justifying these assumptions here.

It is worth pointing out that the final optimal output (O_{1221}) in (44) does not necessarily have to lead to a grammatical sentence. In Weisser's (2015) analysis, MERGE OVER MOVE ensures that the COORDINATE STRUCTURE CONSTRAINT is strict for symmetric coordination – in this case, a continuation of O_{1221} will eventually lead to perdition.[26]

4.6. On the Nature of Minimize Satisfaction

MINSAT is noteworthy in two respects. First, as noted above, it differs from standard constraints of the *H-Eval* part of an optimality-theoretic grammar in being *transderivational* (or, more aptly, *translocal*, in the terminology adopted in Müller & Sternefeld (2001)): In order to find out whether MINSAT is violated by an output O_i, it does not suffice to take into account the intrinsic properties of O_i; rather, O_i's properties must be compared with the properties of competing outputs. In this sense, determining the presence or absence of a MINSAT violation for a given output O_i can be viewed as a sort of sub-optimization routine. Just as, say, the transderivational economy constraint FEWEST STEPS proposed in Chomsky (1991) selects the candidate(s) with the fewest applications of syntactic operations in a given candidate set (or 'reference set', in Chomsky's terminology), MINSAT selects the candidate(s) with the fewest (non-zero) new constraint satisfactions.

However, there is another sense in which MINSAT looks somewhat different from typical constraints in optimality theory. If one assumes that MERGE OVER MOVE effects are a *general, invariant* property of syntactic derivations in the world's languages, then MINSAT must not be violable by optimal outputs; in other words, there is no room for reranking this constraint and demoting it to a position where some optimal output can violate it. This state of affairs suggests that MINSAT might in fact not be part of the *H-Eval* part of the grammar (and might, e.g., better be assigned to the *Gen* part of the grammar instead), as it was assumed above for the STRICT CYCLE CONDITION (see (22) of chapter 2), and for the constraint EXHAUST NUMERATION (see (18) of chapter 1). On the other hand, recall from page 113 that there is clear evidence that there is both opaque rule interaction (as with counter-bleeding) and transparent rule interaction (as with bleeding) in phonology, and if a high ranking of MINSAT is responsible

---

[26] This raises the question of how ineffability (i.e., absolute ungrammaticality) is accounted for in optimality-theoretic syntax. See Müller (2015) for an overview of the options.

for the former, it would seem unavoidable to conclude that a low ranking of MINSAT ensures the latter.

I take this asymmetry between phonology and syntax to be real, and not an artefact of the theory. In what follows, I will presuppose that MINSAT is indeed inviolable in optimal outputs in syntax, but violable in optimal outputs in phonology. I take it that the relevant distinctive property is that syntax is a system in which structure is built up compositionally, whereas phonology is primarily concerned with modifying and licensing an existing structure (which ultimately comes from the lexicon, in the form of an underlying representation), not with building it. Given present assumptions, morphology also intrinsically has the structure-building property. Therefore, it is to be expected that MINSAT is also inviolable for optimal outputs in morphology. Given the ubiquity of extended exponence (as well as contextual allomorphy, to which I will turn in chapter 5), this seems to be the case; therefore, for the remainder of this study, I will simply postulate that MINSAT cannot be violated by optimal outputs in morphology or syntax, leaving it open how this can be derived.[27] The next section then shows how an undominated MINSAT systematically derives extended exponence in harmonic serialism.

5.   Minimize Satisfaction in Morphology: Extended Exponence

5.1.   *Morphological Arrays*

Consider again the options arising for the analysis of (partially superfluous) extended exponence in harmonic serialism. Recall that I have assumed that secondary, contextual features should be abandoned. Furthermore, if all instances of exponence based on all morphological arrays have access to the fully specified feature matrix associated with the stem, an unrestricted system results. In the present harmonic serialist approach, then, the conclusion is that that the challenge posed by (partially superfluous) extended exponence is a genuine one: In all the examples discussed above, the two morphological markers participating in cases of extended exponence belong to a single morphological array, and the question arises why the more specific exponent (realizing $[F_1,F_2]$) does not block the more general one (realizing only $[F_1]$) as suboptimal because the former maximizes the satisfaction of faithfulness constraints. At this point, what is needed is a precise

---

[27] The most obvious way to proceed would be to declare that MINSAT is a part of *Gen* rather than *H-Eval* in the morphological and syntactic components of grammar. Still, so as not to prejudge the issue, I will continue to list MINSAT in the rankings, and indicate its violation profile with candidates; this will arguably also enhance perspicuity.

specification of the concept of morphological array (so far, I have relied on an informal notion of what a morphological array is). I would like to suggest that morphological arrays are defined in a principled and stringent way, as in (45).

(45) *Morphological array$_X$:*
      An exponent α is in the morphological array for a grammatical category X (MA$_X$) in the domain of a syntactic category (part of speech) W iff (i), (ii), or (iii) holds:

   (i) α realizes a grammatical category X in the domain of W by a morpho-syntactic feature that is a (possibly underspecified) instantiation of X.

   (ii) α realizes a grammatical category Y in the domain of W by a morpho-syntactic feature that is a (possibly underspecified) instantiation of Y, and there is an exponent in MA$_X$ that realizes Y.

   (iii) α is a unique radically underspecified exponent for X in the domain of W.

Let me illustrate this concept on the basis of two abstract paradigms. Suppose that there are two grammatical categories in the domain of nouns: On the one hand, there is the grammatical category case with, say, four instantitations: [–obl,–gov] (nominative), [–obl,+gov] (accusative), [+obl,+gov] (dative), and [+obl,–gov] (genitive). On the other hand, there is the grammatical category number, with, e.g., two instantiations: [–pl] (singular) and [+pl] (plural). Now, assume first that language L_1 has the exponents for the categories case and number in the domain of nouns (rather than, e.g., adjectives or determiners) in (46-a). Here, all the βs realize case by being associated with morpho-syntactic features that capture instantiations of this grammatical category (except for the elsewhere marker β_4), and the γs do the same for the grammatical category number. Since there is no β_i that realizes number, and no γ_j that realizes case, a strictly agglutinative system will arise based on two separate morphological arrays: one for case (as in (46-b)), and one for number (as in (46-c)).

(46) *Exponents and morphological arrays of L_1:*
      a. $/\beta_1/ \leftrightarrow$[–obl], $/\beta_2/ \leftrightarrow$[–obl,+gov], $/\beta_3/ \leftrightarrow$[+obl,+gov], $/\beta_4/ \leftrightarrow$[ ], $/\gamma/_1\leftrightarrow$[–pl], $/\gamma/_2\leftrightarrow$[+pl]
      b.   Case: {$/\beta_1/ \leftrightarrow$[–obl], $/\beta_2/ \leftrightarrow$[–obl,+gov], $/\beta_3/ \leftrightarrow$[+obl,+gov], $/\beta_4/ \leftrightarrow$[ ]}
      c.   Num: {$/\gamma/_1\leftrightarrow$[–pl], $/\gamma/_2\leftrightarrow$[+pl]}

In contrast, suppose now that L_2 has the minimally different inventory
of case and number exponents in (47-a). Here the only difference to L_1's
inventory is that β_3 is specified not simply as a dative marker, but as a
dative plural marker. Given (45-ii), this means that MA_{Case} and MA_{Num}
emerge as one and the same set; see (47-bc).

(47) *Exponents and morphological arrays of L_2:*

    a. $/\beta_1/ \leftrightarrow [-\text{obl}]$, $/\beta_2/ \leftrightarrow [-\text{obl},+\text{gov}]$, $/\beta_3/ \leftrightarrow [+\text{obl},+\text{gov},+\text{pl}]$,
       $/\beta_4/ \leftrightarrow [\ \ ]$, $/\gamma/_1 \leftrightarrow [-\text{pl}]$, $/\gamma/_2 \leftrightarrow [+\text{pl}]$

    b.   Case: $\{/\beta_1/ \leftrightarrow [-\text{obl}]$, $/\beta_2/ \leftrightarrow [-\text{obl},+\text{gov}]$,
       $/\beta_3/ \leftrightarrow [+\text{obl},+\text{gov},+\text{pl}]$, $/\beta_4/ \leftrightarrow [\ \ ]$, $/\gamma/_1 \leftrightarrow [-\text{pl}]$, $/\gamma/_2 \leftrightarrow [+\text{pl}]\}$

    c.   Num: $\{/\beta_1/ \leftrightarrow [-\text{obl}]$, $/\beta_2/ \leftrightarrow [-\text{obl},+\text{gov}]$,
       $/\beta_3/ \leftrightarrow [+\text{obl},+\text{gov},+\text{pl}]$, $/\beta_4/ \leftrightarrow [\ \ ]$, $/\gamma/_1 \leftrightarrow [-\text{pl}]$, $/\gamma/_2 \leftrightarrow [+\text{pl}]\}$

A natural assumption is that if two morphological arrays MA_X and MA_Y
are identical, a language accesses them only once. Thus, (47) captures a
fusional system of morphological exponence. Needless to say, a language
may perfectly well employ both kinds of morphological array in its system
of inflectional morphology.

As before, morphological arrays are targeted by designated $[\bullet X \bullet]$ subcategorization features on stems. X stands for the grammatical category that defines the morphological array in purely agglutinative cases
where there is no overlap. Thus, in (46) there are two separate morphological arrays, one consisting of βs bearing the categorial information
case (i.e., $[_{Case} /\beta/_i]$, in the notation introduced in the previous chapter),
and one consisting of γs bearing the categorial information number (i.e.,
$[_{Num} /\gamma/_j]$). However, since there is an overlap in (47) (with one exponent
specified both for case and for number), there is only one combined morphological array consisting of all the βs and the γs. In this scenario, choice
of the category label X is to some extent arbitrary; recall that in chapter 2, K was chosen for the combined case/number/gender category with
determiner inflection in German. Adopting this assumption here, the morphological array would include exponents of the type $[_K /\beta/_i]$, $[_K /\gamma/_j]$,
etc.

The concept of morphological array in (45) has far-reaching consequences. With respect to the issue currently under consideration (viz.,
extended exponence), all the instances of the phenomenon addressed so far
must now involve a single morphological array from which the relevant inflection markers are chosen. Therefore, the problem initially created by partially superfluous extended exponence for optimality-theoretic approaches

(cf. (12)) is real. In the next subsection, I show how MINSAT provides a systematic solution.

5.2. *Extended Exponence by Minimize Satisfaction*

The gist of the MINSAT-based account of extended exponence (of the partially superfluous type) in harmonic serialism is simple: At an early stage of the derivation, a more general exponent α (that is associated with fewer morpho-syntactic features and therefore leads to fewer new constraint satisfactions) is preferred by the undominated MINSAT constraint to a more specific exponent β (that realizes a superset of morpho-syntactic features and therefore fatally yields more new constraint satisfactions). However, at a subsequent stage of the derivation, β is also merged (so as to satisfy more faithfulness constraints), in accordance with MINSAT because (a) the output with the competing more general exponent α is now out of the way (the less specific exponent having been merged earlier), and (b) due to the earlier use of α in an optimal output, choice of β now triggers fewer new constraint satisfactions. In this way, MINSAT brings about an agglutination-like structure on the basis of a single morphological array that would otherwise lead to a fusional system.[28]

To illustrate the working of this general approach to extended exponence, let me look at the case of multiple realization of the grammatical category number in dative plural contexts of noun inflection in German again. Recall from (1) that n in (48) must be specified for both dative ([+obl,+gov]) and plural ([+pl]) since this exponent cannot show up in either singular contexts (where zero exponence or, in more archaic German, e is chosen in dative environments) or nominative, accusative, or genitive contexts (where zero exponence of case is required in the plural). This gives rise to partially superfluous extended exponence because the 'proper' plural exponent er cannot satisfy any faitfhulness constraints that the dative plural exponent n could not also satisfy.

(48) Kind-er-n
      child-PL-DAT.PL

Given (45), it is clear that there can be only one morphological array for noun inflection in German. It comprises pure number exponents (like the

---

[28] In this context, it is worth noting that Don & Blom (2006) propose a constraint *COMPLEX as part of their analysis of Dutch verb inflection that has a similar effect in demanding agglutination and blocking portmanteau morphemes. I will come back to their analysis in chapter 6.

plural exponents *er*, *e*, *n*, and *s*), what is arguably a pure case exponent (viz., the *n* of the weak masculine declension), and fusional case/number exponents (like genitive singular *s*, and the dative plural *n* currently at issue). In the analysis of determiner inflection based on morphological arrays that was presented in the previous chapter (and that will be substantially revised in the following chapter in the light of a MINSAT-based approach to extended exponence), the MC-related feature picking out the morphological array for case/number inflection was identified as [•K•]. Since we are dealing with an entirely different morphological array, a different label suggests itself for nouns; here I will assume the relevant feature identifying the case/number morphological array for nouns in German to be [•Cn•].

Next, all of the exponents involved in German noun inflection show sensitivity to inflection class: Despite the scarcity of exponents, the system of noun inflection in German can be shown to be composed of a fairly big number of separate inflection classes; see Wiese (2000), among others. For now, suppose that inflection class compatibility of exponents is captured by primitive inflection class features [cl] whose values are numbers identifying the individual inflection classes; e.g.: [cl:I], [cl:II], [cl:III], etc. As before, IDENT-F ensures compatibility (it is violated if a [cl:I] exponent is used with a stem bearing the inflection class information [cl:III]). However, for present purposes, I will not assume that MAX constraints are relevant for inflection class; their irrelevance follows if the feature [cl] is inherently present on all exponents of the morphological array identified by Cn.[29]

Finally, the constraints that are needed in the analysis have basically all been introduced already. They are listed in (49).

(49) a.   MINSAT (MINIMIZE SATISFACTION):
           Assign * to an output O_i iff
           (i) O_i has x new constraint satisfactions ($0 \leq x \leq n$).

---

[29] Ultimately, there is more to be said about inflection class features, though. Inflection classes are often quite similar to one another; i.e., they typically share exponents with other inflection classes, giving rise to what can be called transparadigmatic syncretism. Transparadigmatic syncretism can be accounted for decomposing inflection class features and underspecifying morphological exponents with respect to inflection class information; cf., e.g., Corbett & Fraser (1993), Halle (1992), Nesset (1994), Oltra Massuet (1999), Müller (2005; 2007b), and Trommer (2008b). For the system of German noun inflection, it is indeed argued in Alexiadou & Müller (2008) that the (primary) inflection classes are captured by cross-classifications of three primitive inflection class features [±α], [±β], [±γ], and exponents can be underspecified with respect to this information. From this perspective, the question of whether MAX constraints are relevant does in principle arise. I will return to this issue in chapter 4.

      (ii)   There is an output O_j ($j \neq i$) in the same candidate set such that:

               O_j has y new constraint satisfactions ($0 \leq y \leq n$); and

$$0 < y < x.$$

b.   MERGE CONDITION(CN) (MC(CN)):

   [•Cn•] participates in Merge.

c.   IDENT-F:

   Morpho-syntactic features of input and output cannot have different values.

d.   MAX(PL):

   [pl] of the input is realized on an exponent in the output.

e.   MAX(OBL):

   [obl] of the input is realized on an exponent in the output.

f.   MAX(GOV):

   [gov] of the input is realized on an exponent in the output.

g.   *STRUC ('*Structure'):

   Adding exponents is prohibited.

By assumption, MINSAT, MC(CN), and IDENT-F are not violable by optimal outputs. Furthermore, *STRUC must be ranked low, and MAX(PL) outranks MAX(OBL) and MAX(GOV). An overall ranking compatible with the evidence is one that corresponds to the order in (49). Based on these assumptions, consider now the sequence of optimization procedures underlying the generation of extended exponence in (48).[30]

---

[30] Note that the inventory of the morphological array defined by Cn is incomplete, and simplified in various respects (e.g., as regards umlaut). In the morphological array given here, the exponent /er/ is assumed to be composed of a consonantal and a vowel part (with the latter realized as ə). In principle, it would also have been possible to assume a bare /r/ marker instead, with a preceding ə analyzed as phonological epenthesis, as it must independently be possible for the plural exponent /n/ (cf., e.g., the plural form *Strahl-en* ([ən]), where /n/ is attached to a stem ending in a consonant, vs. the plural form *Auge-n*, where /n/ is attached to a stem ending in a vowel. However, /er/ only attaches to consonant-final stems, so the initial vocalic element ə need not be considered to be phonologically conditioned (but, as just noted, it could be). Note also that a plural marker /e/ is usually realized as ə; however, if the noun stem itself already meets the trochaic ideal of the language (as in *Adler* ('eagle'), *Wagen* ('carriage')), /e/ is phonologically realized as null. Finally, for the time being, zero exponence in singular contexts is ignored; see chapter 4.

(50) *Extended exponence in dative plural contexts* (harmonic serialism, step 1):

I_1: Kind$_{\text{III}}$:[•Cn•] [+pl,+obl,+gov], {[$_{\text{Cn}}$ /e/↔[+pl,I]], [$_{\text{Cn}}$ /n/↔[+pl,II]] [$_{\text{Cn}}$ /er/↔[+pl,III]], [$_{\text{Cn}}$ /s/↔[+pl,IV]], [$_{\text{Cn}}$ /e/↔[−pl,+obl,+gov]], [$_{\text{Cn}}$ /s/↔[−pl,+obl,−gov]], [$_{\text{Cn}}$ /n/↔[+pl,+obl,+gov]]...}	MIN SAT	MC CN	ID F	MAX PL	MAX OBL	MAX GOV	*STRUC
O_{11}: Kind$_{\text{III}}$[+pl,+obl,+gov]:[•Cn•]		*!		*	*	*	
O_{12}: Kind$_{\text{III}}$[+pl,+obl,+gov]-e[+pl,I]			*!		*	*	*
O_{13}: Kind$_{\text{III}}$[+pl,+obl,+gov]-n[+pl,II]			*!		*	*	*
☞O_{14}: Kind$_{\text{III}}$[+pl,+obl,+gov]-er[+pl,III]					*	*	*
O_{15}: Kind$_{\text{III}}$[+pl,+obl,+gov]-s[+pl,IV]			*!		*	*	*
O_{16}: Kind$_{\text{III}}$[+pl,+obl,+gov]-e[−pl,+obl,+gov]]	*!		*				*
O_{17}: Kind$_{\text{III}}$[+pl,+obl,+gov]-s[−pl,+obl,−gov]]	*!		**				*
O_{18}: Kind$_{\text{III}}$[+pl,+obl,+gov]-n[+pl,+obl,+gov]]	*!						*

O_{11} is the output that leaves the input intact. Since it does not give rise to any new constraint satisfaction, it cannot block another output via MINSAT (note also that *STRUC is not violated by the input, so not violating it in the output does not count from the perspective of MINSAT); and it fatally violates high-ranked MC(CN). Outputs O_{12}, O_{13}, and O_{15} use a wrong plural marker, in violation of ID(ENT)-F. Note that these candidates cannot block the intended winner O_{14} via MINSAT either because the latter candidate's ID-F satisfaction is not a new constraint satisfaction in the sense of (49-a): The input I_1 satisfies ID-F vacuously.[31] Next, O_{16} and O_{17} use exponents which show up in singular contexts; this would suffice to fatally violate ID-F, which is ranked higher than MAX(PL), MAX(OBL), and MAX(GOV), the markedness constraints that they satisfy. In addition, however, since O_{16} and O_{17} satisfy all three MAX constraints at once, these candidates are already excluded via MINSAT. In (50), O_{17} violates ID-F twice (because of a non-matching value for [gov], and because of a wrong value for [pl]), whereas O_{16} violates ID-F once (because of a wrong value for [pl]). The crucial competition, then, is the one between O_{14}, which satisfies MAX(PL) but not yet MAX(OBL) and MAX(GOV) by using a pure number exponent *er*, and O_{18}, which satisfies all these three constraints in one go by using an exponent *n* that realizes both number and case features in accordance with ID-F. O_{18} would give rise to a better constraint profile, were it not for MINSAT, which excludes it and thereby ensures that O_{14} is the optimal output of the first optimization procedure.

---

[31] I will come back to this fundamental difference between ID-F and MAX with respect to MINSAT at the end of the chapter.

In the next step, O_{14} is used as the input for further output generation and optimization. All of the items of the initial morphological array are still accessible, except, of course, for bare plural /er/, which has been used up in the first step. The resulting competition is shown in (51).

(51) *Extended exponence in dative plural contexts* (harmonic serialism, step 2):

I_{14}: Kind$_{III}$[+pl,+obl,+gov]-er[+pl,III] [+pl,+obl,+gov], {[Cn /e/↔[+pl,I]], [Cn /n/↔[+pl,II]] [Cn /s/↔[+pl,IV]], [Cn /e/↔[−pl,+obl,+gov]], [Cn /s/↔[−pl,+obl,−gov]], [Cn /n/↔[+pl,+obl,+gov]]...}	MIN SAT	MC CN	ID F	MAX PL	MAX OBL	MAX GOV	*STRUC
O_{141}: Kind$_{III}$[+pl,+obl,+gov]-er[+pl,III]					*!	*	
O_{142}: Kind$_{III}$[+pl,+obl,+gov]-er[+pl,III]-e[+pl,I]			*!		*	*	*
O_{143}: Kind$_{III}$[+pl,+obl,+gov]-er[+pl,III]-n[+pl,II]			*!		*	*	*
O_{144}: Kind$_{III}$[+pl,+obl,+gov]-er[+pl,III]-s[+pl,IV]			*!		*	*	*
O_{145}: Kind$_{III}$[+pl,+obl,+gov]-er[+pl,III]-e-[−pl,+obl,+gov]			*!				*
O_{146}: Kind$_{III}$[+pl,+obl,+gov]-er[+pl,III]-s[−pl,+obl,−gov]			*!*				*
☞O_{147}: Kind$_{III}$[+pl,+obl,+gov]-er[+pl,III]-n[+pl,+obl,+gov]							*

Candidate O_{141} does not carry out any operation, therefore fails to improve the constraint profile further, and is thus blocked as suboptimal (since it does not lead to any new constraint satisfaction, it also cannot block other candidates via MINSAT). O_{142}, O_{143}, and O_{144} also do not trigger any new constraint satisfactions; by using yet another bare plural marker (with the wrong inflection class information), they induce gratuitous violations of ⁺STRUC and ID-F while maintaining the input's MAX(OBL) and MAX(GOV) violations. O_{145} and O_{146} add a singular case exponent (/e/ or /s/) to the extended stem that realizes both [obl] and [gov]; thus they satisfy MAX(OBL) and MAX(GOV). This is the minimal number of new constraint satisfactions available in the competition. However, both these candidates violate ID-F (the former once, the latter twice). These violations turn out to be fatal since O_{147}, which adds the plural dative exponent /n/, does not lead to more new constraint satisfactions than O_{145} and O_{146} (recall that ID-F does not count for the purposes of MINSAT since it is always vacuously satisfied in the input). Consequently, O_{147} is correctly classified as optimal. This illustrates how extended exponence can become optimal: Unlike what was the case in the first optimization step, at this stage of the derivation, the realization of [+pl] by /n/ cannot violate MINSAT because [+pl] has already been satisfied (by /er/) in the prior optimization step.

The final optimization procedure leads to convergence, see (52).

(52) *Extended exponence in dative plural contexts* (harmonic serialism, step 3):

I_{147}: Kind_{III}[+pl,+obl,+gov]-er[+pl,III]–n[+pl,+obl,+gov] [+pl,+obl,+gov], {[$_{Cn}$ /e/↔[+pl,I]], [$_{Cn}$ /n/↔[+pl,II]] [$_{Cn}$ /s/↔[+pl,IV]], [$_{Cn}$ /e/↔[−pl,+obl,+gov]], [$_{Cn}$ /s/↔[−pl,+obl,−gov]], ...}	Min Sat	MC Cn	Id F	Max pl	Max obl	Max gov	*Str
☞O_{1471}: Kind_{III}[+pl,+obl,+gov]-er[+pl,III]-n[+pl,+obl,+gov]							
O_{1472}: Kind_{III}[+pl,+obl,+gov]-er[+pl,III]-n[+pl,+obl,+gov]-e[+pl,I]			*!				*
O_{1473}: Kind_{III}[+pl,+obl,+gov]-er[+pl,III]-n[+pl,+obl,+gov]-n[+pl,II]			*!				*
O_{1474}: Kind_{III}[+pl,+obl,+gov]-er[+pl,III]-n[+pl,+obl,+gov]-s[+pl,IV]			*!				*
O_{1475}: Kind_{III}[+pl,+obl,+gov]-er[+pl,III]-n[+pl,+obl,+gov]-e[−pl,+obl,+gov]			*!				*
O_{1476}: Kind_{III}[+pl,+obl,+gov]-er[+pl,III]-n[+pl,+obl,+gov]-s[−pl,+obl,−gov]			*!*				*

More generally, the way in which the competition is resolved in (52) illustrates how the absence of fully superfluous extended exponence in the world's languages is accounted for.

It should be clear that this account entirely depends on the adoption of an approach to inflectional morphology based on harmonic serialism. Other things being equal, in a standard parallel optimality-theoretic approach, either O_{14} (*Kind-er*) would wrongly be predicted as the optimal form in a dative plural environment with the noun *Kind* (because of MIN-SAT); or, alternatively, *Kind-n* would wrongly be expected to be optimal if MINSAT is not active (because the bare plural exponent would emerge as superfluous). So the problem raised by partially superfluous extended exponence for standard parallel optimality theory (see (12)) persists even if MINSAT is adopted. To see that an approach in terms of standard parallel optimality theory is not feasible, consider first the scenario where MINSAT is undominated and active. Other things being equal, optimization will invariably pick the candidate that just realizes the bare plural exponent; see (53) (where many irrelevant suboptimal competitors are left out to enhance perspicuity).

(53) *Extended exponence in dat. pl. contexts* (standard parallel OT, with MINSAT):

I_1: Kind_{III}:[•Cn•] [+pl,+obl,+gov], {[$_{Cn}$ /e/↔[+pl,I]], [$_{Cn}$ /n/↔[+pl,II]] [$_{Cn}$ /er/↔[+pl,III]], [$_{Cn}$ /s/↔[+pl,IV]], [$_{Cn}$ /e/↔[−pl,+obl,+gov]], [$_{Cn}$ /s/↔[−pl,+obl,−gov]], [$_{Cn}$ /n/↔[+pl,+obl,+gov]]...}	Min Sat	MC Cn	Id F	Max pl	Max obl	Max gov	*Struc
O_{11}: Kind_{III}[+pl,+obl,+gov]:[•Cn•]		*!		*	*	*	
O_{12}: Kind_{III}[+pl,+obl,+gov]-e[+pl,I]			*!		*	*	*
O_{13}: Kind_{III}[+pl,+obl,+gov]-n[+pl,II]			*!		*	*	*
☛O_{14}: Kind_{III}[+pl,+obl,+gov]-er[+pl,III]					*	*	*
O_{15}: Kind_{III}[+pl,+obl,+gov]-s[+pl,IV]			*!		*	*	*
O_{16}: Kind_{III}[+pl,+obl,+gov]-n[+pl,+obl,+gov]	*!						*
☆O_{17}: Kind_{III}[+pl,+obl,+gov]-er[+pl,III]-n[+pl,+obl,+gov]	*!						**
O_{18}: Kind_{III}[+pl,+obl,+gov]-n[+pl,+obl,+gov]-er[+pl,III]	*!						**

ation approach, either because it is ranked low (notwith-

Alternatively, suppose that MINSAT is not active in a standard parallel optimality-theoretic approach, either because it is ranked low (notwithstanding the considerations above suggesting an invariant inviolability in structure-building areas of grammar), or because it does not exist in the first place. In this case, global, parallel optimization will converge on the output that employs the most specific exponent, essentially as in (12); see (54).

(54) *Extended exponence in dat. pl. contexts* (standard parallel OT, without MINSAT):

	MC CN	ID F	MAX PL	MAX OBL	MAX GOV	*STRUC
I_1: $[_{V_1}$ Kind$_{III}$]:[•Cn•] $[+pl,+obl,+gov]$, {$[_{Cn}$ /e/↔[+pl,I]], $[_{Cn}$ /n/↔[+pl,II]] $[_{Cn}$ /er/↔[+pl,III]], $[_{Cn}$ /s/↔[+pl,IV]], $[_{Cn}$ /e/↔[−pl,+obl,+gov]], $[_{Cn}$ /s/↔[−pl,+obl,−gov]], $[_{Cn}$ /n/↔[+pl,+obl,+gov]]...}						
O_{11}: Kind$_{III}$[+pl,+obl,+gov]:[•Cn•]	*!		*	*	*	
O_{12}: Kind$_{III}$[+pl,+obl,+gov]-e[+pl,I]		*!		*	*	*
O_{13}: Kind$_{III}$[+pl,+obl,+gov]-n[+pl,II]		*!		*	*	*
O_{14}: Kind$_{III}$[+pl,+obl,+gov]-er[+pl,III]				*	*	*
O_{15}: Kind$_{III}$[+pl,+obl,+gov]-s[+pl,IV]		*!		*	*	*
☞O_{16}: Kind$_{III}$[+pl,+obl,+gov]-n[+pl,+obl,+gov]]						*
☆O_{17}: Kind$_{III}$[+pl,+obl,+gov]-er[+pl,III]-n[+pl,+obl,+gov]						**!
O_{18}: Kind$_I$[+pl,+obl,+gov] n[+pl,+obl,+gov]-er[+pl,III]						**!

More generally, under standard parallel optimization, the candidate that has extended exponence will always be harmonically bounded by a candidate that leaves out one of the two markers. If MINSAT is abandoned (or demoted to a sufficiently low position in the ranking), as in (54), the optimal candidate will always be one where there is a sole exponent that is maximally specific (/n/, in the case at hand); and if MINSAT is inviolable in optimal outputs, as in (53), the optimal candidate will always be one where the sole exponent is maximally general (/er/, in the case at hand).

In contrast, harmonic serialism makes possible scenarios where some form is temporarily optimal that does not correspond to the eventual output, but that determines the latter's properties in important respects.[32]

Thus, extended exponence in German dative plural environments with nouns is accounted for. At this point, it remains to be shown that a MINSAT-based approach to extended exponence is capable of capturing the phenomenon more generally. In some cases, this should be obvious.

---

[32] One might think that because of its extremely general formulation, there could be a danger that MINSAT selects the wrong intermediate winner at an early stage of the derivation. I will come back to this issue at the end of the chapter.

An account of extended exponence in ergative plural contexts with Archi
nouns (see (2)), e.g., will look almost exactly like the one just developed for
German, the only relevant difference being that the case feature in question is [–obl,+gov] (ergative) rather than [+obl,+gov] (dative). The basic
pattern also emerges as identical in the other cases of extended exponence
discussed above, but there are some interesting twists, relating to (a) subanalysis, and (b) movement in morphology. I will address these two issues
in the following two subsections.

5.3.   Extended Exponence and Subanalysis

Recall that extended exponence of number in Sierra Popoluca does not involve complete instantiations of this grammatical category, but more primitive features resulting from decomposition (which in turn is motivated by
systematic partial syncretism); see the examples in (4) and (5), and the
pattern of distribution in (7). More specifically, in a form like the one in
(55), the prefixal ergative marker is actually composed of three exponents
of segment-like size: There is a pure ergative case marker /n/ (which undergoes assimilation before the velar consonant), preceding it there is a
person exponent /a/↔[+1], and in front of that there is a more specific
person exponent /t/↔[+1,+2] signalling first person inclusive; it is this
latter marker that gives rise to extended exponence.

(55)   Ø-Taŋ-koʔc-pa
       3.ABS-1.INCL.ERG-hit-INC
       'You and I hit him.'

The complex ergative/person exponent in (55) is preceded by a (potentially
also complex) absolutive/person exponent, which happens to be Ø in third
person environments. Following the stem are exponents for number, voice,
and aspect (only the latter one shows up in the case at hand).[33] The fully
specified set of morpho-syntactic features associated with the verb stem in
the numeration for an example like (55) encodes two syntactic arguments
(an ergative one and an absolutive one), and thus presupposes that V in this
context is equipped with two [•Agr•] features for morphological structure-
building; in other words, the single morphological array Agr encompassing
case and person (but not number) in Sierra Popoluca must be accessed

---

[33] The number marker is of secondary importance in Sierra Popoluca (on nouns as well
as on verbs; see Elson (1960b, 209, 219), Noyer (1992, 211–215)), and it is not involved in
argument encoding (i.e., number markers are not sensitive to the absolutive or ergative
status of the number-marked argument).

twice, first for the ergative argument, and then for the preceding accusative argument.[34]

For present purposes, we can abstract away from both the aspect marker and the (zero) absolutive marker in (55) (this includes the second [•Agr•] feature that must show up on V); I will return to issues raised by the latter below. The set of constraints that are relevant then includes the un-dominated, inviolable MINIMIZE SATISFACTION (MINSAT); the high-ranked MERGE CONDITION for [•Agr•] features (MC(AGR)); ID-F, which guaran-tees compatibility; the MAX constraints MAX(GOV), MAX(1), and MAX(2); a linearization constraint L⇐AGR ensuring that the Agr exponents real-izing case and person show up as prefixes (rather than as suffixes);[35] and finally, as before, a low-ranked markedness constraint *STRUC which blocks unmotivated exponence. Based on these assumptions, the first relevant op-timization procedure is shown in (56): V discharges its [•Agr•] feature for ergative argument encoding and is merged with an exponent that is part of the morphological array Agr.

(56) *Extended exponence in ergative first pers. incl. contexts* (harmonic serialism, step 1):

I_1: [v koʔc-pa]:[•Agr•] [+gov,+1,+2], {[Agr /n/↔[+gov]], [Agr /Ø/↔[−gov]], [Agr /a/↔[+1]], [Agr /i/↔[−1]], [Agr /m/↔[+2,−gov]], [Agr /t/↔[+1,+2]],...}	Min Sat	MC Agr	Id F	Max Gov	Max 1	Max 2	L⇐ Agr	*Struc
O_{11}: [v koʔc-pa]:[•Agr•]		*!		*	*	*		
☞O_{12}: n-[v koʔc-pa]					*	*		*
O_{13}: [v koʔc-pa]-n					*	*	*!	*
O_{14}: Ø-[v koʔc-pa]			*!		*	*		*
O_{15}: a-[v koʔc-pa]				*!		*		*
O_{16}: [v koʔc-pa]-a				*!		*	*	*
O_{17}: i-[v koʔc-pa]			*!	*		*		*
O_{18}: m-[v koʔc-pa]	*!		*		*			*
O_{19}: t-[v koʔc-pa]	*!			*				*

---

[34] Note that given the definition in (45), case and person exponents must belong to one and the same morphological array in Sierra Popoluca since there is an exponent /m/ for second person absolutive contexts which must be specified as [+2,−gov]; see Müller (2006b).

[35] Satisfying an alignment constraint like L⇐AGR cannot violate MINSAT for principled reasons at the start of the derivation, given vacuous satisfaction in initial inputs. The same conclusion also holds for later stages, assuming that there is also always a counter-acting (albeit low-ranked) constraint R⇐AGR in the system, and every candidate that improves the constraint profile at all has to violate one of the two constraints.

As illustrated in (56), output O_{12}, which merges the pure ergative exponent /n/ as a prefix, is optimal. O_{11} leaves the input unchanged, which fatally violates MC(AGR). O_{13} has /n/ merged as a suffix, in fatal violation of L⇐AGR. O_{14} has an absolutive ([–gov]) rather than ergative ([+gov]) exponent, which fatally violates ID-F. In O_{15}, the pure number marker /a/ is merged as a prefix; since MAX(GOV) dominates MAX(1), this candidate is suboptimal. O_{16} has the same violation with /a/ as a suffix, triggering a L⇐AGR violation in addition. O_{17}, using /i/, gives rise to an ID-F violation that removes the candidate from the competition. The exponent /m/ in O_{18} would do the same, but this candidate is already excluded by MINSAT since two MAX constraints that are not satisfied in the input are satisfied in the output (viz., MAX(GOV) and MAX(2)). O_{19} uses the more specific person exponent /t/, which fatally violates MINSAT in the same way (but would independently also be excluded by the ranking MAX(GOV) ≫ MAX(1), MAX(2)). Realizing the exponents as suffixes in minimally different versions of O_{14}, O_{17}, O_{18} and O_{19} would also not change the general outcome; in addition, these candidates are also excluded by L⇐AGR. Thus, O_{12} is used as the input for the next optimization procedure in (57).

(57) *Extended exponence in ergative first pers. incl. contexts* (harmonic serialism, step 2):

I_{12}: n-[$_V$ ko$^{\gamma}$c-pa] [+gov,+1,+2], {[$_{Agr}$ /Ø/↔[–gov]], [$_{Agr}$ /a/↔[+1]], [$_{Agr}$ /i/↔[–1]], [$_{Agr}$ /m/↔[+2,–gov]], [$_{Agr}$ /t/↔[+1,+2]],...}	MIN SAT	MC AGR	ID F	MAX GOV	MAX 1	MAX 2	L⇐ AGR	*STRUC
O_{121}: n-[$_V$ ko$^{\gamma}$c-pa]					*!	*		
O_{122}: Ø-n-[$_V$ ko$^{\gamma}$c-pa]			*!		*	*		*
☞O_{123}: a-n-[$_V$ ko$^{\gamma}$c-pa]						*		*
O_{124}: i-n-[$_V$ ko$^{\gamma}$c-pa]			*!			*		*
O_{125}: m-n-[$_V$ ko$^{\gamma}$c-pa]	*!		*		*			*
O_{126}: t-n-[$_V$ ko$^{\gamma}$c-pa]	*!							*

(57) shows that in order to satisfy MAX(PERSON) constraints in the best possible way, given MINSAT, /a/ (which only realizes [+1]) is next selected, as in O_{123}; merging /t/ (which realizes [+1] *and* [+2]) at this point, as in O_{126}, would improve the output's satisfaction of the MAX(PERSON) constraints but would lead to a fatal violation of MINSAT since two constraints that are violated by I_{12} are now satisfied. In contrast, O_{123} brings about a more gradual improvement by satisfying MAX(1) and still violating MAX(2). All the remaining outputs (only some of which are shown here – items that place the Agr exponent on the wrong side of the stem and thus

violate L⇐AGR are ignored here and in the following two tableaux) are blocked by virtue of the same considerations as before.[36]

The optimal output O_{123} of (57) is now used as the input for further optimization. The new competition is documented in (58).

(58) *Extended exponence in ergative first pers. incl. contexts* (harmonic serialism, step 3):

I_{123}: a-n-[$_V$ ko$^{\text{?}}$c-pa] [+gov,+1,+2], {[$_{Agr}$ /Ø/↔[–gov]], [$_{Agr}$ /i/↔[–1]], [$_{Agr}$ /m/↔[+2,–gov]], [$_{Agr}$ /t/↔[+1,+2]],...}	MIN SAT	MC AGR	ID F	MAX GOV	MAX 1	MAX 2	L⇐ AGR	*STRUC
O_{1231}: a-n-[$_V$ ko$^{\text{?}}$c-pa]						*!		
☞O_{1232}: t-a-n-[$_V$ ko$^{\text{?}}$c-pa]								*
O_{1233}: i-a-n-[$_V$ ko$^{\text{?}}$c-pa]			*!			*		*
O_{1234}: Ø-a-n-[$_V$ ko$^{\text{?}}$c-pa]			*!			*		*
O_{1235}: m-a-n-[$_V$ ko$^{\text{?}}$c-pa]			*!					*

At this stage of the derivation, /t/ ceases to violate MINSAT despite bearing two MAX-relevant person features ([+1], [+2]); the reason is that the earlier exponent /a/ (bearing [+1]) has ensured that one of the two MAX constraints (viz., MAX(1)) is already satisfied by the current input. For this reason, merging /t/ from the morphological array Agr, as in O_{1232}, is the optimal solution at this point; in particular, O_{1232} cannot accidentally be blocked via MINSAT by some other exponent that minimally improves the current constraint profile (like /m/ in O_{1235}, which, like /t/ in O_{1232}, improves the satisfaction of MAX(2) but not of any other constraint, and which thus has the same status from the perspective of MINSAT, and is blocked by an ID-F violation). Finally, all the remaining outputs that do not improve the constraint profile at all cannot block O_{1232} via MINSAT either, and they are filtered out as suboptimal – either because they do not carry out any operation whatsoever (in the case of O_{1231}), or because they carry out an operation whose only relevant consequence is that some ID-F violation occurs (in the case of O_{1233} and O_{1234}).

---

[36] Strictly speaking, the question arises of whether L⇐AGR is now also violated by all the outputs that add a person exponent in front of the case exponent, i.e., by O_{122}–O_{126}. Depending on the exact formulation of L⇐AGR, this may or may not be the case. The deeper issue here is whether an exponent α that belongs to the same morphological array as another exponent β and precedes β can in and of itself trigger a violation of an alignment constraint that holds for both α and β (because it singles out the feature capturing the grammatical function which both α and β realize). In the case at hand, it is clear that the two options do not make different predictions, so I will refrain from deciding this issue and committing to one of the two options.

The final optimization step yields convergence; see (59).

(59) *Extended exponence in ergative first pers. incl. contexts* (harmonic serialism, step 4):

I_{1232}: t-a-n-[$_V$ ko?c-pa] $[+gov,+1,+2]$, $\{[_{Agr} /\emptyset/\leftrightarrow[-gov]], [_{Agr} /i/\leftrightarrow[-1]], [_{Agr} /m/\leftrightarrow[+2,-gov]],...\}$	MIN SAT	MC AGR	ID F	MAX GOV	MAX 1	MAX 2	L⇐ AGR	*STRUC
☞O_{12321}: t-a-n-[$_V$ ko?c-pa]								
O_{12322}: i-t-a-n-[$_V$ ko?c-pa]			*!					*
O_{12323}: $\emptyset$-t-a-n-[$_V$ ko?c-pa]			*!					*
O_{12324}: m-t-a-n-[$_V$ ko?c-pa]			*!					*

This basically concludes the account of extended exponence of subanalyzed person exponents of segment-like size in Sierra Popoluca based on MINSAT. However, it turns out that a bit more must be be said in view of the fact that there is an additional prefix slot for argument encoding in the language, viz., the position for absolutive exponents preceding the ergative exponents. Here the present account in terms of harmonic serialism faces two challenges (which are both entirely independent of the gist of the analysis, i.e., the derivation of extended exponence by MINSAT). First, the usual linking problem must be addressed: How can it be ensured that, given two separate feature structures like $[-gov,-1,-3]$ and $[+gov,+1,+2]$ encoding the two arguments of the verb in a case like (55), the ergative exponents (/t/, /a/, /n/) realizing the latter features ends up closer to the verb than the (zero) absolutive exponents realizing the former features?[37] And second, given that the two morphological arrays spring into action as a consequence of designated [•Agr•] features, how can an order of structure-building operations within and across morphological arrays be guaranteed that respects the STRICT CYCLE CONDITION?

As regards the first question, various options to bring about linking in derivational approaches suggest themselves. Here I will adopt just one possible approach, without further discussion or justification: Suppose that

---

[37] Of course, this order of absolutive and ergative exponents cannot be directly verified by just inspecting (55), where one of the two exponents is null, but it can be on the basis of forms like the one in (i).

(i)   M(i)-aŋ-ko?c-pa
       2.ABS-1.ERG-hit-INC
       'I hit you.'

Here both slots for argument encoding are overtly realized.

V in the numeration is associated with two fully specified feature structures for the two arguments – [–gov,–1,–3] and [+gov,+1,+2], in the case
at hand. Consequently, as noted, V needs to bear two [•Agr•] features to
trigger individual exponence of the two feature sets. However, it does not
have to be stipulated which of the two [•Agr•] features encodes which feature set ([–gov,–1,–3] and [+gov,+1,+2]); rather the association can come
about freely, so that two general options arise: In one legitimate derivation, first the optimal exponent(s) for [–gov,–1,–3] are derived, and then
the optimal exponent(s) for [+gov,+1,+2], yielding the order in (60-a); in
another legitimate derivation, the reverse order is chosen; see (60-b).

(60) a.   [+gov,+1,+2]-[–gov,–1,–3]-V
      b.   [–gov,–1,–3]-[+gov,+1,+2]-V

In addition, there is a more specific constraint L⇐ABS outranking the general constraint L⇐AGR, which induces left-alignment of exponents realizing [–gov] in the word; this constraint is vacuously satisfied under the order
in (60-b) and simply requires an additional movement step in morphology
under the order chosen in (60-a).[38]

The second question is related but slightly more involved. By assumption, [•F•] features that trigger the initial step of each morphological
structure-building operation represent a grammatical category (or several
grammatical categories), but not an instantiation of a grammatical category. In the case at hand, Agr encodes the grammatical categories case and
person, but not, say, absolutive and person (or absolutive and first person
inclusive). Thus, there can only be one MERGE CONDITION triggering exponence of both ergative first person inclusive *and* third person absolutive.
So far, MC constraints have always outranked the ID-F and, in particular,
MAX faithfulness constraints; let us continue to assume that this is the
case more generally. Then it would seem that the analysis of ergative and
absolutive exponence in Sierra Popoluca demands MC-driven merging of
the two respective pure case exponents for the two (identical) morphological arrays (in either order, given the solution to the first problem) *before*
MAX(1/2)-driven extended exponence within a given argument slot can

---

[38] This would require a kind of pied piping of exponents which belong to the absolutive array without being themselves marked [–gov]; or some similar means ensuring that
ABS stands for all the items realizing features in the morphological array for the absolutive argument, including the pure person exponents. I take the first solution to be
conceptually preferable, given that it can be implemented straightforwardly by means
of Trommer's (2008a) COHERENCE constraint introduced in section 3.2. of chapter 2.

take place. This, however, could create a violation of the STRICT CYCLE CONDITION, which is repeated here in (61) from (22) of chapter 2 – at least, this is so if one assumes (as seems plausible) that each morphological structure-building operation defines a domain in the sense of (61).

(61) STRICT CYCLE CONDITION (SCC; Chomsky (1973)):
      Within the current domain δ, an operation may not target a position that is included within another domain ϵ that is dominated by δ.

To see what the issue is, consider a sequence of optimization steps where the ergative argument is encoded first (as in (60-b)), by virtue of [•Agr•] on V. In this scenario, the exponent in the morphological array Agr that is required by the highest-ranked MAX constraint will be combined with the stem first; as we have seen, this is the ergative exponent /n/ (see (56)). At this point, we might expect the next step to be a combination of the extended stem with the exponent in this very morphological array realizing the ergative argument that is required by the next-lower MAX constraint, which would be /a/ (see (57)); then, optimization should merge the exponent of the same array demanded by the lowest-ranked relevant MAX constraint, viz., /t/ (see (58)); and only *then* should the derivation move on to the next MC-driven Merge operation targeting the zero absolutive exponent, followed by exponents for person (also zero in the example (55) currently under consideration). However, such a derivation is not possible if both morphological arrays (encoding the ergative and absolutive arguments, respectively) are targeted by the same MC constraint, which must then invariably outrank all MAX constraints throughout.

Now, the problem is that the alternative derivation based on (60-b) that recognizes the high ranking of MC is at variance with the STRICT CYCLE CONDITION: Here, ergative /n/ would be merged first, as before, but then absolutive /Ø/ would be combined with the stem, which would require going back to lower positions for the ergative person exponents /a/, /t/ in the next steps. In principle, this dilemma could be solved in the particular scenario currently under consideration, by simply choosing the alternative order in (60-a) to begin with. On this view, both (60-a) (with late movement) and (60-b) (without such movement) are basically possible, but only the former derivation would be compatible with the SCC in the case at hand. However, it is clear that this solution cannot be generalized. The problem will show up in all contexts where both arguments visibly require more than one exponent from the morphological arrays that encode them; and it will arise much more generally if MC constraints of all types outrank all faithfulness constraints in morphology.

The solution I would like to propose relies on the hypothesis that in the same way that harmonic serialist optimization in syntax needs a constraint like EXHAUST NUMERATION (ExNUM; see (18) of chapter 1) which ensures that optimization proceeds stepwise from embedded to higher domains, harmonic serialist optimization in morphology needs a constraint EXHAUST MORPHOLOGICAL ARRAY (ExMORAR) that guarantees that the derivation optimizes a word form based on the current morphological array before moving on to the next one. The constraint is formulated in (62).

(62) EXHAUST MORPHOLOGICAL ARRAY (ExMORAR):
      [•X•] cannot participate in Merge if the constraint profile of an output can be improved by accessing the current morphological array.

This constraint, like EXHAUST NUMERATION (and like MINSAT) must be assumed to be necessarily undominated and inviolable for optimal outputs; as before, an option that suggests itself is that it captures a restriction on *Gen* and does not in fact belong to the *H-Eval* part of the grammar. Checking ExMORAR can be implemented in such a way that a series of optimization procedures based on a given morphological array must end in what may be called "sub-convergence" (i.e., the optimal output is the same as the input) before a further [•X•]-driven operation to satisfy MC can be carried out.

A final remark before I turn to an analysis of the next case of extended exponence (where the two items participating in it are not adjacent): One may ask oneself why the question of how to reconcile realization based on morphological arrays with the STRICT CYCLE CONDITION hand has not arisen before. The reason is twofold. First, the issue of *multiple* selection of items from what is originally a single morphological array simply does not come up in chapters 1 and 2. And second, the phenomenon of extended exponence that brings this issue to the fore has so far been analyzed only on the basis of case/number inflection in German (and Archi), where there is only *a single* morphological array in addition to the stem.

The next section deals with a second special type of multiple exponence, viz., discontinuous extended exponence.

5.4. *Discontinuous Extended Exponence*

5.4.1. *Discontinuous Extended Exponence of Person and Case in Timucua*

Consider again instances of extended exponence of person and case on the verb in Timucua (see (3)); the relevant examples are repeated in (63).

(63) a.   ni-huba-so-si-bo-te-la
            1.NOM-love-TR-REC-1/2.NOM.PL-ASP-LOC
            'We love each other.'

      b.   ci-huba-so-bo-te-le
            2.NOM-love-TR-1/2.NOM.PL-ASP-LOC
            'You$_{pl}$ love (someone).'

      c.   Ø-ini-ma-bi-la
            3.NOM-be-3.NOM.PL-ASP-LOC
            'They are just now.'

Given the concept of morphological array in (45), all six underlined exponents in (63) will have to show up in a single morphological array Agr. Suppose that the lexical entries for these exponents look as in (64).[39]

(64) a.   /mi,ho/ ↔ [+1,–3,–gov]
      b.   /ci/ ↔ [–1,–3,–gov]
      c.   /Ø/ ↔ [–1,+3,–gov]
      d.   /bo/$_1$ ↔ [+1,–3,–gov,+pl]
      e.   /bo/$_2$ ↔ [–1,–3,–gov,+pl]
      f.   /ma/ ↔ [–1,+3,–gov,+pl]

From the perspective of standard parallel optimality theory, the question arises why, say, /ci/ is possible, given that /bo/$_2$ realizes a proper superset of morpho-syntactic features (but cf. the last footnote); or why /Ø/ is possible, given that /ma/ realizes a proper superset. As before, MINSAT provides a systematic answer against the background of harmonic serialism. However, what distinguishes the Timucua scenario of extended exponence from the ones addressed so far is the discontinuous realization of the more general exponent (as a prefix) and the more specific exponent (as a suffix).

---

[39] This implies an unresolved syncretism with /bo/, which should arguably be treated as a single exponent associated with underspecified person information: [–3,–gov,+pl]. However, such a specification gives rise to questions about how to derive disjunctive blocking in the present approach that will only be addressed in the next chapter; hence the simplified assumption of double entries for /bo/ in (64). – Still, the person features that will eventually be needed – [±1], [±3] – are already in place. Also note that the ultimately more plausible, underspecified feature specification for /bo/ would imply that for first and second person environments, extended exponence is actually of the overlapping type, not of the partially superfluous type. For this reason, I will focus on third person exponents at this point already, even if the evidence for extended exponence is empirically somewhat weaker in this case (given that one of the markers is zero), and given that linearization properties can thus only be detected via equivalence class formation. (However, the analysis to be developed below carries over to first or second person contexts without any further assumptions.)

As a first step towards an analysis, suppose that constraints of the type employed so far in analyses of extended exponence (MinSat, MC(Agr), Id-F, Max(gov), Max(1), Max(3), Max(pl) and *Str(uc)) are now accompanied by two linearization constraints Num⇒R and L⇐Pers that impose conflicting requirements on exponents specified for both number and person; and a low-ranked constraint Coherence that is evidentially violated by the very existence of discontinuous extended exponence.[40] Furthermore, I will abstract away from (and will not specifically list in the following tableaux) exponents realizing grammatical categories like transitivity and reciprocity, which are closer to the stem than suffixal Agr exponents; I will simply presuppose that V in the following derivation stands for a potentially extended stem that may already have undergone several MC-based structure-building operations.

Based on these assumptions, consider the initial competition in (65) underlying argument encoding in Timucua in a third person environment.

(65) *Discontinuous extended exponence in third pers. pl. contexts* (harmonic serialism, step 1):

I_1: V :[●Agr●] [−gov,−1,+3,+pl], {[$_{Agr}$ /mi,ho/↔[−gov,+1,−3]], [$_{Agr}$ /ci/↔[−gov,−1,−3]], [$_{Agr}$ /Ø/↔[−gov,−1,+3]], [$_{Agr}$ /bo/$_1$⟨⟩[gov,|1, 3,+pl]], [$_{Agr}$ /bo/$_2$↔[−gov,−1,−3,+pl]], [$_{Agr}$ /ma/↔[−gov,−1,+3,+pl]]}	Min Sat	MC Agr	Id F	Max Gov	Max 1	Max 3	Max Pl	Num ⇒R	L⇐ Pers	*Str	Coh
O_{11}: V:[●Agr●]		*!		*	*	*	*				
O_{12}: mi,ho-V			*!*				*			*	
$O_{12'}$: V-mi,ho			*!*				*		*	*	
O_{13}: ci-V			*!				*			*	
$O_{13'}$: V-ci			*!				*		*	*	
☞O_{14}: Ø-V							*			*	
$O_{14'}$: V-Ø							*		*!	*	
O_{15}: bo$_1$-V	*!		**					*		*	
$O_{15'}$: V-bo$_1$	*!		**						*	*	
O_{16}: bo$_2$-V	*!		*					*		*	
$O_{16'}$: V-bo$_2$	*!		*						*	*	
O_{17}: ma-V	*!							*		*	
$O_{17'}$: V-ma	*!								*	*	

$O_{15(')}$, $O_{16(')}$, and $O_{17(')}$ introduce exponents that lead to new satisfactions of all four Max constraints relevant here; in contrast, the other outputs only

---

[40] Instead of person, the relevant grammatical category mentioned by one of the two conflicting linearization constraints could also be assumed to be case.

generate three new MAX constraint satisfactions, except for O_{11}, which preserves the input and does not create any new constraint satisfactions. Since all other constraints are either irrelevant with respect to MINSAT (because they are not violated by the input even in cases where they are satisfied in the output), or do not discriminate between the remaining candidates, MINSAT excludes $O_{15(')}$, $O_{16(')}$, and $O_{17(')}$. Next, MC(AGR) blocks O_{11}, as before. ID-F then removes all remaining outputs from the competition that have affixation but do not employ /Ø/ (or /ma/ – but outputs using /ma/ are already excluded by MINSAT). All outputs that satisfy MINSAT will have to violate MAX(PL). At this point, only O_{14} and $O_{14'}$ are left in the competition; and $O_{14'}$ is then blocked because it realizes the person exponent as a suffix rather than as a prefix.[41] Thus, O_{14} becomes the input for the next optimization round; see (66).

(66) *Discontinuous extended exponence in third pers. pl. contexts* (harmonic serialism, step 2):

I_{14}: Ø-V [−gov,−1,+3,+pl], {[Agr /mi,ho/↔[−gov,+1,−3]], [Agr /ci/↔[−gov,−1,−3]], [Agr /bo/$_1$↔[−gov,+1,−3,+pl]], [Agr /bo/$_2$↔[−gov,−1,−3,+pl]], [Agr /ma/↔[−gov,−1,+3,+pl]]}	MIN SAT	MC AGR	ID F	MAX GOV	MAX 1	MAX 3	MAX PL	NUM ⇒R	L⇐ PERS	*STR	COH
O_{141}: Ø-V							*!				
O_{142}: mi,ho-Ø-V			*!*				*		*	*	
$O_{142'}$: Ø-V-mi,ho			*!*				*		**	*	*
O_{143}: ci-Ø-V			*!				*		*	*	
$O_{143'}$: Ø-V-ci			*!				*		**	*	*
O_{144}: bo$_1$-Ø-V			*!*					**	*	*	
$O_{144'}$: Ø-V-bo$_1$			*!*						**	*	*
O_{145}: bo$_2$-Ø-V			*!					**	*	*	
$O_{145'}$: Ø-V-bo$_2$			*!						**	*	*
O_{146}: ma-Ø-V								*!*	*	*	
☞ $O_{146'}$: Ø-V-ma									**	*	*

I_{14} still has a violation of MAX(PL); so further improvement is potentially possible. This excludes O_{141} (which leaves the input as is) and $O_{142(')}$ and $O_{143(')}$ (which merge an exponent that is not specified for [±pl]). Crucially, at this stage MINSAT does not discriminate between the remaining candidates anymore: All outputs have the same number of new constraint

---

[41] Note that L⇐PERS is assumed to be violated once here (and in other outputs where the person exponent is on the right-hand side of the word) because L⇐PERS violations are evaluated for *exponents*, not for individual *features* of exponents (of which there are two in the cases at hand).

satisfactions at this point, except for O_{141} (which has none).[42] Consequently, harmony evaluation picks an output as optimal that gets rid of the remaining MAX(PL) violation of I_{14} by adding an exponent marked for [+pl] (/bo/$_1$, /bo/$_2$, or /ma/) without inducing an ID-F violation; this leaves only /ma/, as in O_{146} and $O_{146'}$. This exponent has both person features ([−1,+3]) and a number feature ([+pl]), but given the ranking NUM⇒R ≫ L⇐PERS, it is clear that violating the latter constraint by merging /ma/ as a suffix yields the better constraint profile. Therefore, $O_{146'}$ emerges as optimal.

Given that all (relevant) MAX constraints are satisfied at this point, the next optimization procedure based on $O_{146'}$ as the input will produce convergence; see (67).

(67) *Discontinuous extended exponence in third pers. pl. contexts*
   (harmonic serialism, step 3):

$I_{146'}$: Ø-V-ma$_2$ [−gov,−1,+3,+pl], {[$_{Agr}$ /mi,ho/↔[−gov,+1,−3]], [$_{Agr}$ /ci/↔[−gov,−1,−3]], [$_{Agr}$ /bo/$_1$↔[−gov,+1,−3,+pl]], [$_{Agr}$ /bo/$_2$↔[−gov,−1,−3,+pl]]}	MIN SAT	MC AGR	ID F	MAX GOV	MAX 1	MAX 3	MAX PL	NUM ⇒R	L⇐ PERS	*STR	COH
☞$O_{146'1}$: Ø-V-ma									**		*
$O_{146'2}$: ci-Ø-V-ma			*!						****	*	*
$O_{146'3}$: ma-Ø-V								*!*	*		
. . .											

Carrying out movement at this stage of the derivation, as in $O_{146'3}$, is an option that needs to be considered; but it is obvious that this cannot lead to a better constraint profile of the candidate (essentially, $O_{146'3}$ reproduces the fatal violations of NUM⇒R incurred by O_{146} in (66), the only difference being that there is no *STRUC violation involved this time).[43]

<hr>

[42] Note that the satisfactions of the linearization constraints NUM⇒R and L⇐PERS of the individual outputs in the tableau in (66) are either old (because they are already present in O_{14}) or not relevant (because the exponent that gives rise to them in the output is not yet attached to the stem in the input). Similarly, COHERENCE is irrelevant from this perspective because it is vacuously satisfied in the input.

[43] I do not assume here that movement in morphology qualifies as an instance of Merge that is prohibited by *STRUC (as one might perhaps expect in analogy to Chomsky's (2013) assumptions about syntactic movement as internal Merge); i.e. *STRUC exclusively punishes taking items from the morphological array, and merging it with the current stem (and not taking items from the current word form and merging it in a different position). Therefore, $O_{146'3}$ in the tableau in (67) does not register a *STRUC violation. However, nothing really hinges on this. – That said, it seems clear that there

More generally, we arrive at the conclusion that the case of discontinuous extended exponence in Timucua argument encoding can be successfully handled in an analysis that does not rely on movement. That said, an alternative analysis in terms of movement could in principle also be devised, and would technically also work; it's just that there is no need for it in the case at hand. The situation is different with extended exponence of negation in past tense contexts in Swahili.

5.4.2. Discontinuous Extended Exponence of Negation in Swahili

Recall the particular problem that extended exponence of negation in Swahili (as in (9), repeated here as (68)) poses: As argued by Stump (2001), this case is a challenge for theories of inflection where extended exponence is a priori unexpected, and requires a recourse to a concept like secondary (contextual features) to be derivable at all, because it looks as though the bare negative exponent *ha*, which is further away from the stem than the exponent *ku* that realizes both past tense and negation, must be viewed as a secondary exponent in cases like (68-b) (i.e., it is associated with zero primary features in the context of negation here) whereas it looks like the primary exponent in other contexts, e.g., in future tense environments (see (10-b) above). Analogous conclusions obtain with standard parallel optimality-theoretic approaches.

(68) a.   tu-li-taka   (positive)
           1.PL-PAST-want
           'We wanted'
      b.   ha-tu-ku-taka   (negative)
           NEG-1.PL-NEG.PAST-want
           'We did not want'

In contrast, in an approach based on harmonic serialism that systematically predicts movement in morphology to be an option, this problem can be solved in a fairly straightforward manner. Under present assumptions, the more general exponent *ha* that is only associated with the feature [+neg] is indeed merged with the verb stem before *ku* (which is associated with both the feature [+neg] and the feature [+past]) is merged, as required by MINSAT. However, at a later stage of the derivation, a linearization constraint becomes relevant that forces the bare [+neg] marker *ha* to move to the left edge of the word, thereby rendering its status as the first-merged

---

will have to be some faithfulness constraint that is violated by movement in morphology, disrupting an order that is established earlier. I will briefly come back to this issue in chapter 5 (cf. (16) there).

exponent opaque. As noted in chapter 2 (see page 83), this corresponds to the standard, well-established way in transformational grammar to resolve conflicting evidence for structure assignments: Some item (here, the bare negative marker *ha*) overtly shows up in peripheral position A but behaves in certain respects (here: those determined by the strict locality requirement imposed on extended exponence in the present approach, and by the fact that the more general marker has to be merged before the more specific marker according to MinSat) as if it occupied a position B that is lower in the structure.

In what follows, I lay out the derivation in more detail. First, it is clear that since there is an exponent encoding both tense ([+past]) and polarity ([+neg]) on the verb, the two grammatical categories must belong to a single morphological array in Swahili (see (45)). In what follows, I will refer to this morphological array as Tp (which stands for tense/polarity). Second, in contrast, there is a distinct morphological array for agreement with respect to ϕ-features that I will refer to as Agr (as before). Finally, the core building blocks that the analysis depends on are the inviolable constraint MinSat, which should be familiar by now; the inviolable Ex-MorAr, which demands that a given morphological array feeds further optimization before an item from the next morphological array is merged; MC(Tp) and MC(Agr) targeting the two morphological arrays just introduced; standard Id-F and Max(neg), Max(past), and Max(ϕ) constraints ensuring compatiblity and specificity; and a low-ranked constraint against morphological structure-building (*Struc). In addition, there are three constraints on linearization of morphological exponents that prove highly relevant in the analysis of extended exponence of negation in Swahili: L⇐Neg and L⇐T demand left-alignment of [±neg]-marked and [±past] (more generally, tense-marked) exponents in the word.[44] Finally, Agr⇒T is a constraint that requires exponents that realize ϕ-features to precede exponents that realize tense features.[45] Crucially, this last constraint does

---

[44] Note that this implies that L⇐T does not hold for all exponents in the morphological array identified by the feature [Tp]; pure negative markers which do not bear a tense feature like [±past] do not obey this requirement.

[45] Here the same reasoning applies as before: Bare negative markers lacking a specification of a tense feature like [±past] are not subject to the requirement even though they are contained in the morphological array defined by Tp.

not care about the absolute position of these items in the word; only the relative order is of relevance.[46]

With these assumptions in mind, consider now the serial optimization of extended exponence of negation in past tense contexts in Swahili, as in the example *ha-tu-ku-taka* (NEG-1.PL-NEG.PAST-want; 'We did not want') in (68-b). The initial step of the derivation looks as in (69). The verb stem *taka* is accompanied by a [•Tp•] feature and by a [•Agr•] feature, for structure-building based on the two morphological arrays Tp and Agr, respectively. In addition, it is associated with a fully specified feature matrix encoding a negated past tense first person plural environment.

(69)   *Discontinuous extended exponence in neg. past contexts* (harmonic serialism, step 1):

I_1: [$_V$ taka]: [•Tp•], [•Agr•] [+past,+neg,+1,−2,+pl], {[$_{Tp}$ /li/↔[+past,−neg]], [$_{Tp}$ /ku/↔[+past,+neg]], [$_{Tp}$ /ha/↔[+neg]], ...} {[$_{Agr}$ /tu/↔[+1,−2,+pl]], ...}	MIN SAT	EX MOR AR	MC TP	MC AGR	ID F	MAX NEG	MAX PAST	MAX φ	AGR ⇒T	L⇐ NEG	L⇐ T	*STR
O_{11}: taka:[•Tp•], [•Agr•]			*!	*		*	*	*				
O_{12}: li-taka:[•Agr•]	*!			*	*			*				*
O_{13}: taka-li:[•Agr•]	*!			*	*			*		*	*	*
O_{14}: tu-taka:[•Tp•]			*!			*	*		*			*
O_{15}: taka-tu:[•Tp•]			*!			*	*		*			*
O_{16}: ku-taka:[•Agr•]	*!			*				*				*
O_{17}: taka-ku:[•Agr•]	*!			*				*		*	*	*
☞O_{18}: ha-taka:[•Agr•]				*			*	*				*
O_{19}: taka-ha:[•Agr•]				*			*	*		*!		*

As before, leaving the input unchanged is not an option at this earliest stage; see O_{11}. Next, other things being equal, the ranking MC(TP) $\gg$ MC(AGR) ensures that an exponent specified for tense/polarity is merged before an exponent specified for φ is; this excludes O_{14} and O_{15}.[47] Crucially,

---

[46] Thus, AGR⇒T is again reminiscent of bigram constraints of the type adopted in Ryan (2010); see footnote 37 in chapter 2 above, also as regards the difference between the two concepts (centred around whether adjacency is required or not).

[47] Depending on the exact specification of the Agr exponent (here, /tu/, which is assumed to be specified as [+1,−2,+pl] but could in principle also be underspecified in various ways), selecting a marker from this morphological array may also be blocked by MINSAT at this point; the reason is that MAX(φ) is of course a placeholder for several individual faithfulness constraints: MAX(1), MAX(2), and MAX(PL). For present purposes, I abstract away from this issue since it is orthogonal to the central topic at hand (which is how discontinuous exponence with tense/polarity markers in Swahili is brought about); I will return to it at the end of the chapter.

MinSat guarantees that of the three potentially relevant Tp exponents /li/, /ku/, and /ha/, it is the last one that is selected at this point: /li/ in O_{12}, O_{13} satisfies Max(Neg) and Max(Past) (although it violates Id-F), as does /ku/ in O_{16}, O_{17} (without violating Id-F at the same time); but the bare negation exponent /ha/ in O_{18}, O_{19} makes do with only one new constraint satisfaction (of Max(Neg)), and is therefore preferred by MinSat. Finally, the decision between O_{18} (where /ha/ is a prefix) and O_{19} (where /ha/ is a suffix) is made by the alignment constraint L⇐Neg, with O_{18} emerging as optimal. This candidate is then used as the input for the next optimization step in (70).

(70) *Discontinuous extended exponence in neg. past contexts* (harmonic serialism, step 2):

I_{18}: ha-taka:[•Agr•] [+past,+neg,+1,−2,+pl], {[Tp /li/↔[+past,−neg]], [Tp /ku/↔[+past,+neg]],...} {[Agr /tu/↔[+1,−2,+pl]], ...}	Min Sat	Ex Mor Ar	MC Tp	MC Agr	Id F	Max Neg	Max Past	Max ϕ	Agr ⇒T	L⇐ Neg	L⇐ T	*Str
O_{181}: ha-taka:[•Agr•]				*			*!	*				
O_{182}: taka-ha:[•Agr•]				*			*!	*		*		
O_{183}: tu-ha-taka		*!					*		*	*		*
O_{184}: ha-taka-tu		*!					*		*			*
☞O_{185}: ku-ha-taka:[•Agr•]				*				*		*		*
O_{186}: ha-taka-ku:[•Agr•]				*				*		**!	**	*
O_{187}: li-ha-taka:[•Agr•]				*	*!			*		*		*
O_{188}: ha-taka-li:[•Agr•]				*	*!			*		**	**	*

The high-ranked constraint MC(Agr) would trigger the concatenation of an exponent from the morphological array Agr, as in O_{183}, O_{184} in (70), if not for ExMorAr, which ensures that the derivation first tries to improve the constraint profile by carrying out an operation based on exponents from the original morphological array Tp. Leaving the input unchanged (as in O_{181}) and moving the sole exponent attached to the stem so far to the right (as in O_{182}) are evidently not operations that improve the constraint profile. However, merging the exponent /ku/, as in O_{185} and O_{186}, does improve the candidate's satisfaction of Max(Past), and this time the improvement happens in accordance with MinSat (given that Max(Neg) was satisfied in the earlier optimization procedure); this gives rise to extended exponence of negation in the word. A use of /li/, as in O_{187}, O_{188}, would also generate a new satisfaction of Max(Neg) but would violate Id-F at the same time, and is therefore blocked. Finally, the question is whether /ku/ is realized as a prefix, as in O_{185} (in front of /ha/, given the Strict Cycle Condition), or as a suffix, as in O_{186}. Since there are now two exponents specified for [±neg] in the word, a violation of L⇐Neg is unavoidable in the optimal output at this point. Still, such a violation needs to be kept minimal; therefore /ku/ must show up as a prefix rather than as a suffix. Hence, O_{185} is optimal, and becomes the input for the next optimization procedure in (71).

(71)　*Discontinuous extended exponence in neg. past contexts* (harmonic serialism, step 3):

I_{185}: ku-ha-taka:[•Agr•] [+past,+neg,+1,–2,+pl], {[$_{Tp}$ /li/↔[+past,–neg]], ...} {[$_{Agr}$ /tu/↔[+1,–2,+pl]], ...}	MIN SAT	EX MOR AR	MC TP	MC AGR	ID F	MAX NEG	MAX PAST	MAX ϕ	AGR ⇒T	L⇐ NEG	L⇐ T	*STR
O_{1851}: ku-ha-taka:[•Agr•]				*!				*		*		
O_{1852}: ha-taka-ku:[•Agr•]				*!				*		**	**	
O_{1853}: ku-taka-ha:[•Agr•]				*!				*		**		
O_{1854}: ha-ku-taka:[•Agr•]				*!				*		*	*	
☞O_{1855}: tu-ku-ha-taka										***	*	*
O_{1856}: ku-ha-taka-tu									*!	*		*
O_{1857}: li-ku-ha-taka:[•Agr•]				*!	*			*		*		*
O_{1858}: ku-ha-taka-li:[•Agr•]				*!	*			*		*		*

Now the constraint profile cannot be improved any more by operations based on the first morphological array: Moving /ku/ or /ha/ to the right (as in O_{1852} and O_{1853}, respectively) and moving /ha/ to the left, around /ku/ (as in O_{1854}) are all strategies whose sole effect is to add violations of alignment constraints. Essentially the same goes for merging /li/ from the original morphological array, which does nothing but add a violation of ID-F; see O_{1857}, O_{1858}. Therefore, MC(AGR) is addressed next, by selecting /tu/ and merging it in a prefix (rather than suffix) position (as demanded by AGR⇒T); see O_{1855} vs. O_{1856}.[48] Interestingly, by satisfying the higher-ranked constraint AGR⇒T, the optimal output O_{1855} introduces *new* violations of linearization constraints that O_{185} (hence O_{1851}) does not have: In O_{1855}, /ku/ is now not at the left edge anymore, which gives rise to one violation of L⇐NEG and one violation of L⇐T; and /ha/ is now two positions removed from the left edge, which incurs two violations of L⇐NEG. These new violations are taken care of in the final part of the derivation, based on O_{1855} as the input; see (72). At this point, the only option for further improving the constraint profile consists in movement of

---

[48] Note that O_{1855} has two new constraint satisfactions – one of MC(AGR) and one of MAX(ϕ) (though recall the qualifications in footnote 47). Still, this candidate is not blocked by MINSAT because there is no competitor that would improve the constraint profile more minimally.

an exponent to the left or the right periphery. The resulting competition is illustrated in (72).[49]

(72) *Discontinuous extended exponence in neg. past contexts* (harmonic serialism, step 4):

I_{1855}: tu-ku-ha-taka [+past,+neg,+1,−2,+pl], {[$_{Tp}$ /li/↔[+past,−neg]], ...} {...}	MIN SAT	EX MOR AR	MC TP	MC AGR	ID F	MAX NEG	MAX PAST	MAX ϕ	AGR ⇒T	L⇐ NEG	L⇐ T	*STR
O_{18551}: tu-ku-ha-taka										***!	*	
O_{18552}: ku-tu-ha-taka	*!								*	**		
☞O_{18553}: ha-tu-ku-taka										**	**	
O_{18554}: ku-ha-taka-tu	*!								*	*		
O_{18555}: tu-ha-taka-ku										***!	***	
O_{18556}: tu-ku-taka-ha										***!*	*	

In (72), any output that reverses the order of the Agr-item /tu/ (which is subject to AGR⇒T) and the Tp-item /ku/ (which, being specified for [±past], is also subject to AGR⇒T) leads to a fatal violation of high-ranked AGR⇒T; this excludes O_{18552} (with leftward movement of /ku/) and O_{18554} (with rightward movement of /tu/). Next, movement of either /ku/ or /ha/ to the right periphery, as in O_{18555} and O_{18556}, respectively, is not an option either; in fact, this strategy only amasses further violations of L⇐NEG and (in the former case) L⇐T and is thus harmonically bounded by the output O_{18551} that leaves the input unchanged. This leaves O_{18553} as the optimal candidate in (72). Here /ha/ moves from its base position across the intervening items /ku/ and /tu/ to the word-initial slot. With this movement step, satisfaction of the highest-ranked linearization constraint AGR⇒T remains intact. Crucially, however, violations of L⇐NEG are reduced (from three to two), at the cost of a further violation of low-ranked L⇐T (because /ku/ is one more slot removed from the left periphery).[50]

---

[49] Candidates gratuitously adding /li/ from the morphological array based on Tp are not listed again here; these outputs will be excluded on the basis of the other constraints active in this derivation.

[50] Note incidentally that O_{18552} and O_{18554} are also excluded by MINSAT under present assumptions since they both have more new constraint satisfactions than O_{18553}; cf. the violation profiles for L⇐NEG and L⇐T. We will later encounter evidence suggesting that MINSAT might have to be revised in such a way that O_{18552} and O_{18554} would not violate it anymore; but these outputs will then still fatally violate AGR⇒T. The same considerations apply to the MINSAT-violating candidates O_{185533} and O_{185535} in (73) below, which are blocked by MINSAT under present assumptions but will eventually not be blocked by the revised version of this constraint.

The subsequent optimization step yields convergence; any further movement operation results in a worse constraint profile. This is shown in (73).

(73) *Discontinuous extended exponence in neg. past contexts* (harmonic serialism, step 5):

I_{18553}: ha-tu-ku-taka [+past,+neg,+1,–2,+pl], $\{[_{Tp}$ /li/$\leftrightarrow$[+past,–neg]], ...$\}$ $\{...\}$	Min Sat	Ex Mor Ar	MC Tp	MC Agr	Id F	Max Neg	Max Past	Max ϕ	Agr $\Rightarrow$T	L$\Leftarrow$ Neg	L$\Leftarrow$ T	*Str
☞O_{185531}: ha-tu-ku-taka										**	**	
O_{185532}: tu-ha-ku-taka										***!	**	
O_{185533}: ku-ha-tu-taka	*!								*	*		
O_{185534}: tu-ku-taka-ha										***!*	*	
O_{185535}: ha-ku-taka-tu	*!								*	*	*	
O_{185536}: ha-tu-taka-ku										***!	***	

Thus, the existence of discontinuous extended exponence of negation in Swahili past tense contexts is accounted for. Since here, the eventual positions of the two markers involved in extended exponence are unequivocally such that the more general marker is further away from the basic stem than the more specific marker, a movement analysis not only suggests itself but is in fact unavoidable (given the MinSat-based approach to extended exponence); recall from (65) and (66) that the situation is different in the case of discontinuous exponence of person in Timucua, where the more general (prefix) marker can be assumed to be closer to the basic stem than the more specific (suffix) marker (and where nothing rules out a derivation where these two items are merged directly one after the other in their surface positions).

Finally, some remarks are due on positive past tense contexts (cf. (9-a)) and positive and negative future tense contexts (cf. (10-a) and (10-b), respectively). Since there is no bare positive exponent, MinSat does not block an early use of the [–past,–neg] marker /li/ in positive past contexts such as (9-a), followed by structure-building via the ϕ-exponent /tu/, yielding *tu-li-taka* (1.PL-PAST-want). Basically the same goes for positive future contexts as in (10-a), where forms like *tu-ta-taka* (1.PL-FUT-want) become optimal. As concerns negative future environments as in (10-b), which do not exhibit extended exponence of negation, under present assumptions the bare negative exponent /ha/ needs to be merged first, as in the negative past environment – assuming, that is, that the tense feature involved in future contexts is subject to a similarly ranked Max constraint as the [±past] feature. This then holds independently of the specification of the future exponent /ta/, which eventually also must be a bare exponent specified just for tense information since it shows up in both positive and negative contexts and thus cannot be disfavoured by MinSat: The order of Merge operations applying to the Tp members /ha/ (bare negation) and /ta/ (bare tense) follows from the ranking Max(Neg) ≫ Max(Past) (more precisely, Max(Future), or a similar faithfulness constraint singling out future tense information).

After this, one might expect that the Agr exponent /tu/ is merged in the derivation of (10-b), in analogy to what happens in step 3 of the derivation in negative past environments (see (71)). This would produce an intermediate form *tu-ta-ha-taka* (1.PL-FUT-NEG-want). However, there is a fundamental difference between the two scenarios: In negative past contexts, moving the bare negative exponent /ha/ across the past/negative exponent /ku/ does not locally improve the constraint profile (on the contrary, it gives rise to an additional violation of L⇐T since /ku/ is not at the left edge anymore as a result; cf. O_{1854} of (71)). On the other hand, in negative future contexts, where there is no extended exponence, local movement of the bare negative exponent /ha/ across the bare future exponent /ta/ *does* improve the constraint profile because it manages to (temporarily) get rid of the earlier L⇐Neg violation (at the cost of a violation of the lower-ranked L⇐T). Consequently, this is what ExMorAr forces the derivation to do, yielding the intermediate form *ha-ta-taka* (NEG-FUT-want). The rest of the derivation is basically as in steps 3, 4, and 5 of the negative past derivation (cf. (71), (72), and (73)). The Agr exponent (here: /tu/) is merged, triggered by MC(Agr), giving rise to *tu-ha-ta-taka* (1.PL-NEG-FUT-want); then /ha/ is moved around it, triggered by L⇐Neg, in accordance with higher-ranked Agr⇒T; and finally the derivation converges on the output form *ha-tu-ta-taka* (NEG-1.PL-FUT-want).

5.5.   Stratal Optimality Theory

As regards the basic logic of the account of extended exponence, the present analysis has a predecessor. Caballero & Inkelas (2013) introduce a stratal optimality-theoretic approach (cf. references in footnote 15) that can also cover extended exponence by relying on the hypothesis that when the more general exponent is merged, the more specific exponent is not yet available. For instance, for the case of extended exponence of number in Archi (recall, e.g., *gel-um-čaj* (cup-PL-ERG.PL) in (2)), Caballero & Inkelas (2013, 124–126) assume that there are two separate strata (a first root to stem stratum and a second stem to word stratum), which are subject to two consecutive optimization procedures. By stipulation, a bare number exponent like *um* belongs to the first stratum, and *čaj*, which counts as a case exponent (although it is also specified for number) belongs to the second stratum.

Thus, the latter marker cannot block the former one because it comes too late to have a chance to do so.

Whereas this core aspect of Caballero & Inkelas's (2013) analysis in terms of stratal optimality theory is similar to the gist of the present approach in terms of harmonic serialism, there are significant differences. The first, and perhaps most important, difference is that what needs to be *stipulated* in the stratal approach (viz., that *um* comes first, and *čaj* comes second) is actually *derived* in the harmonic serialism approach, via MIN-SAT, which exploits the fact that the sets of (relevant) morpho-syntactic features of the two exponents are in a subset relation and gives preference to the less specific exponents at an early stage of the derivation. In contrast, this fact does not play a role in the stratal approach, where the assignment of exponents to different strata proceeds by fiat.

Second, and this is related to the property just mentioned, depending on a number of further assumptions, the stratal approach is compatible with fully superfluous extended exponence. Deriving fully superfluous extended exponence is impossible under the harmonic serialism analysis, though, because in this case the second exponent cannot possibly improve the constraint profile further (whereas it can be the optimal marker in a second stratum where the first exponent is not available). Assuming fully superfluous extended exponence not to exist in the world's languages (see footnote 7 above), I take this to be a welcome consequence of the harmonic serialist approach.

Third, it is highly questionable whether a postulation of two separate morphological strata can be independently motivated in all the cases of extended exponence discussed so far. I don't know of evidence that would bear on the issue with respect to exponence of number vs. case in Archi, so it is unclear whether there is a good independent reason to treat extended exponence of plural in ergative contexts in this language in this way. With respect to dative plural nouns in German, where plural is realized by a bare plural marker and by a dative plural marker, the evidence is inconclusive: It is unclear whether the two markers participating in extended exponence here (like plural /er/ and dative plural /n/ in an example like (1)) can successfully be argued to belong to two different strata. There would seem to be one environment where one might possibly argue that there are operations that can apply to a plural form like *Kind-er* ('child-PL') but not to a larger form with a case marker *Kind-er-n* ('child-PL-DAT.PL'), viz., compounds; cf. well-formed *[Kind-er]-betreuung* ('child-care') vs. ill-formed **[Kind-er-n]-dank* ('child-gratitude') (where the verb *betreuen* ('take care of so.') governs the accusative case, syncretic with the nominative in the plural, and the verb *danken* ('thank') governs the dative case). However, the standard view about these markers accompanying the first member of an N-N compound is that they are not plural exponents but special linking morphemes ('Fugenmorpheme') that happen to be homonymous with plural markers (see, e.g., Eisenberg (2000b)). In line with this, it is worth pointing out that the other main type of linking morpheme in German compounding looks like a canonical genitive exponent *s*, as in *[Tag-es]-licht* ('day light'). This might suggest that if a linking morpheme that looks like a plural exponent is analyzed as a number exponent after all, there is reason to analyze the linking morpheme that looks like a genitive exponent as a case exponent as well, in which case compounding again does not distinguish between forms inflected for number and forms inflected for case. Finally, Wiese (1996, 143–146) argues that whereas linking morphemes that take the form of plural markers are indeed plural markers (even if they do not have to give rise to a plural interpretation of the noun that they are attached to as suffixes), the linking morpheme *s* has a different status, and does not represent a case marker. However, based on examples like *[Stern-en]-glanz* ('star brightness') and *[Instrument-en]-bauer* ('instrument builder'), Wiese eventually concludes that the dative plural *n* may also show up in the position of a linking morpheme in compounding, which (against the background of an approach recognizing strata) would then provide even more direct evidence that the two kinds of exponents belong to the same stratum. However, the evidence from Sierra Popoluca (taken here as representative of all instances of extended exponence involving subanalysis) appears categorical in this respect: Recall that in an example like (55) – Ø-*Taŋ-koʔc-pa* (3.ABS-1.INCL.ERG-hit-INC) –, /a/ is specified as [+1], and /t/ as [+1,+2]. There does not seem to be an obvious way to argue that two bare person exponents (each the size of a segment) belong to different strata.

The final consideration is also based on the evidence from Sierra Popoluca discussed above: If "root → stem" defines the first stratum, as assumed by Caballero & Inkelas (2013), then a partially superfluous exponent like /a/↔[+1] can never be non-adjacent to the root. This is certainly not the case for absolutive markers like /t/-/a/ on verbs in Sierra Popoluca. The example in (4-c) involves an intransitive scenario, but /t/↔[+1,+2] and /a/↔[+1] can also occur in the absolutive slot if they precede an extended stem containing an ergative prefix in transitive contexts.

For all these reasons, I contend that the approach to extended exponence in terms of harmonic serialism outlined above is superior to one in terms of stratal optimality theory.

6. Conclusion and Outlook

To sum up, I have shown that cases of extended exponence that qualify as partially superfluous in the sense that one of two exponents in a word realizes a proper subset of the other pose a signficant problem for standard parallel optimality-theoretic approaches (as well as other approaches to inflectional morphology) but can be successfully addressed in an approach based on harmonic serialism that incorporates a general, inviolable constraint MINSAT. By demanding a minimal satisfaction of constraints from input to output, MINSAT initially prefers a more general exponent to a more specific one, with the latter getting a chance to also become optimal at a later stage of the derivation. I have argued that MINSAT also plays an important role elsewhere in the grammar, in accounts of counter-bleeding in phonology and Merge over Move effects in syntax.[51] More generally, it turns out that, in line with the specific nature of MINSAT as a transderivational (or translocal) constraint, it can have a special status in the grammar; to wit, it seems to be inviolable in the grammatical subcomponents of morphology and syntax, which are concerned with structure-building, but in principle violable (and then yielding bleeding instead of

---

[51] There are further potential applications of MINSAT in morphology and syntax. For instance, as regards morphology, Weisser (2017b) argues that an analysis of the interaction of *suspended affixation* (i.e., deletion of right-peripheral inflectional exponents of number (plural) and local case (e.g., inessive) in coordination structures) and two separate *affix reordering* operations (involving (i) plural and possessive exponents, and (ii) possessive and local case exponents) in Mari (as analyzed in Guseva & Weisser (2018)) poses a problem for harmonic serialism. The reason is that the intermediate output that is required to bring about suspended affixation (i.e., deletion of plural and local case exponents in a right-peripheral position in the word) on the basis of an initial order PL-POSS-LOCAL CASE is one that exhibits an exponent order POSS-PL-LOCAL CASE, with local metathesis of PL and POSS. However, this order POSS-PL-LOCAL CASE cannot be generated in the course of the derivation since the two constraints that trigger the individual exponent reorderings can *both* be satisfied in the environment at hand by *one* reordering that yields the sequence PL-LOCAL CASE-POSS on the basis of an initial input PL-POSS-LOCAL CASE – but in this representation, the right-peripheral POSS would block the application of PL and LOCAL CASE deletion. It should be clear that this problem is of exactly the same type as the counter-bleeding effects in phonology discussed above; accordingly, an additional high-ranked (or inviolable) constraint MINSAT would slow down the derivation in the required manner, by changing PL-POSS-LOCAL CASE to POSS-PL-LOCAL CASE first, and then carrying out deletion of the LOCAL CASE and PL exponents in right-peripheral positions.

Similarly, MINSAT could perhaps shed some light on the existence of a constraint like the SPECIFIER-HEAD BIAS adhered to in chapter 1 (see (40-c) there) that cannot be violated by optimal outputs, and ultimately derive it as a theorem: If it is the case that Agree with a specifier is ceteris paribus always preferred to Agree into (or with) the

counter-bleeding) in the grammatical subcomponent of phonology, which is primarily concerned with modifications of existing structures.

In the highly general form that MINSAT takes under current assumptions (see (13), repeated here once more in (74)), it has potentially far-reaching consequences.

(74) MINSAT (MINIMIZE SATISFACTION):
      Assign * to an output O_i iff

   a. O_i has x new constraint satisfactions $(0 \leq x \leq n)$.
   b. There is an output O_j $(j \neq i)$ in the same candidate set such that
       (i) O_j has y new constraint satisfactions $(0 \leq y \leq n)$; and
       (ii) $0 < y < x$.

The question arises of whether (74) is *too* general, thereby predicting unwanted MINSAT effects. As a matter of fact, there would be various simple and coherent ways to narrow down the effects of MINSAT.

One option would be to restrict MINSAT blocking to the same *local domain*; in morphology, this could, e.g., be defined via morphological arrays: In all the applications of MINSAT in morphology that we have seen so far, MINSAT was crucial in blocking some output that applied an operation giving rise to a new satisfaction of more than the minimal number of constraints on the basis of the same morphological array.

Another natural option would be to impose a further requirement to (74) according to which the new constraint satisfactions of O_j form *a proper subset* of the new constraint satisfactions of O_j (in the technical sense of 'new constraint satisfaction' that is relevant here throughout, based on counting constraint satisfactions that are present in the output but not in the input). It can easily be verified that in all the cases where MINSAT has proved relevant so far (in phonology, syntax, and morphology), the new constraint satisfactions of the output O_i that is blocked are a proper superset of the new constraint satisfactions of the output O_j that acts as the blocker.[52] This way, it would be ensured that only those new constraint

---

complement (see Müller (2013b)), this might be derivable from MINSAT, assuming that the latter option involves the satisfaction of two constraints – concerning matching and Agree under c-command – whereas the former option only gives rise to a new satisfaction of a matching requirement.

[52] To give a few examples: The optimal intermediate output O_{11} that carries out palatalization and thus eventually gives rise to a counter-bleeding effect in Bedouin Arabic in the phonological competition in (25) has a new constraint satisfaction of *ki whereas

satisfactions need to be evaluated by MINSAT that pull candidates in the same general direction (whereas, given just the formulation in (74), MINSAT can choose among two candidates O_i and O_j even if the new satisfactions of O_i and O_j are completely independent of one another).

A third possible option might be to add a further condition to (74) which ensures that an output O_j can block another output O_i via MINSAT only if O_j itself improves the constraint profile of the input underlying the current optimization procedure. Again, such a condition would be met in all the instances where MINSAT has been crucially invoked to exclude an output so far, in phonology, syntax, and morphology.

Based on evidence of the type addressed so far, it is not clear whether the extremely general version of MINSAT in (74) leads to empirical problems. A central precondition for a constraint satisfaction to become relevant for MINSAT is that a defective property can be identified in an input (base input or derived input). This is the case with markedness constraints in phonology, with constraints like MC and AC in syntax (where features are involved that are designed to trigger an operation and thus render an input defective unless the required operation is in fact applied), and with MC and MAX constraints triggering exponence in morphology: Recall from the last paragraph of section 2 in chapter 2 (see page 53) that the relevant correspondence relation mediated by MAX constraints in exponence is one between features on the stem and features on the inflection marker; on this view, every stem in a derivation (including the original input) bearing a feature [•F•] is defective as long as there is no inflectional exponent in the same word with a matching feature F. In contrast, other faithfulness constraints that do not *trigger* operations (but, as a tendency, *block* operations, or maximally *restrict* operations) will be irrelevant from the perspective of MINSAT. This holds, inter alia, for ID-F; and it also holds for MAX constraints that do not cover syntagmatic relations between features (which can trigger operations) but rather paradigmatic relations between features

---

the transparent output O_{13} has new constraint satisfactions of *ki and *iCV. Similarly, the optimal intermediate output O_{12} that carries out a Merge operation in the syntactic competition in (42) has a new constraint satisfaction of MC whereas the output that needs to be excluded by MINSAT has new constraint satisfactions of MC and AC. And, of course, scenarios with partially superfluous extended exponence in morphology show this pattern almost by definition: For instance, the optimal intermediate output O_{14} in the competition in (50) that underlies extended exponence in dative plural environments in German has a new satisfaction of MAX(PL) whereas the output in O_{18} that is blocked by it has new satisfactions of both MAX(PL) and the faithfulness constraints for case features MAX(OBL), MAX(GOV). And so on.

(such as a MAX constraint demanding preservation of a given feature on a stem in the input on the same stem in the output; see chapter 6 below).

As already indicated in footnote 42, analogous conclusions hold for alignment constraints. Such constraints determining the placement of a morphological exponent (at the left or right periphery, given the STRICT CYCLE CONDITION) were discussed in section 3 of chapter 2, and they have also figured prominently in section 5.4 of the present chapter. Alignment constraints normally do not interfere with MINSAT if (i) they are always vacuously satisfied by the initial input (when the exponent is still part of the morphological array), and (ii) for every constraint that demands left-alignment of an item bearing [+X], there is a (lower-ranked, inactive) constraint that demands right-alignment of [+X] items, and vice versa.[53] Furthermore, a constraint like Trommer's (2008a) COHERENCE (see chapter 2) does not apply at very early stages of the derivation, where MINSAT is most relevant; etc.

For these reasons, I will, for the time being, continue to adopt MINSAT in the maximally general form in (74), noting that more restrictive versions with less far-reaching consequences that incorporate local domains or a subset restriction are readily available.[54]

More generally, I have now addressed three of the four questions posed on page 106 with respect to MINSAT, concerning independent evidence for the constraint, its nature and role in the overall system, and how it helps to derive extended exponence in harmonic serialism. Still, one question remains open at this point: How can the gist of the analysis of disjunctive blocking in harmonic serialism (highlighted in section 2 of chapter 2) be maintained in an approach that relies on MINSAT? The problem is that any optimality-theoretic approach to disjunctive blocking that models standard (non-optimality-theoretic) analyses relying on compatibility and specificity would seem to depend on a *maximization* of MAX satisfactions; but MINSAT

---

[53] Ultimately, a bit more may have to be said here, though. Suppose that there are two exponents α, β, where α is specified as [+X,+Y], and β is only specified as [+X]. Suppose furthermore that there are two pairs of alignment constraints, demanding left-alignment of [+X], right-alignment of [+X], left-alignment of [+Y], and right-alignment of [+Y], with the left-alignment constraints higher-ranked in both cases. Then, ceteris paribus, an output employing the exponent α can in principle generate more new constraint satisfactions at a non-initial stage of the derivation (viz., 2) than a competing output employing the exponent β (which only has 1 new constraint satisfaction).

[54] However, as will be shown in the next chapter, there are indeed contexts that require a modfication along the lines envisaged here.

seems to demand a *minimization* of Max satisfactions. This apparent paradox will be resolved in the next chapter.

Chapter 4

Disjunctive Blocking Revisited

1. The Problem

In disjunctive blocking environments, only one exponent out of a set of competing exponents is chosen. The standard way to account for this in theoretical approaches to inflectional morphology (like Distributed Morphology, Paradigm Function Morphology, Network Morphology or Minimalist Morphology) is to invoke the concepts of compatibility and specificity. As shown in chapter 2, optimality-theoretic analyses do not have to stipulate these compatibility and specificity requirements; they follow from the independently required presence of IDENT and MAX constraints, respectively. Recall furthermore from section 2.4. of chapter 2 that a transfer of standard parallel optimality-theoretic analyses of disjunctive blocking to harmonic serialism emerged as entirely unproblematic as such. However, with the advent of the constraint MINSAT in chapter 3, things have changed: By demanding the minimal number of new constraint satisfactions from input to output, MINSAT favours the more general exponent over the more specific one. To see this, consider once more the paradigm of determiner inflection in German (with inflection of the determiner *dies* ('this') as a representative example), which is repeated here in (1) (from (1) in chapter 2).

(1)   *Determiner inflection in German:*

dies	MASC.SG	NEUT.SG	FEM.SG	PL
NOM	dies-r	dies-s	dies-e	dies-e
ACC	dies-n	dies-s	dies-e	dies-e
DAT	dies-m	dies-m	dies-r	dies-n
GEN	dies-s	dies-s	dies-r	dies-r

The set of (underspecified) underlying exponents is repeated from (5) of chapter 2 in (2).

(2)   *Underspecified exponents*:

a.	$/\text{m}/^1 \leftrightarrow [+\text{masc},+\text{obl},+\text{gov}]$	(DAT.MASC.SG./NEUT.SG.)
b.	$/\text{s}/^2 \leftrightarrow [+\text{masc},+\text{obl}]$	(GEN.MASC.SG./NEUT.SG.)
c.	$/\text{s}/^3 \leftrightarrow [+\text{masc},+\text{fem}]$	(NOM./ACC.NEUT.SG.)
d.	$/\text{n}/^4 \leftrightarrow [+\text{masc},+\text{gov}]$	(ACC.MASC.SG.)
e.	$/\text{r}/^5 \leftrightarrow [+\text{masc}]$	(NOM.MASC.SG.)
f.	$/\text{r}/^6 \leftrightarrow [+\text{obl},+\text{fem}]$	(DAT./GEN.FEM.SG.)
g.	$/\text{n}/^7 \leftrightarrow [+\text{obl},+\text{gov}]$	(DAT.PL.)
h.	$/\text{r}/^8 \leftrightarrow [+\text{obl}]$	(GEN.PL.)
i.	$/\text{e}/^9 \leftrightarrow [\ ]$	(NOM./ACC.FEM.SG./PL.)

To account for the systematic syncretism in, e.g., dative masculine singular contexts and dative neuter singular contexts, the exponent /m/ is underspecified with respect to gender information (it is marked [+masc] rather than [+masc,–fem] or [+masc,+fem]); however, it qualifies as the most specific exponent (i.e., the exponent that best satisfies the MAX constraints for decomposed case and gender features) among the ones that are compatible with the fully specified feature matrix associated with the input stem (i.e., among the exponents that satisfy IDENT-F). This is shown in the tableau in (23) in chapter 2. In contrast, (3) is a minimally modified version of that tableau that includes an inviolable MINSAT constraint. Instead of the intended winning candidate O_{11}, which uses the most specific $/\text{m}/^1$ exponent satisfying MAX(MASC), MAX(OBL), and MAX(GOV), MINSAT picks candidate O_{19}, which has the least specific elsewhere exponent $/\text{e}/^9$ that does not lead to any new satisfaction of MAX constraints.[1]

---

[1] As in chapter 2, underlining of a decomposed gender or case feature on the D stem signals satisfaction of the corresponding MAX constraint by an exponent, and a superscript ^{i} indicates a violation of IDENT-F; thus the marker entries can in effect be recovered from the effects that they have on the fully specified feature matrix associated with the stem. In addition, the analysis of course presupposes alignment constraints ensuring that the exponents are realized as suffixes rather than prefixes; since this issue does not play a role for current considerations pertaining to specificity, I do not add these constraints (or the relevant candidates that violate them) here. As before, ☛ indicates the wrong winner, and ☆ accompanies the intended winner that emerges as suboptimal.

(3)   *Dative masculine singular contexts* (harmonic serialism, with MIN-SAT):

I_1: [D dies]: [•K•], [+m,–f,+o,+g], {[K e^9], [K r^8], [K n^7], [K r^6], [K r^5], [K n^4], [K s^3], [K s^2], [K m^1]}	MINSAT	MC	ID-F	MAXM	MAXO	MAXF	MAXG
☆ O_{11}: D[+m,–f,+o,+g]-m^1	*!**					*	
O_{12}: D[+m,–f,+o,+g]-s^2	*!*					*	*
O_{13}: D[+m,–f^i,+o,+g]-s^3	*!*		*		*		*
O_{14}: D[+m,–f,+o,+g]-n^4	*!*				*	*	
O_{15}: D[+m,–f,+o,+g]-r^5	*!				*	*	*
O_{16}: D[+m,–f^i,+o,+g]-r^6	*!*		*	*			*
O_{17}: D[+m,–f,+o,+g]-n^7	*!*			*		*	
O_{18}: D[+m,–f,+o,+g]-r^8	*!			*		*	*
☞O_{19}: D[+m,–f,+o,+g]-e^9				*	*	*	*
O_{20}: D[+m,–f,+o,+g]$_{[•K•]}$		*!		*	*	*	*

O_{19} minimizes new constraint satisfactions by satisfying only MC (which is violated in the input). All the other candidates employing more specific exponents in O_{11}–O_{18} also satisfy MAX constraints (whether they violate IDENT-F or not), and are therefore blocked by MINSAT. Finally, O_{20}, which leaves the input unchanged and does not lead to any new constraint satisfactions, cannot block O_{19} via MINSAT for this very reason.

So the analysis faces a paradox: The constraint MINSAT that proved indispensable in the account of extended exponence developed in chapter 3 seems to make radically wrong predictions for disjunctive blocking.

However, closer inspection reveals that even though this problem might be fatal for standard parallel optimality theory, it is far from fatal under harmonic serialism. The reason is that in harmonic serialism, optimization does not stop after the first round; it continues until the constraint profile cannot be improved any further, and convergence is reached. And indeed, *ultimately* a derivation starting out as in (3) will converge on the most specific exponent; it's just that it also predicts other exponents that emerge as optimal at intermediate stages to show up in addition in the eventual output form. Essentially, this is the correct result for cases of extended exponence, but not for cases of disjunctive blocking. Viewed from this angle, the present approach in terms of MINSAT merely faces a problem that arises in some form in virtually all theoretical approaches to inflectional morphology: It has to be ensured that in some cases, a given set of fully specified features can lead to multiple realization (extended exponence) whereas in other cases, it can only give rise to a single inflection marker (disjunctive blocking).

I would like to suggest that the difference between extended exponence and disjunctive blocking can be captured by postulating that structure that is generated by Merge can subsequently be removed again by an elementary operation Remove which acts as the mirror image of Merge: In a nutshell, if Remove is active in a morphological array, disjunctive blocking arises; if Remove is not active, there is extended exponence.

2. Structure Removal

2.1. *Structure Removal in Syntax*

In Müller (2016; 2017; 2018b), it is proposed that syntactic derivations employ not one, but two elementary operations modifying the size of representations: In addition to an operation that *builds* structure, viz., *Merge* (see Chomsky (2001; 2008; 2013)), there is a complementary operation that *removes* structure: *Remove*. From this perspective, one expects that Remove obeys the same kinds of constraints as Merge, and it is postulated that this is indeed the case. One assumption about Merge is that it is feature-driven; it is triggered by designated [•F•] features, which show up on lexical items and are discharged one after the other.[2] Accordingly, Remove is also assumed to be feature-driven; it is triggered by designated [–F–] features on lexical items which are discharged in a certain order (determined by constraint ranking). Next, Merge can apply to heads (yielding head movement in cases of internal Merge) or phrases (yielding XP movement in cases of internal Merge); this difference needs to be encoded somehow, e.g., by diacritics 0 (for heads) and 2 (for phrases): [•F_0•], [•F_2•]. The same assumption is made for Remove: [–F_0–] removes a head of type F, and [–F_2–] removes a phrase of type F. Third, Merge obeys the STRICT CYCLE CONDITION (see (22) in chapter 2, (61) in chapter 3); and the same goes for Remove. This means that neither Merge nor Remove can affect deeply embedded material in syntactic structures. Finally, Merge can be external or internal (yielding movement in the latter case). Similarly, both options exist in principle for Remove, but most of the relevant cases involve internal Remove, i.e., removal of structure that is present in syntactic derivations.[3]

Consider Remove applying to phrases first. (4) illustrates a case where a head X equipped with a structure-building feature [•Y_2•] and a removal feature [–Y_2–] first combines with a YP complement and subsequently removes the whole YP subtree from the representation again. (ZP, WP could

---

[2] See Heck & Müller (2007), Abels (2012), Stabler (2013), Georgi (2014), Müller (2014), and references cited there; also cf. chapter 1 above.

[3] In contrast, external Remove applies to material in the numeration that thus never gets a chance to enter a syntactic derivation.

not be removed by X in this configuration even if X were equipped with
$[-Z_2-]$ or $[-W_2-]$ features because of the STRICT CYCLE CONDITION: These
phrases are too deeply embedded.)

(4)   *Syntactic removal of phrases:*

a.   Merge($X_{[\bullet Y_2 \bullet] \succ [-Y_2-]}$,YP):   b.   Remove($X_{[-Y_2-]}$,YP):

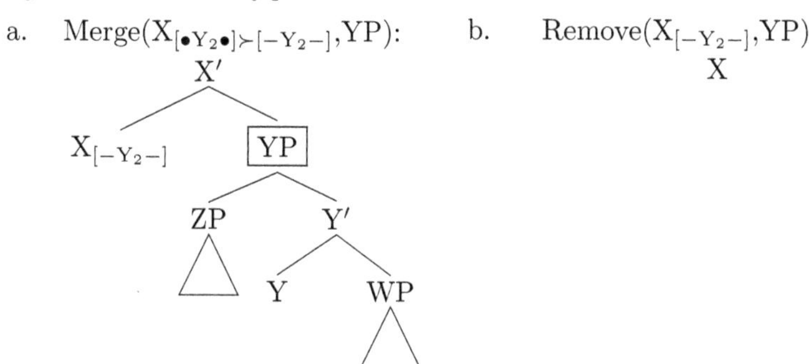

(4) qualifies as a Duke-of-York derivation (see Pullum (1976), McCarthy
(2003), Lechner (2010)). Of course, between the two steps of Merge in
(4-a) and Remove (4-b), in the representation generated in (4-a), YP is
syntactically accessible and can participate in various operations. This type
of structure removal of subtrees has been argued to account for conflicting
evidence with respect to the accessibility of external arguments in passive
derivations in Müller (2016); further domains where it is relevant include
applicative constructions (see Müller (2017)), as well as certain phenomena
involving ellipsis (see Murphy & Müller (2016)).

In contrast, (5) shows what happens if Remove applies to heads in the
syntax. Since $[-F_0-]$ removes the head, it takes away the highest projection, but no more than that. More deeply embedded material (like ZP) is
attached to the head responsible for removal and replaces the original item
(YP).[4]

---

[4] If there were two or more items in YP to begin with (e.g., ZP as a specifier of Y, and
WP as a complement of Y), they would reassemble in their original structural and linear
order in the XP domain.

(5)   *Syntactic removal of heads*:

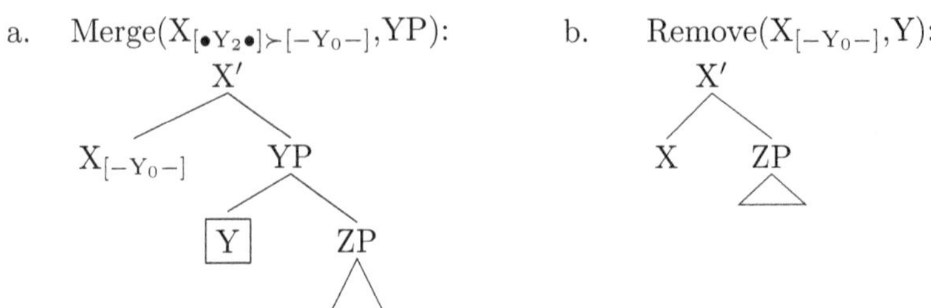

Syntactic removal of heads has been argued to underlie phenomena where there is conflicting evidence with respect to the accessibility of XP shells above structure that is visible in the final representation. Applications include restructuring phenomena (where there is evidence both for and against CP and TP shells on top of embedded vP infinitives; see Müller (2017), Dschaak (2017)), *tough*-movement constructions (see Schwarzer (2016)), DP-NP oscillation phenomena (see Puškar (2016)), pseudo-incorporation of nouns (see Müller (2018a)), complex prefields (see Müller (2018b)), and clausal determiners (see Korsah & Murphy (2018)). Predecessors bringing about effects that are very similar, or even extensionally identical, to Remove applying to heads are Ross (1967, ch. 3) on tree pruning, which gets rid of clause boundaries in clitic climbing and scrambling constructions in languages like Serbo-Croatian and Latin; Aissen & Perlmutter (1983) on clause reduction in similar contexts in Spanish; Chomsky (1981; 2015) (and Hornstein (2014b)) on *that*-trace effects; and Heycock & Kroch (1994) and Stepanov (2012) on structure removal after head movement. Furthermore, the more recent concept of exfoliation (cf. Pesetsky (2016), Pietraszko (2017), Stojković (2019)) also boils down to removal of functional XP shells in the course of the derivation;[5] and Heck's (2016) approach to selective avoidance of intervention effects with XP movement (in the presence of head movement) relies on the idea that there is the option

---

[5] Unlike structure removal via Remove, exfoliation is not feature-driven. In Pesetsky's (2016) approach, it is a repair operation that can resolve a dilemma created by the need of an embedded subject DP to undergo movement to the matrix clause across a phase (viz., an embedded CP) without violating either a phase-based concept of antilocality (by movement to the specifier of the phase) or phase impenetrability (by skipping over the specifier of the phase): Exfoliation can delete the CP phase (plus, possibly, a TP below it) and thereby make subject movement to the matrix clause possible. Stojković (2019) applies the same logic to extraction from DP in Bulgarian, and Pietraszko (2017) to the variability of clause sizes in Ndebele.

of temporary structure removal applying to both heads and phrases in the course of the derivation.

This may suffice as a brief illustration of structure removal in syntax. As it turns out, the concept of structure removal is not unheard of in morphology either.

2.2. *Structure Removal in Morphology*

The first thing to note is that an operation widely adopted in work in Distributed Morphology is post-syntactic *impoverishment*; see Bonet (1991), Noyer (1992; 1998), Halle & Marantz (1993; 1994), Halle (1997), Bobaljik (2002b), Frampton (2002), Harley (2004), Embick & Noyer (2007), and Arregi & Nevins (2012), among many others; also see chapter 6 below. Impoverishment deletes features or sets of features. It is not standardly assumed to delete full syntactic categories, but given that categories are generally assumed to be nothing more than sets of features (see Gazdar et al. (1985)), the difference is a quantative rather than a qualititative one.

In a similar vein, Arregi & Nevins (2012) propose that in addition to impoverishment, the morphological systems of natural languages also have access to the more radical operation of *obliteration*, which leads to deletion of terminal nodes; i.e., it explicitly removes whole categories. The same idea is also pursued by Harbour (2003, 561), who argues that both *impoverishment at the node* (standard impoverishment) and *impoverishment of the node* (postsyntactic deletion of the whole category) are options.

Furthermore, also based on a Distributed Morphology approach, Embick (2003; 2010) argues that there is post-syntactic *pruning* of Ø-affixes, according to which nodes are removed if the exponents of these elements are null exponents.[6]

Against this background (which is comprehensively laid out in Keine & Müller (2020)), I would like to put forward the hypothesis that Remove is active in inflectional morphology. Given that I have identified Merge as a core operation of morphological structure-building, and given the complementarity of the two operations, such an assumption suggests itself for conceptual reasons alone. In a sense, one may assume structure removal in morphology to be even more straightforward than structure removal in syntax. Here is why: Structure removal in the syntax is heavily constrained by *recoverability*. In particular, this holds for removal of whole XP subtrees; removal of functional heads (hence, functional XP shells, like DP or CP)

---

[6] The underlying rationale is to ensure locality for the purposes of contextual allomorphy; I address this issue in the next chapter.

is typically much less restricted for this reason (here it is easier to ensure that all removed information required for semantic interpretation is recoverable). Interestingly, if inflectional morphology is strictly realizational, as assumed throughout this monograph (see chapter 1), the issue of recoverability can never arise with removal of inflectional exponents, for principled reasons: An inflectional exponent does not contribute anything that is not already there, so if it undergoes removal, no information can ever be lost.[7]

Assuming a general availability of Remove in inflectional morphology, disjunctive blocking can be derived if morphological realization proceeds gradually, by merging more and more specific matching exponents, in line with MINSAT. The exponents that were merged earlier are successively removed by their (slightly) more specific successors. The difference between extended exponence and disjunctive blocking boils down to whether or not [–X–] features for Remove are present in the morphological array that assembles the set of all possible exponents for a given position.

3. Disjunctive Blocking by Structure Removal

3.1. Introduction

Consider once more the MERGE CONDITION (MC) introduced in (19) in chapter 1 (also see (21) and (41-a) in chapters 2 and 3, respectively), which is repeated here in a minimally different version as (6).

(6)   MERGE CONDITION (MC):
      A structure-building feature [•X•] that is accessible in the input participates in (and is deleted by) a Merge operation in the output.

In addition, the discharge of Remove features is governed by an analogous REMOVE CONDITION, as in (7).

(7)   REMOVE CONDITION (RC):
      A removal feature [–X–] that is accessible in the input participates in (and is deleted by) a Remove operation in the output.

As just noted, the format of the definitions of the two conditions in (6) and (7) is not fully identical to the format adopted for MC so far. In particular, these conditions are here formulated as constraints on outputs

---

[7] Things are different with the original stem, which, among other things, carries all the relevant features that are subject to morphological realization; such a head can therefore never undergo removal. (Removing it would in fact be compatible with locality considerations; see below.)

in the presence of some property of the input even though they are not faithfulness constraints. I will come back to the reason for the slightly different rendering of the conditions. For the time being, it may suffice to note that markedness constraints of exactly this type, which are both output-sensitive and input-sensitive, have been argued for on the basis of different aspects of optimality-theoretic morphology, and independently of the issues currently under consideration, in Trommer (2001; 2003; 2006a) and Müller & Thomas (2017) (Trommer calls these constraints "two-level markedness constraints").

By assumption, $[-X-]$ features for Remove can show up on exponents. Exponents are assembled into morphological arrays. For now, suppose that it is an inherent property of a morphological array defined by some property (e.g., a grammatical category) α that all members have a $[-\alpha-]$ Remove feature instantiated on them – all, that is, but the least specified, elsewhere marker in the array (because there is no other exponent that could be removed by the elsewhere marker). Thus, so far I have assumed that the morphological array for disjunctive blocking in determiner inflection with German *dies* ('this') in dative masculine singular contexts looks as in (8).

(8)   *Morphological array for dative masculine singular contexts* (old):

     a.   Stem:

       $[_D \text{ dies}]_{[\bullet K \bullet]}$, $[+\text{masc},-\text{fem},+\text{obl},+\text{gov}]$

     b. $\{[_K e^9], [_K r^8], [_K n^7], [_K r^6], [_K r^5], [_K n^4], [_K s^3], [_K s^2], [_K m^1]\}$

However, according to the new, Remove-based approach, the initial morphological array for this environment looks as in (9), where all exponents (but one) are accompanied by a $[-K-]$ feature.

(9)   *Morphological array for dative masculine singular contexts* (new):

     a.   Stem: $[_D \text{ dies}]_{[\bullet K \bullet]}$, $[+\text{masc},-\text{fem},+\text{obl},+\text{gov}]$

     b.   Morphological array:

       $\{[_K e^9], [_K r^8]_{[-K-]}, [_K n^7]_{[-K-]}, [_K r^6]_{[-K-]}, [_K r^5]_{[-K-]},$
       $[_K n^4]_{[-K-]}, [_K s^3]_{[-K-]}, [_K s^2]_{[-K-]}, [_K m^1]_{[-K-]}\}$

Furthermore, it seems natural to assume that a $[-K-]$ feature on a morphological exponent is not yet accessible (in the sense of the REMOVE CONDITION (RC) (7)) as long as the exponent is embedded in the morphological array; it only becomes accessible (and visible for the purposes of (7)) once the exponent has been taken from the morphological array, and merged with a stem.[8]

Two further interrelated issues need to be clarified before we can go through some sample derivations. First, given that structure removal in syntax can affect either heads or phrases, the question arises of whether there could be a similar split in the morphological component where, of course, there are no phrases virtually by definition. Here the relevant distinction might be between (i) removal of exponents attached to the stem (as analogous to removal of heads) and (ii) removal of non-trivial subtrees headed by the stem (as analogous to removal of phrases). However, since the latter option would give rise to fundamental recoverability problems in most (perhaps all) of the relevant configurations, I will assume that only the former option is in fact available – in other words: If, say, a morphological exponent realizing K were to come equipped with a [–D–] feature for removing the stem to which it has been attached, this would lead to an ill-formed result, in violation of recoverability. Second, the question arises which of two exponents β, δ bearing a feature γ that have undergone Merge with some stem Σ is removed by a subsequent exponent α with a Remove feature $[-\gamma-]$, as in the scenario in (10).

(10) $[_\Sigma\ [_\Sigma\ [_\Sigma\ \Sigma\ [_\gamma\ \beta\ ]]\ [_\gamma\ \delta\ ]]\ [_\gamma\ \alpha_{[-\gamma-]}]]$

If the "current domain" in the definition of the STRICT CYCLE CONDITION stops below items that have participated in the preceding structure-building operation, it can be derived that α can remove δ in (10), but not β, which is more deeply embedded. In what follows, I will assume that this is correct; this consequence will not play a role in the actual derivations that will momentarily be addressed, but it will become important in section 5 below.[9]

On this basis, let me now return to the problem MINSAT raises for disjunctive blocking in German determiner inflection (see (3)), and see how the assumption that the K exponents bear features for K removal in the morphological array helps to solve it.

---

[8] See Heck & Müller (2013; 2016) for independent evidence for this concept of accessibility within a derivational approach to syntax in terms of harmonic serialism.

[9] An alternative way of bringing about this locality restriction would be to invoke a constraint like Relativized Minimality (see Rizzi (1990)) or the Minimal Link Condition (see Fanselow (1991), Chomsky (2001)).

3.2. Dative Masculine Singular Contexts

As before, consider dative masculine singular contexts first. As we will see, the derivation here is somewhat more involved – though no less principled – than in other environments.

The first step is exactly as before (see (3)): The elsewhere exponent $/e^9/$ is merged because it can get rid of the structure-building feature [•K•] on D, thereby satisfying high-ranked MC, without triggering any new satisfaction of faithfulness constraint; recall that, by assumption, this marker lacks [–K–] even if the other exponents in the same morphological array all have this feature. This is illustrated in (11).

(11) *Dative masculine singular contexts* (harmonic serialism, step 1):

I_0: [D dies]: [•K•], [+m,–f,+o,+g], {[K e^9], [K r^8], [K n^7], [K r^6], [K r^5], [K n^4], [K s^3], [K s^2], [K m^1]}	MinSat	RC	MC	Id-F	MaxM	MaxO	MaxF	MaxG
O_1: D[+m,–f,+o,+g]-m^1	*!**						*	
O_2: D[+m,–f,+o,+g]-s^2	*!*						*	*
O_3: D[+m,–f,+o,+g]-s^3	*!*			*		*		*
O_4: D[+m,–f,+o,+g]-n^4	*!*					*	*	
O_5: D[+m,–f,+o,+g]-r^5	*!					*	*	*
O_6: D[+m,–f,+o,+g]-r^6	*!*			*	*			*
O_7: D[+m,–f,+o,+g]-n^7	*!*				*		*	
O_8: D[+m,–f,+o,+g]-r^8	*!				*		*	*
☞O_9: D[+m,–f,+o,+g]-e^9					*	*	*	*
O_{10}: D[+m,–f,+o,+g]$_{[•K•]}$			*!		*	*	*	*

In standard parallel optimality theory, optimization would stop at this point. However, in harmonic serialism, the output O_0 is used as the input for further optimization, and there will be a follow-up operation improving the overall constraint profile. As shown in (12), the next-specific exponent from the same morphological array K (as selected by MinSat in interaction with the ranked Max constraints) is merged with the extended stem; this is $/r/^5$.[10]

___

[10] Recall that an exponent that has been taken from the morphological array and shows up in an optimal output form is permanently gone from the array, and need not be considered again in the remainder of the derivation. In the present context, this holds for $/e/^9$, which is not present in the morphological array of (12) anymore.

(12) *Dative masculine singular contexts* (harmonic serialism, step 2):

I_9: D[+m,−f,+o,+g]-e^9 {[$_K$ r^8], [$_K$ n^7], [$_K$ r^6], [$_K$ r^5], [$_K$ n^4], [$_K$ s^3], [$_K$ s^2], [$_K$ m^1]}	MinSat	RC	MC	Id-F	MaxM	MaxO	MaxF	MaxG
O_{91}: D[+m,−f,+o,+g]-e^9-m^1	*!*						*	
O_{92}: D[+m,−f,+o,+g]-e^9-s^2	*!						*	*
O_{93}: D[+m,−f,+o,+g]-e^9-s^3	*!			*		*		*
O_{94}: D[+m,−f,+o,+g]-e^9-n^4	*!					*	*	
☞O_{95}: D[+m,−f,+o,+g]-e^9-r^5						*	*	*
O_{96}: D[+m,−f,+o,+g]-e^9-r^6	*!			*	*			*
O_{97}: D[+m,−f,+o,+g]-e^9-n^7	*!				*		*	
O_{98}: D[+m,−f,+o,+g]-e^9-r^8					*!		*	*
O_{99}: D[+m,−f,+o,+g]-e^9					*!	*	*	*

At this point, two exponents accompany the D stem, thereby creating an instance of pseudo-agglutination. This effect, however, is a temporary one because O_{95}'s constraint profile leaves room for massive improvement: Not only is it the case that this candidate still violates three MAX constraints; as an input for a subsequent optimization procedure, it now also violates RC. Note that it is here that the particular formulation of the conditions MC (in (6)) and RC (in (7)) as constraints referring to both output and input is justified: An output that has an accessible feature for structure removal on an exponent that was still part of the morphological array in the input does not violate RC (so introducing the relevant feature – [–K–], in the present context – on an exponent in an output like O_{95} is harmless); but a (derived) input where such a feature is already accessible on a merged exponent leads to a violation of the constraint in an output if it is still present there, and demands immediate action in the presence of a high-ranked RC.[11] Consequently, the next optimal step on the basis of input I_{95} consists in removing an exponent bearing the categorial information K. The competition is illustrated in (13).

---

[11] A side remark: Rasin (2018) shows that the feeding Duke-of-York interaction observable with (i) lengthening before morpheme boundaries, (ii) stress assignment, and (iii) shortening of stressless vowels in Palestinian Arabic poses problems if it is to be transferred to harmonic serialism (as it poses problems for standard parallel optimality theory). The reason is that the constraint triggering lengthening (*V̆+, where + stands for the morpheme boundary and V̆ is a short vowel) must outrank STRESS, which in turn must outrank the constraint triggering shortening of stressless vowels (*V:$_{[−stress]}$) – but, by transitivity, this will make it impossible for shortening to apply to stressless vowels before a morpheme boundary. Again, it seems that by reinterpreting *V̆+ as a two-level markedness constraint, this problem could be solved. On this view, *V̆+ only requires vowels that are short in the input to be long in the output (before a morpheme boundary); thus, vowels that are long in the input (at a later stage of the derivation) can still legitimately be affected by shortening.

(13) *Dative masculine singular contexts* (harmonic serialism, step 3):

I_{95}: $D[\underline{+m},-f,+o,+g]$-$e^9$-$r^5{}_{[-K-]}$ $\{[_K r^8], [_K n^7], [_K r^6],$ $[_K n^4], [_K s^3], [_K s^2], [_K m^1]\}$	MINSAT	RC	MC	ID-F	MAXM	MAXO	MAXF	MAXG
O_{951}: $D[\underline{+m},-f,\underline{+o},+g]$-$e^9$-$r^5$-$m^1$	*!	*					*	
O_{952}: $D[\underline{+m},-f,\underline{+o},+g]$-$e^9$-$r^5$-$s^2$		*!					*	*
O_{953}: $D[\underline{+m},\underline{-f},+o,+g]$-$e^9$-$r^5$-$s^3$		*!		*		*		*
O_{954}: $D[\underline{+m},-f,+o,\underline{+g}]$-$e^9$-$r^5$-$n^4$		*!				*	*	
O_{955}: $D[\underline{+m},-f,+o,+g]$-$e^9$-$r^5$		*!				*	*	*
☞O_{956}: $D[\underline{+m},-f,+o,+g]$-$r^5$						*	*	*
O_{957}: $D[+m,-f,+o,+g]$-e^9					*!	*	*	*
O_{958}: $D[\underline{+m},\underline{-f},\underline{+o},+g]$-$e^9$-$r^5$-$r^6$	*!	*		*				*
O_{959}: $D[\underline{+m},-f,\underline{+o},+g]$-$e^9$-$r^5$-$n^7$	*!	*					*	
O_{959a}: $D[\underline{+m},-f,\underline{+o},+g]$-$e^9$-$r^5$-$r^8$		*!					*	*

The optimal candidate is O_{956}. It discharges the $[-K-]$ feature of $/r/^5$ in the input (I_{95}) by removing the elsewhere exponent $/e/^9$ merged earlier; this gets rid of the RC violation that would otherwise arise in the output. In contrast, outputs that do not carry out any operation (see O_{955}) and outputs that add a third exponent in order to improve the candidate's profile vis-à-vis MAX constraints (see O_{951}-O_{954}, O_{958}-O_{959a}) can never become optimal because they violate RC. Still, there is one further competitor to consider, viz., O_{957}. So far, it has been tacitly presupposed that an item bearing a Remove feature can only remove some other item. However, this would be a stipulation, and there is no independent evidence for this.[12] So the assumption is that the null hypothesis holds: Remove is *reflexive*, i.e., [X] can bring about removal of a category X on which it shows up. However, self-removal of $/r/^5$ in O_{957} in (13) reintroduces a MAX(MASC) violation that leads to harmonic bounding of the output by the optimal output O_{956}, which removes the earlier exponent $/e/^9$. Consequently, the candidate employing self-removal of $/r/^5$, viz., O_{957}, is successfully blocked as suboptimal by the candidate in which the elsewhere exponent $/e/^9$ is removed: O_{956}. Finally, note that MINSAT is satisfied with O_{956} in (13): Among the outputs that lead to some improvement, there is no competitor which gives rise to fewer new constraint satisfactions. As a matter of fact, only O_{951}, O_{958}, and O_{959} violate MINSAT in this competition (because they give rise to two new MAX satisfactions that were absent in the input, whereas other outputs make do with only one new MAX satisfaction, or none at all).

---

[12] Also note that none of the possible instances of structure removal in syntax I am aware of would involve a situation where some head could legitimately remove itself, due to absence of feature matching, recoverability, etc.

In the next step, further improvement of MAX constraints is sought. Such improvement must be gradual, as required by MINSAT; so the number of constraints that are not satisfied in the input but are satisfied by the new optimal output must be minimal. At this point, an interesting case of *optionality* emerges: The derivation splits into two possible continuations because optimization does not distinguish between two scenarios.

In the first scenario, the MAX(MASC) satisfaction continues to come from the earlier exponent $/r/^5$, and Merge of $/r/^8$ (with the feature [+obl]) with D-$/r/^5$ gets rid of the violation of the next-highest faithfulness constraint (but not of other constraints), viz., MAX(OBL), in accordance with MINSAT.

In the second scenario, the continued MAX(MASC) satisfaction is (also) ensured by the newly merged exponent $/s/^2$ (which bears the features [+masc,+obl]), as is the new satisfaction of MAX(OBL). Since so far no constraints discriminate between the two options (note in particular that *STRUC does not distinguish between them), temporary optionality is expected.

The tableau in (14) shows that both O_{9562}, with gradual improvement as a result of merging $/s/^2$, and O_{9568}, with gradual improvement by merging $/r/^8$, emerge as optimal. O_{9561}, O_{9567}, and O_{9566} lead to additional MAX satisfactions, in violation of MINSAT (and at the cost of an additional ID-F violation in the last case); other outputs have fewer (non-zero) new constraint satisfactions. O_{9563}, which employs an incompatible ([+fem]) exponent $/s/^3$, is excluded by ID-F. Finally, O_{9564} and O_{9565} are outputs that are filtered out by MAX constraints: The latter candidate simply leaves the input unchanged, and the former candidate, using $/n/^4$, exchanges the new satisfaction of the higher-ranked MAX(OBL) in the optimal outputs for a new satisfaction of the lower-ranked MAX(GOV).

(14)   *Dative masculine singular contexts* (harmonic serialism, step 4):

I_{956}: D[+m,−f,+o,+g]-r^5 {[κ r^8], [κ n^7], [κ r^6], [κ n^4], [κ s^3], [κ s^2], [κ m^1]}	MINSAT	RC	MC	ID-F	MAXM	MAXO	MAXF	MAXG
O_{9561}: D[+m,−f,+o,+g]-r^5-m^1	*!						*	
☞O_{9562}: D[+m,−f,+o,+g]-r$^5_{[+m]}$-s$^2_{[+m,+o]}$							*	*
O_{9563}: D[+m,−f,+o,+g]-r^5-s^3				*!		*		*
O_{9564}: D[+m,−f,+o,+g]-r^5-n^4						*!	*	
O_{9565}: D[+m,−f,+o,+g]-r^5						*!	*	*
O_{9566}: D[+m,−f,+o,+g]-r^5-r^6	*!			*				*
O_{9567}: D[+m,−f,+o,+g]-r^5-n^7	*!						*	
☞O_{9568}: D[+m,−f,+o,+g]-r$^5_{[+m]}$-r$^8_{[+o]}$							*	*

Thus, optionality arises: An optimal output on the basis of I_{956} may add either $/s/^2$ (O_{9562}) or $/r/^8$ (O_{9568}). Naturally, the question arises of whether intermediate optionality leads to any unwanted consequences, and whether there might be ways to avoid this instance of indeterminacy. In fact, there are pretty obvious ways to get around this consequence; it is a straightforward option to introduce additional constraints that distinguish between the two outputs. Since one exponent is associated with two features and the other exponent only with one feature, this could straightforwardly be done, in any direction (economy vs. specificity). However, it turns out that such a step is in fact not needed; the temporary indeterminacy turns out to be innocuous and will invariably be resolved by subsequent optimization procedures. So, now there are two possible continuations, one based on $D[\underline{+m},-f,\underline{+o},+g]$-$r^5_{[+m]}$-$r^8_{[+o]}$ (O_{9568} as input, step 5-a), and one for $D[\underline{+m},-f,\underline{+o},+g]$-$r^5_{[+m]}$-$s^2_{[+m,+o]}$ (O_{9562} as input, step 5-b).

Let us first look at the case where O_{9568} is used as the input. It is clear that since all non-elsewhere exponents in the morphological array defined by K come with a feature $[-K-]$ for exponent removal, and RC outranks all MAX constraints, the optimal step based on I_{9568} will be removal of one of the two exponents that are present in the form. This leaves O_{95686} (with removal of $/r/^5$) and O_{95687} (with reflexive removal of $/r/^8$) as the only relevant options.

(15) *Dative masculine singular contexts* (harmonic serialism, step 5-a):

I_{9568}: $D[\underline{+m},-f,\underline{+o},+g]$-$r^5$-$r^8_{[-K-]}$ { [ᴋ n^7], [ᴋ r^6], [ᴋ n^4], [ᴋ s^3], [ᴋ s^2], [ᴋ m^1]}	MɪɴSᴀᴛ	RC	MC	Iᴅ-F	MᴀxM	MᴀxO	MᴀxF	MᴀxG
O_{95681}: $D[\underline{+m},-f,\underline{+o},+g]$-$r^5$-$r^8$-$m^1$		*!					*	
O_{95682}: $D[\underline{+m},-f,\underline{+o},+g]$-$r^5$-$r^8$-$s^2$		*!					*	*
O_{95683}: $D[\underline{+m},-f,\underline{+o},+g]$-$r^5$-$r^8$-$s^3$		*!		*		*		*
O_{95684}: $D[\underline{+m},-f,+o,+g]$-$r^8$-$r^5$-$n^4$		*!					*	
O_{95685}: $D[\underline{+m},-f,\underline{+o},+g]$-$r^5$-$r^8$		*!					*	*
O_{95686}: $D[+m,-f,\underline{+o},+g]$-$r^8$					*!		*	*
☞O_{95687}: $D[\underline{+m},-f,+o,+g]$-$r^5$						*	*	*
O_{95688}: $D[\underline{+m},\underline{-f},\underline{+o},+g]$-$r^5$-$r^8$-$r^6$		*!	*					*
O_{95689}: $D[\underline{+m},-f,\underline{+o},+g]$-$r^5$-$r^8$-$n^7$		*!					*	

As indicated in (15), the output with reflexive removal carried out by $/r/^8$ emerges as optimal. Like the output that removes $/r/^5$, this output reintroduces a faithfulness violation, but since all other candidates fatally violate RC by not discharging $/r/^8$'s $[-K-]$ that is present in the input, reintroducing a violation of MAX(OBL) by getting rid of $/r/^8$ via self-removal emerges as the optimal solution, better than reintroducing a MAX(MASC) violation by carrying out removal of $/r/^5$.

This, in effect, means that the optimization procedure yielding O_{9568} as an optimal output in (14) has proven to be a dead end. O_{95687}, the optimal output in (15), can be used for further optimization, but essentially we are back to square one. O_{95687} is identical to O_{956}, the optimal output of step 3; the only difference to the continuation 5-b based on the other winning candidate in step 4 is that $/r/^8$ has now irrevocably gone, and need not be considered anymore in this continuation. Since the subsequent optimization steps based on O_{95687} will be fully identical to those based on O_{956} where O_{9562} is chosen as the input for further optimization in step 4, I will disregard this continuation in what follows, and focus on I_{9562} as the input of step 5-b, as in (16).

(16)   *Dative masculine singular contexts* (harmonic serialism, step 5-b):

I_{9562}: D[+m,-f,+o,+g]-r^5-s$^2{}_{[-K-]}$ {[K r^8], [K n^7], [K r^6], [K n^4], [K s^3], [K m^1]}	MinSat	RC	MC	Id-F	MaxM	MaxO	MaxF	MaxG
O_{95621}: D[+m,-f,+o,+g]-r^5-s^2-m^1		*!					*	
O_{95622}: D[+m,-f,+o,+g]-r^5-s^2		*!					*	*
☞ O_{95623}: D[+m,-f,+o,+g]-s^2							*	*
O_{95624}: D[+m,-f,+o,+g]-r^5						*!	*	*
O_{95625}: D[+m,-f,+o,+g]-r^5-s^2-s^3		*!		*				*
O_{95626}: D[+m,-f,+o,+g]-r^5-s^2-n^4		*!					*	
O_{95627}: D[+m,-f,+o,+g]-r^5-s^2-r^6		*!		*				*
O_{95628}: D[+m,-f,+o,+g]-r^5-s^2-n^7		*!					*	
O_{95629}: D[+m,-f,+o,+g]-r^5-s^2-r^8		*!					*	*

As before, since the input in (16) now contains an accessible [–K–] feature, RC will force removal of one of the two exponents, either of $/r/^5$, as in O_{95623}, or (via self-removal) of $/s/^2$, as in O_{95624}. This time, the new exponent prevails; O_{95623} is the optimal output. The reason is that unlike O_{95686}'s $/r/^8$ in (15), O_{95623}'s $/s/^2$ in (16) can maintain the removed exponent's (i.e., $/r/^5$'s) earlier MAX satisfactions; and this is so because the feature specification of $/s/^2$ ([+masc,+obl]) is a superset of the feature specification of $/r/^5$ ([+masc]) whereas the feature specification of $/r/^8$ ([+obl]) is not. More generally, the following theorem can be derived:

(17)   *Intermediate Optionality Theorem*:
     When two intermediate optimal outputs in an optionality scenario differ only with respect to exponents that have feature sets which are in a subset relation, the output with the superset exponent will prevail.

Returning to the derivation at hand, O_{95623} in (16) cannot yet lead to convergence since it still violates MAX(FEM) and MAX(GOV), and there are exponents which can get rid of a violation of the latter faithfulness constraint. Consequently, in the next step, a further Merge operation is carried out. And again, temporary optionality arises, for exactly the same reason as before, and this time even with *three* exponents: Merge operations using $/n/^7$ (cf. O_{956236}), n^4 (see O_{956234}) and $/m/^1$ (in O_{956231}) can all improve the constraint profile (conservatively, i.e., in accordance with MINSAT) by getting rid of the MAX(GOV) violation. This is illustrated in (18).

(18) *Dative masculine singular contexts* (harmonic serialism, step 6):

I_{95623}: $D[\underline{+m},-f,\underline{+o},+g]-s^2$ $\{[\text{K } r^8], [\text{K } n^7], [\text{K } r^6],$ $[\text{K } n^4], [\text{K } s^3], [\text{K } m^1]\}$	MINSAT	RC	MC	ID-F	MAXM	MAXO	MAXF	MAXG
☞O_{956231}: $D[\underline{+m},-f,\underline{+o},+g]-s^2-m^1$							*	
O_{956232}: $D[\underline{+m},-f,\underline{+o},+g]-s^2$							*	*!
O_{956233}: $D[\underline{+m},\underline{-f},\underline{+o},+g]-s^2-s^3$				*!				*
☞O_{956234}: $D[\underline{+m},-f,\underline{+o},+g]-s^2-n^4$							*	
O_{956235}: $D[\underline{+m},\underline{-f},\underline{+o},+g]-s^2-r^6$				*!				*
☞O_{956236}: $D[\underline{+m},-f,\underline{+o},+g]-s^2-n^7$							*	
O_{956237}: $D[\underline{+m},-f,\underline{+o},+g]-s^2-r^8$							*	*!

However, as before, continuations based on $/n/^4$ and $/n/^7$ (steps 7-a and steps 7-b, not shown here) will immediately lead to (permanent) self-removal of these exponents: Adding a further exponent fatally violates RC, as does leaving the candidate as is; and carrying out removal of the inner exponent $/s/^2$ (so as to delete the feature triggering removal from the new exponent) reintroduces a fatal violation of a high-ranked faithfulness constraint that only the continued presence of $/s/^2$ can avoid (MAXOBL with $/n/^4$, and MAX(MASC) with $/n/^7$). The problem is that that neither $/n/^4$ nor $/n/^7$ can maintain $/s/^2$'s earlier MAX satisfactions since they are not associated with supersets of the morpho-syntactic features of $/s/^2$. Reflexive removal will reintroduce a non-fatal violation of MAX(GOV), and the derivation will continue with an optimization that looks exactly like the one shown here as step 7-c, based on O_{956231} as the input (the only difference being that $/n/^4$ and/or $/n/^7$ are permanently gone from the morphological array, and the corresponding outputs thus removed from the candidate set). The relevant optimization step 7-c based on I_{956231}, with $/m/^1$ as the added exponent, is shown in (19).

(19) *Dative masculine singular contexts* (harmonic serialism, step 7-c):

I_{956231}: D$[\underline{+m},-f,\underline{+o},+g]$-s^2-m$^1_{[-K-]}$ $\{[\text{K r}^8], [\text{K n}^7], [\text{K r}^6],$ $[\text{K n}^4], [\text{K s}^3]\}$	MINSAT	RC	MC	ID-F	MAXM	MAXO	MAXF	MAXG
$O_{9562311}$: D$[\underline{+m},-f,\underline{+o},+g]$-s^2-m^1		*!					*	
☞$O_{9562312}$: D$[\underline{+m},-f,\underline{+o},+g]$-m^1							*	
$O_{9562313}$: D$[\underline{+m},-f,\underline{+o},+g]$-s^2							*	*!
$O_{9562314}$: D$[\underline{+m},\underline{-f},\underline{+o},+g]$-s^2-m^1-s^3		*!	*					
$O_{9562315}$: D$[\underline{+m},-f,\underline{+o},+g]$-s^2-m^1-n^4		*!					*	
$O_{9562316}$: D$[\underline{+m},\underline{-f},\underline{+o},+g]$-s^2-m^1-r^6		*!	*					
$O_{9562317}$: D$[\underline{+m},-f,\underline{+o},+g]$-s^2-m^1-n^7		*!					*	
$O_{9562318}$: D$[\underline{+m},-f,\underline{+o},+g]$-s^2-m^1-r^8		*!					*	

Since /m/^{1} *can* maintain /s/^{2}'s earlier MAX satisfactions (given the fact
that [+masc,+obl,+gov] is a superset of [+masc,+obl]), reflexive removal
does not take place; rather, /s/^{2} is removed by virtue of /m/^{1}'s [–K–] feature. Thus, the derivation has finally reached the correct, most specific
exponent that it could not reach directly in the first step, because of MIN-
SAT: The next optimization procedure is the last one because it yields
convergence; see step 8 in (20). Here the low-ranked constraint *STRUC
that prohibits adding exponents (see (11) from chapter 3) is integrated into
the ranking. This constraint has been tacitly presupposed throughout the
discussion of disjunctive blocking in this chapter even if it does not show
up in the above tableaux, for the sake of readability: It has not played a
role yet, but it does now.

(20) *Dative masculine singular contexts* (harmonic serialism, step 8):

$I_{9562312}$: D$[\underline{+m},-f,\underline{+o},+g]$-m^1 $\{[\text{K r}^8], [\text{K n}^7], [\text{K r}^6],$ $[\text{K n}^4], [\text{K s}^3]\}$	MINSAT	RC	MC	ID-F	MAXM	MAXO	MAXF	MAXG	*STR
☞$O_{95623121}$: D$[\underline{+m},-f,\underline{+o},+g]$-m^1							*		
$O_{95623122}$: D$[\underline{+m},\underline{-f},\underline{+o},+g]$-m^1-s^3				*!					*
$O_{95623123}$: D$[\underline{+m},-f,\underline{+o},+g]$-m^1-n^4							*		*!
$O_{95623124}$: D$[\underline{+m},\underline{-f},\underline{+o},+g]$-m^1-r^6				*!					*
$O_{95623125}$: D$[\underline{+m},-f,\underline{+o},+g]$-m^1-n^7							*		*!
$O_{95623126}$: D$[\underline{+m},-f,\underline{+o},+g]$-m^1-r^8							*		*!

From a slightly more general perspective, the derivation that ultimately
yields the most specific exponent /m/^{1} as the sole optimal marker in the
word in dative masculine singular contexts can be depicted in an abstract
manner by the diagram in (21).

(21) *Dative masculine singular contexts – derivation:*

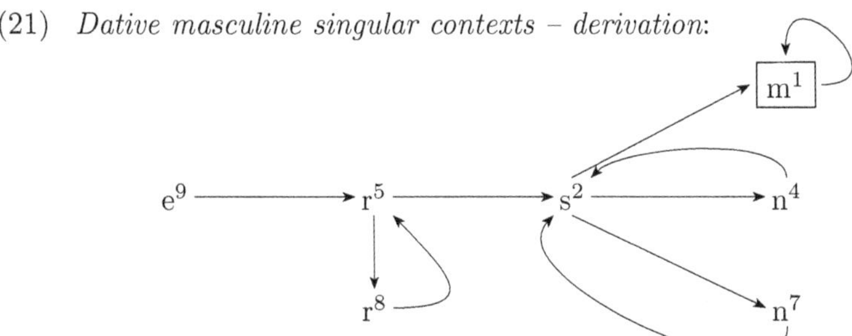

To sum up so far, the immediate problem encountered at the outset of the present chapter is solved: Despite MINSAT, the harmonic serialist derivation is able to converge on the most specific compatible exponent in dative masculine singular contexts. To document that this result is not accidental, I will address a few other environments of the same paradigm (German determiner inflection) in the next two subsections.

3.3. *Genitive Neuter Singular Contexts*

The correct exponent in genitive neuter singular contexts with determiner inflection in German is $/s/^2$. However, because of MINSAT, an output with this exponent cannot directly emerge as optimal; as before, it takes a number of optimization procedures to let the derivation eventually converge on this output. In the beginning, the elsewhere exponent $/e/^9$ is part of the optimal output, exactly as in dative masculine singular contexts. All other outputs either violate MINSAT (O_1–O_8) or do not improve the constraint profile at all (O_{11}); see (22).

(22) *Genitive neuter singular contexts* (harmonic serialism, step 1):

I_0: [$_D$ dies]: [•K•], [+m,+f,+o,−g], {[$_K$ e⁹], [$_K$ r⁸], [$_K$ n⁷], [$_K$ r⁶], [$_K$ r⁵], [$_K$ n⁴], [$_K$ s³], [$_K$ s²], [$_K$ m¹]}	MINSAT	RC	MC	ID-F	MAXM	MAXO	MAXF	MAXG
O_1: D[+m,+f,+o,−g]-m¹	*!**			*			*	
O_2: D[+m,+f,+o,−g]-s²	*!*						*	*
O_3: D[+m,+f,+o,−g]-s³	*!*					*		*
O_4: D[+m,+f,+o,−g]-n⁴	*!*			*		*	*	
O_5: D[+m,+f,+o,−g]-r⁵	*!					*	*	*
O_6: D[+m,+f,+o,−g]-r⁶	*!*				*			*
O_7: D[+m,+f,+o,−g]-n⁷	*!*			*	*		*	
O_8: D[+m,+f,+o,−g]-r⁸	*!				*		*	*
☞O_9: D[+m,+f,+o,−g]-e⁹					*	*	*	*
O_{10}: D[+m,+f,+o,−g][•K•]			*!		*	*	*	*

Next, $/r/^5$ is merged in addition, yielding a temporary presence of two exponents in the word; see O_{95} in (23). This candidate improves the satisfaction of one faithfulness constraint (viz., of MAX(MASC)), but no more than that (as required by MINSAT). The only remaining outputs that are not at variance with MINSAT in this competition are O_{99}, which does not carry out any operation whatsoever, and O_{98}, which, by merging $/r/^8$, improves the satisfaction of MAX(OBL), which is ranked lower MAX(MASC).

(23) *Genitive neuter singular contexts* (harmonic serialism, step 2):

I_9: D[+m,+f,+o,−g]-e^9, {[ᴋ r^8], [ᴋ n^7], [ᴋ r^6], [ᴋ r^5], [ᴋ n^4], [ᴋ s^3], [ᴋ s^2], [ᴋ m^1]}	MINSAT	RC	MC	ID-F	MAXM	MAXO	MAXF	MAXG
O_{91}: D[+m,+f,+o,−g]-e^9-m^1	*!*			*			*	
O_{92}: D[+m,+f,+o,−g]-e^9-s^2	*!						*	*
O_{93}: D[+m,+f,+o,−g]-e^9-s^3	*!					*		*
O_{94}: D[+m,+f,+o,−g]-e^9-n^4	*!			*		*	*	
☞O_{95}: D[+m,+f,+o,−g]-e^9-r^5						*	*	*
O_{96}: D[+m,+f,+o,−g]-e^9-r^6	*!				*			*
O_{97}: D[+m,+f,+o,−g]-e^9-n^7	*!			*	*		*	
O_{98}: D[+m,+f,+o,−g]-e^9-r^8					*!		*	*
O_{99}: D[+m,+f,+o,−g]-e^9					*!	*	*	*

As an output of the optimization procedure in (23), O_{95} does not violate RC; but as an input for further optimization, it does; cf. O_{955} in (24). Consequently, the next step is removal of the elsewhere exponent $/e/^9$ from I_{95} by $/r/^5$'s [−K−] feature; see O_{959}. The competition is illustrated in (24).

(24) *Genitive neuter singular contexts* (harmonic serialism, step 3):

I_{95}: D[+m,+f,+o,−g]-e^9-r$^5_{[-K-]}$, {[ᴋ r^8], [ᴋ n^7], [ᴋ r^6], [ᴋ n^4], [ᴋ s^3], [ᴋ s^2], [ᴋ m^1]}	MINSAT	RC	MC	ID-F	MAXM	MAXO	MAXF	MAXG
O_{951}: D[+m,+f,+o,−g]-e^9-r^5-m^1	*!	*		*			*	
O_{952}: D[+m,+f,+o,−g]-e^9-r^5-s^2		*!					*	*
O_{953}: D[+m,+f,+o,−g]-e^9-r^5-s^3		*!				*		*
O_{954}: D[+m,+f,+o,−g]-e^9-r^5-n^4		*!		*		*	*	
O_{955}: D[+m,+f,+o,−g]-e^9-r^5		*!				*	*	*
O_{956}: D[+m,+f,+o,−g]-e^9-r^5-r^6		*!			*			*
O_{957}: D[+m,+f,+o,−g]-e^9-r^5-n^7		*!	*	*			*	
O_{958}: D[+m,+f,+o,−g]-e^9-r^5-r^8		*!			*!		*	*
☞O_{959}: D[+m,+f,+o,−g]-r^5						*	*	*
O_{959a}: D[+m,+f,+o,−g]-e^9					*	*	*	*

At this point, further improvement of the constraint profile is possible. Again, it turns out that ceteris paribus there are two exponents which can induce a gradual improvement of constraints violated by the input (I_{959}). Both O_{9591} (which merges $/s/^2$) and O_{9597} (which merges $/r/^8$) manage to get rid of the MAX(OBL) violation; so temporary optionality arises. All alternative candidates that are compatible with MINSAT exhibit a worse constraint profile; incidentally, the same would go for the candidates that *do* incur fatal MinSat violations.

(25) *Genitive neuter singular contexts* (harmonic serialism, step 4):

I_{959}: $D[\underline{+m},+f,+o,-g]$-$r^5$, $\{[_K r^8], [_K n^7], [_K r^6],$ $[_K n^4], [_K s^3], [_K s^2], [_K m^1]\}$	MinSat	RC	MC	Id-F	MaxM	MaxO	MaxF	MaxG
O_{9590}: $D[\underline{+m},+f,\underline{+o},-g]$-$r^5$-$m^1$	*!			*			*	
☞O_{9591}: $D[\underline{+m},+f,\underline{+o},-g]$-$r^5{}_{[+m]}$-$s^2{}_{[+m,+o]}$							*	*
O_{9592}: $D[\underline{+m},+f,+o,-g]$-$r^5$-$s^3$						*!		*
O_{9593}: $D[\underline{+m},+f,+o,-g]$-$r^5$-$n^4$				*!		*	*	
O_{9594}: $D[\underline{+m},+f,+o,-g]$-$r^5$						*!	*	*
O_{9595}: $D[\underline{+m},\underline{+f},\underline{+o},-g]$-$r^5$-$r^6$	*!				*			*
O_{9596}: $D[\underline{+m},+f,\underline{+o},-g]$-$r^5$-$n^7$				*!	*		*	
☞O_{9597}: $D[\underline{+m},+f,\underline{+o},-g]$-$r^5{}_{[+m]}$-$r^8{}_{[+o]}$							*	*

Therefore, at this point the derivation branches, as we have seen before. In the continuation based on O_{9597} ($D[\underline{+m},+f,\underline{+o},-g]$-$r^5{}_{[+m]}$-$r^8{}_{[+o]}$), the next optimal output involves self-removal by /r/^{8}; see step 5-a in (26). Again, the reason is that /r/^{8} can temporarily improve the constraint profile by satisfying Max(Obl), but it cannot maintain /r/^{5}'s satisfaction of the higher-ranked constraint Max(Masc) because its feature specification is not a superset of the latter exponent's specification.

(26) *Genitive neuter singular contexts* (harmonic serialism, step 5-a):

I_{9597}: $D[\underline{+m},+f,\underline{+o},-g]$-$r^5$-$r^8{}_{[-K-]}$, $\{[_K n^7], [_K r^6],$ $[_K n^4], [_K s^3], [_K s^2], [_K m^1]\}$	MinSat	RC	MC	Id-F	MaxM	MaxO	MaxF	MaxG
O_{95971}. $D[\underline{+m},+f,\underline{+o},-g]$-$r^5$-$r^0$-$m^1$		*!		*			*	
O_{95972}: $D[\underline{+m},+f,\underline{+o},-g]$-$r^5$-$r^8$-$s^2$		*!					*	*
O_{95973}: $D[\underline{+m},\underline{+f},\underline{+o},-g]$-$r^5$-$r^8$-$s^3$		*!						*
O_{95974}: $D[\underline{+m},+f,\underline{+o},-g]$-$r^5$-$r^8$-$n^4$		*!		*			*	
O_{95975}: $D[\underline{+m},+f,\underline{+o},-g]$-$r^5$-$r^8$		*!					*	*
O_{95976}: $D[\underline{+m},\underline{+f},\underline{+o},-g]$-$r^5$-$r^8$-$r^6$		*!						*
O_{95977}: $D[\underline{+m},+f,\underline{+o},-g]$-$r^5$-$r^8$-$n^7$		*!		*			*	
☞O_{95978}: $D[\underline{+m},+f,+o,-g]$-$r^5$						*	*	*
O_{95979}: $D[+m,+f,\underline{+o},-g]$-$r^8$					*!		*	*

Thus, choosing /r/^{8} in step 4 turns out to lead to a dead end; the derivation via step 5-a continues as in step 4, the only difference being that /r/^{8} is not available anymore.

The other optimal output in step 4 in (25), O_{9591} ($D[\underline{+m},+f,\underline{+o},-g]$-$r^5{}_{[+m]}$-$s^2{}_{[+m,+o]}$), proves more successful. As shown in (27), the $[-K-]$ feature on /s/^{2} is able to remove prior /r/^{5} rather than /s/^{2} itself in step 5-b because /s/^{2} can maintain /r/^{5}'s Max(Masc) satisfaction, in addition to producing a Max(Obl) satisfaction.

(27) *Genitive neuter singular contexts* (harmonic serialism, step 5-b):

I_{9591}: D[±m,+f,±o,−g]-r^5-s$^2_{[-\text{K}-]}$, {[K r^8], [K n^7], [K r^6], [K n^4], [K s^3], [K m^1]}	MinSat	RC	MC	Id-F	MaxM	MaxO	MaxF	MaxG
O_{95911}: D[±m,+f,±o,−g]-r^5-s^2-m^1		*!		*			*	
O_{95912}: D[±m,+f,±o,−g]-r^5-s^2		*!					*	*
O_{95913}: D[±m,+f,±o,−g]-r^5-s^2-s^3		*!						*
O_{95914}: D[±m,+f,±o,−g]-r^5-s^2-n^4		*!		*			*	
O_{95915}: D[±m,+f,±o,−g]-r^5-s^2-r^6		*!						*
O_{95916}: D[±m,+f,±o,−g]-r^5-s^2-n^7		*!		*			*	
O_{95917}: D[±m,+f,±o,−g]-r^5-s^2-r^8		*!					*	*
O_{95918}: D[±m,+f,+o,−g]-r^5						*!	*	*
☞O_{95919}: D[±m,+f,±o,−g]-s^2							*	*

As a matter of fact, the derivation has now reached the intended final optimum, with /s/^{2} as the sole inflectional exponent. Still, it turns out that further local improvement is possible on the basis of O_{95919} since this candidate has violations of Max(Fem) and Max(Gov), and there are two exponents left in the morphological array – /s/^{3} and /r/^{6} – which can satisfy Max(Fem) without violating higher-ranked Id-F. Thus, at first sight, this may look like a potential problem of roughly the same type as the problem with deriving counter-feeding in phonology in harmonic serialism (see McCarthy (2007) and the discussion on pp. 110–111 in chapter 3), where the derivation reaches the intended final output too early and then has to change it again. However, closer scrutiny reveals that local improvement of the current optimal output in the next optimization step 6 is actually harmless. Consider (28).

(28) *Genitive neuter singular contexts* (harmonic serialism, step 6):

I_{95919}: D[±m,+f,±o,−g]-s^2, {[K r^8], [K n^7], [K r^6], [K n^4], [K s^3], [K m^1]}	MinSat	RC	MC	Id-F	MaxM	MaxO	MaxF	MaxG
O_{959191}: D[±m,+f,±o,−g]-s^2-m^1				*!			*	
O_{959192}: D[±m,+f,±o,−g]-s^2							*	*
☞O_{959193}: D[±m,+f,±o,−g]-s^2-s^3								*
O_{959194}: D[±m,+f,±o,−g]-s^2-n^4				*!			*	
☞O_{959195}: D[±m,+f,±o,−g]-s^2-r^6								*
O_{959196}: D[±m,+f,±o,−g]-s^2-n^7				*!			*	
O_{959197}: D[±m,+f,±o,−g]-s^2-r^8							*	*

As indicated in (28), both adding /s/^{3} (which bears the features [+masc] and [+fem]) and adding /r/^{6} (which bears the features [+obl] and [+fem]) can locally improve the constraint profile by getting rid of the Max(Fem) violation incurred by O_{959192} (i.e., the candidate that corresponds to the input and tries to achieve convergence). Thus, not only does the derivation continue in a seemingly unwanted way, there is temporary optionality again in addition. Still, since $/s/^3$ and $/r/^6$ come equipped with $[-K-]$ features, the question arises whether they can successfully remove the earlier exponent $/s/^2$ by maintaining this latter marker's constraint satisfactions. And of course, they cannot do so. (29) illustrates step 7-a on the basis of O_{959193} as the new input: $/s/^3$ cannot preserve $/s/^2$'s MAX(OBL) satisfaction, and therefore has to undergo self-removal, producing, again, an output with only $/s/^2$ as the optimal candidate (see $O_{9591937}$). This output is then used as the input in (a step like) step 6, the only difference being that $/s/^3$ is not available anymore.

(29) *Genitive neuter singular contexts* (harmonic serialism, step 7-a):

I_{959193}: D[$\underline{+m},\underline{+f},\underline{+o},-g$]-s^2-s$^3_{[-K-]}$, {[$_\text{K}$ r^8], [$_\text{K}$ n^7], [$_\text{K}$ r^6], [$_\text{K}$ n^4], [$_\text{K}$ m^1]}	MinSat	RC	MC	Id-F	MaxM	MaxO	MaxF	MaxG
$O_{9591931}$: D[$\underline{+m},\underline{+f},\underline{+o},\underline{-g}$]-s^2-s^3-m^1		*!		*				
$O_{9591932}$: D[$\underline{+m},\underline{+f},\underline{+o},-g$]-s^2-s^3		*!						*
$O_{9591933}$: D[$\underline{+m},\underline{+f},\underline{+o},\underline{-g}$]-s^2-s^3-n^4		*!		*				
$O_{9591934}$: D[$\underline{+m},\underline{+f},\underline{+o},-g$]-s^2-s^3-r^6		*!						*
$O_{9591935}$: D[$\underline{+m},\underline{+f},\underline{+o},\underline{-g}$]-s^2-s^3-n^7		*!		*				
$O_{9591936}$: D[$\underline{+m},\underline{+f},\underline{+o},-g$]-s^2-s^3-r^8		*!						*
☞$O_{9591937}$: D[$\underline{+m},+f,\underline{+o},-g$]-s^2							*	*
$O_{9591938}$: D[$\underline{+m},\underline{+f},+o,-g$]-s^3						*!		*

Alternatively, the derivation proceeds on the basis of the other optimal output O_{959195} (with $/r/^6$) in step 6 in (28), as in (30). Again, the candidate that keeps $/r/^6$ rather than the original exponent $/s/^2$ cannot become optimal because it fails to maintain $/s/^2$'s satisfaction of a higher-ranked faithfulness constraint; this time it is MAX(MASC) which is fatally violated by the output preserving the newly added exponent. This is shown in (30).

(30) *Genitive neuter singular contexts* (harmonic serialism, step 7-b):

I_{959195}: D[$\underline{+m},\underline{+f},+o,-g$]-s^2-r$^6_{[-K-]}$, {[$_\text{K}$ r^8], [$_\text{K}$ n^7], [$_\text{K}$ n^4], [$_\text{K}$ s^3], [$_\text{K}$ m^1]}	MinSat	RC	MC	Id-F	MaxM	MaxO	MaxF	MaxG
$O_{9591951}$: D[$\underline{+m},\underline{+f},\underline{+o},-g$]-s^2-r^6-m^1		*!		*				
$O_{9591952}$: D[$\underline{+m},\underline{+f},\underline{+o},-g$]-s^2-r^6		*!						*
$O_{9591953}$: D[$\underline{+m},\underline{+f},\underline{+o},-g$]-s^2-r^6-s^3		*!						*
$O_{9591954}$: D[$\underline{+m},\underline{+f},\underline{+o},-g$]-s^2-r^6-n^4		*!		*				
$O_{9591955}$: D[$\underline{+m},\underline{+f},\underline{+o},-g$]-s^2-r^6-n^7		*!		*				
$O_{9591956}$: D[$\underline{+m},\underline{+f},\underline{+o},-g$]-s^2-r^6-r^8		*!						*
☞$O_{9591957}$: D[$\underline{+m},+f,\underline{+o},-g$]-s^2							*	*
$O_{9591958}$: D[$\underline{+m},\underline{+f},+o,-g$]-r^6					*!			*

Eventually we are back at (a step like) step 6 again, the only difference from the original step 6 being that two further exponents – $/s/^3$ and $/r/^6$ – have been tried out and rejected, and as a consequence have been permanently removed from the morphological array. The final version of step 6 that the derivation goes through is shown in (31); this is identical to the original step 6 in (28) except for the fact that $/s/^3$ and $/r/^6$ are not present in the morphological array anymore, and candidates that merge these exponents therefore cannot be generated in the first place.

(31)   *Genitive neuter singular contexts* (harmonic serialism, step 6″):

I_{95919}: $D[\underline{+m},+f,\underline{+o},-g]$-$s^2$, $\{[_K r^8], [_K n^7], [_K n^4], [_K m^1]\}$	MinSat	RC	MC	Id-F	MaxM	MaxO	MaxF	MaxG
O_{959191}: $D[\underline{+m},+f,\underline{+o},-g]$-$s^2$-$m^1$				*!			*	
☞O_{959192}: $D[\underline{+m},+f,\underline{+o},-g]$-$s^2$							*	*
O_{959194}: $D[\underline{+m},+f,\underline{+o},-g]$-$s^2$-$n^4$				*!			*	
O_{959196}: $D[\underline{+m},+f,\underline{+o},-g]$-$s^2$-$n^7$				*!			*	
O_{959197}: $D[\underline{+m},+f,\underline{+o},-g]$-$s^2$-$r^8$							*	*

As a result, the output using $/s/^2$ emerges as optimal, and with (ultimately) all outputs using exponents that give rise to temporary improvement gone from the competition, it is clear that from this point onwards, no further improvement is possible: The derivation will converge on this form in the next and final step, which is not shown here (see (20) above); and $/s/^2$ remains the optimal exponent for genitive neuter singular contexts.[13]

From a more general point of view, we now have a first strong argument for postulating the morphological array. To eventually let the derivation converge, it is crucial that $/s/^3$ and $/r/^6$ disappear once they have been tried out: In contrast to what was the case with the first case study on dative masculine singular contexts, there is no legitimate derivation to the end that does without (permanent) reflexive removal. The progress of the derivation can again be illustrated by a diagram; see (32).

---

[13] Note that the numbering of outputs in (31) is not strictly speaking correct: The input is a descendant of optimal outputs in which all the loops generated by temporary improvement that could not be sustained have been gone through. Also, note that $/r/^8$ of O_{959197} fatally violates *Struc, which is not shown here.

(32)   *Genitive neuter singular contexts – derivation:*

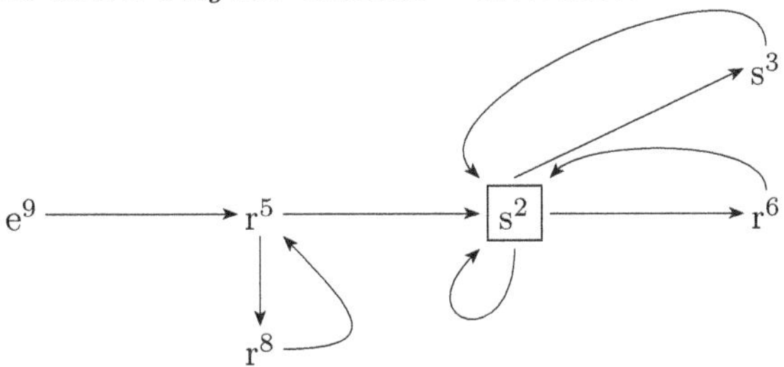

3.4.   Other Contexts

The two environments in German determiner inflection discussed so far belong to the more complex derivations of exponence with disjunctive blocking. Most other derivations take fewer derivational steps. As an example,
consider dative feminine singular contexts. The target exponent is $/r/^6$.
As before, the exponent chosen in the first optimization step (by MIN-
SAT) is the radically underspecified $/e/^9$, which satisfies MC but no MAX
constraint yet. In the next steps, $/e/^9$ is first accompanied (in line with
MINSAT), and then removed, by $/r/^8$ (specified as [+obl]), which gives
rise to a new satisfaction of MAX(OBL). And then, $/r/^8$ is joined by $/r/^6$
(specified as [+obl,+fem]), which triggers a new satisfaction of MAX(FEM),
and subsequently replaced by the new exponent (since $/r/^6$ can maintain
$/r/^8$'s MAX(OBL) satisfaction). At this point, the derivation converges. A
diagram of the results of the sequence of optimization steps is given in (33).

(33)   *Dative feminine singular contexts – derivation:*

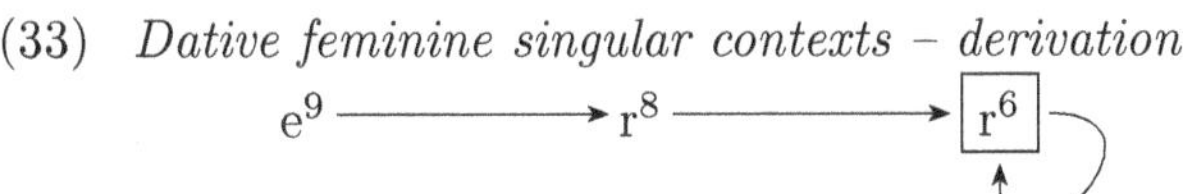

A derivation of a similar length underlies the optimization of exponence in
accusative masculine singular contexts; see (34). Here, an initial elsewhere
exponent $/e/^9$ is first replaced by the more specific exponent $/r/^5$ (realizing [+masc]), and the latter is then replaced by the target exponent $/n/^4$
(bearing the features [+masc,+gov]), on which the derivation converges.

(34)   *Accusative masculine singular contexts – derivation:*

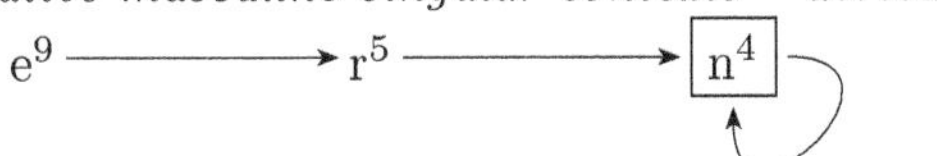

Finally, a very short derivation takes place in, e.g., nominative plural contexts, as in (35). Again, in the first step the elsewhere exponent $/e/^9$ is selected, which continues to violate all four MAX constraints. However, this time, no further improvement of the constraint profile (be it gradual, as required by MINSAT, or not) is possible (because all other exponents are incompatible; they thus trigger violations of the higher-ranked constraint ID-F). For this reason, the derivation uncharacteristically converges on the very first optimal output.

(35) *Nominative plural contexts – derivation:*

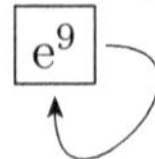

4. Bigger Leaps

So far, we have only seen instances of disjunctive blocking where the move from one exponent α to the next (more specific) exponent β in the course of optimization that is required by MINSAT is a very gradual one, with β giving rise to one new constraint satisfaction that could not be triggered by α. However, in the way in which it is defined in the present monograph (see (74) in the previous chapter), MINSAT is also compatible with scenarios where the optimal step involves a new satisfaction of two (or more) faithfulness constraints, as long as there is no competing output with fewer new constraint satisfactions; i.e., bigger leaps from one output to the next, harmonically improving output are possible in principle.

This property is required to account for certain elsewhere distributions where the elsewhere exponent uniformly shows up in a number of different contexts but its distribution is selectively interrupted in one particular context, which, hence, requires a highly specific characterization of the non-elsewhere exponent. The scenario is schematically illustrated in (36).

(36) *A simple elsewhere distribution:*

x	y
x	x

Suppose that the exponent x is the elsewhere marker specified as [ ], and that y is specified as $[+\alpha,-\beta]$. Then, optimization first merges x with some stem (triggerd by MC), and subsequently y needs to replace x in $[+\alpha,-\beta]$ contexts. This will satisfy two MAX constraints at once which were not satisfied before (MAX(α), MAX(β)), which is unproblematic as long as there is no other exponent that makes do with fewer new constraint satisfactions *and* leads to a constraint profile that cannot legitimately be improved upon by subsequent steps.

To check these predictions with an actual example, let us look at verb inflection in English present tense contexts.

(37) *Regular English verbs, present tense:*

	Singular	Plural
1	-Ø	-Ø
2	-Ø	-Ø
3	-s	-Ø

It seems clear that whereas /Ø/ must be assumed to be a radically under-specified elsewhere marker, /s/ must bear at least two separate features, one encoding number ([–pl]), and one encoding third person. This latter information is either provided by means of two primitive person features ([–1,–2]), or, alternatively, by means of a single feature [+3], which directly singles out first and second person as a natural class (see Cysouw (2001), Baerman et al. (2005) for empirical evidence, and Trommer (2006b;c) and Nevins (2007) for arguments for postulating a feature [±3]; also cf. chapter 2 above). In the first case, the step from an initial exponent /Ø/ to a final exponent /s/ would involve three new MAX satisfactions; in the second case, it would still involve two new MAX satisfactions. Both kinds of derivations, as such, are unproblematic; sequential optimization can apply as depicted in (38).

(38) *Third person singular contexts – derivation:*

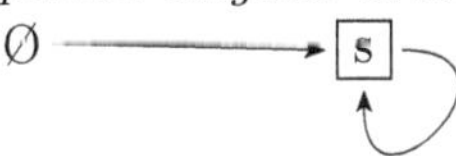

There is a caveat, though. The elsewhere marker /Ø/ in (37) is not specified for either person or number, and given the assumptions in chapter 3 about morphological arrays, it must minimally bear categorial information ([T]) to satisfy the encoding the categorial feature [T] sought for by [•T•] on V, via MC. At this point, the question arises of whether /Ø/ (and /s/) in (37) are also specified for present tense, by a feature like [–past]; if so, the initial elsewhere marker /Ø/ already gives rise to two new constraint satisfactions (viz., MC and MAX(PAST)). Whereas the two options (with and without [–past] for both present tense exponents) as such yield the same results if only the paradigm in (37) is considered, there may be different consequences when past tense environments are also taken into account; see (39).

(39) *Regular English verbs, past tense:*

	Singular	Plural
1	-ed	-ed
2	-ed	-ed
3	-ed	-ed

Given the concept of morphological array in (45) of chapter 3, the [+past]-marked exponent /ed/ in (39) belongs to the same morphological array T as the exponents /Ø/ and /s/. Consider now first the scenario where /ed/ is specified as [+past] whereas /Ø/ and /s/ are specified as [–past], as in (40).[14]

(40) a. /Ø/ ↔ [T], [–past]
      b. /s/ ↔ [T], [+3,–pl,–past], [–T–]
      c. /ed/ ↔ [T], [+past]

In a first person singular present tense environment, optimization is entirely straightforward. In the first step, /Ø/ is chosen as the best exponent; see (41), where O_{12} discharges [•T•], thereby satisfying MC, and also satisfies MAX(PAST) by realizing [–past]. Among the outputs that give rise to new constraint satisfaction, there is no competitor that has fewer new constraint satisfactions; so MINSAT is not violated either.

(41) *First person singular present tense contexts* (harmonic serialism, step 1):

I_1: [$_V$ work]: [•T•], [+1,–3,–pl,–past], {[$_T$ Ø], [$_T$ s], [$_T$ ed]}	MIN SAT	RC	MC	ID F	MAX 3	MAX 1	MAX PAST	MAX PL	*STR
O_{11}: [$_V$ work]:[+1,–3,–pl,–past],[•T•]			*!		*	*	*	*	
☞O_{12}: [$_V$ work]:[+1,–3,–pl,–past]-Ø					*	*		*	*
O_{13}: [$_V$ work]:[+1,–3,–pl,–past]-s	*!			*		*			*
O_{14}: [$_V$ work]:[+1,–3,–pl,–past]-ed				*!	*	*		*	*

As shown in (42), the next step yields convergence. Note that adding the exponent /s/ as in O_{122} does not violate MINSAT (because there is no competing output with fewer new constraint satisfactions, O_{123} being harmonically bounded by O_{121}); however, O_{122} fatally violates ID-F because /s/'s person feature [+3] is incompatible with the feature structure in need of realization.

---

[14] Note that since /Ø/ and /ed/ are both maximally non-specific elsewhere markers in this morphological array, none of them is accompanied by a removal feature [–T–].

(42) *First person singular present tense contexts* (harmonic serialism, step 2):

I_{12}: [v work]:[+1,–3,–pl,–past]-Ø, {[T s], [T ed]}	Min Sat	RC	MC	Id F	Max 3	Max 1	Max Past	Max Pl	*Str
☞O_{121}: [v work]:[+1,–3,–pl,–past]-Ø					*	*		*	
O_{122}: [v work]:[+1,–3,–pl,–past]-Ø-s				*!		*			*
O_{123}: [v work]:[+1,–3,–pl,–past]-Ø-ed				*!	*	*		*	*

Turning to third person singular present tense environments next, the first step is identical to the previous derivation: MinSat prefers /Ø/ over /s/ at this point, and /Ø/ blocks /ed/ via Id-F. This is shown in (43).

(43) *Third person singular present tense contexts* (harmonic serialism, step 1):

I_1: [v work]: [•T•], [–1,+3,–pl,–past], {[T Ø], [T s], [T ed]}	Min Sat	RC	MC	Id F	Max 3	Max 1	Max Past	Max Pl	*Str
O_{11}: [v work]:[–1,+3,–pl,–past],[•T•]			*!		*	*	*	*	
☞O_{12}: [v work]:[–1,+3,–pl,–past]-Ø					*	*		*	*
O_{13}: [v work]:[–1,+3,–pl,–past]-s	*!					*			*
O_{14}: [v work]:[–1,+3,–pl,–past]-ed				*!	*	*		*	*

In the following step, /s/ is added to the extended stem V-Ø. This is compatible with MinSat since there is no other competitor that would improve the constraint profile in any other (let alone more gradual) way; see (44).

(44) *Third person singular present tense contexts* (harmonic serialism, step 2):

I_{12}: [v work]:[–1,+3,–pl,–past]:-Ø, {[T s], [T ed]}	Min Sat	RC	MC	Id F	Max 3	Max 1	Max Past	Max Pl	*Str
O_{121}: [v work]:[–1,+3,–pl,–past]-Ø					*!	*		*	
☞O_{122}: [v work]:[–1,+3,–pl,–past]-Ø-s						*			*
O_{123}: [v work]:[–1,+3,–pl,–past]-Ø-ed				*!	*	*		*	*

Next, /s/'s removal feature [–T–] is discharged. Since there is no question whether /s/ can maintain /Ø/'s original constraint satisfactions, /Ø/ is removed at this point, and self-removal is blocked; see (45).

(45)   *Third person singular present tense contexts* (harmonic serialism, step 3):

I_{122}: [v work]:[−1,+3,−pl,−past]:-Ø-s, {[T ed]}	Min Sat	RC	MC	Id F	Max 3	Max 1	Max Past	Max Pl	*Str
O_{1221}: [v work]:[−1,+3,−pl,−past]-Ø-s		*!				*		*	
☞O_{1222}: [v work]:[−1,+3,−pl,−past]-s						*		*	
O_{1223}: [v work]:[−1,+3,−pl,−past]-Ø					*!	*	*	*	
O_{1224}: [v work]:[−1,+3,−pl,−past]-Ø-s-ed		*!		*	*	*		*	*

Finally, there is convergence; see (46).

(46)   *Third person singular present tense contexts* (harmonic serialism, step 4):

I_{1222}: [v work]:[−1,+3,−pl,−past]-s, {[T ed]}	Min Sat	RC	MC	Id F	Max 3	Max 1	Max Past	Max Pl	*Str
☞O_{12221}: [v work]:[−1,+3,−pl,−past]-s						*		*	
O_{12222}: [v work]:[−1,+3,−pl,−past]-s-ed				*!	*	*		*	*

So far, so good. Let me now turn to the alternative feature assignment envisaged above for the three exponents /Ø/, /s/, and /ed/, where the first two markers are in fact not at all specified for tense information; accordingly, /ed/ is now more specific than /Ø/, and consequently receives a [−T−] feature, too. Cf. (47) vs. (40).

(47)   a.   /Ø/ ↔ [T]
       b.   /s/ ↔ [T], [+3,−pl], [−T−]
       c.   /ed/ ↔ [T], [+past], [−T−]

In a standard parallel optimality-theoretic analysis, this would give rise to the same optimal outputs. However, ceteris paribus this is not quite the case in an analysis in terms of harmonic serialism that incorporates MinSat. Whereas first person singular present tense contexts (and almost all other environments) would work as before, third person singular present tense contexts would not.

The first optimization procedure in third person singular present tense contexts would still look quite similar, and would give rise to the same winner; but note that O_{14} would now be excluded by MinSat at this early stage, just like O_{13} (O_{14} satisfies MC and Max(Past), as before, whereas O_{12}, without tense information on /Ø/, only satisfies MC, and is thus preferred over O_{14} by MinSat). This illustrated in (48).

(48) *Third person singular present tense contexts* (version; harmonic
serialism, step 1):

I_1: [v work]: [•T•], [−1,+3,−pl,−past], {[T Ø], [T s], [T ed]}	Min Sat	RC	MC	Id F	Max 3	Max 1	Max Past	Max Pl	*Str
O_{11}: [v work]:[+1,+3,−pl,−past],[•T•]			*!		*	*	*	*	
☞O_{12}: [v work]:[−1,+3,−pl,−past]-Ø					*	*	*	*	*
O_{13}: [v work]:[−1,+3,−pl,−past]-s	*!					*	*		*
O_{14}: [v work]:[−1,+3,−pl,−past]-ed	*!			*	*	*		*	*

The next round of optimization then gives rise to a fatal consequence,
given the marker entries in (47). As shown in (49), when O_{121} violates
Max(Past) because /Ø/ is not specified as [−past] anymore, O_{123}, which
uses the incompatible exponent /ed/, can trigger a new constraint satisfaction (even though it cannot actually improve the constraint profile), and
it can do so in a more economical way than the intended winner O_{122} introducing /s/ (which triggers two new constraint satisfactions, of Max(3)
and of Max(Pl)); the fact that the new Max(Past) satisfaction by O_{123}
comes at the price of a violation of higher-ranked Id-F does not play a role
from the perspective of MinSat.

(49) *Third person singular present tense contexts* (version; harmonic
serialism, step 2):

I_{12}: [v work]:[−1,+3,−pl,−past]:-Ø, {[T s], [T ed]}	Min Sat	RC	MC	Id F	Max 3	Max 1	Max Past	Max Pl	*Str
☞O_{121}: [v work]:[−1,+3,−pl,−past]-Ø					*	*	*	*	
☆ O_{122}: [v work]:[−1,+3,−pl,−past]-Ø-s	*!					*	*		*
O_{123}: [v work]:[−1,+3,−pl,−past]-Ø-ed				*!	*	*		*	*

This, in a nutshell, is the problem: O_{123} in (49) cannot itself become
optimal (which would enable an output merging /s/ to become optimal
in a later optimization step), but its local new satisfaction of Max(past)
vis-à-vis output O_{121}, which keeps the input fully intact, suffices to block
the intended winner O_{122}, and effectively keeps the latter in limbo: The
derivation has now prematurely converged on the wrong final output: O_{121}.

In view of this state of affairs, two general possible conclusions suggest
themselves. First, for the case at hand, it can simply be assumed that the
morphological array underlying finite verb inflection in English is the one
incorporating the exponents in (40) (with tense features for all exponents)
and *not* the one based on the exponents in (47) (with tense features only
for the past exponent).

However, there is also a second, somewhat more principled solution,
and that is to revise MinSat (repeated here once more in (50)) in such a
way that the wrong prediction in (49) can be avoided.

(50) MinSat (Minimize Satisfaction):
      Assign * to an output O_i iff (a) and (b) hold.

   a. O_i has x new constraint satisfactions ($0 \leq x \leq n$).
   b.   There is an output O_j ($j \neq i$) in the same candidate set such
        that
        (i) O_j has y new constraint satisfactions ($0 \leq y \leq n$); and
        (ii) $0 < y < x$.

In fact, towards the end of chapter 3 (cf. pp. 157–159), I have discussed
three possible ways to restrict MinSat further, and thereby reduce its
empirical effects:

   1. O_j and O_i have to be part of the same local domain.
   2. O_j's new constraint satisfactions are a proper subset of O_i's new
      constraint satisfactions.
   3. O_j improves the constraint profile of the input.

As it turns out, the last two additions to the definition of MinSat in (50)
each suffice to ensure that O_{122} in (49) is not blocked by O_{123} via MinSat
(while being compatible with all the other analyses in this chapter). Adding
restriction 2 directly removes the MinSat violation of O_{122} because this
output's new constraint satisfactions are of Max(3) and Max(Pl) whereas
O_{123}'s new constraint satisfaction is one of Max(Past). Similarly, adding
restriction 3 has the desired effect since O_{123}'s constraint profile is actually
worse than the constraint profile of the input (which is also represented
by O_{121}). For the sake of concreteness, and even though it is not actually
required by the analysis currently under consideration as a solution to the
problem posed by (49), I will assume from now on that MinSat is modified
by integrating restriction 3 in addition, as in (51).

(51) MinSat (Minimize Satisfaction, revised):
      Assign * to an output O_i iff (a) and (b) hold.

   a. O_i has x new constraint satisfactions ($0 \leq x \leq n$).
   b.   There is an output O_j ($j \neq i$) in the same candidate set such
        that
        (i) O_j has y new constraint satisfactions ($0 \leq y \leq n$);
        (ii) $0 < y < x$; and
        (iii) O_j improves the constraint profile of the input.

This new version of MinSat solves the problem that would arise with (49)
if the inventory in (47) were postulated. More importantly, however, it
will be shown in the next section to be required for other contexts. The
following section sets out to address a question that is not directly related,

viz., that of combining disjunctive blocking and extended exponence on the basis of a single morphological array.

5. Disjunctive Blocking and Extended Exponence Intertwined

5.1. A Problem

So far, I have shown how the concepts of disjunctive blocking and extended exponence can be reconciled in principle: MinSat always favours the more general exponent, but repeated optimization eventually leads to the most specific exponent becoming optimal. On this view, the only remaining difference between disjunctive blocking and extended exponence based on a given morphological array containing two exponents ρ and ω is whether the newly optimal exponent introduced in the course of the derivation (ω in (52)) removes the previous optimal exponent (ρ in (52)), thereby giving rise to disjunctive blocking, or leaves it in place, which produces extended exponence.

(52) $[_\Sigma\ [_\Sigma\ [_\Sigma\ \Sigma\ ]\ \rho\ ]\ \omega\ ]$

However, closer inspection reveals that even in scenarios of extended exponence, where ρ and ω both survive, both ρ and ω may in principle be involved in disjunctive blocking relations with other exponents. This option does not yet follow from the analysis, which is based on the hypothesis that morphological arrays either have a [–F–] removal feature instantiated on all items (except for the least specific one) or do not come equipped with such a feature. If disjunctive blocking and extended exponence can be intertwined, a somewhat more flexible approach is needed.

I will look at two case studies suggesting (strongly in one case, more tentatively in the other) a co-existence of extended exponence and disjunctive blocking in a single morphological array: First, I address Udihe subject agreement marking; and after that, I return to case marking of German nouns, advancing a possible reanalysis of the material in chapter 3.

5.2. Disjunctive Blocking and Extended Exponence in Subject Agreement in Udihe

Subject agreement marking on verbs in the Tungusic language Udihe (see Nikolaeva & Tolskaya (2001)) involves extended exponence; simplifying somewhat, tense/mood information can show up on two distinct exponents in the language. Schematically, the verb stem (Σ in (52)) is accompanied by an exponent registering tense/mood information that may act like a stem extension (ρ in (52)), which in turn is followed by a subject agreement exponent that is not merely specified for person and number but is also sensitive to tense/mood information (ω in (52)).

Instantiations of the grammatical category tense/mood are PRS (present), SUBJ (subjunctive), PRF (perfect), FUT (future), PST (past), IMP (imperative), and several others; instantiations of the grammatical category person are 1. person, 2. person, 3. person, and 1. person inclusive; and instantiations of the grammatical category number are singular and plural.

The ρ slot does not necessarily host fully-fledged tense/mood categories throughout. First, ρ may employ a zero exponent. This is the present stem, used in PRS, SUBJ, FUT, and many other instantiations of tense/mood; this suggests massive underspecification. Second, ρ may host another exponent that is segmentally zero, but whose presence can be detected by suprasegmental effects that can be traced back to a floating mora μ; μ triggers lengthening of non-high stem-final vowels, and diphthongization of high vowels (/i/ and /u/; see Nikolaeva & Tolskaya (2001, 209)). This is the past stem, which is used in regular PST environments (and two further environments building on PST, viz., (i) active past participles and (ii) intensive). Third, ρ may be occupied by an abstract exponent /ge/ that is realized in this segmental form after high vowels, and as laryngealization of the stem-final vowel otherwise. This is the perfect stem, which is used in PRF contexts (and with perfective converbs); see Nikolaeva & Tolskaya (2001, 210). Furthermore, the zero-marked present stem can be extended by a variety of exponents in other tense/mood environments based on it, like subjunctive, imperative, future, or conditional contexts.[15]

Some complete tense/mood specifications that capture the contexts against which these exponent specifications are matched are given in (53) (note that this is just a selection; there are several more). For present purposes, it may suffice to postulate abstract primitive tense/mood features $[\pm\alpha]$, $[\pm\beta]$, $[\pm\gamma]$ that capture natural classes.

(53) *Tense/mood types*:

    a.   PRS: $[+\alpha,-\beta,-\gamma]$

    b.   SUBJ: $[+\alpha,+\beta,-\gamma]$

    c.   PRF: $[+\alpha,+\beta,+\gamma]$

    d.   FUT: $[+\alpha,-\beta,+\gamma]$

    e.   PAST: $[-\alpha,+\beta,-\gamma]$

---

[15] It should be noted that these regularities hold for verb stems of class I; verb stems of class II behave somewhat differently (but not in qualitatively different ways); they will be disregarded in what follows.

The tense/mood-based exponents for the ρ slot suggest underspecification, with the present stem exponent /Ø/ emerging as substantially underspecified. I assume that the tense/mood exponents in (54) receive the feature specifications indicated here.

(54) *Exponents for tense/mood:*
    a.   /Ø/ $\leftrightarrow$ [+α]
    b.   /Ø$^\mu$/ $\leftrightarrow$ [−α,+β,−γ]
    c.   /ge/ $\leftrightarrow$ [+α,+β,+γ]
    d.   /zA/ $\leftrightarrow$ [+α,+β,−γ]
    e.   /zAŋA/ $\leftrightarrow$ [+α,−β,+γ]

Here, /Ø/ can be viewed as the default exponent used in contexts where no other exponent is compatible (PRS). The fully specified PRF and PAST exponents /Ø$^\mu$/ and /ge/ have the potential to induce stem mutations; exponents like the SUBJ marker /zA/ and the FUT marker /zAŋA/ do not have this ability, and thus look like they are built on the basis of the present stem.[16]

Next, the agreement marking system in the second slot (ω) exhibits a lot of syncretism. First, the optimal exponents for some person/number combinations can be identical for some tense/mood specifications but not for others. This implies that some of the agreement exponents are underspecified with respect to tense/mood information. Furthermore, some of the agreement exponents show syncretism across different persons. This implies that there can be underspecification with respect to person as well. The distribution of the agreement exponents over PRS, SUBJ, PRF, FUT, and PAST tense/mood categories is shown in the two paradigms in (55), for singular and plural environments, respectively.

(55) a. *Singular:*

	PRS	SUBJ	PRF	FUT	PAST
1.SG	mi				mi
2.SG			i		
3.SG	ini/ili		Ø		ni

---

[16] As a matter of fact, since the present stem leaves the basic stem unchanged, it would in principle also have been possible to postulate a fully specified /Ø/ exponent ([+α,−β,−γ]), rather than an underspecified /Ø/ exponent, as in (54) ([+α]), in the analysis given below. At least for expository purposes, though, the present approach based on (54) seems preferable: It presupposes that there is disjunctive blocking in the ρ slot.

b.   *Plural:*

	PRS	SUBJ	PRF	FUT	PAST
1.PL.INCL	fi		ti_1	fi	
1.PL.EXCL					mu
2.PL	u				
3.PL	iti	du		ti_2	

Against the background of a Distributed Morphology approach, the paradigms in (55) have been given an analysis in terms of underspecification in Pyatigorskaya (2015). In what follows, I will for the most part follow her analysis, and confine myself to showing how it can be transferred to an approach based on harmonic serialism that incorporates MinSat.[17] The person and number features assumed by Pyatigorskaya are entirely standard: The cross-classification of $[\pm 1]$, $[\pm 2]$ yields the four persons active in Udihe; and $[\pm pl]$ can be assumed to capture the singular/plural distinction in the language.

The decomposed tense/mood features in (53) ensure that the instances of syncretism across tense/mood categories visible in (55) with agreement exponents in the second (ω) slot can be systematically derived. For instance, SUBJ and PRF qualify as a natural class that is referred to by the 3. person exponents /Ø/ (in the singular paradigm) and /du/ (in the plural paradigm); assuming that SUBJ is specified as $[+\alpha,+\beta,-\gamma]$ and PRF is specified as $[+\alpha,+\beta,+\gamma]$, /Ø/ and /du/ can be underspecified with respect to tense/mood information by only bearing the tense/mood features $[+\alpha,+\beta]$. Also, PRS, SUBJ, and PAST form a natural class referred to by the singular exponent /mi/. Assuming that PRS is specified as $[+\alpha,-\beta,-\gamma]$, SUBJ is specified as $[+\alpha,+\beta,-\gamma]$, and PAST as $[-\alpha,+\beta,-\gamma]$, /mi/ can be underspecified as $[-\gamma]$.

The complete set of agreement marker specifications is given in (56).

(56) *Exponents for person/number:*

    a.   /ini/ $\leftrightarrow [-1,-2,-pl,+\alpha,-\beta,-\gamma]$

    b.   /iti/ $\leftrightarrow [-1,-2,+pl,+\alpha,-\beta,-\gamma]$

---

[17] The one domain where I will not follow Pyatigorskaya's analysis concerns the handling of extended exponence as such: Pyatigorskaya (2015) assumes that there is separate post-syntactic realization (by vocabulary insertion) of separate tense (T) and agreement (Agr) morphemes; extended exponence is assumed to be brought about by a post-syntactic copying operation (enrichment; see Müller (2007a)) that provides the full set of tense/mood features on both heads. See chapter 3 for critical remarks on such a concept from the present perspective.

c.   /mu/ $\leftrightarrow$ [+1,–2,+pl,–α,+β,–γ]
d.   /ti$_1$/ $\leftrightarrow$ [+1,+2,+pl,+α,+β,+γ]
e.   /du/ $\leftrightarrow$ [–1,–2,+pl,+α,+β]
f.   /Ø/ $\leftrightarrow$ [–1,–2,–pl,+α,+β]
g.   /mi/ $\leftrightarrow$ [+1,–2,–pl,–γ]
h.   /ni/ $\leftrightarrow$ [–1,–2,–pl]
i.   /ti$_2$/ $\leftrightarrow$ [–1,–2]
j.   /fi/ $\leftrightarrow$ [+1,+2]
k.   /i/ $\leftrightarrow$ [–pl]
l.   /u/ $\leftrightarrow$ [+pl]

On the basis of the marker entries in (56), extended exponence arises in abundance, both of the partially superfluous type (in particular, this holds for those exponents in (56) that carry fully specified tense/mood information), and of the overlapping type (where underspecified tense/mood information is involved). In addition, some of the inflection markers in (56) do not give rise to extended exponence because they are not specified for tense/mood information at all.

Given the concept of morphological array adopted here (see (45) of chapter 3), it is clear that the tense/mood exponents bringing about extended stems in (54) and the ϕ exponents encoding person and number in (56) will all be part of a single morphological array. This morphological array can be captured by the categorial label [T]. At this point, the question arises how [–T–] features for exponent removal in disjunctive blocking contexts are distributed over the exponents in this morphological array – where they are absent, extended exponence will arise.

Suppose first that there were no [–T–] features whatsoever here. In that case, long sequences of exponents with increasing specificity (i.e., increasing numbers of MAX constraint satisfactions) would wrongly be expected to arise. Suppose next that all exponents in this morphological array, except for one maximally underspecified elsewhere exponent (perhaps /Ø/ in (54), or /u/ or /i/ in (56)), bear a [–T–] feature for structure removal. In that case, it would wrongly be predicted that there is no extended exponence, and only one exponent (i.e., the one that is most specific among the compatible ones) can survive in each context.

In view of this situation, I would like to introduce the concept of a *morphological subarray*, according to which the morphological array (see (45) of chapter 3) is further partitioned into two (or more) disjoint sets

of featurally homogeneous members.[18] For the case at hand, I would like
to suggest that the property giving rise to two separate subarrays in the
morphological array defined by T is the presence vs. absence of ϕ features
(person and/or number) on an exponent. Thus, one subarray of the morphological array defined by [T] in Udihe consists of the exponents in (54);
and another subarray of the same morphological array is composed of the
exponents in (56).

Of course, postulating morphological subarrays only has interesting effects if there are rules or constraints that refer to them. I assume subarrays
to have a dual function. First, they regulate the distribution of [–F–] features for removal of exponents classified as optimal in an earlier step. The
central claim here is that the least specific exponents in morphological subarrays are exempt from bearing a feature for structure removal. In the
case at hand, this holds for /Ø/ in the subarray based on absence of ϕ
feature information; and for /i/ and /u/ in the subarray based on person
and number information. This then implies that disjunctive blocking and
extended exponence can be interspersed in just the way that the data suggest: Within a morphological subarray, each new optimal exponent removes
another one that was earlier classified as optimal (which yields disjunctive
blocking); but there is no such removal outside the morphological subarray
(which permits extended exponence).

The second function of the morphological subarray is to provide a local
assembly of items that the derivation needs to comprehensively deal with
before it can move on to the next one. As with the inviolable constraint
EXHAUST NUMERATION (EXNUM) based on the concept of a numeration
in syntax (see (18) of chapter 1), and as with the inviolable constraint
EXHAUST MORPHOLOGICAL ARRAY (EXMORAR) based on the concept of
a morphological array in morphology (see (62) of chapter 3), I postulate
that there is an inviolable constraint EXHAUST SUBARRAY (EXS) based
on the concept of a morphological subarray which ensures that once a
given subarray has been accessed, the derivation disregards all exponents
of another subarray (for operations like Merge, but also for a constraint like
MINSAT) as long as the constraint profile can still be improved by accessing
the current subarray; see (57).

---

[18] See Chomsky (2000, 110) for the analogous distinction between a *lexical array* (or
numeration), which assembles lexical material underlying a complete derivation, and a
subarray, which only consists of items used in a given phase.

(57) EXHAUST SUBARRAY (ExS):
      An exponent from a morphological subarray S_j is not accessible if the
      current input has been derived by accessing a morphological subarray
      S_i (where i $\neq$ j, and S_i and S_j belong to the same morphological
      array) and the constraint profile of the input can be improved based
      on material from S_i.

On the basis of these assumptions, let me now go through a few harmonic
serialist derivations of verb inflection in Udihe that show how disjunctive
blocking can be combined with extended exponence. The constraints that
are of relevance in the analysis include inviolable ExS and MINSAT, RC
and MC, ID-F, a low-ranked constraint *STRUC banning structure-building
by morphological exponence, and MAX constraints for the features that are
involved: MAX(PL), MAX(1), MAX(2), plus three faithfulness constraints
for the abstract tense/mood features: MAX(α), MAX(β), MAX(γ). To
make extended exponence possible, the MAX constraints for tense/mood
features must outrank those for person and number.

As a first example, consider first person inclusive PRF environments. For
a verb stem *bu* ('give'), the correct final output in this context is *bu-ge-ti*. In
the first optimization step, MC needs to be satisfied, and given MINSAT,
this satisfaction must proceed in a way that minimizes new satisfaction
of MAX constraints. Consequently, a maximally non-specific exponent is
chosen; and given that MAX(α) outranks MAX(PL), this will have to be
/Ø/ rather than /i/ or /u/. This is illustrated in (58), where O_2 is selected as optimal over O_6 and O_7 (i.e., the only other candidates satisfying
MINSAT).[19]

---

[19] The two distinct subarrays are indicated here by subscripts – i for the non-ϕ exponents, and j for the ϕ exponents. Note also that the morphological array provided here is
not complete; in particular, many (pure) tense/mood exponents that extend the present
stem are ignored here, so as to enhance readability. For the same reason, features for
structure removal are not systematically indicated on exponents; but recall that only
three exponents do *not* come with a [–T–] feature, viz., /Ø/$_i$, /u/$_j$, and /i/$_j$ – the markers for which there is no less specific marker in the morphological subarray. Finally, I am
abstracting away here from alignment constraints, which guarantee that all exponents
(with one systematic exception that I will address below) have to emerge as suffixes.

(58)   *First person inclusive plural perfect contexts* (harmonic serialism, step 1):

Input I_0: [$_\mathrm{V}$ bu]: [•T•], [$+1,+2,+pl,+\alpha,+\beta,+\gamma$], {[$_{\mathrm{T}_i}$ Ø], [$_{\mathrm{T}_i}$ Ø$^\mu$], [$_{\mathrm{T}_i}$ ge], [$_{\mathrm{T}_i}$ zA], … [$_{\mathrm{T}_j}$ u], [$_{\mathrm{T}_j}$ i], [$_{\mathrm{T}_j}$ ni], [$_{\mathrm{T}_j}$ ti$_2$], [$_{\mathrm{T}_j}$ fi], [$_{\mathrm{T}_j}$ mi], [$_{\mathrm{T}_j}$ Ø], [$_{\mathrm{T}_j}$ du], [$_{\mathrm{T}_j}$ ti$_1$], [$_{\mathrm{T}_j}$ mu], [$_{\mathrm{T}_j}$ iti], [$_{\mathrm{T}_j}$ ini]}

Candidate	ExS	MinSat	RC	MC	IdF	Maxα	Maxβ	Maxγ	Max1	Max2	MaxPl	*Str
O_1: [$_\mathrm{V}$ bu]$_{:[+1,+2,+pl,+\alpha,+\beta,+\gamma]}$, [•T•]				*!		*	*	*	*	*	*	
☞ O_2: [$_\mathrm{V}$ bu]$_{:[+1,+2,+pl,\pm\alpha,+\beta,+\gamma]}$-Ø$_i$							*	*	*	*	*	*
O_3: [$_\mathrm{V}$ bu]$_{:[+1,+2,+pl,\pm\alpha,\pm\beta,\pm\gamma]}$-Ø$^\mu_i$		*!			**				*	*	*	*
O_4: [$_\mathrm{V}$ bu]$_{:[+1,+2,+pl,\pm\alpha,\pm\beta,\pm\gamma]}$-ge$_i$		*!							*	*	*	*
O_5: [$_\mathrm{V}$ bu]$_{:[+1,+2,+pl,\pm\alpha,\pm\beta,\pm\gamma]}$-zA$_i$		*!			*				*	*	*	*
O_6: [$_\mathrm{V}$ bu]$_{:[+1,+2,\pm pl,+\alpha,+\beta,+\gamma]}$-u$_j$					*!	*	*	*	*	*		*
O_7: [$_\mathrm{V}$ bu]$_{:[+1,+2,\pm pl,+\alpha,+\beta,+\gamma]}$-i$_j$					*!	*	*	*	*	*		*
O_8: [$_\mathrm{V}$ bu]$_{:[\pm1,\pm2,\pm pl,+\alpha,+\beta,+\gamma]}$-ni$_j$		*!			***	*	*	*				*
O_9: [$_\mathrm{V}$ bu]$_{:[\pm1,\pm2,+pl,+\alpha,+\beta,+\gamma]}$-ti$_{2j}$		*!			**	*	*	*			*	*
O_{9a}: [$_\mathrm{V}$ bu]$_{:[\pm1,\pm2,+pl,+\alpha,+\beta,+\gamma]}$-fi$_j$		*!				*	*	*			*	*
O_{9b}: [$_\mathrm{V}$ bu]$_{:[\pm1,\pm2,\pm pl,+\alpha,+\beta,\pm\gamma]}$-mi$_j$		*!			***	*	*					*
O_{9c}: [$_\mathrm{V}$ bu]$_{:[\pm1,\pm2,\pm pl,\pm\alpha,\pm\beta,+\gamma]}$-Ø$_j$		*!			***			*				*
O_{9d}: [$_\mathrm{V}$ bu]$_{:[\pm1,\pm2,\pm pl,\pm\alpha,\pm\beta,+\gamma]}$-du$_j$		*!			**			*				*
O_{9e}: [$_\mathrm{V}$ bu]$_{:[\pm1,\pm2,\pm pl,\pm\alpha,\pm\beta,\pm\gamma]}$-ti$_{1j}$		*!										*
O_{9f}: [$_\mathrm{V}$ bu]$_{:[\pm1,\pm2,\pm pl,\pm\alpha,\pm\beta,\pm\gamma]}$-mu$_j$		*!			***							*
O_{9g}: [$_\mathrm{V}$ bu]$_{:[\pm1,\pm2,\pm pl,\pm\alpha,\pm\beta,\pm\gamma]}$-iti$_j$		*!			****							*
O_{9h}: [$_\mathrm{V}$ bu]$_{:[\pm1,\pm2,\pm pl,\pm\alpha,\pm\beta,\pm\gamma]}$-ini$_j$		*!			*****							*

As a result, one subarray has been activated (viz., the one indicated by subscript i), and the other subarray (viz., the one signalled by subscript j) cannot be accessed at this point as long as further improvement based solely on the first subarray is possible. As shown in (59), where O_2 is used as the new input, this is indeed the case. Since improvement based on the currently activated subarray is still possible, all outputs based on the ϕ-related subarray (with subscript j) fatally violate ExS, and can thus be ignored in this competition; therefore, I confine myself to listing just two of these candidates.

(59)   *First person inclusive plural perfect contexts* (harmonic serialism, step 2):

Input I_2: [$_\mathrm{V}$ bu]–Ø$_i$ [$+1,+2,+pl,+\alpha,+\beta,+\gamma$], {[$_{\mathrm{T}_i}$ Ø$^\mu$], [$_{\mathrm{T}_i}$ ge], [$_{\mathrm{T}_i}$ zA], … [$_{\mathrm{T}_j}$ u], [$_{\mathrm{T}_j}$ i], [$_{\mathrm{T}_j}$ ni], [$_{\mathrm{T}_j}$ ti$_2$], [$_{\mathrm{T}_j}$ fi], [$_{\mathrm{T}_j}$ mi], [$_{\mathrm{T}_j}$ Ø], [$_{\mathrm{T}_j}$ du], [$_{\mathrm{T}_j}$ ti$_1$], [$_{\mathrm{T}_j}$ mu], [$_{\mathrm{T}_j}$ iti], [$_{\mathrm{T}_j}$ ini]}

Candidate	ExS	MinSat	RC	MC	IdF	Maxα	Maxβ	Maxγ	Max1	Max2	MaxPl	*Str
O_{21}: [$_\mathrm{V}$ bu]$_{:[+1,+2,+pl,\pm\alpha,+\beta,+\gamma]}$-Ø$_i$						*!	*	*	*	*		
O_{22}: [$_\mathrm{V}$ bu]$_{:[+1,+2,+pl,\pm\alpha,\pm\beta,\pm\gamma]}$-Ø$_i$-Ø$^\mu_i$					*!*				*	*	*	*
☞ O_{23}: [$_\mathrm{V}$ bu]$_{:[+1,+2,+pl,\pm\alpha,\pm\beta,\pm\gamma]}$-Ø$_i$-ge$_i$									*	*	*	*
O_{24}: [$_\mathrm{V}$ bu]$_{:[+1,+2,+pl,\pm\alpha,\pm\beta,\pm\gamma]}$-Ø$_i$-zA$_i$					*!				*	*	*	*
O_{25}: [$_\mathrm{V}$ bu]$_{:[+1,+2,\pm pl,\pm\alpha,+\beta,+\gamma]}$-Ø$_i$-u$_j$	*!						*	*	*	*		*
O_{26}: [$_\mathrm{V}$ bu]$_{:[\pm1,\pm2,+pl,\pm\alpha,\pm\beta,\pm\gamma]}$-Ø$_i$-ti$_{1j}$	*!	*										*

O_{23} is optimal in (59) because, by merging /ge/, it adds $\text{MAX}(\beta)$ and $\text{MAX}(\gamma)$ satisfactions to the $\text{MAX}(\alpha)$ satisfaction of the input, in line with MINSAT. Since /ge/ bears a $[-T-]$ feature, RC becomes active in the next step, where O_{23} is used as the new input; RC needs to be satisfied immediately by carrying out structure removal affecting the prior exponent. This is shown in (60).

(60) *First person inclusive plural perfect contexts* (harmonic serialism, step 3):

I_{23}: $[_V \text{bu}]$–$\varnothing_i$-$\text{ge}_{i[-T-]}$ $[+1,+2,+\text{pl},+\alpha,+\beta,+\gamma]$, $\{[_{T_i} \varnothing^\mu], [_{T_i} \text{zA}], \dots [_{T_j} \text{u}], [_{T_j} \text{i}], [_{T_j} \text{ni}], [_{T_j} \text{ti}_2], [_{T_j} \text{fi}], [_{T_j} \text{mi}], [_{T_j} \varnothing], [_{T_j} \text{du}], [_{T_j} \text{ti}_1], [_{T_j} \text{mu}], [_{T_j} \text{iti}], [_{T_j} \text{ini}]\}$	Ex S	Min Sat	R C	M C	Id F	Max α	Max β	Max γ	Max 1	Max 2	Max Pl	*Str
O_{231}: $[_V \text{bu}]_{:[+1,+2,+\text{pl},\underline{+\alpha,+\beta,+\gamma}]}$-$\varnothing_i$-$\text{ge}_{i[-T-]}$			*!						*	*	*	
O_{232}: $[_V \text{bu}]_{:[+1,+2,+\text{pl},\underline{+\alpha,+\beta,+\gamma}]}$-$\varnothing_i$							*!	*	*	*	*	
☞O_{233}: $[_V \text{bu}]_{:[+1,+2,+\text{pl},\underline{+\alpha,+\beta,+\gamma}]}$-$\text{ge}_i$									*	*	*	
O_{234}: $[_V \text{bu}]_{:[+1,+2,+\text{pl},\underline{+\alpha,+\beta,+\gamma}]}$-$\varnothing_i$-$\text{ge}_{i[-T-]}$-$\text{u}_j$	*!		*						*	*		*

Reflexive removal, as in O_{232}, is blocked by removal of the earlier exponent /Ø/, as in O_{233}, since /ge/ can maintain /Ø/'s $\text{MAX}(\alpha)$ satisfaction. At this stage, no further improvement is possible based on the first morphological subarray (identified by index i), and the derivation can now access exponents from the second morphological subarray (identified by index j), in accordance with ExS. (61) illustrates that the best operation at this point is to merge the least specific marker /u/ from the second subarray, which gives rise to improved behaviour of the candidate vis-à-vis $\text{MAX}(\text{PL})$; see O_{2332}. Adding another exponent from this subarray will either lead to a fatal ID-F violation (see O_{2333}), or will be excluded by MINSAT (see O_{2334}–O_{2339d}).

(61) *First person inclusive plural perfect contexts* (harmonic serialism, step 4):

I_{233}: [v bu]-ge$_i$ [+1,+2,+pl,+α,+β,+γ], {[T$_i$ Ø$^\mu$], [T$_i$ zA], ... [T$_j$ u], [T$_j$ i], [T$_j$ ni], [T$_j$ ti$_2$], [T$_j$ fi], [T$_j$ mi], [T$_j$ Ø], [T$_j$ du], [T$_j$ ti$_1$], [T$_j$ mu], [T$_j$ iti], [T$_j$ ini]}	Ex S	Min Sat	R C	M C	Id F	Max α	Max β	Max γ	Max 1	Max 2	Max Pl	*Str
O_{2331}: [v bu]:[+1,+2,+pl,±α,±β,±γ]-ge$_i$									*	*	*!	
☞ O_{2332}: [v bu]:[+1,+2,±pl,±α,±β,±γ]-ge$_i$-u$_j$									*	*		*
O_{2333}: [v bu]:[+1,+2,±pl,±α,±β,±γ]-ge$_i$-i$_j$					*!				*	*		*
O_{2334}: [v bu]:[±1,±2,+pl,±α,±β,±γ]-ge$_i$-ni$_j$		*!			***							*
O_{2335}: [v bu]:[±1,±2,+pl,±α,±β,±γ]-ge$_i$-ti$_{2j}$		*!			**						*	*
O_{2336}: [v bu]:[±1,±2,+pl,±α,±β,±γ]-ge$_i$-fi$_j$		*!									*	*
O_{2337}: [v bu]:[±1,±2,±pl,±α,±β,±γ]-ge$_i$-mi$_j$		*!			***							*
O_{2338}: [v bu]:[±1,±2,±pl,±α,±β,±γ]-ge$_i$-Ø$_j$		*!			***							*
O_{2339}: [v bu]:[±1,±2,±pl,±α,±β,±γ]-ge$_i$-du$_j$		*!			**							*
O_{2339a}: [v bu]:[±1,±2,±pl,±α,±β,±γ]-ge$_i$-ti$_{1j}$		*!										*
O_{2339b}: [v bu]:[±1,±2,±pl,±α,±β,±γ]-ge$_i$-mu$_j$		*!			***							*
O_{2339c}: [v bu]:[±1,±2,±pl,±α,±β,±γ]-ge$_i$-iti$_j$		*!			****							*
O_{2339d}: [v bu]:[±1,±2,±pl,±α,±β,±γ]-ge$_i$-ini$_j$		*!			*****							*

Since /u/$_j$, as a maximally non-specific exponent of the second morphological subarray, does not bear a [–T–] feature for structure removal, RC is vacuously satisfied when O_{2332} is used as the new input. Min Sat now permits the next optimal candidate to add /fi/$_j$ (as in O_{23322}) or /ti$_1$/$_j$ (as in O_{23323}); see (62).[20]

(62) *First person inclusive plural perfect contexts* (harmonic serialism, step 5):

I_{2332}: [v bu]-ge$_i$-u$_j$ [+1,+2,+pl,+α,+β,+γ], {[T$_i$ Ø$^\mu$], [T$_i$ zA], ... [T$_j$ i], [T$_j$ ni], [T$_j$ ti$_2$], [T$_j$ fi], [T$_j$ mi], [T$_j$ Ø], [T$_j$ du], [T$_j$ ti$_1$], [T$_j$ mu], [T$_j$ iti], [T$_j$ ini]}	Ex S	Min Sat	R C	M C	Id F	Max α	Max β	Max γ	Max 1	Max 2	Max Pl	*Str
O_{23321}: [v bu]:[+1,+2,±pl,±α,±β,±γ]-ge$_i$-u$_j$									*	*		
☞ O_{23322}: [v bu]:[±1,±2,±pl,±α,±β,±γ]-ge$_i$-u$_j$-fi$_j$												*
☞ O_{23323}: [v bu]:[±1,±2,±pl,±α,±β,±γ]-ge$_i$-u$_j$-ti$_{1j}$												*

Note, however, that even though /fi/$_j$ and /ti$_1$/$_j$ both lead to full satisfaction of all Max constraints in interaction with /ge/$_i$ and /u/$_j$, there is a crucial difference between the two new ϕ exponents in (62): /ti$_1$/$_j$ can maintain /u/$_j$'s Max(Pl) satisfaction if the latter exponent goes away

---

[20] To simplify exposition, all outputs that give rise to Id-F violations are here left out of this and the following tableaux, even where the Id-F violation's fatality is masked by a violation of the higher-ranked Min Sat constraint (i.e., with highly specific exponents that do not meet the compatibility requirement).

again; but $/\text{fi}/_j$ cannot do so. Consequently, in a continuation based on O_{23322}, the constraint profile in the MAX area deteriorates again temporarily: Exponent removal needs to take place so as to satisfy the $[-\text{T}-]$ feature on $/\text{fi}/_j$; cf. (63), where O_{23322} acts as the new input.

(63) *First person inclusive plural perfect contexts* (harmonic serialism, step 6-a):

I_{23322}: $[\text{v bu}]\text{-ge}_i\text{-u}_j\text{-fi}_{j[-\text{T}-]}$ $[+1,+2,+\text{pl},+\alpha,+\beta,+\gamma]$, $\{[_{\text{T}_i} \varnothing^\mu], [_{\text{T}_i} \text{zA}], \ldots$ $[_{\text{T}_j} \text{i}], [_{\text{T}_j} \text{ni}], [_{\text{T}_j} \text{ti}_2],$ $[_{\text{T}_j} \text{mi}], [_{\text{T}_j} \varnothing], [_{\text{T}_j} \text{du}],$ $[_{\text{T}_j} \text{ti}_1], [_{\text{T}_j} \text{mu}], [_{\text{T}_j} \text{iti}], [_{\text{T}_j} \text{ini}]\}$	Ex S	Min Sat	R C	M C	Id F	Max α	Max β	Max γ	Max 1	Max 2	Max Pl	* Str
O_{233221}: $[\text{v bu}]_{:[\pm 1,\pm 2,+\text{pl},+\alpha,\pm\beta,\pm\gamma]}\text{-ge}_i\text{-u}_j\text{-fi}_{j[-\text{T}-]}$			*!									
O_{233222}: $[\text{v bu}]_{:[+1,+2,\pm\text{pl},\pm\alpha,\pm\beta,\pm\gamma]}\text{-ge}_i\text{-u}_j$									*!	*		
☞O_{233223}: $[\text{v bu}]_{:[\pm 1,\pm 2,+\text{pl},\pm\alpha,\pm\beta,\pm\gamma]}\text{-ge}_i\text{-fi}_j$											*	

There is one further potential RC-compatible output competing with those in (63) based on removal of $/\text{u}/_j$ and self-removal of $/\text{fi}/_j$ that needs to be excluded, viz., a candidate that removes the *initial* exponent /ge/. In the case at hand, such an output would straightforwardly be ruled out because it would yield a suboptimal constraint profile (with fatal violations of MAX constraints for primitive tense/mood features reappearing). However, independently of this consideration, recall from page 170 that such cases of non-local removal are at variance with the STRICT CYCLE CONDITION (alternatively, minimality constraints; see footnote 9 above).

Thus, O_{233223} is taken as the new input for the next optimization procedure; and given that this input still violates MAX(PL), further improvement is possible. Focussing, as before, exclusively on exponents whose addition respects ID-F, there is now one competing output left: $O_{2332232}$ merges $/\text{ti}_1/_j$ from the second subarray; this step is compatible with MINSAT, and emerges as optimal since $/\text{ti}_1/_j$ can maintain both $/\text{fi}/_j$'s satisfactions of MAX(1) and MAX(2), *and* the original satisfaction of MAX(PL) by the earlier marker $/\text{u}/_j$. This is shown in (64) and (65).

(64) *First person inclusive plural perfect contexts* (harmonic serialism, step 7-a):

I_{233223}: $[\text{v bu}]\text{-ge}_i\text{-fi}_j$ $[+1,+2,+\text{pl},+\alpha,+\beta,+\gamma]$, $\{[_{\text{T}_i} \varnothing^\mu], [_{\text{T}_i} \text{zA}], \ldots$ $[_{\text{T}_j} \text{i}], [_{\text{T}_j} \text{ni}], [_{\text{T}_j} \text{ti}_2],$ $[_{\text{T}_j} \text{mi}], [_{\text{T}_j} \varnothing], [_{\text{T}_j} \text{du}],$ $[_{\text{T}_j} \text{ti}_1], [_{\text{T}_j} \text{mu}], [_{\text{T}_j} \text{iti}], [_{\text{T}_j} \text{ini}]\}$	Ex S	Min Sat	R C	M C	Id F	Max α	Max β	Max γ	Max 1	Max 2	Max Pl	* Str
$O_{2332231}$: $[\text{v bu}]_{:[\pm 1,\pm 2,+\text{pl},\pm\alpha,\pm\beta,\pm\gamma]}\text{-ge}_i\text{-fi}_j$											*!	
☞$O_{2332232}$: $[\text{v bu}]_{:[\pm 1,\pm 2,\pm\text{pl},\pm\alpha,\pm\beta,\pm\gamma]}\text{-ge}_i\text{-fi}_j\text{-ti}_{1j}$												*

The new exponent brings with it a [–T–] feature for structure removal. Therefore, in the next step, RC becomes active for the new input $I_{2332232}$, and self-removal of $/ti_1/_j$ is blocked in favour of removal of the prior exponent $/fi/_j$; see the tableau in (65).

(65) *First person inclusive plural perfect contexts* (harmonic serialism, step 8-a):

$I_{2332232}$: $[_V \text{bu}]$-ge_i-fi_j-ti_{1j} $[+1,+2,+pl,+\alpha,+\beta,+\gamma]$, $\{[_{T_i} \varnothing^\mu], [_{T_i} zA], \dots [_{T_j} i], [_{T_j} ni], [_{T_j} ti_2], [_{T_j} mi], [_{T_j} \varnothing], [_{T_j} du], [_{T_j} mu], [_{T_j} iti], [_{T_j} ini]\}$	Ex S	Min Sat	R C	M C	Id F	Max α	Max β	Max γ	Max 1	Max 2	Max Pl	*Str
$O_{23322321}$: $[_V \text{bu}]_{:[+1,+2,+pl,+\alpha,+\beta,+\gamma]}$-$ge_i$-$fi_j$-$ti_{1j}$			*!									
$O_{23322322}$: $[_V \text{bu}]_{:[+1,+2,+pl,+\alpha,+\beta,+\gamma]}$-$ge_i$-$fi_j$											*	
☞ $O_{23322323}$: $[_V \text{bu}]_{:[+1,+2,+pl,+\alpha,+\beta,+\gamma]}$-$ge_i$-$ti_{1j}$												

Since the new optimal output does not violate any of the relevant constraints anymore, it is clear that convergence will be reached in the next, and final, optimization procedure. Of course, given that O_{23323} is also optimal in step 5 in (62), there is another continuation leading to the same eventual form in a more direct way: Structure removal applies to $/u_j/$ in I_{23323} in step 6-b (not shown here). Schematically, the sequence of optimization procedures can be illustrated by the diagram in (66).

(66) *First person inclusive plural perfect contexts – derivation:*

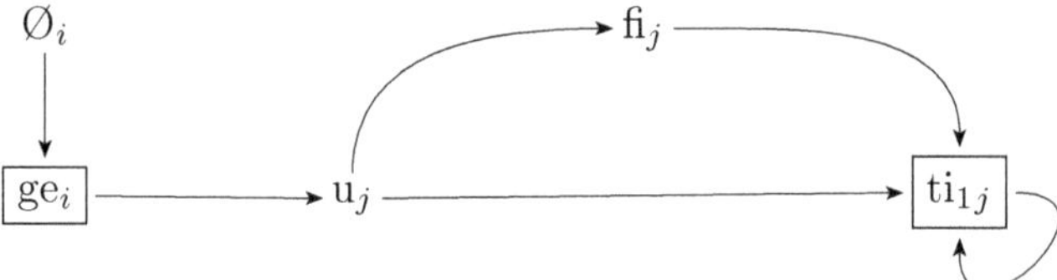

At this point, one may ask oneself whether the new constraint ExS is actually needed for the analysis to work. In the optimization steps 2 (see (59)) and 3 (see (60)), ExS does indeed exclude certain outputs. However, most of these outputs (cf. O_{26} in (59), O_{234} in (60)) would be independently blocked because of fatal MinSat or RC violations. Things are different with O_{25} in (59); if ExS did not hold, this output (which, by prematurely merging $/u/_j$, would minimize new constraint satisfactions, adding only a satisfaction of Max(Pl) but thereby improving the input's constraint profile) would block nearly all the other ones (except for the one adding $/i/_j$, which violates Id-F), among them the intended winner O_{23}, which merges $/ge/_i$ (and thus gives rise to two new Max constraint satisfactions, as opposed to only one new constraint satisfaction induced by $/u/_j$). However, whether or not relying on ExS would pose severe problems in this case would depend on what assumptions are made about $/\mathrm{u}/_j$ and structure removal: If $/\mathrm{u}/_j$ does not have a $[-\mathrm{T}-]$ feature (as assumed throughout), $/\emptyset/$ is wrongly predicted to be fixed once and for all as a tense/mood exponent in this context; if it does, self-removal will ensue, which solves this particular problem but requires additional stipulations about which items do not come equipped with a removal feature in environments that mix extended exponence and disjunctive blocking. Furthermore, early self-removal of $/\mathrm{u}/_j$ in the presence of $/\emptyset/_i$ would also have negative consequences in environments where $/\mathrm{u}/_j$ needs to be part of the final optimal output (like all 2. person plural contexts, and most 1. person exclusive plural contexts) – recall that an item that is taken from the morphological array and subsequently removed will never have a chance to reappear in the derivation. For these reasons, I conclude that ExS does not just suggest itself on the basis of conceptual considerations (given the existence of ExNum and ExMorAr) but is also empirically motivated.

From a more general perspective, one may also ask whether ExS threatens to undermine the present account of extended exponence, by implicitly reintroducing a stratal account like the one discussed, and rejected, in chapter 3. This is not the case. The arguments for (i) harmonic serialism and (ii) MinSat in an account of phenomena involving extended exponence are not affected by the existence of ExS: As before, an approach in terms of standard parallel optimality theory ceteris paribus makes wrong predictions by prohibiting the first (more general) exponent in favour of the second (more specific) exponent in this case of partially superfluous extended exponence. Thus, under standard parallel optimality theory, the optimal output would wrongly be predicted to be *bu-ti* rather than *bu-ge-ti*. Also, as before, without MinSat an approach in terms of harmonic serialism would ceteris paribus give rise to the same fatal consequence (because it would favour initial selection of the most specific exponent from the second subarray, thereby invariably blocking the more general exponent from the first subarray for the remainder of the derivation). Thus, ExS itself does not contribute to an account of extended exponence, in stark contrast to the concept of a stratum.

Let me consider some other environments in Udihe subject agreement (albeit in less detail). In first person singular present tense contexts, the features associated with the V stem in the numeration are $[+1,-2,-\mathrm{pl},+\alpha, -\beta,-\gamma]$. Here the analysis proceeds as schematically depicted in (67).

(67) *First person singular present tense contexts – derivation:*

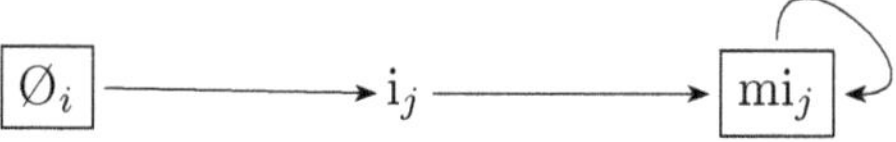

As before, $/\emptyset/_i$ is merged first (given MinSat, and given that Max(Pl) is outranked by Max(α)). This time, though, the derivation cannot proceed to a more specific exponent in the i-subarray; the reason is that all available exponents are incompatible with the target tense/mood specification [$+\alpha$, $-\beta,-\gamma$]. Thus, the derivation moves to the j-subarray, merging the maximally general marker $/i/_j$ first (both $/i/_j$ and $/u/_j$ lead to only one new constraint satisfaction, viz., of Max(Pl), and are thus favoured by Min-Sat, but in the present context $/u/_j$ triggers a fatal Id-F violation). Next, $/mi/_j$ is merged, bearing the features [$+1,-2,-pl,-\gamma$], and subsequently replacing less specific $/i/_j$. Finally, the derivation converges; the eventual inflected word for a stem like *bu* ('give') is *bu-$\emptyset$-mi*. Again, there is a kind of extended exponence, but it is not even one of the overlapping type: $/\emptyset/_i$ and $/mi/_j$ both bear tense/mood features, but $/\emptyset/_i$ realizes [$+\alpha$], whereas $/mi/_j$ realizes [$-\gamma$] ($/mi/_j$ can also appear in PAST environments, and can thus not be specified as [$+\alpha$] since PAST is specified as [$-\alpha,+\beta,-\gamma$]).

Recall now that at the end of section 4 I proposed a revision of MinSat in (51) according to which an output O_j can block another output O_i with fewer new constraint satisfactions only if O_j itself improves the input's constraint profile. I noted there that this additional assumption might not be absolutely necessary for the data discussed in section 4, but will become indispensable in the present section. The derivation in (67) makes it clear why this is so. The step from $/i/_j$ to $/mi/_j$ involves a bigger leap (in the sense of section 4 above): Merging $/mi/_j$ gives rise to three new constraint satisfactions (of Max(1), Max(2), and Max(γ)). However, there are competing exponents, like $/fi/_j$ (which is specified as [$+1,+2$] only), which trigger fewer new constraint satisfactions (only of Max(1) and Max(2), to be precise). Consequently, without clause (51-b-iii), we would end up with the fatal consequence that an output introducing less specific $/fi/_j$ in the presence of $/i/_j$ would invariably block the intended winner introducing more specific $/mi/_j$ without ever having a chance of becoming (temporarily) optimal itself, due to a high-ranked Id-F violation ([$+1,+2$] on $/fi/_j$ is incompatible with the target specification [$+1,-2$]). As a result, the derivation would converge on the input, and $/i/_j$ would wrongly be expected to be the final optimal exponent for the person/number (ω) slot. All of this is shown in the tableau in (68), which zooms in on the derivation at the stage where $/i/_j$ has successfully been merged in the previous step, and is now part of the input.

(68) *An argument for modifying* MINSAT *by adding (51-b-iii)* (harmonic serialism):

I_{122}: [v bu]-Ø$_i$-i$_j$, $[+1,-2,-pl,+\alpha,-\beta,-\gamma]$, {[T$_i$ Ø$^\mu$], [T$_i$ ge], [T$_i$ zA], ... [T$_j$ u], [T$_j$ ni], [T$_j$ ti$_2$], [T$_j$ fi], [T$_j$ mi], [T$_j$ Ø], [T$_j$ du], [T$_j$ ti$_1$], [T$_j$ mu], [T$_j$ iti], [T$_j$ ini]}	Ex S	Old Min Sat	R C	M C	Id F	Max α	Max β	Max γ	Max 1	Max 2	Max Pl	* Str
☞ O_{1221}: [v bu]:$[+1,-2,\underline{-pl},\underline{+\alpha},-\beta,-\gamma]$-Ø$_i$-i$_j$							*	*	*	*		
☆ O_{1222}: [v bu]:$[+1,-2,\underline{-pl},\underline{+\alpha},-\beta,\underline{-\gamma}]$-Ø$_i$-i$_j$-mi$_j$		*!					*					*
O_{1223}: [v bu]:$[+1,-2,\underline{-pl},\underline{+\alpha},-\beta,\underline{-\gamma}]$-Ø$_i$-i$_j$-fi$_j$					*!		*	*				*

The requirement (51-b-iii) in the revised MINSAT constraint solves this problem: O_{1223} cannot block O_{1222} via MINSAT because O_{1223} does not improve the constraint profile of the input (due to the ID-F violation); hence, O_{1222} can become optimal instead of O_{1221}.

As a third example, consider first person exclusive plural past tense contexts. Here the derivation proceeds as illustrated in (69).

(69) *First person exclusive plural past tense contexts – derivation:*

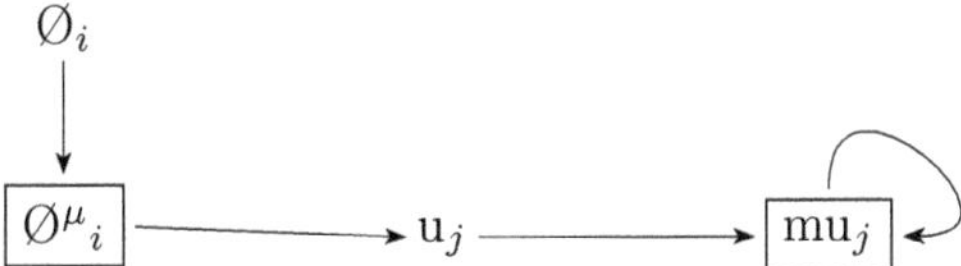

Again, this instantiates partially superfluous extended exponence: The tense/mood features that /Ø$^\mu$/$_i$ contributes (viz., $[-\alpha,+\beta,-\gamma]$) are all also available from /mu/$_j$, which bears ϕ features in addition (it is a fully specified exponent marked $[+1,-2,+pl,-\alpha,+\beta,-\gamma]$). The final output form for the verb stem *bu* ('give') is *bu-oː-mu* (< *bu-Ø$^\mu$-mu*).

Finally, third person plural perfect scenarios ($[-1,-2,+pl,+\alpha,+\beta,+\gamma]$) produce an interesting effect. The optimal exponents for the ρ and ω slots are /ge/$_i$ ($[+\alpha,+\beta,+\gamma]$) and /du/$_j$ ($[-1,-2,+pl,+\alpha,+\beta]$), respectively; and the derivation that generates inflected words with these exponents is given in (70).

(70) *Third person plural perfect contexts – derivation:*

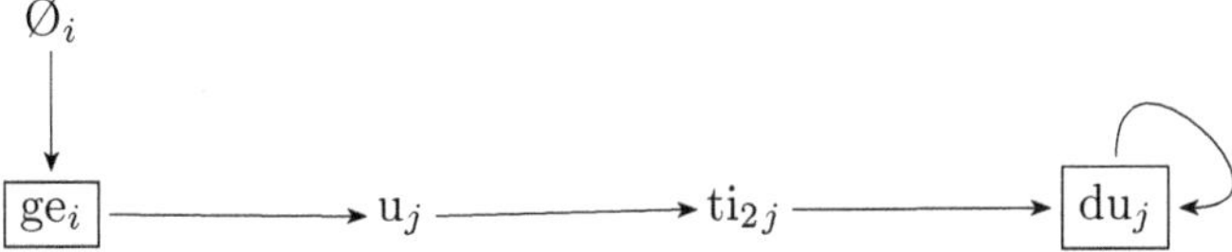

For the verb stem *bu* ('give'), one would therefore be led to expect the final form to be **bu-ge-du*. However, this is not the right output; rather, there is a local permutation affecting the two inflectional exponents, with the output form that is eventually optimal emerging as *bu-du-ge*. The same effect also arises in third person plural subjunctive environments (which use the same ϕ marker in this context: /du/). As argued in Nikolaeva & Tolskaya (2001) and Pyatigorskaya (2015), there is reason not to assume that this exponent reversal is phonologically conditioned. Against the background of what was said about movement in morphology in chapter 2 and 3 (and what will be said about this issue in the next chapter), it is clear that such an effect does not need to be regarded as a peculiarity; it can be integrated straightforwardly into the overall system. Various possibilities to implement the reversal suggest themselves; for present purposes, it may suffice to adopt the linearization constraint in (71) (again, cf. Ryan (2010) on bigram constraints, and in particular the precedence constraints employed in a lot of work on word order variation in syntax).

(71) $3{\Leftarrow}\mathrm{T}$:
    A $[-1,-2]$ exponent precedes a $[+\alpha,+\beta]$ exponent.

The features $[+\alpha,+\beta]$ capture the natural class of PRF and SUBJ, which both show the reversal effect. Furthermore, in the general way it is formulated in (71), the constraint does not just apply to the plural exponent /du/ ($[-1,-2,+\mathrm{pl},+\alpha,+\beta]$), but also the the singular exponent /Ø/ ($[-1,-2,-\mathrm{pl},+\alpha,+\beta]$). In other words: The analysis also postulates a reversal in third person singular contexts where, however, it cannot be easily detected because one of the two markers involved is phonologically null. I take this to be entirely unproblematic.[21]   That said, it would also be unproblematic to minimally complicate (71) by adding the information $[+\mathrm{pl}]$. Finally, it needs to be ensured that $3{\Leftarrow}\mathrm{T}$ is ranked below the MAX constraints that bring about concatenation of /du/ (and /Ø/) with the extended stem that already has /ge/ at its right edge: Given the STRICT CYCLE CONDITION, it is impossible to satisfy $3{\Leftarrow}\mathrm{T}$ by adding /du/ (/Ø/) as a suffix; but this violation is then repaired by moving /ge/ to the right.

5.3.   Disjunctive Blocking and Extended Exponence in Case Marking in German

Recall the account of extended exponence of plural in German nouns developed in section 5.2. of chapter 3: As shown by the sequence of optimization procedures in (50)–(52) of that chapter, first a plural marker is added that

---

[21] Note also that $3{\Leftarrow}\mathrm{T}$ cannot trigger inversion of other third person exponents (/ini/, /iti/, /ni/, /ti$_2$/) because these exponents do not show up in $[+\alpha,+\beta]$ contexts.

matches the inflection class of the noun stem (e.g., /er/ is merged with the noun stem /Kind/, yielding *Kind-er*) and satisfies MAX(PL). Then a dative plural marker (/n/) is attached to the extended stem (giving rise to the word form *Kind-er-n* in the case at hand) that manages to satisfy MAX(OBL) and MAX(GOV) but in addition, from a global perspective, would alone have sufficed to also satisfy MAX(PL) since the two exponents must belong to one and the same morphological array (captured by the feature [cn]) – this fact produces a problem for standard parallel optimality theory (see (53), (54)) but is fully expected under the present approach in terms of harmonic serialism. Finally, convergence is reached. I would like to contend that this analysis works well as such as an account of this particular instance of extended exponence.

However, as noted in footnote 29 of chapter 3, as it stands, the analysis rests on the assumption that whereas inflection class information on a noun stem requires compatibility as regards inflection class information on a plural exponent, inflection class information, by itself, cannot act as a *trigger* for inflection, via MAX constraints. In this respect, inflection class information is unlike other instantiations of grammatical categories, which, as we have seen in numerous cases, can act as triggers of exponence, based on MAX constraints. This conclusion may well be tenable (and arguably receives independent support based on the observation that inflection class features are purely morphomic whereas features capturing other grammatical categories play a role in both morphology and syntax). Still, the reasoning presupposes that there is no decomposition and underspecification with respect to inflection class, and there is some evidence that this may not be correct since the phenomenon of syncretism *across* inflection classes (i.e., transparadigmatic syncretism) is widespread and often systematic; see, again, footnote 29 in chapter 3.

As a matter of fact, there is also transparadigmatic syncretism with plural exponents belonging to different inflection classes in German (see Wiese (2000) and Alexiadou & Müller (2008), among others). This is illustrated for a number of different plural exponents occurring with Ns belonging to different inflection classes (as evidenced by different patterns of exponence in the singular) in (72).[22]

---

[22] To simplify exposition, I continue to abstract away from umlaut, here in and what follows. As observed by Wiese (2000), eventually two /e/ exponents need to be postulated – one which triggers umlaut (with both the masculine and the feminine inflection classes that it can be part of), and one which systematically does not (with the masculine, neuter, and feminine inflection classes that it can show up in). In contrast, the plural exponent /n/ never induces umlaut; and the plural exponent /er/ always does.

(72) *Syncretism within and across inflection classes in German:*

	I	II	III	IV	V	VI	VII	VIII
	Hund$_m$ (dog) *Schaf$_n$* (sheep)	*Maus$_f$* (mouse) *Drangsal$_f$* (distress)	*Strahl$_m$* (ray) *Auge$_n$* (eye)	*Ziege$_f$* (goat)	*Planet$_m$* (planet) *Dirigent$_m$* (conductor)	*Buch$_n$* (book) *Mann$_m$* (man)	*Pizza$_f$* (pizza)	*Park$_m$* (park)
NOM/SG	Ø	Ø	Ø	Ø	Ø	Ø	Ø	Ø
ACC/SG	Ø	Ø	Ø	Ø	n$_2$	Ø	Ø	Ø
GEN/SG	s$_2$	Ø	s$_2$	Ø	n$_2$	s$_2$	Ø	s$_2$
NOM/PL	e	e	n	n	n	er	s	s

There are four different plural markers (but cf. the remarks in the last
footnote), and three of these show up in more than one inflection class (as
is clear from the fact that different inflection markers can be chosen in genitive and, in one case, accusative/dative environments). In view of this state
of affairs, a straightforward way to maintain a unique feature specification
for each of the four plural markers is to assume that inflection class features
(like I–VIII in (72)) are decomposed into more primitive features, so that
the plural exponents that exhibit transparadigmatic syncretism – /e/, /n/,
and /s/ – can be underspecified with respect to this information.[23] Thus,
suppose that inflection classes in German noun declension are composed of
three abstract, primitive inflection class features, which can be called $[\pm\alpha]$,
$[\pm\beta]$, $[\pm\gamma]$; see Alexiadou & Müller (2008).[24] Whereas a cross-classification

---

Also note that m, f, and n in (72) stand for masculine, feminine, and neuter, respectively.

[23] One might assume that another way out would be to postulate that the different
inflectional patterns arising with one and the same plural marker do not involve genuine
inflection classes but rather gender-related distinctions within what would then be a
single inflection class; see Carstairs (1983; 1987), Carstairs-McCarthy (1986) for such
a proposal (under the label of "macroparadigm"), but also Müller (2007b) for critical
comments. While such an enterprise might not be inherently doomed to fail, it faces a
serious challenge with the plural exponent /n/, which shows up both with "strong" masculine nouns like *Strahl* ('ray') and with "weak" masculine nouns like *Planet* ('planet')
and *Dirigent* ('conductor'), where, as (72) shows, the inflectional patterns are very different in the presence of identical gender information. (Eisenberg (2000a) has argued that
weak masculine nouns might actually count as a separate "fourth gender" in German,
but this assessment is obviously incorrect, essentially because gender is a grammatical
category that is defined purely syntactically, by the behaviour of items in the syntactic
context with respect to operations like agreement, concord, or pronominal resumption –
but with weak and strong masculine nouns in German, no differences with respect to
such operations can ever be detected; see Hoberg (2004), among others.)

[24] These features are not to be confused with the features introduced in the previous
section for Udihe tense/mood categories. In the former case, these features encoded

of these features yields the fully specified individual inflection classes, underspecification with respect to abstract inflection class feature information captures natural classes of inflection classes, and thereby makes a systematic account of the transparadigmatic syncretism visible in (72) possible.

For concreteness, the eight inflection classes in (72) can be assumed to exhibit the fine structure in (73).

(73) *Decomposed inflection class features in German noun declension:*

a.

I	II
$[-\alpha,+\beta,+\gamma]$	$[-\alpha,-\beta,+\gamma]$

b.

III	IV	V
$[+\alpha,+\beta,+\gamma]$	$[+\alpha,-\beta,+\gamma]$	$[+\alpha,+\beta,-\gamma]$

c.

VI
$[+\alpha,-\beta,-\gamma]$

d.

VII	VIII
$[-\alpha,+\beta,-\gamma]$	$[-\alpha,-\beta,-\gamma]$

The number markers can then be underspecified, capturing natural classes of inflection classes, as in (74).[25]

(74) *Exponents for number:*

a. $/\emptyset/ \leftrightarrow [-]$
b. $/n/ \leftrightarrow [+\text{pl}], [+\alpha]$
c. $/e/ \leftrightarrow [+\text{pl}], [-\alpha,+\gamma]$
d. $/s/ \leftrightarrow [+\text{pl}], [-\alpha,-\gamma]$
e. $/er/ \leftrightarrow [+\text{pl}], [+\alpha,-\beta,-\gamma]$

Under these assumptions, extended exponence of plural in dative plural environments with nouns in German must also involve disjunctive blocking;

---

meaningful aspects of a grammatical category that is relevant in the syntax; in the case at hand, the features encode abstract, meaningless aspects of a morphomic grammatical category that is irrelevant outside of the morphological component.

[25] There is disagreement in the literature as to what counts as the default (elsewhere) plural exponent in the system of German noun inflection. Clahsen (1999) and Pinker (1999) identify /s/ as the default marker (also see Wiese (1996)); in contrast, Wurzel (1998), Wunderlich (1999), and Wegener (1999) postulate that /e/ is the default marker. I here follow Alexiadou & Müller (2008), where it is proposed that /n/ is the elsewhere exponent. Note that this issue, while ultimately important, is orthogonal to my present concerns – as long as there is *some* elsewhere plural exponent that is compatible with many (or all) relevant environments, disjunctive blocking will become relevant.

i.e., the two phenomena are again interspersed. Therefore, the morphological array defined by the feature Cn that includes number exponents, case exponents, and exponents that combine the two grammatical categories (in particular, the dative plural /n/ that is at the heart of the analysis of extended exponence in chapter 3), must be divided into two subarrays – one for number (corresponding to the set of markers in (74), and signalled by an index i), and one for case (signalled by index j). The decisive feature distinguishing the subarrays is whether case information is present on a marker or not. The zero marker in (74-a) is a radically underspecified elsewhere exponent that only bears the categorial feature [Cn] sought for by the N stem's [•Cn•] feature; thus, this exponent will always be merged first (given MinSat). Furthermore, given the conventions introduced in the previous section, /Ø/ in (74) is not associated with a structure remvoval feature [–Cn–], whereas the other exponents in (74) are. As for the exponents in the morphological subarray based on case specification (essentially, genitive singular /s/, and accusative/genitive/dative singular /n/ in (72), archaic dative singular /e/, and dative plural /n/), I will assume that none of them is equipped with a more general application domain than the one where it can actually be observed in well-formed outputs; in other words, there is no competition, and hence no need for a means to bring about disjunctive blocking, here. Consequently, these exponents all lack [–Cn–] features.[26]

On this view, the derivation producing optimal exponents /er/ and /n/ in dative plural contexts of a noun stem like *Kind* ('child') does not exactly look as in (50)–(52) of chapter 3; rather, it takes the form shown on the following pages.[27]

In the first step, the maximally underspecified exponent /Ø/ is merged with N. Output O_2 is selected by MinSat because it gives rise to a satisfaction of high-ranked MC (by discharging N's [•Cn•] feature) without introducing a new satisfaction of any other relevant constraint violated by the input – in particular, due to maximal underspecification of /Ø/, there is no new satisfaction of a Max constraint. See (75).

---

[26] That said, if this subarray were to exhibit disjunctive blocking, too, implementing it along the lines shown for Udihe verb inflection in the previous section would be straightforward.

[27] As before, the derivation is simplified in various respects, e.g., as regards the composition of the morphological array, and the competing output representations. And as before, I presuppose that there are high-ranked alignment constraints which ensure that all exponents are added as suffixes.

(75) *Dative plural contexts, revised* (harmonic serialism, step 1):

I_0: Kind$_{[+\alpha,-\beta,-\gamma]}$:[•Cn•]
[+pl,+obl,+gov],
{[$_{Cn_i}$ /Ø/↔[–]], [$_{Cn_i}$ /n/↔[+pl,+α]
[$_{Cn_i}$ /e/↔[+pl,–α,+γ],
[$_{Cn_i}$ /s/↔[+pl,–α,–γ],
[$_{Cn_i}$ /er/↔[+pl,+α,–β,–γ],
[$_{Cn_j}$ /n/↔[+pl,+obl,+gov], ...}

	ExS	MinSat	RC	MC	IdF	MaxPl	MaxObl	MaxGov	Maxα	Maxβ	Maxγ	*Str
O_1: N$_{[+\alpha,-\beta,-\gamma]}$,[+pl,+obl,+gov], [•Cn•]			*!			*	*	*	*	*	*	
☞O_2: N$_{[+\alpha,-\beta,-\gamma]}$,[+pl,+obl,+gov]-Ø$_i$						*	*	*	*	*	*	*
O_3: N$_{[+\alpha,-\beta,-\gamma]}$,[+pl,+obl,+gov]-n$_i$		*!					*	*		*	*	*
O_4: N$_{[+\alpha,-\beta,-\gamma]}$,[+pl,+obl,+gov]-e$_i$		*!			**		*	*		*		*
O_5: N$_{[+\alpha,-\beta,-\gamma]}$,[+pl,+obl,+gov]-s$_i$		*!			*		*	*		*		*
O_6: N$_{[+\alpha,-\beta,-\gamma]}$,[+pl,+obl,+gov]-er$_i$		*!					*	*				*
O_7: N$_{[+\alpha,-\beta,-\gamma]}$,[+pl,+obl,+gov]-n$_j$		*!							*	*	*	*

The following optimization procedure is based on O_2 as the new input. ExS and MinSat ensure that the next least specific plural exponent is now merged with the extended stem; this is /n/$_i$ in O_{22}. The competition is illustrated in (76).

(76) *Dative plural contexts, revised* (harmonic serialism, step 2):

I_2: Kind$_{[+\alpha,-\beta,-\gamma]}$-Ø$_i$
[+pl,+obl,+gov],
{[$_{Cn_i}$ /n/↔[+pl,+α]
[$_{Cn_i}$ /e/↔[+pl,–α,+γ],
[$_{Cn_i}$ /s/↔[+pl,–α,–γ],
[$_{Cn_i}$ /er/↔[+pl,+α,–β,–γ],
[$_{Cn_j}$ /n/↔[+pl,+obl,+gov], ...}

	ExS	MinSat	RC	MC	IdF	MaxPl	MaxObl	MaxGov	Maxα	Maxβ	Maxγ	*Str
O_{21}: N$_{[+\alpha,-\beta,-\gamma]}$,[+pl,+obl,+gov]-Ø$_i$						*!	*	*	*	*	*	
☞O_{22}: N$_{[+\alpha,-\beta,-\gamma]}$,[+pl,+obl,+gov]-Ø$_i$-n$_i$							*	*	*	*	*	*
O_{23}: N$_{[+\alpha,-\beta,-\gamma]}$,[+pl,+obl,+gov]-Ø$_i$-e$_i$		*!			**		*	*		*		*
O_{24}: N$_{[+\alpha,-\beta,-\gamma]}$,[+pl,+obl,+gov]-Ø$_i$-s$_i$		*!			*		*	*		*		*
O_{25}: N$_{[+\alpha,-\beta,-\gamma]}$,[+pl,+obl,+gov]-Ø$_i$-er$_i$		*!					*	*				*
O_{26}: N$_{[+\alpha,-\beta,-\gamma]}$,[+pl,+obl,+gov]-Ø$_i$-n$_j$	*!	*							*	*	*	*

Since, by assumption, all Cn$_i$ exponents except for maximally non-specific /Ø/ bear a [–Cn–] feature for structure removal, RC now becomes active with the new input I_{22}, and /Ø/ is removed from the word as a consequence; cf. O_{223} in (77). Note in passing that O_{224} and O_{225} do not violate MinSat anymore (even though their adding /e/$_i$ and /s/$_i$ did violate MinSat in the previous round) because they both only give rise to one new constraint satisfaction (viz., of Max(γ)) at this point, just like O_{223} does. O_{226} and O_{227}, on the other hand, violate MinSat since they both add two new constraint satisfactions: For O_{226}, the newly satisfied constraints are Max(β) and Max(γ); for O_{227}, the constraints in question are Max(Obl) and Max(Gov). O_{227} fatally violates ExS in addition because it has moved prematurely from the currently active subarray to the second subarray.

(77) *Dative plural contexts, revised* (harmonic serialism, step 3):

I_{22}: Kind$_{[+\alpha,-\beta,-\gamma]}$,[+pl,+obl,+gov]-Ø$_i$-n$_i$ [+pl,+obl,+gov], {[$_{Cn_i}$ /e/↔[+pl,−α,+γ], [$_{Cn_i}$ /s/↔[+pl,−α,−γ], [$_{Cn_i}$ /er/↔[+pl,+α,−β,−γ], [$_{Cn_j}$ /n/↔[+pl,+obl,+gov], ...}	Ex S	Min Sat	R C	M C	Id F	Max Pl	Max Obl	Max Gov	Max α	Max β	Max γ	* Str
O_{221}: N$_{[+\alpha,-\beta,-\gamma]}$,[+pl,+obl,+gov]-Ø$_i$-n$_i$			*!				*	*		*	*	
O_{222}: N$_{[+\alpha,-\beta,-\gamma]}$,[+pl,+obl,+gov]-Ø$_i$					*!	*	*	*	*	*	*	
☞O_{223}: N$_{[+\alpha,-\beta,-\gamma]}$,[+pl,+obl,+gov]-n$_i$							*	*		*	*	
O_{224}: N$_{[+\alpha,-\beta,-\gamma]}$,[+pl,+obl,+gov]-Ø$_i$-n$_i$-e$_i$			*!		**		*	*		*		*
O_{225}: N$_{[+\alpha,-\beta,-\gamma]}$,[+pl,+obl,+gov]-Ø$_i$-n$_i$-s$_i$			*!		*		*	*		*		*
O_{226}: N$_{[+\alpha,-\beta,-\gamma]}$,[+pl,+obl,+gov]-Ø$_i$-n$_i$-er$_i$		*!	*				*	*				*
O_{227}: N$_{[+\alpha,-\beta,-\gamma]}$,[+pl,+obl,+gov]-Ø$_i$-n$_i$-n$_j$	*!	*	*						*	*	*	*

In the fourth step in (78), further improvement of the constraint profile is achieved by merging /er/$_i$ with I_{223} (= O_{223} in (77)). O_{2232} and O_{2233} cannot preclude O_{2234} from becoming optimal via MinSat because these outputs do not improve the constraint profile vis-à-vis the input (due to the new Id-F violation); recall the addition of clause (51-b-iii) to the definition of MinSat.

(78) *Dative plural contexts, revised* (harmonic serialism, step 4):

I_{223}: Kind$_{[+\alpha,-\beta,-\gamma]}$,[+pl,+obl,+gov]-n$_i$ [+pl,+obl,+gov], {[$_{Cn_i}$ /e/↔[+pl,−α,+γ], [$_{Cn_i}$ /s/↔[+pl,−α,−γ], [$_{Cn_i}$ /er/↔[+pl,+α,−β,−γ], [$_{Cn_j}$ /n/↔[+pl,+obl,+gov], ...}	Ex S	Min Sat	R C	M C	Id F	Max Pl	Max Obl	Max Gov	Max α	Max β	Max γ	* Str
O_{2231}: N$_{[+\alpha,-\beta,-\gamma]}$,[+pl,+obl,+gov]-n$_i$							*	*		*!	*	
O_{2232}: N$_{[+\alpha,-\beta,-\gamma]}$,[+pl,+obl,+gov]-n$_i$-e$_i$					*!*		*	*		*		*
O_{2233}: N$_{[+\alpha,-\beta,-\gamma]}$,[+pl,+obl,+gov]-n$_i$-s$_i$					*!		*	*		*		*
☞O_{2234}: N$_{[+\alpha,-\beta,-\gamma]}$,[+pl,+obl,+gov]-n$_i$-er$_i$							*	*				*
O_{2235}: N$_{[+\alpha,-\beta,-\gamma]}$,[+pl,+obl,+gov]-n$_i$-n$_j$	*!								*	*	*	*

The new optimal output has an exponent bearing [−Cn−] (viz., /er/$_i$); therefore, structure removal applies in the next step, and it affects the earlier exponent /n/$_i$ rather than the newly added exponent /er/$_i$ (via self-removal); see (79).

(79) *Dative plural contexts, revised* (harmonic serialism, step 5):

I_{2234}: Kind$_{[+\alpha,-\beta,-\gamma],[\underline{+pl},+obl,+gov]}$-n$_i$-er$_i$ [+pl,+obl,+gov], {[Cn$_i$ /e/↔[+pl,−α,+γ], [Cn$_i$ /s/↔[+pl,−α,−γ], [Cn$_j$ /n/↔[+pl,+obl,+gov], ...]}	Ex S	Min Sat	R C	M C	Id F	Max Pl	Max Obl	Max Gov	Max α	Max β	Max γ	* Str
O_{22341}: N$_{[+\alpha,-\beta,-\gamma],[\underline{+pl},+obl,+gov]}$-n$_i$-er$_i$			*!				*	*				
O_{22342}: N$_{[+\alpha,-\beta,-\gamma],[\underline{+pl},+obl,+gov]}$-n$_i$							*	*		*!	*	
☞O_{22343}: N$_{[+\alpha,-\beta,-\gamma],[\underline{+pl},+obl,+gov]}$-er$_i$							*	*				
O_{22344}: N$_{[+\alpha,-\beta,-\gamma],[\underline{+pl},+obl,+gov]}$-n$_i$-er$_i$-e$_i$			*!	**			*	*				*
O_{22345}: N$_{[+\alpha,-\beta,-\gamma],[\underline{+pl},+obl,+gov]}$-n$_i$-er$_i$-s$_i$			*!	*			*	*				*
O_{22346}: N$_{[+\alpha,-\beta,-\gamma],[\underline{+pl},\underline{+obl},+gov]}$-n$_i$-er$_i$-n$_j$		*!	*									*

At this point, no further improvement is possible on the basis of the exponents in the first subarray (ρ in (52)), and ExS permits the derivation to use exponents from the second subarray (ω in (52)). As shown in (80), by merging /n/$_j$, Max(Obl) and Max(Gov) can now also be satisfied.

(80) *Dative plural contexts, revised* (harmonic serialism, step 6):

I_{22343}: Kind$_{[+\alpha,-\beta,-\gamma],[\underline{+pl},+obl,+gov]}$-er$_i$ [+pl,+obl,+gov], {[Cn$_i$ /e/↔[+pl,−α,+γ], [Cn$_i$ /s/↔[+pl,−α,−γ], [Cn$_j$ /n/↔[+pl,+obl,+gov], ...]}	Ex S	Min Sat	R C	M C	Id F	Max Pl	Max Obl	Max Gov	Max α	Max β	Max γ	* Str
O_{223431}: N$_{[+\alpha,-\beta,-\gamma],[\underline{+pl},+obl,+gov]}$-er$_i$							*	*				
O_{223432}: N$_{[+\alpha,-\beta,-\gamma],[\underline{+pl},+obl,+gov]}$-er$_i$-e$_i$					*!*		*	*				*
O_{223433}: N$_{[+\alpha,-\beta,-\gamma],[\underline{+pl},+obl,+gov]}$-er$_i$-s$_i$					*!		*	*				*
☞O_{223434}: N$_{[+\alpha,-\beta,-\gamma],[\underline{+pl},\underline{+obl},+gov]}$-er$_i$-n$_j$												*

Since /n/$_j$ does not carry a [–Cn–] feature, there is no further structure removal, and extended exponence can arise: Plural is realized both by /er/$_i$ and by /n/$_j$. It is worth pointing out that under this analysis, extended exponence of plural in German noun inflection actually is an instance of *overlapping multiple exponence* rather than an instance of *partially superfluous multiple exponence*, in Caballero & Harris's (2012) terminology. The reason is that if inflection class information is subject to Max constraints, there *is* something that the first participant in an extended exponence relation (here: /er/$_i$) contributes that the second participant (here: /n/$_j$) does not. As alluded to above, I will refrain from taking a firm position as regards the question of whether inflection class information should be subjected to Max constraints, on a par with features encoding grammatical categories that play a role outside morphology; for this reason, extended exponence of plural in German noun declension may or may not continue to pose a severe problem to standard parallel optimality-theoretic approaches.

To sum up, if inflection class information is subject to Max constraints, the derivation of inflectional exponence in dative plural contexts for a noun like *Kind* ('child') in German proceeds as depicted in (81).

(81) *Dative plural contexts – derivation:*

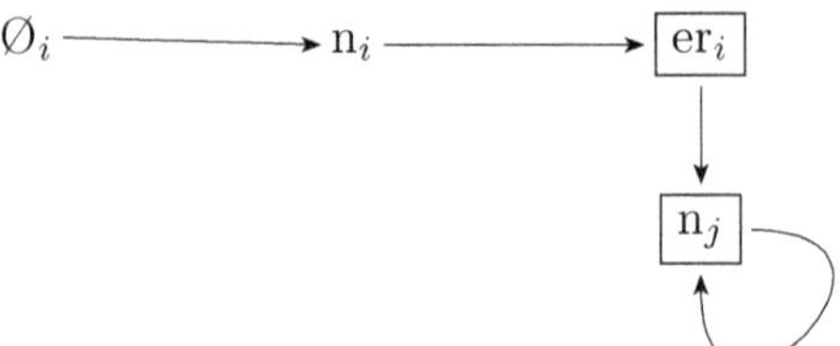

6. Outlook

The main goal of this chapter has been to reconcile the MINSAT-based account of extended exponence developed in chapter 3 with the existence of disjunctive blocking. The problem to be solved here was that MINSAT favours the more general exponent over the more specific one, whereas disjunctive blocking demands a selection of the most specific exponent (among those that are compatible with the contextual specification). I have argued that the apparent paradox finds a natural and conceptually simple solution if structure removal is an option in natural languages: On this view, in addition to the elementary structure-building operation Merge, there is a mirror-image operation Remove. By alternating Merge and Remove operations in morphology, the derivation can gradually move towards, and ultimately converge on, the most specific exponent, even though it always needs to start out with the most general exponent (because of MINSAT). This way, the difference between extended exponence and disjunctive blocking can be reduced to the presence or absence of [–X–] features for structure removal on the exponents in a morphological array. Furthermore, it turns out that there is evidence that extended exponence and disjunctive blocking can co-occur in a single morphological array; this scenario has been accomodated by introducing the concept of a morphological subarray, accompanied by principled assumptions about which exponents in which subarray can or cannot carry Remove features, and by a designated constraint ExS that demands accessing one subarray for as long as possible before moving on to the next one.

It goes without saying that the new approach to disjunctive blocking raises a number of non-trivial questions, and may eventually require additional assumptions and further restrictions. However, for the time being, I would like to confine myself to pointing out two noteworthy characteristics. First, notwithstanding its merits and shortcomings, it seems that the present approach to disjunctive blocking can only be implemented in a theory of inflectional morphology that adheres to the tenets of harmonic serialism; as far as I can tell, there is no obvious way to transfer its gist to any other morphology theory in existence. Here is why: On the one hand, the analysis crucially relies on violability (and ranking) of the constraints encoding specificity; in fact, the violability needs to be massive where the most general exponent favoured by MINSAT is selected. This property virtually excludes non-optimality-theoretic approaches. On the other hand, the analysis also relies on a derivational approach where building and removal of structure alternate, and intermediate stages that are not visible or accessible in the final output are nevertheless required to determine the latter. This rules out all non-derivational theories. Thus, the analysis of disjunctive blocking developed here can only be implemented in an approach to inflectional morphology that envisages constraint violability, constraint ranking, and strict derivationalism; and it would seem that harmonic serialism is the only such theory around at this point in time.

Second and finally, it may be instructive to note that the partitioning of competing exponents in a morphological array (or whatever the local domain is that defines a competition among markers) works somewhat differently in the present approach from standard approaches relying on compatibility and specificity. In standard approaches (as developed in, e.g., Distributed Morphology or Paradigm Function Morphology), for each syntactically defined environment, one can distinguish between (i) the optimal, grammatical exponent (which satisfies both compatibility and specificity), (ii) ungrammatical compatible exponents (which satisfy compatibility but not specificity), and (iii) ungrammatical incompatible exponents (which do not satisfy compatibility). The distinction between class (ii) and class (iii) is potentially very interesting: If it can be independently substantiated, this can then be viewed as a good argument for distinguishing between compatibility and specificity requirements in morphological theories, and consequently, for the concept of underspecification that gives rise to the two different sources of ungrammaticality in the first place. In contrast, standard parallel optimality-theoretic approaches to inflection do not permit distinguishing between class (ii) (of compatible, not sufficiently specific exponents) and class (iii) (of incompatible exponents) so easily – given usual assumptions about suboptimality, all suboptimal candidates are ill-formed to the same degree, independently of the ranking of the constraint that is responsible for their suboptimality.[28]

---

[28] See, however, Keller (2001) for a different view; but also Müller (2000a, ch. 6) for arguments against such an approach, based on existing studies in optimality-theoretic syntax – the upshot here is that there is no sense in which the second-best candidate in a syntactic competition would standardly qualify as less ill formed than, say, the third-best candidate.

Grouping suboptimal exponents according to the constraints they fatally violate (ID-F or MAX) will yield the desired result, but such a step is arguably ad hoc, and certainly at variance with the core conceptual assumptions of the surrounding framework.

Against this background, consider the neurophysiological study of strong adjective inflection in German reported in Opitz, Regel, Müller & Friederici (2013). In general, strong adjective inflection is nearly identical to determiner inflection; the only difference shows up in genitive singular masculine/neuter contexts, which have an /n/ instead of an /s/. The study shows that class (iii) exponents violating compatibility behave differently from class (ii) exponents violating only specificity, with the former evoking a much stronger electroencephalography (EEG) potential; and of course, there is a substantial difference between the grammatical class (i) exponent and class (ii) and class (iii) exponents. In Opitz, Regel, Müller & Friederici (2013), we thus take this three-way distinction as an independent confirmation of compatibility and specificity as two separate requirements for morphological inflection, and hence, as support for the concept of underspecification itself.

From the present perspective, an alternative approach to establishing three-way distinctions in morphological arrays suggests itself. Rather than distinguishing between (i) grammatical exponents, (ii) fatally non-specific exponents, and (iii) fatally non-compatible exponents, the new analysis suggests a partitioning of competing exponents into (i) grammatical (= finally optimal) exponents, (ii) temporarily optimal exponents, and (iii) consistently suboptimal exponents.

As a matter of fact, in the main environment focussed on in Opitz, Regel, Müller & Friederici (2013), viz., accusative singular neuter contexts, the present approach would make the desired distinctions: $/s/^5$ is eventually optimal, $/e/^9$ is temporarily (i.e., initially) optimal, but $/n/^4$ is never optimal at any stage of the sequence of optimization procedures. For other environments, additional assumptions (or changes to the exact specification of exponents, as they are also discussed for various extensionally identical approaches in Opitz, Regel, Müller & Friederici (2013) in terms of the meta-concepts of maximal underspecification and minimal underspecification) may be called for.

More generally, though, I would like to conclude that the difference between (ii) temporarily optimal and (iii) consistently suboptimal outputs that comes for free under present assumptions might qualify as a viable alternative to (ii) compatible but not sufficiently specific and (iii) incompatible exponents, especially in view of the fact that the two partitionings are far from equivalent: There can be compatible exponents that never become temporarily optimal during derivations; and, in principle, there can also be incompatible exponents that become temporarily optimal at the start of a derivation (although we have not seen such a case yet). However, pursuing this question is beyond the scope of the present monograph.[29]

---

[29] A related question that one might ask oneself is whether temporarily optimal exponents might leave phonological reflexes in the same way that moved grammatical exponents can do (see sections 7 and 8 of chapter 2). Here the answer would seem to be unequivocally negative; and this does in fact follow from the assumption that a phonological cycle can only be triggered if all morphological arrays are exhausted – this precludes phonological reflexes of temporarily optimal exponents.

Chapter 5

Suppletion

This chapter addresses two distinct but related issues arising with stem suppletion. First, recently instances of non-local stem suppletion in the world's languages have come to the fore, and it turns out that this phenomenon poses a problem for morphological theories. And second, it has been observed that stem allomorphy obeys an *ABA constraint that can, under certain assumptions, be derived from compatibility and specificity requirements. In both cases, the question arises what the present approach in terms of harmonic serialism has to say about the phenomenon. I address the two issues in turn, starting with non-local allomorphy.

1. Non-Local Allomorphy

1.1. *The Phenomenon*

A standard assumption in much work on Distributed Morphology is that the phenomenon of stem suppletion, i.e., the choice between two or more different stems for a single lexical entry based on non-inherent morpho-syntactic features, extrinsic to the lexical information of the stem as such (like case, person, tense), is a strictly local one. For instance, Bobaljik (2000) assumes that only features in terminal nodes that are structurally adjacent can play a role in allomorph selection. Assuming a slightly less rigid concept of locality, Embick (2010) postulates that contextual information can be relevant for allomorph selection only if it is contained in the same local domain (phase), and if the information is present on a linearly (rather than structurally) adjacent node; in addition, as already noted in the previous chapter, a pruning operation bringing about structure removal of empty intervening nodes can lead to adjacency. For stem allomorphy regulated by non-inherent morpho-syntactic features (i.e., suppletion), both approaches imply that in an environment like (1), where Σ is a stem and ρ and ω are inflectional exponents, the morpho-syntactic features borne by ρ

(or, given the option of underspecification, the morpho-syntactic features that ρ realizes) can determine the choice of Σ but the morpho-syntactic features borne by ω (or, again, the features that ω realizes) cannot influence Σ choice.[1]

(1) $\Sigma - \rho - \omega$

However, more recent research has identified various phenomena in typologically diverse languages where it looks as though the morpho-syntactic features of (or associated with) ω can indeed determine selection of the stem Σ.[2]

A first example illustrating this comes from personal pronouns in Tamil (see Lehmann (1989) and Schiffman (1999)). As observed by Moskal & Smith (2016), in first and second person scenarios, there are two different stems for the realization of D whose choice seems to be non-locally determined: There is both a standard stem, which is chosen in nominative contexts, and a so-called oblique stem, which is chosen whenever an overt case marker shows up (accusative /ai/, dative /(a/u)kku/, instrumental /aal/, sociative /ooṭu/, or locative /il/). Interestingly, the case exponent that determines selection of the stem allomorph does not need to be adjacent (neither structurally, nor linearly), given that a number exponent (which itself cannot trigger stem allomorphy) can intervene. This number exponent is zero in singular contexts, but non-zero (/(n)ga(l)/) in plural

---

[1] Two remarks. First, throughout this chapter, I will only be concerned with *morpho-syntactically* governed allomorphy, not with *phonologically* determined allomorphy, where the phonological context determines exponent choice; in the latter case, locality would seem to be much less of a controversial issue. See Wolf (2008), Bonet et al. (2015a), Bye (2015), Paster (2015), Trommer (2015b), and several other contributions in Bonet et al. (2015b). Second, I will only address morpho-syntactically conditioned *stem* allomorphy, not morpho-syntactically conditioned allomorphy of *inflectional exponents*. The reasons for this are twofold. On the one hand, as observed by Božič (2017; 2019), far fewer cases of affix allomorphy have been documented so far (among them the case of modality exponents determined by non-local exponents registering (in)transitivity in Kiowa reported in Bonet & Harbour (2012)). On the other hand, as we will see, modelling stem allomorphy in the present approach poses a somewhat greater challenge – but, as we will also see, for reasons that are actually independent of the locality issue. In fact, what will be said about non-local stem allomorphy will automatically carry over to cases of non-local affix allomorphy.

[2] That said, some instances of what initially looks like extremely non-local allomorphy may upon closer inspection turn out to be more local after all. See, e.g., Bobaljik & Harley (2013) on suppletive verb stems in Hiaki, conditioned by the number specification of a subject DP; but Bobaljik and Harley show that the subject DPs in question should be analyzed as underlying objects (and the verbs, correspondingly, as unaccusative).

contexts. Consider as an example the data in (2-ab), where D shows up in nominative and dative environments.

(2)   a.   (i)   1.SG.NOM: naan-Ø-Ø
           (ii)   1.PL.NOM: naan-ga-Ø
           (iii) 1.SG.DAT: en-Ø-akku
           (iv) 1.PL.DAT: en-ga(l)-ukku
      b.   (i)   2.SG.NOM: nii-Ø-Ø
           (ii)   2.PL.NOM: nii-(n)ga-Ø
           (iii) 2.SG.DAT: on-Ø-akku
           (iv) 2.PL.DAT: on-ga(l)-ukku

The relevant pronoun forms are those in (2-a-iv) and (2-b-iv). In (2-a-iv), a dative exponent /(a/u)kku/ determines choice of the first person D oblique stem /en/ instead of an otherwise expected stem /naan/ across an intervening plural exponent /(n)ga(l)/. In (2-b-iv), the presence of /(a/u)kku/ ensures that an oblique stem /on/ is chosen for D realization in a second person context, instead of the standard stem /nii/; again, the determination of the correct stem looks like it must take place across an intervening plural exponent /(n)ga(l)/.

As a second example of non-local stem allomorphy, consider the case of Slovenian verbs discussed in Božič (2017; 2019). Relevant examples are given in (3).

(3)

ROOT	VERB:1.SG	PARTICIPLE:F.SG	
√žanj-	žanj-e-m	ž-e-l-a	('reap')
√koln-	koln-e-m	kl-e-l-a	('swear')
√boj-	boj-i-m	b-a-l-a	('fear')

Here the choice of stem (e.g., /žanj/ vs. /ž/) can be conditioned by an inflectional exponent (viz., the participle affix /l/) that is separated from it by an intervening theme vowel (/e/ or /a/).[3]

A third example mentioned and analyzed in Božič (2019) comes from Tariana (based on Brown et al. (2003), based in turn on Aikhenvald (2003)). Here there are two stems for the adjective 'big', viz., /hanu/ and /male/, and the first form is chosen in singular contexts whereas the second is chosen in plural contexts. Crucially, the conditioning number exponent is

---

[3] Following Božič (2017), I assume here that stem alternations of the type in (3) cannot be insightfully handled by phonological truncation operations.

separated from the stem by an intervening class marker exponent that does
not interact with stem choice; see (4).

(4) a. hanu-pua-Ø   b. male-pua-pe
         big-CLASS-SG   big-CLASS-PL

A fourth, slightly different kind of example of non-local stem allomorphy
is investigated in Merchant (2015). In Greek, there are a few verbs which
have three different stems (Σ in (1)), depending on (i) the features realized
by a right-adjacent voice exponent (ACTIVE or NON-ACTIVE) corresponding
to ρ in (1), and (ii) the features of a suffixal aspect exponent (PERFECTIVE
or IMPERFECTIVE) corresponding to ω in (1). In the inflected verb, these
exponents are then followed by exponents for person and number that do
not interact with stem choice. (5) illustrates the three stems for the verb
'eat' in 1.SG environments: /tro(ɣ)/ is the (active or non-active) imperfective stem, /fa(ɣ)/ is the active perfective stem, and /faɣo/ is the non-active
perfective stem.

(5) a. 1.SG.ACT.IMP.NONPAST: tró-Ø-Ø-o
     b. 1.SG.NONACT.IMP.NONPAST: tróɣ-Ø-Ø-ome
     c. 1.SG.ACT.IMP.PAST: é-troɣ-Ø-Ø-a
     d. 1.SG.NONACT.IMP.PAST: troɣ-Ø-Ø-ómun
     e. 1.SG.ACT.PERF.NONPAST: fá-Ø-Ø-o
     f. 1.SG.NONACT.PERF.NONPAST: faɣo-θ-Ø-ó
     g. 1.SG.ACT.PERF.PAST: é-faɣ-Ø-Ø-a
     h. 1.SG.NONACT.PERF.PAST: faɣó-θ-ik-a

This pattern of non-local stem allomorphy differs from the other patterns
above in that it is not merely the remote ω exponent that determines stem
selection, but the intervening ρ exponent, too: If voice is [+ACT] *and* aspect
is [+PERF], /fa(ɣ)/ is selected; if voice is [−ACT] *and* aspect is [+PERF],
/fa(ɣ)o/ becomes optimal; and if none of these contexts is present, the stem
exponent is /tro(ɣ)/. Thus, stem suppletion in Greek obeys a contiguity
requirement; the features of (or realized by) the intervening exponent in
non-local allomorphy also matter.

   Several more cases of non-local stem allomorphy have been identified,
but for present purposes I will leave it at that.[4]

---

[4] See in particular the collection in Kastner & Moskal (2018).

1.2. State of the Art

Several approaches to non-local stem allomorphy have been developed in the recent literature. They all have in common that the non-locality of the phenomenon is taken at face value, and strategies are accordingly contemplated to ensure that the existence of long-distance suppletion can be reconciled with the theories of inflection otherwise employed.

First, observing that the Greek pattern in (5) poses severe problems for strictly local analyses of contextual allomorphy as devised by Bobaljik (2000) (based on structural adjacency) and Embick (2010) (based on linear adjacency), Merchant (2015, 288) proposes that the relevant locality domain is the *span*, where a span is a contiguous sequence of heads in an extended projection (see Svenonius (2016)); i.e., the idea that morphological realization should be of *constituents* in a two-dimensional space is abandoned. Against this background, Merchant suggests that "a span and only a span can be targeted for Vocabulary Insertion" (i.e., morphological realization). This works well for the Greek data in (5), where Σ allomorphy is conditioned both by ρ and by ω in (1). However, as noted by Moskal & Smith (2016) and Božič (2019), inter alia, other data illustrating non-local stem allomorphy – like the ones involving stem variation with personal pronouns in Tamil, stem alternation with verbs in Slovenian, and stem alternation with adjectives in Tariana – do not lend themselves to a span-based analysis as straightforwardly. The reason is that spans by definition obey a strict contiguity requirement; but the Tamil, Slovenian, and Tariana data show that it can be the case that the intermediate exponent (viz., ρ in (1)) must be ignored for morphological realization.

In contrast, Moskal & Smith (2016) argue that non-local stem allomorphy should be handled by (i) stipulating accessibility domains as the local domains that can contain information required for the realization of a given morphological exponent, and (ii) postulating designated so-called *hyper-contextual* realization rules, where contextual information is not confined to an adjacent slot but may involve multiple nodes in the structure.[5]

Yet another extra tool to account for non-local suppletion is introduced in Božič (2017; 2019). Based on a typological survey of data exhibiting non-local stem allomorphy, Božič concludes that virtually all of the core cases involve relatively local relations after all, with at most one (non-empty) intervening head. This empirical finding is then implemented by postulating *buffers* which are associated with functional heads that in turn

---

[5] Also see Gazdar (1982, 176) for discussion of the analogous use of such non-local information in the modelling of restrictions on movement.

collect all the relevant information by means of a specific SCAN operation before vocabulary insertion (i.e., morphological realization) takes place. So, SCAN itself is a non-local operation, but it makes contextual information locally accessible.

The fourth and final special approach to non-local stem allomorphy to be mentioned here goes back to Weisser (2017a). According to this proposal, non-local allomorphy does indeed presuppose the availability of a larger accessible domain (rather than just adjacent slots). However, there is a restriction: Context-sensitive morphological realization of a functional head α can only involve information located in a separate head β if there is a *selection* relation between α and β (in either direction).

At this point, it is not my goal to discuss the virtues and shortcomings of these individual proposals. I will confine myself to noting that they all require additional stipulations as regards morphological realization and its locality. Thus, the question arises of whether instances of non-local allomorphy be accounted for without extending locality domains for suppletion, without introducing hyper-contextual realization rules (as in Moskal & Smith (2016)), without other operations that are not strictly local, like spanning (see Merchant (2015)) or selection-tracking allomorphy (see Weisser (2017a)), and without postulating non-local operations that make the relevant features required for morphological realization locally accessible and necessitate additional assumptions about the place where this information is put (like scanning plus buffers in Božič (2017; 2019)).

Of course, non-local stem allomorphy does not pose the slightest problem for analyses employing realizational-inferential theories, like Paradigm Function Morphology (cf. Stump (2001; 2016)) or Network Morphology (cf. Corbett & Fraser (1993) and Brown & Hippisley (2012)). This is so because, by assumption, *all* morpho-syntactic features that define a given paradigm cell are *always* accessible by *all* possible exponents (or, more precisely, rules of exponence) in a word. Consequently, there is no problem to account for (what, under these assumptions, only looks like) non-local allomorphy. However, this option comes at the price of a massive loss of restrictiveness: As already noted in chapter 3 (see page 101), these kinds of approaches have nothing insightful to say about the fact that the individual slots for exponence in a word are typically *relatively* homogeneous as far as the features that are realized are concerned. Or, at the very least, it should be uncontroversial that they are not at all arbitrary. However, such arbitrariness is what one would expect in such a framework: Each feature contained in the fully specified matrix can be accessed by each rule block.

In the following section, I will argue that the present approach in terms of harmonic serialism offers a straighforward solution to the problem posed by apparently non-local stem allomorphy, one that does not necessitate any special assumptions about the phenomeon: In cases of non-local suppletion, morphological realization is strictly local (as required under the concept of morphological array), but this locality is masked by subsequent morphological *movement*.

1.3. Non-Local Stem Allomorphy in Harmonic Serialism

1.3.1. Morphological Arrays and Movement

The first thing to note is that stem allomorphy (suppletion) conditioned by morpho-syntactic features, whether local or non-local, is always an instance of extended exponence: The stem Σ realizes a morpho-syntactic feature $[F_1]$ (among many other features) that is also realized by a designated inflectional exponent ω in the same word. However, unlike a priori challenging core cases of extended exponence as they figured prominently in chapter 3, stem allomorphy typically does not involve *partially superfluous* multiple exponence, but rather *overlapping* multiple exponence; i.e., both the stem Σ and an inflectional exponent ω realize morpho-syntactic features other than the shared feature $[F_1]$ (or, more generally, shared features $[F_1], \ldots, [F_n]$). As shown in chapter 3, overlapping extended exponence is much less of a problem for theories of inflection than partially superfluous extended exponence is; recall, e.g., that standard parallel optimality theory faces severe problems with the latter kind of morphological realization but can easily handle the former one. Arguably, this fact can be held responsible for the tendency observable in the literature on suppletion not to discuss the phenomenon under this rubric. Be this as it may, it seems clear that *local* suppletion can then be accounted for in roughly the same way as other cases of overlapping exponence, and *non-local* suppletion can be derived along essentially the same lines as shown for discontinuous partially superfluous extended exponence in Swahili in section 5.4. of chapter 3.[6]

To be a bit more specific, given that contextual (or secondary) features are to be abandoned (cf. chapter 3), Σ stems that participate in suppletion must bear not only the features that one would normally attribute to a stem of their particular type, but also features that are borne by inflectional exponents ω. Given the definition in (45) of chapter 3, if a stem Σ

---

[6] As a matter of fact, nothing in principle rules out stem allomorphy involving partially superfluous multiple exponence, and there is also no reason why it should not be able to be non-local on the surface. Hungarian personal pronouns are a case in point. (Thanks to Daniel Gleim for pointing this out to me.) Thus, in a form like *eng-em-et* (1.SG.ACC-1.POSS-ACC, 'me'), the exponent *eng* unambiguously indicates accusative (the nominative stem form would be *én*), and the exponent *et* is a pure accusative marker.

and an inflectional exponent ω share a morpho-syntactic feature, it follows that they must belong to the same morphological array. This, in turn, ensures that they will be merged in contiguous steps in the morphological derivation, and will consequently be adjacent in the inflected word (with a minor qualification that I will turn to immediately) if nothing else happens. This covers local suppletion. As for non-local suppletion, there is also initial adjacency of the stem Σ and the inflectional exponent ω (again, with the qualification just alluded to). However, subsequently movement may apply in the morphological component, which disrupts the initial proximity of Σ and ω in the surface representation and counter-bleeds the adjacency requirement. On this view, the form of the first person plural dative personal pronoun in Tamil (see (2-a-iv)) in (6-b) is derived from the base order in (6-a) by (rightward) *morphological* movement in the same way that, say, the word order with an extraposed object DP in Tamil in (6-d) is derived from the base order in (6-c) by (rightward) *syntactic* movement (see Sarma (2003)).

(6)   a.   en - (a/u)kku - (n)ga(l)
       b.   en - (n)ga(l) - (a/u)kku

       c.   shakuni   dharmaa-kku daayatt-ai koṭut-tt-aan
            Shakuni$_{nom}$ Dharma$_{dat}$ dice$_{acc}$ give-PAST-3.SG.MASC
       d.   shakuni   daayatt-ai koṭut-tt-aan   dharmaa-kku
            Shakuni$_{nom}$ dice$_{acc}$ give-PAST-3.SG.MASC Dharma$_{dat}$

According to present assumptions, movement is ubiquitous in morphology as it is in syntax; and morphological displacement is triggered by aligment constraints as they have been proposed for entirely independent reasons (i.e., reasons not related to movement) in analyses couched in standard parallel optimality theory.

Viewed from this perspective, the (surface) non-locality of suppletion does not come as a surprise, and certainly does not necessitate any new assumptions with potentially far-reaching consequences. However, the phenomenon of suppletion nonetheless poses a challenge for the present approach because it raises the question how the initial step of structure-building proceeds.[7] Therefore, before turning to case studies showing how

---

[7] Closer scrutiny reveals that this issue is by no means confined to the present approach; it also shows up in many other approaches which are not strictly realizational-inferential (in Stump's (2001) terms), where it is often swept under the carpet.

non-local stem allomorphy can be addressed in the current approach based
on harmonic serialism, I address the issue of how stem alternation can come
about in the first place in the following subsection.

1.3.2. Stem Allomorphy

So far, I have presupposed that a basic stem comes from the lexicon with
its inherent features, is enriched by non-inherent features that provide a
fully specified contextual information for morphological realization (see (2)
in chapter 1), and then induces Merge operations (triggered first by MC
constraints and subsequently by MAX constraints) and Move operations
(triggered by COHERENCE and alignment constraints). In view of the existence of stem allomorphy, which suggests that choice of stem is itself the
outcome of an optimization procedure, this approach may be in need of
modification.

I will make the following assumptions. First, stems are themselves
members of morphological arrays, defined by their belonging to the same
abstract lexeme. In addition, they do not necessarily have this morphological array all to themselves: If there is more than one stem in a single
morphological array, with the selection determined by morpho-syntactic
information (i.e., in cases of morpho-syntactically governed stem allomorphy), there also have to be inflectional exponents bearing identical features
in the same array. Within these latter composite morphological arrays,
stems establish separate subarrays (cf. chapter 4); this ensures that stems
can be underspecified, with the most specific compatible stem eventually
being selected after a sequence of optimization procedures that start out
with the most general initial stem (as required by MinSat), before the
derivation moves on to the first inflectional exponent that is part of the
same morphological array (because it shares a morpho-syntactic feature,
or several of them, with the stem).[8]

---

[8] These considerations also shed some light on the ontological status of morphological
arrays. Note that the definition of morphological arrays adopted here (see (45) in chapter 3) is basically compatible with both (i) a view as a filter on certain abstract objects
(viz., morphological arrays, and morphological subarrays) that are stored in the mental
lexicon, and (ii) a view as a generative procedure creating certain abstract objects (viz.,
morphological arrays, and a fortiori morphological subarrays) in the numeration, envisaged here as the locus of inflectional morphology (cf. chapter 1). Given that stems can
show up in morphological arrays *together with inflectional exponents*, it follows that only
the latter view can be the correct one: It would be clearly absurd to assume that for each
stem (or, at least, for each stem that is subject to suppletion) of a certain category in a
given language, all the inflectional exponents that can in principle be attached to it are
stored together with it to begin with, thereby giving rise to a proliferation of – otherwise

Second, suppose that stems cannot actually be enriched with non-inherent morpho-syntactic features (providing a fully specified environment for morphological realization by inflectional exponents) in the numeration. Rather, they have the same status as inflectional exponents in this respect, with one exception: Some of a stem's intrinsic morpho-syntactic features (e.g., animacy, gender or inflection class features with noun stems, or binyanim, inflectional class, and possibly aspect/aktionsart with verbs; see Aronoff (1994)) can still be used as part of the fully specified matrix that provides the context for realization. However, other morpho-syntactic features associated with a stem (e.g., those that are shared with an inflectional exponent in the case of stem allomorphy) are purely realizational; these features, which are typically underspecified (see below), do not provide the context for realization but are used for the morphological realization of an independently existing fully specified feature matrix. In line with this, [•F•] features that trigger the first selection of an exponent from a morphological array are not attributed to stems anymore; rather, the stem's category feature is itself one that defines a morphological array, and is sought for by something else.

Third, this then raises the question of where all non-inherent morpho-syntactic features, and [•F•] features inducing initial Merge operations (including those affecting stems themselves), are located if they are not on stems. Here I will assume that there are separate *categorizing heads* that can be referred to as v, n, a, p, d, etc., which combine with stems of type V, N, A, P, D, respectively, before any inflectional exponent is attached. Assuming that membership in the mental lexicon is confined to items whose properties are not fully predictable by the rules of grammar (see, e.g., Di Sciullo & Williams (1987)), these items do in fact *not* belong to the lexicon. And, as a matter of fact, the items v, n, a, etc. ultimately reduce to *a single* item that we can call x: On this view, x is just a placeholder for any combination of non-inherent fully specified morpho-syntactic features that are instantiated on x in the numeration, and that are well-formed for a given part of speech in the language (see Stump (2001) and chapter 1). If non-inherent features that are compatible with, say, verbs in a given language are instantiated on x in the numeration (e.g., ϕ-features, tense features, etc.), and if a verb stem-selecting feature [•V•] is also instantiated on x (plus other [•F•] features that capture morphological arrays containing the kinds of exponents that can be combined with verb stems

---

identical – inflectional exponents in the lexicon. Also see the remarks on pages 230–231 on what the lexicon can and cannot consist of.

in the language), the resulting item can be dubbed v; similarly for other categories. The non-inherent, purely grammatical features of the categorizing head x added to x in the numeration and the inherent features of a stem Σ that is merged with x then together make up the fully specified morpho-syntactic context that needs to be realized by (further) inflectional exponence.

Clearly, x and Σ have a privileged relationship. It must be ensured that the categorizing head merges with a stem before it can merge with any other exponent. For the most part, this may well follow from assuming the respective MC for the category feature of the stem to outrank all other MCs in every language. However, there might then still be a danger that MinSat could select an inflectional exponent yielding fewer new (Max) constraint satisfactions. In view of this state of affairs, two possible solutions suggest themselves. First, the condition that stems are combined with the categorizing head x before anything else is might be hardwired into the concept of MinSat. Alternatively, an inherent preference to stem concatenation over concatenation of an inflectional exponent follows directly if one assumes that inflectional exponents can only ever be merged in the presence of a *fully articulated* feature specification. Thus, if every stem contributes inherent features to the environment capturing the paradigm cell or syntactic context for exponent realization, adding the stem must come before adding an inflectional exponent.[9] In what follows, I will not take a firm stand on this issue. Both approaches yield the desired result that stem exponence always comes before inflection marker exponence. Still, for concreteness I will provisionally adopt the second option.

There is also another sense in which the Σ-x connection is special: x cannot be overtly realized. Again, there are various ways to bring about this consequence; but the simplest solution is straightforward: Only items in the lexicon can have a phonological representation; categorizing heads, which under present assumptions arise from a radically underspecified placeholder

---

[9] Two remarks as regards the second view: First, the idea of what counts as a 'fully articulated' feature matrix might need to diverge from the simplest possible approach if *impoverishment* is assumed, and given an optimality-theoretic implementation not in terms of unfaithful (ID-F-violating) realization of features by exponents (as in Trommer (2003), Wunderlich (2004), and Don & Blom (2006)), but in terms of actual deletion of features (as in Keine & Müller (2011; 2014)); cf. chapter 6. Also see the proposal on page 297 in chapter 6, which basically suggests implementing impoverishment by permitting selective violations of the principle at hand. And second, as will be demonstrated in the second part of the present chapter, the assumption that only complete feature matrices can serve as a context against which morphological items are matched during exponence does not necessarily hold for *stems*.

item via feature enrichment, are not part of the lexicon (in this sense, they qualify as syncategorematic), and can therefore never be overt.[10] In line with this, it seems plausible to assume that categorizing heads are also not registered by alignment constraints; thus, a stem Σ that shows up to the right of a categorizing head x can never violate a constraint demanding left-alignment because of x.[11]

Finally, consider the question of headedness. It is typically the case in morphology and syntax that if some item item α is combined with some item β as a consequence of α selecting β, α counts as the head of the composite category (see Adger (2003), among many others). However, in the case at hand, a categorizing head x does not by itself have any category feature that might differ from the one that characterizes its structure-building feature [•F•]. Therefore, the category feature of the stem will always provide the label of the composite morphological category (also see Williams (1981); Di Sciullo & Williams (1987) on the concept of 'relativized head'), and this label will be maintained for all subsequent Merge operations adding inflectional exponents. Thus, the eventual category of a complex morphological category going back to an initial categorizing head x:[•V•] will always be V; this complex V will then later be subjected to the syntactic derivation, where the *syntactic* features triggering syntactic Merge and Agree operations that come from the stem will get the syntactic derivation going.

To illustrate how the resulting system works, let me first go through an example instantiating stem allomorphy of a *local* type; after that I will address an instance of *non-local* suppletion.

1.3.3. A Case Study of Local Stem Allomorphy: Russian Nouns

A simple case of local suppletion involves number-governed noun stem allomorphy in Russian (see Brown et al. (2003), among others). The noun

---

[10] This is one of the differences between categorizing heads in the present approach and categorizing heads as they have first been proposed in Distributed Morphology; see, e.g., Marantz (1998), Harley (2014), Borer (2014), Alexiadou et al. (2014), and the contributions in Alexiadou et al. (2015). Other differences are that Σ, which I take to be a stem with a category feature (and other morpho-syntactic features that are relevant for inflectional exponence), is a category-neutral root in Distributed Morphology analyses; and that, correspondingly, the categorizing head x does not actually bear a category feature [F] in the present approach but merely a subcategorization feature [•F•] that selects for a stem with the respective category feature.

[11] More generally, of course, this means that it does not matter whether Σ is merged with x as an item preceding x ('prefix') or as an item following x ('suffix'); see below.

stem for the lexeme denoting 'child' is *rebënok* in singular environments, and *det′* in plural environments; see the paradigm in (7).[12]

(7)

	SG	PL
NOM	rebënok-Ø	det′-i
ACC	rebënk-a	det′-ej
DAT	rebënk-u	det′-am
GEN	rebënk-a	det′-ej
INSTR	rebënk-om	det′-mi
LOC	rebënk-e	det′ax

Suppose, at least for the sake of the argument, that /rebënOk/ (cf. the last footnote on the abstract yer vowel /O/) is the elsewhere stem exponent, and /det′/ is the marked stem exponent characterized by the feature [+pl]. Both stem exponents come with intrinsic features; and some of these are relevant for inflection, like the gender feature [+masc] in the case of /rebënOk/, the feature [+animate], and (assuming for present purposes the analysis in Müller (2004)) the decomposed inflection class features $[+\alpha,-\beta]$ which characterize the standard masculine declension pattern in Russian, which /rebënOk/, /det′/ follows.[13]

Now recall the concept of morphological array in (45) of chapter 3. Given that there are stems like, by assumption, /det′/, which bear *both* a category label ([N]) *and* a number feature ([+pl]), these stems will have to show up in a single morphological array with *all* inflectional exponents in the language that bear a number feature, and since there are, furthermore,

---

[12] There is also a plural form *rebjata* partially sharing stem shape with *rebënok*, but this is a colloquial form with a highly restricting meaning that cannot be viewed as a general option for realizing plural with the meaning 'child', and that can therefore be disregarded in the present context; see Isačenko (1975, 126). Also note that the realization of the abstract yer vowel /O/ (as *o* or zero) in underlying /rebënOk/ in (7) is phonologically conditioned and will be ignored in what follows; see Kenstowicz & Rubach (1987) on Slavic yers, Halle (1994) on the role of yers in Russian declension, and, more generally, references cited in these articles.

[13] Assuming the standard neuter declension to be characterized by the features $[+\alpha,+\beta]$, exponents that are underspecified with respect to inflection class information and only bear the feature $[+\alpha]$ are predicted to capture transparadigmatic syncretism (see page 209) involving only these two inflection classes; similarly, exponents specified as just $[-\beta]$ capture a natural class of inflection classes consisting of the standard masculine declension, and the marked (predominantly) feminine so-called i-declension, which show transparadigmatic syncretism in genitive plural contexts; see Müller (2004) for extensive discussion. Also cf. the discussion of the status of inflection class information vis-à-vis underspecification and MAX constraints in section 5.3. of chapter 4.

inflectional exponents in Russian that bear both number and case features (like, incidentally, all plural exponents, in the analysis in Müller (2004)), *all* inflectional exponents bearing case or number information will be part of the same morphosyntactic array (formed in the numeration) as /det′/; in addition, a default exponent for case/number information in Russian (/a/, according to the analysis in Müller (2004), but nothing depends on this assumption in the present context) will also be included in this morphosyntactic array. Next, the alternative stem /rebënOk/ will of course also be part of this morphological array. This means that both in the case at hand, and more generally in the system of Russian noun inflection even where there is no stem allomorphy, there is always a single morphological array, which we can assume to be captured by the category feature [N], that provides all the material for an inflected noun (i.e., stem and ending). This morphological array is then naturally divided into two subarrays, one composed of the stem(s), and one composed of the inflectional exponents for case and number. Within both subarrays, there is disjunctive blocking, brought about by [–F–] features for structure removal, as shown for combinations of extended exponence and disjunctive blocking in Udihe subject agreement and German case marking in the previous chapter.[14]

Suppose further that a categorizing head x has been chosen, and enriched by a feature [•N•] demanding an item from the morphological array identified by [N] (two stems and all inflectional exponents for N, in the case at hand), and by fully specified features capturing, say, a nominative plural context. Again following the analysis in Müller (2004), these latter features may be something like [+pl] and [+subj,–obl,–gov].[15]

The initial competition is one where x's [•N•] feature is discharged by merging an item from the morphological array defined by [N] that consists of /det′/, /rebënOk/, and inflectional exponents like those in (8).[16]

---

[14] A remark is due here on the stems that can show up in a single morphological array. Strictly speaking, (45) in chapter 3 is compatible with the view that the morphological array in which /det′/ and /rebënOk/ show up also includes all other noun stems in the language, which is implausible. So, what is tacitly presupposed here but would eventually have to be added to the concept of a morphological array is a condition that any given morphological array can only host stems belonging to the same lexeme.

[15] Since Russian has six cases, there have to be at least three binary case features to characterize all existing cases by a cross-classification of primitive case features.

[16] Since the present focus is on stem selection and not on selection of inflectional exponents, I confine myself to a small subset of the actual inflectional exponents involved in noun declension in Russian here. Furthermore, I have assumed here that there can be

(8)   *Some exponents for case/number:*
   a. $/a/_1 \leftrightarrow$ [N,+subj]
   b. $/u/ \leftrightarrow$ [N,–subj,+gov]
   c. $/i/ \leftrightarrow$ [N,+pl,–obl,–gov]
   d. $/a/_2 \leftrightarrow$ [N,+pl,+α,+β]
   e. $/am/ \leftrightarrow$ [N,+pl,–subj,+gov,+obl]
   f. $/ov/ \leftrightarrow$ [N,+pl,–β,+subj,+gov,+obl]

Here, $/a/_1$ is an underspecified exponent that shows up in nominative and
genitive singular contexts (with different inflection classes); $/u/$ occurs in
accusative and dative singular environments (again, with different inflection
classes); $/i/$ is an exponent for nominative and accusative plural contexts;
$/a/_2$ is an exponent for nominative and accusative plural contexts with the
neuter inflection class ([+α,+β]); $/am/$ is a general dative plural marker;
and $/ov/$ is a genitive plural marker for two inflection classes (that are
characterized by the feature [+β]). All of this is essentially based on the
analysis in Müller (2004).

The first optimization for nominative plural environments with the noun
'child' is shown in (9). The categorizing head needs to first combine with
a stem. By assumption, the inflectional exponents require a fully specified
feature matrix, which is not yet in place if there is no stem; so outputs directly attaching an inflectional exponent to the categorizing head x cannot
be generated in the first place. Given MinSat, the first optimal output in
both singular and plural environments will invariably have to be /rebënOk/,
which succeeds in discharging [•N•] and thereby satisfies MC, but does not
give rise to a new satisfaction of any other constraint, in contrast to $/det'/$,
which satisfies both MC and Max(Pl).[17]

underspecification of inflectional exponents with respect to inflection class information;
see above.

[17] As before, the two subarrays postulated here are signalled by indices (i, j). Among
the contextual features to be realized by inflectional exponents that are introduced by
stems, only the inflection class features that are relevant in the present context are
indicated here (animacy and gender do not play a role in nominative plural contexts).
Note also that O_1 cannot violate Max([α]), Max([β]) because these contextual inflection
class features in need of morphological realization by exponence are located on stems
and have not been introduced yet.

(9) *Local stem allomorphy in nominative plural contexts* (harmonic serialism, step 1):

I_0: x:[+pl,+subj,−obl,−gov], [•N•]
{[$_{N_i}$ /rebënOk/:[+α,−β] ↔[−]],
[$_{N_i}$ /det′/:[+α,−β] ↔[+pl]],
[$_{N_j}$ /a/$_1$ ↔ [+subj]],
[$_{N_j}$ /u/ ↔ [−subj,+gov]],
[$_{N_j}$ /i/ ↔ [+pl,−obl,−gov]],
[$_{N_j}$ /a/$_2$ ↔ [+pl,+α,+β]],
[$_{N_j}$ /am/ ↔ [+pl,−subj,+gov,+obl],
[$_{N_j}$ /ov/ ↔ [+pl,−β,+subj,+gov,+obl]}

	Ex S	Min Sat	R C	M C	Id F	Max Pl	Max Obl	Max Gov	Max Subj	Max α	Max β	*Str
O_1: x:[+pl,+subj,−obl,−gov], [•N•]				*!		*	*	*	*			
☞O_2: x:[+pl,+subj,−obl,−gov]-rebënOk:[+α,−β]						*	*	*	*			*
O_3: x:[+pl,+subj,−obl,−gov]-det′:[+α,−β]		*!					*	*	*			*

In the second step of the derivation, /det′/ is merged with O_2; this gets rid of the Max(Pl) violation. Since, at this point, fully specified contextual information is available, competing outputs can be generated that merge inflectional exponents; however, given Ex-S, it is clear that other items from the current subarray have to be tried out first (i.e., /det′/), independently of whether this is favoured by Max constraints or not (it is, in the case at hand). The competition is illustrated in (10).

(10) *Local stem allomorphy in nominative plural contexts* (harmonic serialism, step 2):

I_2: x:[+pl,+subj,−obl,−gov]-rebënOk:[+α,−β]
{[$_{N_i}$ /det′/:[+α,−β] ↔[+pl]],
[$_{N_j}$ /a/$_1$ ↔ [+subj]],
[$_{N_j}$ /u/ ↔ [−subj,+gov]],
[$_{N_j}$ /i/ ↔ [+pl,−obl,−gov]],
[$_{N_j}$ /a/$_2$ ↔ [+pl,+α,+β]],
[$_{N_j}$ /am/ ↔ [+pl,−subj,+gov,+obl],
[$_{N_j}$ /ov/ ↔ [+pl,−β,+subj,+gov,+obl]}

	Ex S	Min Sat	R C	M C	Id F	Max Pl	Max Obl	Max Gov	Max Subj	Max α	Max β	*Str
O_{21}: x:[+pl,+subj,−obl,−gov]-rebënOk:[+α,−β]						*!	*	*	*	*	*	
☞O_{22}: x:[+pl,+subj,−obl,−gov]-rebënOk:[+α,−β]-det′:[+α,−β]							*	*	*	*	*	*
O_{23}: x:[+pl,+subj,−obl,−gov]-rebënOk:[+α,−β]-a$_1$	*!						*	*		*	*	*
O_{24}: x:[+pl,+subj,−obl,−gov]-rebënOk:[+α,−β]-u	*!	*			**	*	*			*	*	*
O_{25}: x:[+pl,+subj,−obl,−gov]-rebënOk:[+α,−β]-i	*!	*							*	*	*	*
O_{26}: x:[+pl,+subj,−obl,−gov]-rebënOk:[+α,−β]-a$_2$	*!	*			*		*	*	*			*
O_{27}: x:[+pl,+subj,−obl,−gov]-rebënOk:[+α,−β]-am	*!	*			***					*	*	*
O_{28}: x:[+pl,+subj,−obl,−gov]-rebënOk:[+α,−β]-ov	*!	*			**					*		*

In cases of stem allomorphy, there is disjunctive blocking. This means that all competing stems in a morphological subarray, except for the least specific one, need to be equipped with removal features. In the case at hand, this holds for /det′/. Consequently, in the following step, /det′/'s [−N−] feature triggers removal of /rebënOk/, via RC; cf. O_{222}. (An alternative to satisfy RC would be self-removal of /det′/, as in O_{223}, but this fatally reintroduces the earlier Max(Pl) violation.)

(11) *Local stem allomorphy in nominative plural contexts* (harmonic serialism, step 3):

I$_{22}$: x:[+pl,+subj,–obl,–gov]-rebënOk:[+α,–β]-det':[+α,–β]$_{[-N-]}$
{[$_{N_j}$ /a/$_1$ ↔ [+subj],
[$_{N_j}$ /u/ ↔ [–subj,+gov],
[$_{N_j}$ /i/ ↔ [+pl,–obl,–gov],
[$_{N_j}$ /a/$_2$ ↔ [+pl,+α,+β],
[$_{N_j}$ /am/ ↔ [+pl,–subj,+gov,+obl],
[$_{N_j}$ /ov/ ↔ [+pl,–β,+subj,+gov,+obl]}

	ExS	MinSat	RC	MC	IdF	MaxPl	MaxObl	MaxGov	MaxSubj	Maxα	Maxβ	*Str
O$_{221}$: x:[+pl,+subj,–obl,–gov]-rebënOk:[+α,–β]-det':[+α,–β]$_{[-N-]}$			*!				*	*	*	*	*	
☞ O$_{222}$: x:[+pl,+subj,–obl,–gov]-det':[+α,–β]							*	*	*	*	*	
O$_{223}$: x:[+pl,+subj,–obl,–gov]-rebënOk:[+α,–β]						*!	*	*	*	*	*	
O$_{224}$: x:[+pl,+subj,–obl,–gov]-rebënOk:[+α,–β]-det':[+α,–β]$_{[-N-]}$-a$_1$	*!		*				*	*		*	*	*
O$_{225}$: x:[+pl,+subj,–obl,–gov]-rebënOk:[+α,–β]-det':[+α,–β]$_{[-N-]}$-u	*!	*	*		**		*			*	*	*
O$_{226}$: x:[+pl,+subj,–obl,–gov]-rebënOk:[+α,–β]-det':[+α,–β]$_{[-N-]}$-i	*!	*	*						*	*	*	*
O$_{227}$: x:[+pl,+subj,–obl,–gov]-rebënOk:[+α,–β]-det':[+α,–β]$_{[-N-]}$-a$_2$	*!	*	*		*		*	*	*			*
O$_{228}$: x:[+pl,+subj,–obl,–gov]-rebënOk:[+α,–β]-det':[+α,–β]$_{[-N-]}$-am	*!	*	*		***					*	*	*
O$_{229}$: x:[+pl,+subj,–obl,–gov]-rebënOk:[+α,–β]-det':[+α,–β]$_{[-N-]}$-ov	*!	*	*		**					*		*

O$_{222}$ then forms the input for further optimization. At this stage, the second subarray can be accessed in accordance with ExS. Again, there is a disjunctive blocking relation among the exponents, and MinSat at first chooses the most general marker that can improve the overall constraint profile, viz., /a/$_1$.[18]

(12) *Local stem allomorphy in nominative plural contexts* (harmonic serialism, step 4):

I$_{222}$: x:[+pl,+subj,–obl,–gov]-det':[+α,–β]
{[$_{N_j}$ /a/$_1$ ↔ [+subj],
[$_{N_j}$ /u/ ↔ [–subj,+gov],
[$_{N_j}$ /i/ ↔ [+pl,–obl,–gov],
[$_{N_j}$ /a/$_2$ ↔ [+pl,+α,+β],
[$_{N_j}$ /am/ ↔ [+pl,–subj,+gov,+obl],
[$_{N_j}$ /ov/ ↔ [+pl,–β,+subj,+gov,+obl]}

	ExS	MinSat	RC	MC	IdF	MaxPl	MaxObl	MaxGov	MaxSubj	Maxα	Maxβ	*Str
O$_{2221}$: x:[+pl,+subj,–obl,–gov]-det':[+α,–β]							*	*	*!	*	*	
☞ O$_{2222}$: x:[+pl,+subj,–obl,–gov]-det':[+α,–β]-a$_1$							*	*		*	*	*
O$_{2223}$: x:[+pl,+subj,–obl,–gov]-det':[+α,–β]-u		*!			**		*			*	*	*
O$_{2224}$: x:[+pl,+subj,–obl,–gov]-det':[+α,–β]-i		*!							*	*	*	*
O$_{2225}$: x:[+pl,+subj,–obl,–gov]-det':[+α,–β]-a$_2$		*!			*		*	*	*			*
O$_{2226}$: x:[+pl,+subj,–obl,–gov]-det':[+α,–β]-am		*!			***					*	*	*
O$_{2227}$: x:[+pl,+subj,–obl,–gov]-det':[+α,–β]-ov		*!			**					*		*

In the next step, the derivation seeks to further improve the candidate's behaviour with respect to Max constraints (as far as MinSat permits this), and therefore merges /i/; see (13).

---

[18] The exponent /a/$_1$ is optimal (at the end of the derivation) in nominative environments with the (primarily) feminine declension captured by [–α,+β], and in genitive environments with inflection classes [+α,–β] (the standard masculine declension) and [+α,+β] (the neuter declension) – but as we will see momentarily, it will not survive in the present environment.

(13) *Local stem allomorphy in nominative plural contexts* (harmonic serialism, step 5):

I_{2222}: O_{2222}: x:[+pl,+subj,−obl,−gov]-det′:[+α,−β]-a_1 {[$_{N_j}$ /u/ ↔ [−subj,+gov], [$_{N_j}$ /i/ ↔ [+pl,−obl,−gov], [$_{N_j}$ /a/$_2$ ↔ [+pl,+α,+β], [$_{N_j}$ /am/ ↔ [+pl,−subj,+gov,+obl], [$_{N_j}$ /ov/ ↔ [+pl,−β,+subj,+gov,+obl]}	Ex S	Min Sat	R C	M C	Id F	Max Pl	Max Obl	Max Gov	Max Subj	Max α	Max β	*Str
O_{22221}: x:[+pl,+subj,−obl,−gov]-det′:[+α,−β]-a_1							*!	*		*	*	
O_{22222}: x:[+pl,+subj,−obl,−gov]-det′:[+α,−β]-a_1-u					*!*		*			*	*	*
☞ O_{22223}: x:[+pl,+subj,−obl,−gov]-det′:[+α,−β]-a_1-i										*	*	*
O_{22224}: x:[+pl,+subj,−obl,−gov]-det′:[+α,−β]-a_1-a_2					*!		*	*				*
O_{22225}: x:[+pl,+subj,−obl,−gov]-det′:[+α,−β]-a_1-am					*!**					*	*	*
O_{22226}: x:[+pl,+subj,−obl,−gov]-det′:[+α,−β]-a_1-ov		*!			**					*		*

Note that the optimal output O_{22223}, which merges /i/, is not at variance with MinSat at this point anymore, even though it adds two new Max satisfactions (of Max(Obl) and of Max(Gov)). The reason is that adding /u/ in O_{22222} (which gives rise to only one new constraint satisfaction – viz., of Max(Gov) – since /a/$_1$ has already satisfied Max(Subj)) does not improve the constraint profile of the input because it gives rise to a violation of high-ranked Id-F (and analogous considerations apply in the case of all other exponents with fewer new constraint satisfactions in alternative output candidates that are not listed here).

The following optimization procedure consists of exponent removal, triggered by /i/'s [−N−] feature via RC; see (14). Note that since /i/ does not maintain /a_1/'s earlier Max(Subj) satisfaction (but satisfies the two higher-ranked constraints Max(Obl) and Max(Gov), thereby precluding reflexive removal as in O_{222233}), the constraint profile of the new optimal output O_{222232} is actually *worse* than the constraint profile of the immediately preceding output O_{22223}. This scenario, which may be considered paradoxical at first sight, arises naturally under present assumptions because the removal feature present on O_{22223} leads to an RC violation as soon as this output becomes an input, but not before that.

(14) *Local stem allomorphy in nominative plural contexts* (harmonic serialism, step 6):

I_{22223}: x:[+pl,+subj,−obl,−gov]-det′:[+α,−β]-a_1-i {[$_{N_j}$ /u/ ↔ [−subj,+gov], [$_{N_j}$ /a/$_2$ ↔ [+pl,+α,+β], [$_{N_j}$ /am/ ↔ [+pl,−subj,+gov,+obl], [$_{N_j}$ /ov/ ↔ [+pl,−β,+subj,+gov,+obl]}	Ex S	Min Sat	R C	M C	Id F	Max Pl	Max Obl	Max Gov	Max Subj	Max α	Max β	*Str
O_{222231}: x:[+pl,+subj,−obl,−gov]-det′:[+α,−β]-a_1-i			*!							*	*	
☞ O_{222232}: x:[+pl,+subj,−obl,−gov]-det′:[+α,−β]-i									*	*	*	
O_{222233}: x:[+pl,+subj,−obl,−gov]-det′:[+α,−β]-a_1						*!	*			*	*	
O_{222234}: x:[+pl,+subj,−obl,−gov]-det′:[+α,−β]-a_1-i-u			*!		**							*
O_{222235}: x:[+pl,+subj,−obl,−gov]-det′:[+α,−β]-a_1-i-a_2			*!		*							*
O_{222236}: x:[+pl,+subj,−obl,−gov]-det′:[+α,−β]-a_1-i-am			*!		*!**					*	*	*
O_{222237}: x:[+pl,+subj,−obl,−gov]-det′:[+α,−β]-a_1-i-ov		*!	*		**					*		*

At this point, it is clear that there can be no further improvement by merging additional items from the morphological array: MAX(PL), MAX(OBL) and MAX(GOV) are satisfied in the final optimal output, and there is no inflectional exponent in the system that could also satisfy MAX(SUBJ) or one of the MAX constraints for the inflection class features, without simultaneously inducing a violation of higher-ranked ID-F. Consequently, the next step is the final step leading to convergence; see (15).

(15) *Local stem allomorphy in nominative plural contexts* (harmonic serialism, step 7):

I_{222232}: x:[+pl,+subj,−obl,−gov]-det′:[+α,−β]-i {[$_{N_j}$ /u/ ↔ [−subj,+gov], [$_{N_j}$ /a/$_2$ ↔ [+pl,+α,+β], [$_{N_j}$ /am/ ↔ [+pl,−subj,+gov,+obl], [$_{N_j}$ /ov/ ↔ [+pl,−β,+subj,+gov,+obl]}	Ex S	Min Sat	R C	M C	Id F	Max Pl	Max Obl	Max Gov	Max Subj	α	β	* Str
☞ $O_{2222321}$: x:[+pl,+subj,−obl,−gov]-det′:[+α,−β]-i									*	*	*	
$O_{2222322}$: x:[+pl,+subj,−obl,−gov]-det′:[+α,−β]-i-u					*!*					*	*	*
$O_{2222323}$: x:[+pl,+subj,−obl,−gov]-det′:[+α,−β]-i-a$_2$					*!			*				*
$O_{2222324}$: x:[+pl,+subj,−obl,−gov]-det′:[+α,−β]-i-am					*!**					*	*	*
$O_{2222325}$: x:[+pl,+subj,−obl,−gov]-det′:[+α,−β]-i-ov					*!*					*		*

Finally, it should be pointed out that the analysis of stem allomorphy with /rebënOk/, /det′/ developed here is incomplete in that it does not explicitly list alignment constraints holding for stems and inflectional exponents. Linearization is entirely unproblematic in the case at hand: All the work can be done by a constraint like N⇒R, which ensures (given a sufficiently high ranking) that the noun stem (bearing [N]) shows up to the right of x and the inflection marker (also bearing [N] under present assumptions) shows up to the right of the stem, as required by the STRICT CYCLE CONDITION: Inflectional exponence will then trigger a minimal violation of N⇒R with the stem, but this is unavoidable, and unmotivated subsequent movement of the stem to the right periphery of the word is independently blocked.

Or is it? For such movement that does not improve the constraint profile to be blocked, there has to be *some* constraint that is violated by it. Recall from chapter 3 (footnote 43) that I have assumed throughout that movement in morphology does not violate *STRUC; only adding an item from the morphological array to the current stem does. In view of this, there are (at least) two possible solutions. First, it could be assumed that *STRUC precludes both addition of an item from the morphological array (external Merge) and movement of an item that is already part of the present stem (internal Merge, in Chomsky's terminology); this would in principle be compatible with all the analyses given so far, but I have in fact assumed above that this is not the case. Second, another (typically low-ranked) constraint that is invariably violated by (non-string-vacuous) movement in morphology can be postulated. For the sake of concreteness, I will here adopt the second view and assume a general shape conservation requirement, as in (16) (see Müller (2000b), Williams (2003), and Fox & Pesetsky (2005) for proposals to this effect for syntax, and McCarthy & Prince (1995), McCarthy (2002), and Heinz (2005), among many others, for phonology – more specifically, for metathesis phenomena).[19]

(16) SHAPE CONSERVATION (SC):
      If α precedes β in the input, α precedes β in the output.

Thus, we can conclude that the issue of where to place which item that is part of the inflected word in cases of stem allomorphy with nouns in Russian (and more generally, with instances of local allomorphy) is not a complex one. However, things are slightly different with non-local allomorphy scenarios as they were discussed at the outset of the present chapter. It is to this type of case that I turn next.

1.3.4. A Case Study of Non-Local Stem Allomorphy: Tamil Personal Pronouns

Given the approach to local stem allomorphy detailed in the previous section, and given that the option of movement in morphology follows without further ado from independently motivated constraints in harmonic serialism, the problem posed by non-local allomorphy for most theories of inflectional morphology is resolved: All instances of stem allomorphy are extremely local (this follows from the concept of morphological arrays), but strict locality can be masked by subsequent movement operations, giving rise to what on the surface looks like non-local suppletion. This is a typical counter-bleeding effect, as it can be observed in syntax with sentences like (17), where satisfaction of Principle A of the binding theory is masked by subsequent wh-movement of the DP containing the reflexive pronoun:

---

[19] One might think that versions of Trommer's (2008a) COHERENCE constraint that are sensitive to morphological arrays and morphological subarrays might also suffice (recall from chapter 2 that this constraint is sometimes violated with movement). However, this is not generally the case; in the case at hand, adjacency would not be disrupted if an [N] stem moves across an [N] exponent.

That said, a straightforward alternative would be to adopt (i) a constraint that requires right-alignment only for inflectional exponents, not for stems, and (ii) another, lower-ranked constraint demanding right-alignment for stems. – As a matter of fact, closer inspection reveals that there is no real need for the latter type of constraint: Given that x is a defective item that is invisible for the purposes of alignment constraints, as assumed throughout, it is irrelevant whether the eventual order is x-Σ or Σ-x when the categorizing head is merged with the noun stem.

Wh-movement comes too late to prevent licensing of the reflexive pronoun under c-command by the local (i.e., clause-mate) co-indexed subject DP (see Barss (1986), among others).

(17) [$_{DP_{[wh]}}$ Which book about himself$_1$] does Mary think that John$_1$ likes ?

In addition, recall the counter-bleeding effects with instances of derivational and inflectional morphology in Bemba and Barwar Aramaic, respectively, that were discussed in sections 3.7. and 3.8. of chapter 2.

In what follows, I will illustrate this strictly local approach to non-local suppletion exemplarily by developing a harmonic serialist analysis of case-based suppletion with personal pronoun stems in Tamil. However, it should be clear that this approach will work in basically the same way for all instances of non-local suppletion that have been reported in the literature, including those discussed at the outset of the present chapter (Slovenian verbs, Tariana adjectives, and also the slightly different pattern of Greek verbs).

Recall that in Tamil personal pronouns, the form of the D stem encoding person information is determined by case information (nominative vs. all other cases). However, between the right-peripheral case exponent and the stem, a number exponent can intervene that is overt in the case of plural; cf. the examples in (2), repeated here in (18). In an example like (18-a-iv), /en/ is a first person pronoun stem, /(n)ga(l)/ is a plural marker, and /ukku/ is a non-local exponent for dative case. In contrast, in (18-a-ii), the first person pronoun stem is /naan/, /(n)ga(l)/ is again the intervening plural marker, and the non-local case exponent is zero (i.e., /Ø/).

(18) a. (i)   1.SG.NOM: naan-Ø-Ø
          (ii)   1.PL.NOM: naan-ga-Ø
          (iii) 1.SG.DAT: en-Ø-akku
          (iv)   1.PL.DAT: en-ga(l)-ukku
      b. (i)   2.SG.NOM: nii-Ø-Ø
          (ii)   2.PL.NOM: nii-(n)ga-Ø
          (iii) 2.SG.DAT: on-Ø-akku
          (iv)   2.PL.DAT: on-ga(l)-ukku

The sequence *stem ≻ number exponent ≻ case exponent* is not specific to personal pronouns. It is the general order for nominal categories in Tamil, which also shows up with inflected nouns, independently of stem

alternation (cf., e.g., Lehmann (1989) and Schiffman (1999)).[20] So, for
a noun like /kaal/ ('leg'), the dative plural form is *kaal-kaḷ-ukku* (/kaal/-
/(n)ga(l)/-/ukku/), with noun stem preceding number marker preceding
case marker. In an approach to inflectional morphology where the position
of exponents is crucially determined by alignment constraints (see Trommer
(2001; 2008a) and the preceding chapters), this state of affairs suggests the
constraints in (19) (see (26) in chapter 2).

(19) a.   L⇐PERS:
           A morphological exponent realizing person is aligned with the
           left edge of a word.
      b.   NUM⇒R:
           A morphological exponent realizing number is aligned with the
           right edge of a word.
      c.   CASE⇒R:
           A morphological exponent realizing case is aligned with the right
           edge of a word.

The basic pattern follows under a ranking like that in (20).

(20) L⇐PERS ≫ CASE⇒R ≫ NUM⇒R

(20) ensures that a nominal stem (which is marked for third person in
non-pronominal contexts, i.e., when we are dealing with nouns) is always
left-peripheral in a word, and that a case suffix follows a number affix (since
the right-alignment requirement for case exponents is ranked higher than
the right-alignment requirement for number exponents). In standard noun
inflection scenarios (without suppletion), there will be three morphological
arrays targeted by three structure-building ([•F•]) features, and assuming an appropriate order of the MC constraints involved, there is nothing
that would preclude a simple derivation where the categorizing head x first
combines with the noun stem, the resulting object then merges a number

---

[20] Ultimately, the picture is somewhat more complex with nouns: Whereas the majority
of nouns in Tamil do not show stem alternation between the nominative and other cases,
some nouns do show such alternation, albeit in a much more systematic form (by adding
what has been referred to as an "oblique" suffix *ttu*, or an "oblique" suffix *aṟṟu*, or
by a phonological operation (consonant doubling); see Lehmann (1989) and McFadden
(2018) for further discussion of the phenomenon). These systematic stem extensions in
non-nominative environments with some nouns in Tamil independently pose challenges,
but they do not seem to discriminate between the present approach and other theories
of inflection in this respect. For this reason, I will abstract away from the issue in what
follows, focussing on stem invariance with most nouns in the language in what follows.

exponent on the right, and the extended stem that results as a consequence finally merges a case exponent on its right, thereby inducing a minimal but unavoidable (hence, tolerable) violation of the lower-ranked constraint Num⇒R.

In this kind of derivation, there is no movement involved. However, with personal pronouns, things are different because personal pronoun stems are not merely marked for person, but also for case (nominative vs. other cases). This implies that in these cases, a morphological array is generated that encompasses both stems bearing person and case features, and case exponents. Number exponents, in contrast, have another (small) morphological array all to themselves. I assume that the exponents in (18) belong to the two morphological arrays indicated in (21-a) and (21-b), and are associated with morpho-syntactic features as specified here. The underlying feature system postulated here should for the most part be self-explanatory. Person and number features are as before; as for case features, the assumption is that the nominative is the only case which is not [+gov]; this way, it is systematically singled out among all cases.[21]

(21) a. (i)   /naan/ ↔ [D,+1]
          (ii)   /en/ ↔ [D,+1,+gov]
          (iii) /nii/ ↔ [D,+2]
          (iv)   /on/ ↔ [D,+2,+gov]
          (v)   /Ø/ ↔ [D,−gov,−obl]
          (vi)   /(a/u)kku/ ↔ [D,+gov,+obl]
      b. (i)   /Ø/ ↔ [#,−pl]
          (ii)   /(n)ga(l)/ ↔ [#,+pl]

The morphological array in (21-a) is captured by a feature like [•D•] (collecting all items with person or case information) on the initial categorizing head x, and the morphological array in (21-b) by a feature [•#•] (for number); for each of these features, a designated MC (MC(D), MC(#)) ensures the activation of the morphological array. Furthermore, as noted before, presence vs. absence of person features in a marker entry decides on the attribution of an item in the first morphological array to one or the other of the two subarrays. Under these assumptions, the derivation of a first person

---

[21] Thus, dative ([+gov,+obl]), accusative ([+gov,−obl]), instrumental, sociative, locative, etc. all qualify as extensions of the feature [+gov]. See, however, McFadden (2018) for an alternative way of stating the required distinction.

244   Chapter 5. Suppletion

plural dative form of the personal pronoun, viz., *en-ga(l)-ukku*, works as illustrated in what follows.[22]

Suppose that initially, a categorizing head x is generated that is associated with the contextual features [+pl,+gov,+obl,+1,−2], and that is furthermore equipped with the structure-building features [•D•] and [•#•]. In the first step, x needs to merge with a D stem. MINSAT predicts that of the two possible stem candidates /naan/ (here viewed as underspecified with respect to case information by just being marked [+1]) and /en/ (which bears the case feature [+gov] in addition to [+1]), the former is selected first. This, of course, in turn implies that disjunctive blocking holds for this morphological subarray (i.e., all exponents except for the least specific one(s) – /nii/ has the same status as /naan/ in this respect – are equipped with a [−D−] feature for removal).[23]

(22) *Non-local stem allomorphy in first person dative plural contexts*
       (harmonic serialism, step 1):

I_0: x:[+pl,+gov,+obl,+1,−2], [•D•], [•#•]
{[$_{D_i}$ /naan/ ↔[+1]],
[$_{D_i}$ /en/ ↔[+1,+gov]],
[$_{D_i}$ /nii/ ↔ [+2],
[$_{D_i}$ /on/ ↔ [+2,+gov],
[$_{D_j}$ /Ø/ ↔ [−gov,−obl],
[$_{D_j}$ /(a/u)kku/ ↔ [+gov,+obl]}
{[$_#$ /Ø/ ↔ [−pl],
[$_#$ /(n)ga(l)/ ↔ [+pl]]}

	Min S	R C	MC D	MC #	Id F	Max Pl	Max 1	Max Obl	Max Gov	L⇐ Pers	Case ⇒R	Num ⇒R	* Str	S C
O_1: x:[+pl,+gov,+obl,+1,−2], [•D•], [•#•]			*!	*		*	*	*	*					
☞O_2: x:[+pl,+gov,+obl,+1,−2]-naan, [•#•]				*		*		*	*				*	
O_3: x:[+pl,+gov,+obl,+1,−2]-en, [•#•]	*!			*		*		*					*	
O_4: x:[+pl,+gov,+obl,+1,−2]-nii, [•#•]				*	*!	*	*	*	*				*	
O_5: x:[+pl,+gov,+obl,+1,−2]-on, [•#•]	*!			*	*	*	*	*					*	

Recall that, by assumption, only stems (which can themselves provide contextual features for further exponence) can be considered in the first optimization step. The next step of the derivation further improves the constraint profile; at this point, /en/ can be added so as to get rid of the input's MAX(GOV) violation. Note that EXHAUST SUBARRAY (EXS) ensures that

---

[22] I hasten to add that the sequence of optimization procedures given here is simplified for expository purposes in various ways. Not all relevant constraints are shown, and more exponents in the two morphological arrays would eventually have to be listed.

[23] In principle, it would also have to be possible to come up with an equivalent analysis that does not involve a radically underspecified stem for nominative contexts, but rather one that is characterized by the case feature [−gov]; in such an analysis, MINSAT would not per se favour choice of the "wrong" stem initially. The present choice is mainly motivated by showing that an analysis in terms of underspecification is possible.

only D_i items (i.e., person-marked stems) can be considered; for this reason, all alternative outputs are disregarded in the tableau in (23).

(23) *Non-local stem allomorphy in first person dative plural contexts* (harmonic serialism, step 2):

I₂: x:[+pl,+gov,+obl,±1,–2]-naan, [•#•]
{[D_i /en/ ↔[+1,+gov]],
[D_i /nii/ ↔ [+2],
[D_i /on/ ↔ [+2,+gov],
[D_j /Ø/ ↔ [–gov,–obl],
[D_j /(a/u)kku/ ↔ [+gov,+obl]}
{[# /Ø/ ↔ [–pl],
[# /(n)ga(l)/ ↔ [+pl]]}

	Min S	RC	MC D	MC #	Id F	Max Pl	Max 1	Max Obl	Max Gov	L⇐Pers	Case ⇒R	Num ⇒R	*Str	SC
O₂₁: x:[+pl,+gov,+obl,±1,–2]-naan, [•#•]				*		*		*	*!					
☞ O₂₂: x:[+pl,+gov,+obl,±1,–2]-naan-en, [•#•]				*		*		*		*			*	
O₂₃: x:[+pl,+gov,+obl,±1,–2]-naan-nii, [•#•]				*	*!	*		*		*			*	
O₂₄: x:[+pl,+gov,+obl,±1,–2]-naan-on, [•#•]				*	*!	*		*		*			*	

Incidentally, temporary co-occurrence of two stem exponents as in O₂₂–O₂₄ gives rise to a violation of L⇐Pers. This is unproblematic, given that Max(Gov) outranks this alignment constraint, as assumed here.

Next, since /en/ is equipped with a [–D–] feature, RC becomes active and demands immediate removal of the earlier stem /naan/; see (24).[24]

(24) *Non-local stem allomorphy in first person dative plural contexts* (harmonic serialism, step 3):

I₂₂: x:[+pl,+gov,+obl,±1,–2]-naan-en, [•#•]
{[D_i /nii/ ↔ [+2],
[D_i /on/ ↔ [+2,+gov],
[D_j /Ø/ ↔ [–gov,–obl],
[D_j /(a/u)kku/ ↔ [+gov,+obl]}
{[# /Ø/ ↔ [–pl],
[# /(n)ga(l)/ ↔ [+pl]]}

	Min S	RC	MC D	MC #	Id F	Max Pl	Max 1	Max Obl	Max Gov	L⇐Pers	Case ⇒R	Num ⇒R	*Str	SC
O₂₂₁: x:[+pl,+gov,+obl,±1,–2]-naan-en, [•#•]		*!		*		*		*		*			*	
O₂₂₂: x:[+pl,+gov,+obl,±1,–2]-naan, [•#•]				*		*		*	*!					
☞ O₂₂₃: x:[+pl,+gov,+obl,±1,–2]-en, [•#•]				*		*		*						
O₂₂₄: x:[+pl,+gov,+obl,±1,–2]-naan-en-nii, [•#•]		*!		*	*	*		*		**			*	
O₂₂₅: x:[+pl,+gov,+obl,±1,–2]-naan-en-on, [•#•]		*!		*	*	*		*		**			*	

For the fourth step, Exhaust Morphological Array (ExMorAr, cf. (62) in chapter 3) guarantees that items from the morphological array identified by D need to be considered as long as improvement is still possible on this basis. It is, so outputs involving exponents from the second morphological array identified by # need not yet be taken into account. As shown in (25), the optimal operation at this point is to merge a case exponent that faithfully realizes dative case by producing a satisfaction of Max(Obl) (in

---

[24] From this point onwards, I do not list outputs based on the second person stem exponents /nii/, /on/; it is obvious that they can never become optimal anymore, due to harmonic bounding.

addition to the MAX(GOV) satisfaction already delivered by the D stem /en/). For this purpose, choosing /(a/u)kku/ is the optimal strategy (see O_{2233}); the alternative case exponent /Ø/ (in O_{2232}), as well as all other conceivable exponents of case, lead to a worse constraint profile. This accounts for the pattern of overlapping multiple exponence (see Caballero & Harris (2012)) that typically arises with stem allomorphy under present assumptions.

(25)　*Non-local stem allomorphy in first person dative plural contexts*
　　　　(harmonic serialism, step 4):

I_{223}: x:[+pl,+gov,+obl,±1,–2]-en, [•#•]
{[$_{D_i}$ /nii/ ↔ [+2],
[$_{D_i}$ /on/ ↔ [+2,+gov],
[$_{D_j}$ /Ø/ ↔ [–gov,–obl],
[$_{D_j}$ /(a/u)kku/ ↔ [+gov,+obl]}
{[$_\#$ /Ø/ ↔ [–pl],
[$_\#$ /(n)ga(l)/ ↔ [+pl]]}

	MIN S	R C	MC D	MC #	ID F	MAX PL	MAX 1	MAX OBL	MAX GOV	L⇐ PERS	CASE ⇒R	NUM ⇒R	* STR	S C
O_{2231}: x:[+pl,+gov,+obl,±1,–2]-en, [•#•]				*		*		*!						
O_{2232}: x:[+pl,+gov,+obl,±1,–2]-en-Ø, [•#•]				*	*!	*					*		*	
☞O_{2233}: x:[+pl,+gov,+obl,±1,–2]-en-(a/u)kku, [•#•]				*		*					*		*	
O_{2234}: Ø-x:[+pl,+gov,+obl,±1,–2]-en, [•#•]				*	*!	*				*	*		*	
O_{2235}: (a/u)kku-x:[+pl,+gov,+obl,±1,–2]-en, [•#•]				*		*				*!	*		*	

O_{2234} and O_{2235} are outputs that merge case exponents as prefixes; this gives rise to violations of L⇐PERS and CASE⇒R, which are fatal in the case of /(a/u)kku/ in O_{2235}. Note furthermore that adding a case exponent as a suffix will invariably give rise to a violation of CASE⇒R, given that the D stem also bears the case feature [+gov].

At this stage of the optimization sequence, no further improvement is possible based on the first morphological array, so the derivation turns to the second morphological array. The tableau in (26) illustrates that merging the plural exponent /(n)ga(l)/, which leads to a satisfaction of both MC(#) and MAX(PL), is the optimal strategy now. This operation is compatible with MINSAT because there is no better alternative with fewer new constraint satisfactions.[25] The exponent needs to be merged as a suffix, as in O_{22332}, and not as a prefix, as in O_{22333}: O_{22332} adds more violations of CASE⇒R because (i) /(a/u)kku/ is now not in a right-peripheral position anymore, and (ii) /en/ is now two slots away from the right periphery. However, O_{22333} violates the higher-ranked alignment constraint L⇐PERS (plus, irrelevantly in the present context, the lower-ranked constraint NUM⇒R, due to the plural exponent showing up at the

---

[25] Alternatively, one could have assumed that the singular exponent /Ø/ does not actually bear the feature [–pl]; in that case, the derivation would have had to take a detour via first merging /Ø/ (as would then be demanded by MINSAT), and subsequently merging /(n)ga(l)/ and removing /Ø/ again.

left edge of the word) because the D stem /en/ is not in a left-peripheral position in this candidate.[26]

(26) *Non-local stem allomorphy in first person dative plural contexts* (harmonic serialism, step 5):

I_{2233}: x:[+pl,+gov,+obl,+1,−2]-en-(a/u)kku, [•#•] {[$_{D_i}$ /nii/ ↔ [+2], [$_{D_i}$ /on/ ↔ [+2,+gov], [$_{D_j}$ /Ø/ ↔ [−gov,−obl]} {[# /Ø/ ↔ [−pl], [# /(n)ga(l)/ ↔ [+pl]]}	MIN S	R C	MC D	MC #	ID F	MAX PL	MAX 1	MAX OBL	MAX GOV	L⇐ PERS	CASE ⇒R	NUM ⇒R	* STR	S C
O_{22331}: x:[+pl,+gov,+obl,+1,−2]-en-(a/u)kku, [•#•]				*!		*					*			
☞O_{22332}: x:[+pl,+gov,+obl,+1,−2]-en-(a/u)kku-(n)ga(l)											***		*	
O_{22333}: (n)ga(l)-x:[+pl,+gov,+obl,+1,−2]-en-(a/u)kku										*!	*	**	*	
O_{22334}: x:[+pl,+gov,+obl,+1,−2]-en-(a/u)kku-Ø					*!						***		*	
O_{22335}: Ø-x:[+pl,+gov,+obl,+1,−2]-en-(a/u)kku					*!					*		**	*	

An output that would place the number exponent /(n)ga(l)/ directly between the person-marked D stem and the case suffix can never be an option because it is incompatible with the STRICT CYCLE CONDITION that I have assumed to be inviolable in optimal outputs throughout (see chapter 2). However, this does not mean that the sequence of exponents *stem* ≻ *number exponent* ≻ *case exponent* cannot be reached. On the contrary, further improvement yielding this result via movement is automatically predicted by the independently proposed ranking of constraints, without necessitating any further assumptions.[27] Thus, subjecting the optimal output O_{22332} of step 5 in (26) to a further optimization procedure does not yield convergence; rather, the case exponent /(a/u)kku/ is now predicted to move to the right edge, across the number exponent /(n)ga(l)/. This is shown in (27): Candidate O_{223322} carries out rightward movement, which minimizes violations of CASE⇒R at the price of a violation of the lower-ranked constraint NUM⇒R. Doing nothing, as in O_{223321}, is suboptimal, as is any other type of movement – e.g., movement of the number exponent /(n)ga(l)/ to the left, as in O_{223323}.

---

[26] This presupposes that there is no local reflexive conjunction here, i.e., no cumulative effects; see chapter 2 and references cited there.

[27] As a matter of fact, movement has been an option in candidate generation before in the derivation currently under consideration, but I have not focussed on this because it is clear that it could never have resulted in an optimal strategy before now.

(27) *Non-local stem allomorphy in first person dative plural contexts* (harmonic serialism, step 6):

I_{22332}: x:[+pl,+gov,+obl,+1,−2]-en-(a/u)kku-(n)ga(l) {[D_i /nii/ ↔ [+2], [D_i /on/ ↔ [+2,+gov], [D_i /∅/ ↔ [−gov,−obl]} {[# /∅/ ↔ [−pl]}	Min S	R C	MC D	MC #	Id F	Max Pl	Max 1	Max Obl	Max Gov	L⇐ Pers	Case ⇒R	Num ⇒R	* Str	S C
O_{223321}: x:[+pl,+gov,+obl,+1,−2]-en-(a/u)kku-(n)ga(l)											***!			
☞ O_{223322}: x:[+pl,+gov,+obl,+1,−2]-en-(n)ga(l)-(a/u)kku											**	*		*
O_{223323}: (n)ga(l)-x:[+pl,+gov,+obl,+1,−2]-en-(a/u)kku										*!	*	**		*

Again, we see a general property of analyses in harmonic serialism emerging: A violation that can be perfectly tolerable at one stage of the derivation (of CASE⇒R, in the case at hand) can become fatal at the next stage.

More generally, I would like to conclude that an approach in terms of harmonic serialism makes it possible to solve the conundrum of non-local stem allomorphy in a very simple way: All morpho-syntactically governed allomorphy is extremely local, and where it looks on the surface as though it is not, this is due to movement operations that the language carries out, based on an independently motivated ranking of alignment constraints. This covers seemingly non-local stem allomorphy with Slovenian verbs, Tariana adjectives, and Greek verbs in the same way that non-local stem allomorphy with Tamil personal pronouns could be derived; and it also extends to other instances of seemingly non-local stem allomorphy that have been discussed in the literature.[28]

2. *ABA

2.1. The Phenomenon

There is evidence that stem allomorphy in general obeys an *ABA restriction, in the sense that if there is a default form (A) and a more specific form (B) showing up in certain more specific contexts, the A form can typically not show up again in yet more specific environments. This has been observed by Wiese (2005; 2008) for ablaut with strong verbs in non-past, past, and finite past contexts in German, and independently by Bobaljik (2006; 2012) for adjectives in positive, comparative, and superlative contexts in the world's languages (the so-called "Comparative-Superlative Generalization"). Since then, the phenomenon has figured

---

[28] Among other phenomena, the present approach also directly extends to the apparent non-local determination of negation in Passamaquoddy-Maliseet investigated in Bruening (2017, 4.5.8), and derived there by invoking spans. Interestingly, in a footnote Bruening speculates that movement might in fact be involved here, but he does not pursue this matter further.

prominently in a great number of studies based on these and other empirical domains.[29] In what follows, I address the two original phenomena shown to exhibit an *ABA restriction in turn, beginning with Bobaljik's Comparative-Superlative Generalization.

2.1.1. The Comparative-Superlative Generalization

Based on a detailed typological investigation of suppletion with comparative and superlative forms of adjectives, Bobaljik (2012) arrives at the following generalization.

(28) *Comparative-superlative generalization*:
      If the comparative degree of an adjective is built on a suppletive root, then the superlative will also be suppletive.

The relevant patterns can be illustrated with some simple data from German, English, and Latin. (29-a) shows the unmarked, standard case of there being no stem allomorphy whatsoever; i.e., there is an AAA pattern for the positive, the comparative, and the superlative. In (29-b), an ABB pattern arises: The same suppletive form is used in the comparative and in the superlative. A doubly suppletive ABC pattern shows up in (29-c): There are three different forms for the positive, the comparative, and the superlative with the adjective *bonus* ('good') in Latin. However, what is largely unattested in the languages of the world is an ABA pattern, as in (29-d) (illustrated here for German′ and English′ versions with the adjective *gut* ('good') and *bad*, respectively). Here the positive and the superlative show the same (default) stem, and the comparative takes a different form.

(29) *Gradation patterns*:
      a.   AAA (regular):
           (i)   schlecht ('bad') – schlechter ('worse') – am schlechtesten ('worst')
           (ii)   fine – finer – finest
      b.   ABB (suppletive):
           (i)   gut ('good') – besser ('better') – am besten ('best')
           (ii)   bad – worse – worst
      c.   ABC (doubly suppletive):
           (i)   bonus ('good') – melior ('better') – optimus ('best')

---

[29] There are too many to mention them all, let alone discuss them here. See, among others, Moskal (2015), De Clercq & Vanden Wyngaerd (2017), Caha (2017), Bobaljik & Sauerland (2018), McFadden (2018), and Andersson (2018).

     d. *ABA (unattested):
         (i) *gut – besser – am gutsten
         (ii) *bad – worse – baddest
     e. *AAC (unattested for comparative suppletion):
         (i) *bad – badder – worst

Another pattern that is also unattested for comparative suppletion is the
AAC pattern in (29-e), where positive and comparative share a common
form to the exclusion of the superlative. As we will see below, this pattern is indeed established with other suppletion phenomena; it may thus
seem plausible to assume that the apparent prohibition against *AAC in
comparative formation has a somewhat different explanation than the ban
on *ABA (see Bobaljik (2012), De Clercq & Vanden Wyngaerd (2017) for
further discussion); I will return to this issue.

Bobaljik's explanation for the absence of ABA patterns with comparative formation is as follows.

First, a Distributed Morphology architecture is assumed where stem allomorphy is treated by post-syntactic vocabulary insertion into designated
root positions. Second, syncretism is taken to be systematic in the unmarked case: If two exponents with the same phonological form show up
in two different (but sufficiently similar) contexts, the premise for both
the language learner and the linguist is that they have the same function,
i.e., that they are associated with the same (underspecified) feature set.
Third, the Subset Principle (see (2) of chapter 2) holds, according to which
morphological exponence (here, vocabulary insertion) obeys a compatibility requirement (cf. (2-a) of chapter 2; the exponent must realize a subset
of the morpho-syntactic features provided by the insertion site's context)
and a specificity requirement (cf. (2-b) of chapter 2; more specific exponents – which for present purposes we can assume to mean: exponents
realizing more relevant morpho-syntactic features – block less specific exponents, among the class of exponents that are compatible with the syntactic
context). And fourth, crucially, the morpho-syntactic feature matrices to
be realized by exponence that are associated with positive, comparative,
and superlative are *asymmetric* in the sense that they are characterized by
feature specifications in subset relations. For concreteness, a positive environment can be characterized by the absence of any specific features, a comparative environment is associated with a designated feature like [compr],
and a superlative environment has both the feature [compr] and a further
feature [superl]; as Bobaljik notes, defining the comparative in terms of the
positive plus something else, and defining the superlative in terms of the

comparative (thus eventually including the positive) and something else is
expected from a semantic perspective.

Thus, we end up with feature specifications for syntactic contexts in
need of morphological realization as in (30).[30]

(30) a.   Positive: [–]
      b.   Comparative: [compr]
      c.   Superlative: [compr,superl]

Under these assumptions, the *ABA generalization can be derived. Suppose that there is always one form of the adjectival stem, call it A, that is
not associated with any (relevant) morpho-syntactic features.

The first possibility is that this is the only form. In that case, an AAA
pattern will arise: A is compatible with all three environments, and there
is no more specific form that could ever block it.

The second possibility is that there are also other stem exponents B
and C, where B is characterized by the feature [compr] and C bears the
features [compr] and [superl]. This will give rise to an ABC pattern: A,
B and C are compatible with the superlative environment, but C is most
specific and thus blocks A and B here; A and B are compatible with the
comparative environment, but B is more specific and thus blocks A here;
and only A is compatible with the positive environment, thus precluding a
choice of B or C in this context.

Next, the third a priori possible scenario is one where there is only
an exponent C characterized by both [compr] and [superl] in addition to
unmarked A. Here, the prediction is that A will show up in positive and
comparative contexts, with C confined to the superlative environment; i.e.,
an AAC pattern arises. As noted above, this option may not show up with

---

[30] Actually, the favoured implementation in Bobaljik's work is not via features, but via
separate functional heads Adj, Comp, and Superl, as in (i), with morphological realization proceeding via contextual features. To ensure adjacency of the relevant contextual
information, head movement of A to Compr, and of a complex Compr to Superl can be
postulated.

(i)   a.   Positive:
           [$_{AP}$ ... A ...]
      b.   Comparative:
           [$_{ComprP}$ ... [AP ... A ...] ... Compr ...]
      c.   Superlative:
           [$_{SuperlP}$ ... [ComprP ... [AP ... A ...] ... Compr ...] ... Superl ...]

As noted by Bobaljik, this difference – i.e., sets vs. trees –, while ultimately far from
trivial, is orthogonal as regards the question of how the *ABA generalization is derived.

superlatives in the languages of the world, but it cannot be excluded under the assumptions made thus far.

And fourth, an ABB pattern as it is widely attested can occur if there is only an exponent B bearing the feature [compr], in addition to unmarked A. B is compatible with the target specification in both comparative and superlative environments, and since it is more specific than A, it is chosen in these two contexts.

This latter conclusion, in turn, implies that the a priori conceivable fifth pattern, viz., ABA, can never be generated (at least not as long as it is assumed that the two occurrences of A correspond to a single morphological exponent with a non-disjunctive set of features associated with it). Any instance of morphological exponence referring to the comparative also picks out the superlative, unless there is a more specific exponent that overrides the comparative form. Thus, if an exponent (B) fits into a comparative environment, it will always also fit into a superlative environment, block a less specific exponent (A) in the latter context, and thus emerge as grammatical here – unless, that is, there is an even more specific exponent (C) for the superlative context (which, in turn, is then incompatible with the comparative).

Importantly, for this account of the *ABA generalization to work, the features involved here have to be privative, and not binary. To see this, suppose that they were binary, as in (31) (vs. (30)).

(31) a.   Positive: [–compr,–superl]
      b.   Comparative: [+compr,–superl]
      c.   Superlative: [+compr,+superl]

Now, ABA patterns can be derived after all, by postulating lexical entries for the exponents like the following.

(32) a.   /A/ $\leftrightarrow$ {[–]}
      b.   /B/ $\leftrightarrow$ {[+compr,–superl]}

Given (32), B is compatible (and most specific) in comparative environments, but incompatible in both positive and superlative contexts, where, therefore, maximally non-specific (and maximally compatible) A must be chosen. Thus, it can be concluded that the Subset Principle-based account of *ABA in Bobaljik (2012) presupposes asymmetric feature specifications: The set of features defining comparative environments is a proper subset of the set of features defining superlative environments, and the set of features defining positive environments is a proper subset of the set of features defining comparative environments.

2.1.2. Ablaut in German

Essentially the same distribution of possible and impossible patterns of stem allomorphy can be observed with the various ablaut classes for strong verbs in German. The patterns are identified in Wiese (2005; 2008), and the analysis Wiese gives for ablaut is basically identical to the one given by Bobaljik for adjective gradation.

To begin with, Wiese notes that ablaut with German verbs, despite initial appearances to the contrary and notwithstanding its treatment in standard reference grammars, is actually fully systematic from a synchronic perspective. This becomes evident when one changes the usual order of verb forms: Whereas the traditional order is one in which the infinitival form comes first, the finite first/third person past tense form comes second, and the past participle form comes last (as in *geben* ('give') – *gab* ('gave') – *gegeben* ('given')), Wiese argues that systematic patterns arise once the sequence is reversed, with past participle and finite past changing places (*geben* ('give') – *gegeben* ('given') – *gab* ('gave')). As shown in (33-abc), from this perspetive, regular AAA patterns, suppletive ABB patterns, and doubly suppletive ABC patterns arise as regards stem realization, exactly as with adjective gradation in (29).

(33) *Ablaut patterns*:

    a. AAA (regular):
        (i) arbeiten ('work') – gearbeitet ('worked') – arbeitete ('worked')

    b. ABB (suppletive):
        (i) schreiben ('write') – geschrieben ('written') – schrieb ('wrote')
        (ii) giessen ('pour') – gegossen ('poured') – goss ('poured')

    c. ABC (doubly suppletive):
        (i) werfen ('throw') – geworfen ('thrown') – warf ('threw')
        (ii) sprechen ('speak') – gesprochen ('spoken') – sprach ('spoke')

    d. *ABA (unattested):
        (i) *werfen ('throw') – geworfen ('thrown') – werf ('threw')
        (ii) *schreiben ('write') – geschrieben ('written') – schreib ('wrote')

    e. AAC (attested):
        (i) geben ('give') – gegeben ('given') – gab ('gave')

Unlike what was the case with stem allomorphy in adjective comparatives and superlatives, AAC patterns are attested with German ablaut; cf. (33-e). However, ABA patterns as in (33-d) are conspicuously absent.

Wiese's (2008) explanation for the absence of ABA patterns with strong German verbs is structurally of exactly the same type as Bobaljik's account. By assumption, the feature specification for finite past forms is a proper superset of the feature specifications for past participles, which is a proper superset of the elsewhere basic form. The resulting systems looks as in (34).[31]

(34) a. Infinitive: [–]
      b. Past Participle: [past]
      c. Finite Past Tense: [past,fin]

Consequently, any exponent B bearing only the feature [past] will be compatible not only in past participle contexts, but also in finite past tense context, and it will invariably emerge as more specific than a radically underspecified elsewhere exponent A as it shows up in the infinitive. Therefore, in the absence of a designated (compatible and even more specific) exponent C bearing the features [past] *and* [fin], A is blocked in favour of B in finite past tense environments just as it is blocked in favour of B in past participle contexts. This derives *ABA with German ablaut.

The mechanics of ablaut-based stem allomorphy with strong verbs in German are illustrated by three representative examples in (35): an ABC pattern with the stem *sprech* ('speak') in (35-a), an ABB pattern with the stem *gieß* ('pour') in (35-b), and an AAC pattern with the stem *geb* ('give') in (35-c).

---

[31] In contrast to Bobaljik, Wiese does not embed the analysis in a Distributed Morphology approach, and accordingly does not postulate tree structures plus vocabulary insertion via contextual information for stems; recall (i) in footnote 30. However, transferring Wiese's account to an orthodox Distributed Morphology analysis based on trees and vocabulary insertion dependent on contextual features is straightforward; see (i).

(i)   a. Infinitive:
          [$_{VP}$ ⋯ V ⋯]
      b. Past Participle:
          [$_{TP}$ ⋯ [$_{VP}$ ⋯ V ⋯] ⋯ T$_{[past]}$ ⋯]
      c. Finite Past Tense:
          [$_{AgrP}$ ⋯ [$_{TP}$ ⋯ [$_{VP}$ ⋯ V ⋯] ⋯ T$_{[past]}$ ⋯] ⋯ Agr$_{[fin]}$ ⋯]

Again, it can be assumed that there is head movement of V to T, and of T to Agr, prior to morphological realization (so as to guarantee locality for morphological exponence).

(35) a. (i)   /sprech/ ↔ {[–]}
          (ii)   /sproch/ ↔ {[past]}
          (iii) /sprach/ ↔ {[past,fin]}
      b. (i)   /gieß/ ↔ {[ ]}
          (ii)   /goss/ ↔ {[past]}
      c. (i)   /geb/ ↔ {[ ]}
          (ii)   /gab/ ↔ {[past,fin]}

As before, an indispensable assumption underlying the account is that the
relevant morpho-syntactic features are not binary, but privative; see (34).
If they were binary, as in (36), there would be no subset relations among
the three environments.

(36) a. Infinitive: [–past,–fin]
      b. Past Participle: [+past,–fin]
      c. Finite Past Tense: [+past,+fin]

As a result, the immediate prediction would be that ABA patterns can be
derived after all, by postulating two exponents as in (37).

(37) a. /A/ ↔ {[–]}
      b. /B/ ↔ {[+past,–fin]}

Here, B is compatible with past participles but not with finite past tense
contexts, and this would yield the consequence that only the radically underspecified elsewhere exponent could show up in finite past tense contexts
(as it shows up in infinitives).

Before moving on to a reanalysis of the ban on ABA patterns in the
present approach to morphology based on harmonic serialism, it may be
worth pointing out that both corroborating and contradictory evidence
has been put forward as concerns *ABA in the recent literature on stem
allomorphy in general, and German(ic) ablaut in particular. Focussing on
Germanic languages here, on the one hand Andersson (2018) brings up
some apparent exceptions to the *ABA generalization with verbal ablaut
in Swedish, Gammalsvenskbymålet, and Low German, and he suggests that
there may be extralinguistic factors underlying the phenomenon as a whole.
On the other hand, in Regel, Opitz, Müller & Friederici (2015) we present
experimental evidence in support of the presence of a *ABA restriction
deeply rooted in the grammatical knowledge of speakers of German. Let
me briefly summarize the main findings of this latter study.

According to Wiese's (2008) approach, there should be two different
kinds of ungrammatical ablaut forms: First, there should be non-existent

ablaut forms that are in principle permitted by the grammar but do not actually form part of the language; and second, there should be ungrammatical ablaut forms that are impossible because they instantiate an *ABA pattern, reducible to specificity-driven morphological exponence (i.e., a principle of grammar). Now, based on the assumption that there are two radically different sources of ungrammaticality, the prediction is that different event-related potentials (ERP) should be detectable in EEG studies for the two kinds of ungrammaticality. For concreteness, with actual verbs like *singen* ('sing'), with the actual ablaut pattern in (38-a), the pattern in (38-b) (a non-existing ABB pattern that is compatible with *ABA) should behave differently in the EEG experiment from the pattern in (38-c) (a non-existing ABA pattern that is at variance with *ABA).

(38) a.   singen ('sing') – gesungen ('sung') – sang ('sang')
      b.   singen ('sing') – gesungen ('sung') – *sung ('sang')
      c.   singen ('sing') – gesungen ('sung') – *sing ('sang')

The same predictions can be derived for pseudo-verbs like *tungen*, where both (39-a) and (39-b) conform to *ABA but (39-c) does not.

(39) a.   tingen – getungen – tang
      b.   tingen – getungen – tung
      c.   tingen – getungen – ting

And indeed, the experimental evidence reported in Regel et al. (2015) confirms these predictions: *ABA violations give rise to a very different ERP than other non-existing patterns.

   In what follows, I will assume that the prohibition against ABA patterns with stem allomorphy is real, and should be derived from general principles underlying the mechanism of morphological exponence in the grammar. Accordingly, the question arises as to how *ABA can be accounted for in the present approach based on harmonic serialism.

2.2.   *ABA in Harmonic Serialism

2.2.1.   Initial Considerations

To begin with, it can be noted that if the same central background assumptions are made as in the Bobaljik–Wiese account (viz., that something like the Subset Principle holds, and that the target feature matrices in need of morphological realization are asymmetric, i.e., characterized by subset/superset relations), *ABA can be made to follow in harmonic serialism in much the same way. As shown in chapters 2 and 4, the effects of the compatibility requirement incorporated into the Subset Principle follow from a high-ranked ID-F constraint, and specificity in disjunctive blocking is derived from MAX constraints demanding that the features of contextual feature matrices associated with the selecting input item (encoding the syntactic context, or the paradigm cell) are realized by an exponent that bears them. Thus, suppose, e.g., that we are dealing with a past participle environment that is characterized by the privative feature [past]. If there is an exponent B in the morphological array that is characterized by the feature [past] (and nothing else), then this exponent will eventually be chosen as optimal by the harmonic serialist derivation (after initial selection and subsequent removal of the elsewhere exponent A) because it satisfies MAX(PAST) (whereas A does not). More importantly in the present context, suppose next that the question of morphological realization in a finite past tense environment is at issue, with the context providing the features [past,fin]. Then, if there is no other compatible exponent C in the morphological array that bears the features [past] and [fin], it is clear that the optimal exponent will still be B, and never A: While B does not satisfy MAX(FIN), it minimizes violations of MAX(PAST).

Still, in what follows I would like to pursue a different kind of account of *ABA, based on considerations that are motivated both conceptually and empirically. On the conceptual side, note that asymmetric feature matrices, based on subset/superset relations among paradigm cells in need of morphological exponence (or syntactic contexts demanding morphological realization), have so far not played any role in the analyses developed in the present monograph; so the contexts in which *ABA is discernible would be special in this respect. From this perspective, a case can be made that it is at least worth trying to find out whether *ABA can follow *without* invoking asymmetric feature sets for morphological realization.

Consider next the empirical side. As Bobaljik (2012) shows, it is arguably the case that one can motivate on semantic grounds the assumptions that (i) the superlative consists of the comparative plus some other feature [superl], and that (ii) this other feature [superl] can never directly combine with the positive form of an adjective to yield a fourth category (beyond positive, comparative, and superlative) that would be characterized by the feature specification [−compr,+superl], i.e., the one missing specification arising under a cross-classification as in (31) (but, of course, given that the combination [−compr,+superl] would be uninterpretable, there is no need to block it by resorting to privative features either). The case is different with the features involved in Wiese's (2008) approach to *ABA with strong verbs in German, though. Here, the fourth logically possible specification arising under a cross-classification of [±past] and [±fin] is indeed present:

There are finite present tense contexts in the language.[32] Thus, there is
good reason to postulate the non-asymmetric feature sets in (36) (repeated
here in (40-abc)) resulting from cross-classification of binary (rather than
privative) features, and add the fourth specification in (40-d).

(40) a. Infinitive: [−past,−fin]
      b. Past Participle: [+past,−fin]
      c. Finite Past Tense: [+past,+fin]
      d. Finite Present Tense: [−past,+fin]

What is more, there is empirical evidence that the feature combination in
(40-d) must exist: It can be referred to by strong verbs which show further
stem allomorphy in second and third person singular present tense contexts,
and in the imperative.[33] One such verb is *werfen* ('throw'), which basically
instantiates an ABC pattern but employs a special fourth stem in 2./3.
person singular present tense contexts and in the imperative (singular)
that in effect produces an ABCD pattern; another verb is *geben* ('give'),
which we have so far seen to exhibit an AAC pattern, and which also has
a separate form in these [−past,+fin] contexts, thereby giving rise to an
AACD pattern. The relevant data are repeated from (33) in (41), and
extended by the additional forms.

(41) a. ABCD:
          werfen ('throw') – geworfen ('thrown') – warf ('threw') –
          wirfst ('throw'$_{2.sg.pres}$)
      b. AACD:
          geben ('give') – gegeben ('given') – gab ('gave') –
          gibst ('give'$_{2.sg.pres}$)

This suggests that the privative approach may not be sufficient to account
for all observable systematic stem allomorphy with strong verbs in German.
Rather, an approach based on two binary features like [±past] and [±fin]
is needed. Consequently, the assumption that subset/superset relations

---

[32] Note also that this conclusion is not affected in any way by the observation that
[±past] must get a somewhat more abstract interpretation than simply as past tense to
begin with, so as to be compatible with past participles showing up in non-past contexts
(e.g., as passive participles); see footnote 44 of chapter 2.

[33] Since the imperative in German signals mood and number (as for the latter, compare,
e.g., *Geh!* ('go$_{2.sg.imp}$') with *Geht!* ('go$_{2.pl.imp}$')), it cannot qualify as a [−fin] category;
see Zifonun et al. (1997), among others.

are involved in the target specifications for suppletion may have to be abandoned – and with it goes the Bobaljik/Wiese account of *ABA.[34]

In the next subsection, I will argue that an approach based on harmonic serialism makes it possible to derive *ABA in a way that is compatible with feature matrices as in (40), which do not involve subset/superset relations and thus do not give rise to asymmetric target specifications.

2.2.2. *Analysis*

The analysis of *ABA to be developed here relies on two main ingredients which are both germane to harmonic serialism, and which could not, as far as I can see, be employed in any of the established approaches to inflectional morphology currently around. First, as shown in chapter 4, once an exponent is taken from the morphological array, becomes part of a intermediate optimal output, and is subsequently replaced by another exponent as a consequence of a later optimization procedure, it is gone for good, and can never return in the derivation at hand. I have already presented theory-internal evidence for this assumption in chapter 4 (see page 184); and it will turn out to be central to the account of *ABA. Second, deviating from what has been taken for granted about stem exponence in this chapter so far, I will now assume that the enrichment of categorizing heads with non-inherent features does not have to be completed before morphological realization starts via Merge operations involving stem exponents. For concreteness, suppose that non-inherent features are successively added to a categorizing head *according to the functional sequence f-seq* (that also determines the position of the corresponding heads in the syntax). After the addition of each feature (or, more precisely, class of features), optimization

---

[34] To be sure, the stem allomorphy occurring in second and third person singular present tense and imperative environments is diachronically a different phenomenon from ablaut occurring in the other three environments. In Old High German and Middle High German, the *e/i* alternation that shows up here in the present tense was the outcome of a productive, regular diachronic umlaut process triggered by inflectional exponents with high vowels ('Brechung', a special kind of mutation). However, in standard German, the alternation in, say, *werfen* vs. *wirfst* cannot easily be modelled as a phonologically regular mutation process anymore, and the two stems need to be listed separately, and need to be associated with different morpho-syntactic features so that they can be picked out correctly in the contexts in which they appear. Also, it goes without saying that children acquiring the language do not have access to diachronic information (like the different sources of ablaut and umlaut).

Finally, note that umlaut in second and third person singular present tense environments is far from fully systematic with strong verbs; e.g., the verbs *gehen* ('go'), *stehen* ('stand'), and *weben* ('weave') do not instantiate this *e/i* alternation.

is carried out.[35] These two ingredients of the analysis of *ABA eventually turn out to be two sides of the same coin: In the course of a derivation consisting of a sequence of generation and optimization procedures, the conditions for morphological exponence may change, such that what is impossible at one step becomes possible at a later step (viz., merging a certain stem exponent), and what is possible at one step becomes impossible at a later step (again, merging a certain stem exponent).

In a nutshell, the account of *ABA then works like this. At the beginning of the sequence of optimization steps, the maximally underspecified A form will be optimal. Then, further contextual features are added to the categorizing head, and the B form may become optimal. Note that the feature matrix associated with the categorizing head may not yet be fully specified at this point, and a subsequent addition of morpho-syntactic features may yield the consequence that B, which was optimal in the prior step, now is not optimal anymore because it violates compatibility (i.e., ID-F). At this point, A would again be the optimal stem exponent. However, A is not available anymore since it was taken from the morphological array at the earliest stage of the derivation, and then later discarded via B-induced Remove, a hallmark of disjunctive blocking (see chapter 4 and the previous section). Thus, an ABA pattern cannot be generated.

In the following subsections, I will illustrate the workings of the analysis on the basis of the different possible and impossible ablaut patterns with strong verbs in German; but this solution can be generalized so as to cover other instances of *ABA with stem allomorphy.

2.2.3. AAA Patterns

Consider first the trivial case of a weak ([−str(ong)]) verb that does not show any stem allomorphy. As noted above, if there are verb stems in a language that are marked for some morpho-syntactic feature that inflectional exponents are also marked for, every verb stem will share a morphological array with the relevant inflectional exponents. Since verb stems in German can be marked for both tense information and ϕ information, all inflectional exponents for verbs also have to be part of one and the same morphological array. Consequently, it turns out that there is in fact only one morphological array to be considered for verb inflection in German; and it can simply be assumed that this array is identified by the category feature V, with the respective categorizing head x being equipped with the subcategorization

----

[35] Recall that stems, in contrast to inflectional exponents, do not depend on full feature specifications being in place before morphological realization starts – after all, stem exponents bring with them inherent features for realization.

feature [•V•]. Thus, suppose that a categorizing head x:[•V•] has been formed in the numeration, and a morphological array has been assembled that consists of a verb stem like /arbeit/ ('work') that is not marked for any relevant morpho-syntactic features ([±past] or [±fin] – or, indeed, [–1] and [–pl], as argued for, e.g., ABCD verbs above). This stem forms a sub-array of the current morphological array. It can further be assumed that all the other (non-finite and finite) verbal inflectional exponents included in this morphological array are grouped into further subarrays, according to features like [±fin] and [±tense]. However, since at this point I am only concerned with different patterns of stem selection, I will generally (i.e., beyond the [±fin] and [±tense] information as such) abstract away from these more specific features giving rise to inflectional exponence once the optimal stem has been selected; this will work exactly as before.[36]

By assumption, then, before the first optimization procedure in an AAA scenario (as in all others) can start, the feature (or feature class) that is lowest on f-seq is added to the categorizing head; but the categorizing head does not yet exhibit the final full feature specification (here abridged by [±fin] and [±tense], as just stated). Given that tense information is lower on f-seq than ϕ (more generally, finiteness) information (also cf. the order CP-AgrP-TP-vP in the syntax), what is added at first is just [+past] or [–past]. Assuming for the sake of the argument the former, this yields an an initial input consisting of just x:[+past], [•V•] and the morphological array assembled around the single verb stem /arbeit/ ('work'), as in (42).[37]

---

[36] It needs to ensured that the full feature matrices eventually arrived at provide suffi-ciently many features (of the right kind) so that all inflectional exponents that need to be merged can in fact be merged in accordance with *STRUC (as an instance of over-lapping multiple exponence), by being required by some higher-ranked MAX constraint. For present purposes, I will simply presuppose that this is the case.

[37] The verb is equipped with inflection class information determining the choice of in-flectional exponents later in the derivation; for present purposes, it can be assumed that the relevant feature in the case at hand is [±str(ong)] (although this is a simplification), with [–str] showing up in the case at hand. Also note that [$_{V_j}$ ...] stands for one of the many inflectional exponents belonging to different subarrays, which will not be considered here.

(42) *Stem allomorphy: AAA* (harmonic serialism, step 1):

I_0: x:[+past], [•V•] $\{[_{V_i}$ /arbeit/:[–str] $\leftrightarrow$[–]], $[_{V_j}, \dots] \dots \}$	MIN SAT	RC	MC	ID F	MAX PAST	MAX FIN	*STR
O_1: x:[+past], [•V•]			*!		*		
☞O_2: x:[+past]-$[_{V_i}$ /arbeit/:[–str]]					*		*

The optimization here is trivial: The only way to satisfy MC is to merge
an exponent from the morphological array, and given that stems, which
themselves provide further features for morphological realization, always
have to be merged before inflectional exponents, the only stem available
needs to be merged with the categorizing head. Since, furthermore, the
only stem available is not associated with a [±past] feature, MAX(PAST)
will have to be violated at this point (it may or may not be satisfied later
in the derivation, when inflection markers are added to the word). At
this point, no further improvement based on the initially selected subarray
(consisting of just one stem) is possible, so the next contextual feature is
added to the categorizing head.[38] This might be [+fin]; this feature then
triggers a new optimization step, as in (43).

(43) *Stem allomorphy: AAA* (harmonic serialism, step 2):

I_2: x:[+past,+fin]-$[_{V_i}$ /arbeit/:[–str]] $\{[_{V_j}, \dots] \dots \}$	MIN SAT	RC	MC	ID F	MAX PAST	MAX FIN	*STR
☞O_{21}: x:[+past,+fin]-$[_{V_i}$ /arbeit/:[–str]]					*	*	

Evidently, no further improvement of the candidate is possible this time
(because there is no other stem left that might satisfy one of the two relevant
MAX constraints that are violated by the present output); so the derivation
moves on to inflectional exponence.

The environment underlying the present optimization is [+past,+fin]
(or, more properly, an extension of it, enriched by further morpho-syntactic
features that establish a fully specified matrix), but it should be clear that
this choice has been completely arbitrary: The same outcome is predicted
for [+past,–fin], [–past,+fin], and [–past,–fin] environments.

---

[38] In principle, an alternative possibility would have been that after each addition of a
feature (class), optimization can take place only once. However, the present approach
mirrors what has been assumed about EXHAUST MORPHOLOGICAL ARRAY in (62) of
chapter 3, and EXHAUST SUBARRAY in (57) of chapter 4): Optimization takes place as
long as further improvement is possible; and only then is additional material added.

2.2.4. ABC Patterns

Consider next ABC patterns, as with doubly suppletive *werfen* ('throw') – *geworfen* ('thrown') – *warf* ('threw'). The first scenario to be considered is one where [–past] is first added to the categorizing head (x:[•V•]) before the derivation starts. The morphological array includes three stems, which can be assumed to look as follows: /werf/ ↔ [–], /worf/ ↔ [+past], /warf/ ↔ [+past,+fin].[39] Under these assumptions, the first optimization looks as in (44).[40]

(44) *Stem allomorphy:* $\boxed{A}$ *BC* (harmonic serialism, step 1):

I_0: x:[–past], [•V•] {[$_{V_i}$ /werf/:[+str] ↔[–]], [$_{V_i}$ /worf/:[+str] ↔[+past]], [$_{V_i}$ /warf/:[+str] ↔[+past,+fin]], [$_{V_j}$, ...] ... }	MIN SAT	RC	MC	ID F	MAX PAST	MAX FIN	*STR
O_1: x:[–past], [•V•]			*!		*		
☞O_2: x:[–past]-[$_{V_i}$ /werf/:[+str]]					*		*
O_3: x:[–past]-[$_{V_i}$ /worf/:[+str]]	*!			*			*
O_4: x:[–past]-[$_{V_i}$ /warf/:[+str]]	*!			*			*

As before, MINSAT favours the output O_2 with the least specific exponent; at this stage, O_3 and O_4 are excluded by this constraint since they satisfy both MC and MAX(PAST) (O_3 and O_4 improve the constraint profile of the input and thus need to be considered for MINSAT evaluation). With stem allomorphy, the competing stems are disjunctively ordered, so given the assumptions of chapter 4, the two more specific stems will be equipped with a [–V–] feature for exponent removal within the subarray. However, their satisfaction of MAX(PAST) comes at the price of a violation of the higher-ranked constraint ID-F (because of non-matching feature values). Thus, in the next round of optimization, they still have a worse constraint profile than the candidate with /werf/. Since no further improvement is possible based on the material that is currently available, the next feature is added to x; suppose that this feature is [+fin], as in (45).

---

[39] For now, I abstract away from the fourth stem /wirf/ mentioned above; I will return to this issue, though.

[40] Note that all stems considered from now on qualify as strong verbs, and are thus marked by the inflection class feature [+str] for subsequent inflectional exponence.

(45) *Stem allomorphy:* $\boxed{A}BC$ (harmonic serialism, step 2):

I_2: x:[–past,+fin]-[$_{V_i}$ /werf/:[+str]] {[$_{V_i}$ /worf/:[+str] ↔[+past]], [$_{V_i}$ /warf/:[+str] ↔[+past,+fin]], [$_{V_j}$, …] … }	Min Sat	RC	MC	Id F	Max Past	Max Fin	*Str
☞O_{21}: x:[–past,+fin]-[$_{V_i}$ /werf/:[+str]]					*	*	
O_{22}: x:[–past,+fin]-[$_{V_i}$ /werf/:[+str]]-[$_{V_i}$ /worf/:[+str]]				*!	*		*
O_{23}: x:[–past,+fin]-[$_{V_i}$ /werf/:[+str]]-[$_{V_i}$ /werf/:[+str]]				*!			*

Even with the new, enriched context, neither O_{22} nor O_{23} can block O_{21}. O_{22} fatally violates Id-F. O_{23} can in fact satisfy Max(Fin), in addition to Max(Past). This, as such, would be in accordance with MinSat because there is no competing candidate that would improve O_{21}'s constraint profile with fewer new constraint satisfactions. However, due to Id-F, which is also violated by O_{23}, there is no improvement of the original constraint profile with this candidate either. Consequently, the derivation maintains the radically underspecified stem /werf/ selected originally, and moves on to inflectional exponence.

Turning to the second possible environment next, it can be noted that nothing changes if [–past,+fin] is replaced with [–past,–fin]. The two stems /worf/ and /warf/ are both specified as [+past], so fatal Id-F violations can never be avoided in this context either.

Things get slightly more interesting when the initial feature that is added to the categorizing head is [+past]. The ensuing optimization step is illustrated in (46).

(46) *Stem allomorphy:* $A\boxed{BC}$ (harmonic serialism, step 1):

I_0: x:[+past], [•V•] {[$_{V_i}$ /werf/:[+str] ↔[–]], [$_{V_i}$ /worf/:[+str] ↔[+past]], [$_{V_i}$ /warf/:[+str] ↔[+past,+fin]], [$_{V_j}$, …] … }	Min Sat	RC	MC	Id F	Max Past	Max Fin	*Str
O_1: x:[+past], [•V•]			*!		*		
☞O_2: x:[+past]-[$_{V_i}$ /werf/:[+str]]					*		*
O_3: x:[+past]-[$_{V_i}$ /worf/:[+str]]	*!						*
O_4: x:[+past]-[$_{V_i}$ /warf/:[+str]]	*!						*

Again, O_2 is the initial winner even though it does not satisfy Max(Past) – but it satisfies MC, and the other two outputs' simultaneous satisfaction of these two constraints is fatal at the beginning of the derivation, due to MinSat. However, in the next step, a new stem is added to the currently merged stem, so as to satisfy Max(Past) after all; see (47).

(47) *Stem allomorphy:* $A\boxed{BC}$ (harmonic serialism, step 2):

I_2: x:[+past] {[v_i /worf/:[+str] ↔[+past]], [v_i /warf/:[+str] ↔[+past,+fin]], [v_j, ...] ... }	Min Sat	RC	MC	Id F	Max Past	Max Fin	*Str
O_{21}: x:[+past]-[v_i /werf/:[+str]]					*!		
☞O_{22}: x:[+past]-[v_i /werf/:[+str]]-[v_i /worf/:[+str]]							*
☛O_{23}: x:[+past]-[v_i /werf/:[+str]]-[v_i /warf/:[+str]]							*

Unlike what was the case in tableau (45), there is now no Id-F violation generated by the additional stems, and, if nothing else is said, O_{22} and O_{23} should both emerge as optimal. The reason for this is that both outputs satisfy Max(Past) (unlike O_{21}). Also note that the extra [+fin] feature associated with the stem /warf/ of O_{23} is not registered by any constraint so far. Thus, unless additional assumptions are made that disfavour the surplus feature in O_{23}, there will now be two separate continuations of (47), one based on O_{22} and one based on O_{23}. As it turns out, such a branching of the derivation would in fact be compatible with the existence of ABC patterns if certain assumptions about ineffability (absolute ungrammaticality) are made.[41]

---

[41] Here is what would happen if O_{23} (where /warf/ ↔ [+past,+fin] is added to the initial, underspecified stem /werf/) were to emerge as optimal in (47). First, RC would trigger removal of the earlier stem, much as in the continuation based on O_{22} addressed in the main text. Second, either [–fin] or [+fin] would be added to the feature matrix associated with the categorizing head. If [+fin] is added, the following optimization step would be simple: From the point of view of faithfulness, /warf/ is now the perfect stem since it maximizes satisfaction of the two Max constraints (Max(Past), Max(Fin)). If, on the other hand, [–fin] is added, a violation of Id-F will occur, since /warf/ is marked [+fin]. Still, since the alternative candidate introducing Id-F-respecting /worf/ (which is specified only as [+past]) cannot *simultaneously* remove /warf/ (it could only do so in the subsequent step, and harmonic serialism does not envisage the possibility of look-ahead (only one operation can separate input and output), an additional assumption is required to ensure that the Id-F violation incurred by /warf/ in [–fin] environments is fatal. This additional assumption can then naturally involve whatever is assumed more generally as a means to derive ineffability (or absolute ungrammaticality); see Prince & Smolensky (1993; 2004), Fanselow & Féry (2002), McCarthy (2002), Legendre (2009), Vogel (2009), Müller (2015), and (other) contributions in Rice & Blaho (2009) for overviews and proposals in phonology and syntax. A simple option would be to adopt the *empty output* – or *null parse* (Prince & Smolensky (1993)), or *null output* (McCarthy (2002)) – approach to absolute ungrammaticality (see Prince & Smolensky (1993) for the original proposal for phonology, and Ackema & Neeleman (1998) and Heck & Müller (2013) for applications in syntax): On this view, each candidate set contains an output Ø that leaves the input completely unrealized. The empty output does not violate any faithfulness constraints; in fact, the only constraint that it violates is something like the Empty Output Condition (EOC; *Ø). Id-F might then be assumed to be ranked above

Still, in what follows, I will assume that O_{23} is in fact not optimal because it fatally violates an additional constraint. This decision is motivated by greater simplicity of analysis in the case at hand (i.e., ABC patterns); moreover, it will turn out that there is good reason to adopt it when other patterns (AAC and ABA) are considered. Thus, note first that O_{23} would violate the Subset Principle because it does not bear a subset of the morphological features provided by the environment (here: associated with the categorizing head at this point of the derivation). So far, I have assumed that additional features on morphological exponents do not give rise to compatibility issues (which would then have to be derived as DEP violations); see in particular footnote 9 of chapter 2. However, all relevant cases discussed there involve configurations where the additional feature coming with the exponent is not a morpho-syntactic feature that is part of the (or: a potential) fully specified environment capturing the paradigm cell – i.e., the syntactic context. In fact, given that up to now I have assumed that such syntactic contexts are always fully specified, it is hard to see how such a scenario could have arisen in the first place.[42] With the postulation of a steady growth of feature matrices for morphological realization that are interspersed with optimization procedures, things have changed, though. Now it *can* be the case that an inflectional exponents' morpho-syntactic realizational features are not (yet) present on the categorizing head; and I would like to suggest that this justifies the postulation of DEP constraints precluding certain kinds of morpho-syntactic features on exponents which are not present on categorizing heads (i.e., what used to be stems, up until the present chapter). More specifically, the following constraint will be relevant:[43]

(48) DEP($[+F]$):
      $[+F]$ on an exponent in the output requires the presence of $[F]$ in the input.

---

the EOC (but MC would have to be ranked below it since it is temporarily violable in optimal candidates). This way, the illformedness of maintaining ID-F-violating /warf/ in [+past,–fin] contexts would be ensured in spite of the fact that it cannot be blocked by more faithful /worf/. – The approach laid out in the main text avoids this complication by excluding O_{23} directly, when it first arises.

[42] Note also that I have not yet addressed the issue of impoverishment; see the final chapter for some pertinent remarks.

[43] Here, $[\pm F]$ cannot be just any feature (e.g., one triggering a phonological operation); rather, $[\pm F]$ is a morpho-syntactic feature characterizing fully specified inputs in the language that requires a realization by inflectional exponence.

DEP([+F]) in (48) only formulates a ban on positively specified features in the output that are not matched by the input; the assumption here is that a severe problem can only be created by a positive specification of some property, and not by the negative specification of the absence of some property. This new constraint does not change the outcome of any of the earlier analyses – neither those in the preceding chapters (where it is always vacuously satisfied), nor those in the present chapter that deal with stem optimization. However, it directly excludes O_{23} in (47); the reason is that /warf/ is characterized by [+fin], and [±fin] is not (yet) present in the input. The conclusion is independent of the ranking of DEP([+F]); still, for reasons that will become clear below, I assume that DEP([+F]) outranks the MAX constraints. The resulting competition is illustrated in (49), which is a minimal modification of (47) integrating DEP-F.

(49) *Stem allomorphy:* $A\boxed{BC}$ (harmonic serialism, step 2; modified):

I_2: x:[+past] {[v_i /worf/:[+str] ↔[+past]], [v_i /warf/:[+str] ↔[+past,+fin]], [v_j, …] … }	MIN SAT	RC	MC	ID F	DEP [+F]	MAX PAST	MAX FIN	*STR
O_{21}: x:[+past]-[v_i /werf/:[+str]]						*!		
☞O_{22}: x:[+past]-[v_i /werf/:[+str]]-[v_i /worf/:[+str]]								*
O_{23}: x:[+past]-[v_i /werf/:[+str]]-[v_i /warf/:[+str]]					*!			*

Consequently, now only O_{22} is optimal. In the following step, RC-driven removal of the earlier, radically underspecified stem /werf/ takes place; see (50).

(50) *Stem allomorphy:* $A\boxed{BC}$ (harmonic serialism, step 3):

I_{22}: x:[+past]-[v_i /werf/:[+str]]-[v_i /worf/:[+str]] {[v_i /warf/:[+str] ↔[+past,+fin]], [v_j, …] … }	MIN SAT	RC	MC	ID F	DEP [+F]	MAX PAST	MAX FIN	*STR
O_{221}: x:[+past]-[v_i /werf/:[+str]]-[v_i /worf/:[+str]]		*!						
☞O_{222}: x:[+past]-[v_i /worf/:[+str]]								
O_{223}: x:[+past]-[v_i /werf/:[+str]]						*!		
O_{224}: x:[+past]-[v_i /werf/:[+str]]-[v_i /worf/:[+str]]-[v_i /warf/:[+str]]		*!			*			*

In (50), leaving the input intact, as in O_{221}, fatally violates RC (recall that there is disjunctive blocking among stems, i.e., /worf/ and /warf/ bear [–V–] features). Self-removal, as in O_{223}, reintroduces a fatal MAX(PAST) violation. Adding the third stem, as in O_{224}, does not improve the constraint profile. Therefore, O_{222}, with /worf/ as the sole stem, comes out as optimal.

No further improvement is possible based on the currently accessible material. Therefore, an additional context feature is added to the categorizing head. Suppose first that the feature in question is [–fin]. At this point, MAX(FIN) becomes active. Not changing anything anymore turns out to be the best strategy, and the derivation can continue with inflectional exponence; see (51).

(51) *Stem allomorphy:* $A\boxed{B}C$ (harmonic serialism, step 4a):

I_{222}: x:[+past,–fin]-[$_{V_i}$ /worf/:[+str]] {[$_{V_i}$ /warf/:[+str] ↔[+past,+fin]], [$_{V_j}$, …] … }	MIN SAT	RC	MC	ID F	DEP [+F]	MAX PAST	MAX FIN	*STR
☞O_{2221}: x:[+past,–fin]-[$_{V_i}$ /worf/:[+str]]							*	
O_{2222}: x:[+past,–fin]-[$_{V_i}$ /worf/:[+str]]-[$_{V_i}$ /warf/:[+str]				*!				*

Thus, A forms (in [–past] environments) and B forms (in [+past,–fin] environments) are derived based on a lexical three-way contrast /werf/ ↔ [–], /worf/ ↔ [+past], and /warf/ ↔ [+past,+fin]. It remains to be seen how it can be guaranteed that /warf/ is the sole optimal output for [+past,+fin] environments. For this, we have to consider the optimal output O_{222} (x:[+past]-[$_{V_i}$ /worf/:[+str]]) of (50) again. As before, no futher improvement is possible with this candidate based on the currently available material, so a next contextual feature is added in accordance with f-seq. Suppose that this time the feature that is added is not [–fin], but [+fin]. The continuation looks as in (52).

(52) *Stem allomorphy:* $AB\boxed{C}$ (harmonic serialism, step 4b):

I_{222}: x:[+past,+fin][$_{V_i}$ /worf/:[+str]] {[$_{V_i}$ /warf/:[+str] ↔[+past,+fin]], [$_{V_j}$, …] … }	MIN SAT	RC	MC	ID F	DEP [+F]	MAX PAST	MAX FIN	*STR
$O_{2221'}$: x:[+past,+fin]-[$_{V_i}$ /worf/:[+str]]							*!	
☞$O_{2222'}$: x:[+past,+fin]-[$_{V_i}$ /worf/:[+str]]-[$_{V_i}$ /warf/:[+str]								*

Now the same output that did not violate any of the constraints in (50) (viz., O_{222}) violates MAX(FIN), due to the addition of [+fin] to the categorizing head ($O_{2221'}$). This time, adding a new exponent turns out to be helpful because /warf/ can satisfy MAX(FIN) while only incurring a violation of lower-ranked *STRUC – since the feature values for [±fin] match, there is no violation of ID-F. In the following step, RC requires removal of the earlier stem (/worf/), which is unproblematic because the new stem (/warf/) can maintain the earlier satisfaction of MAX(PAST) (without violating ID-F). This is illustrated in (53).

(53) *Stem allomorphy:* $AB\boxed{C}$ (harmonic serialism, step 5b):

$I_{2222'}$: x:[+past,+fin]-[$_{V_i}$ /worf/:[+str]]-[$_{V_i}$ /warf/:[+str] {–, [$_{V_j}$, …] … }	MIN SAT	RC	MC	ID F	DEP [+F]	MAX PAST	MAX FIN	*STR
$O_{2222'1}$: x:[+past,+fin]-[$_{V_i}$ /worf/:[+str]]-[$_{V_i}$ /warf/:[+str]		*!						
☞$O_{2222'2}$: x:[+past,+fin]-[$_{V_i}$ /warf/:[+str]								

At this point, stem optimization is finished, and the derivation proceeds by merging inflectional material (reflecting whatever other finite verb-related features are present on the categorizing head).

To sum up, all three forms in an ABC pattern can be derived under present assumptions.

2.2.5. AAC Patterns

In AAC patterns, the stem form is identical (A) in all contexts except for [+past,+fin] environments, where a different form is chosen (C). A typical example is the verb *geben* ('give'). Suppose that the two stems are /geb/ ↔ {[ ]} and /gab/ ↔ {[+past,+fin]}, as in Wiese's (2008) proposal. Again, four contexts need to be considered: [–past,–fin], [–past,+fin], [+past,–fin], and [+past,+fin]. The first two are simple: After adding [–past] initially, only an output employing /geb/ can ever become optimal. An output involving /gab/ will always fatally violate Id-F at any stage of the derivation, and independently of whether subsequent feature enrichment applying to the categorizing head involves [+fin] or [–fin]; this is due to the incompatible [+past] specification on /gab/. This accounts for the first A in AAC patterns. Alternatively, [+past] is assigned to the categorizing head at the beginning. As shown in (54), the underspecified stem is again selected as optimal in this case, because of MinSat.

(54) *Stem allomorphy:* A⟨A⟩C (harmonic serialism, step 1):

I_0: x:[+past], [•V•] {[v_i /geb/:[+str] ↔[–]], [v_i /gab/:[+str] ↔[+past,+fin]], [v_j, ...] ... }	Min Sat	RC	MC	Id F	Dep [+F]	Max Past	Max Fin	*Str
O_1: x:[+past], [•V•]			*!			*		
☞O_2: x:[+past]-[v_i /geb/:[+str]]						*		*
O_3: x:[+past]-[v_i /gab/:[+str]]	*!				*			*

Can the constraint profile be further improved on the basis of the current features associated with the categorizing head? As shown in (55), this is not the case: MinSat is not an issue anymore; but merging /gab/ at this point fatally violates Dep([+F]) because there is a [+fin] feature on the exponent but no matching [±fin] on the categorizing head.

(55) *Stem allomorphy:* $A\boxed{A}C$ (harmonic serialism, step 2):

I_2: x:[+past]-[v_i /geb/:[+str]] {[v_i /gab/:[+str] ↔[+past,+fin]], [v_j, ...] ... }	MIN SAT	RC	MC	ID F	DEP [+F]	MAX PAST	MAX FIN	*STR
☞O_{21}: x:[+past]-[v_i /geb/:[+str]]						*		*
O_{22}: x:[+past]-[v_i /geb/:[+str]]-[v_i /gab/:[+str]]					*!			*

In (55), O_{21} violates MAX(PAST) and O_{22} violates DEP([+F]). O_{22} must not become optimal (otherwise, an AAC pattern could not be derived); this motivates the relatively high ranking of DEP([+F]) (above MAX constraints) proposed above.

Next, [–fin] or [+fin] is added; suppose first that the former option is chosen. As illustrated in (56), adding the remaining stem is not possible at this stage because of a fatal ID-F violation (cf. O_{212}). Therefore, the derivation has to make do with both a MAX(PAST) and a MAX(FIN) violation (incurred by optimal O_{211}), as was the case with the past participle stem in an AAA pattern (see (43) above).

(56) *Stem allomorphy:* $A\boxed{A}C$ (harmonic serialism, step 3a):

I_{21}: x:[+past,–fin]-[v_i /geb/:[+str]] {[v_i /gab/:[+str] ↔[+past,+fin]], [v_j, ...] ... }	MIN SAT	RC	MC	ID F	DEP [+F]	MAX PAST	MAX FIN	*STR
☞O_{211}: x:[+past]-[v_i /geb/:[+str]]						*	*	
O_{212}: x:[+past]-[v_i /geb/:[+str]]-[v_i /gab/:[+str]]				*!				*

In contrast, if [+fin] is added to the categorizing head in O_{21} in (55), the outcome of optimization is reversed; see (57). (DEP([+F])) is not relevant anymore at this stage because [±fin] is part of the input.)

(57) *Stem allomorphy:* $AA\boxed{C}$ (harmonic serialism, step 3b):

I_{21}: x:[+past,+fin]-[v_i /geb/:[+str]] {[v_i /gab/:[+str] ↔[+past,+fin]], [v_j, ...] ... }	MIN SAT	RC	MC	ID F	DEP [+F]	MAX PAST	MAX FIN	*STR
$O_{211'}$: x:[+past,+fin]-[v_i /geb/:[+str]]						*	*	
☞$O_{212'}$: x:[+past,+fin]-[v_i /geb/:[+str]]-[v_i /gab/:[+str]]								*

This time, adding /gab/ in $O_{212'}$ manages to avoid an otherwise fatal ID-F violation, and this option is therefore chosen because it satisfies MAX(PAST) and MAX(FIN). It does so in a single step, but this is unproblematic from the point of view of MINSAT because there is no competing output that would lead to an improvement with fewer new constraint satisfactions.

Finally, RC-driven removal of the less specific, earlier stem exponent takes place; see (58).

(58) *Stem allomorphy:* $AA\boxed{C}$ (harmonic serialism, step 4b):

$I_{212'}$: x:[+past,+fin]-[$_{V_i}$ /geb/:[+str]]-[$_{V_i}$ /gab/:[+str]] {–, [v_j, …] … }	Min Sat	RC	MC	Id F	Dep [+F]	Max Past	Max Fin	*Str
$O_{212'1}$: x:[+past,+fin]-[$_{V_i}$ /geb/:[+str]]-[$_{V_i}$ /gab/:[+str]]		*!						
☞$O_{212'2}$: x:[+past,+fin]-[$_{V_i}$ /gab/:[+str]]								

The derivation then continues by adding inflectional exponents.

Thus, all contexts with AAC patterns can be correctly predicted.

2.2.6. ABB Patterns

Let me turn next to ABB patterns, where the [+past,–fin] and [+past,+fin] environments share a single form. This holds, e.g., for the verb *gießen* ('pour'), for which (again essentially following Wiese (2008)) the two stems /gieß/ ↔ {[ ]} and /goss/ ↔ {[+past]} can be postulated. As before, of the four environments to be considered, two are directly accounted for: After adding [–past] to the categorizing head, /gieß/ is merged, in violation of Max(Past) and Max(Fin): /goss/ satisfies Max(Past), but also violates the higher-ranked Id-F (with [–past] in the context vs. [+past] on the exponent) and MinSat, and the latter violation is fatal. In the next optimization step, /goss/ can still not become optimal because, while MinSat can now be respected, Id-F still cannot be satisfied, and is fatally violated. Next, either [–fin] or [+fin] is added; and the following optimization step will identify /gieß/ as the permanently optimal stem because /goss/ is inherently at variance with Id-F. All of this is exactly as before.

If, instead of [–past], [+past] is initially selected for the categorizing head, the first optimal output is again one which merges the underspecified stem so as to satisfy MC but no more constraints than this one; see (59).

(59) *Stem allomorphy:* $A\boxed{BB}$ (harmonic serialism, step 1):

I_0: x:[+past], [•V•] {[$_{V_i}$ /gieß/:[+str] ↔[–]], [$_{V_i}$ /goss/:[+str] ↔[+past]], [v_j, …] … }	Min Sat	RC	MC	Id F	Dep [+F]	Max Past	Max Fin	*Str
O_1: x:[+past], [•V•]			*!			*		
☞O_2: x:[+past]-[$_{V_i}$ /gieß/:[+str]]						*		*
O_3: x:[+past]-[$_{V_i}$ /goss/:[+str]]	*!							*

Next, the stem /goss/ is merged; it is specified as [+past], and can thus give rise to a new satisfaction of Max(Past) at this point (without violating MinSat, as it did in (59)). This is shown in (60).

(60) *Stem allomorphy: A BB* (harmonic serialism, step 2):

I_2: x:[+past]-[$_{V_i}$ /gieß/:[+str]] {[$_{V_i}$ /goss/:[+str] ↔[+past]], [$_{V_j}$, ...] ... }	MIN SAT	RC	MC	ID F	DEP [+F]	MAX PAST	MAX FIN	*STR
O_{21}: x:[+past]-[$_{V_i}$ /gieß/:[+str]]						*!		
☞O_{22}: x:[+past]-[$_{V_i}$ /gieß/:[+str]]-[$_{V_i}$ /goss/:[+str]]								*

After this step, the earlier stem is removed, triggered by RC; see (61).

(61) *Stem allomorphy: A BB* (harmonic serialism, step 3):

I_{22}: x:[+past]-[$_{V_i}$ /gieß/:[+str]]-[$_{V_i}$ /goss/:[+str]] {−, [$_{V_j}$, ...] ... }	MIN SAT	RC	MC	ID F	DEP [+F]	MAX PAST	MAX FIN	*STR
O_{221}: x:[+past]-[$_{V_i}$ /gieß/:[+str]]-[$_{V_i}$ /goss/:[+str]]		*!						
☞O_{222}: x:[+past]-[$_{V_i}$ /goss/:[+str]]								
O_{223}: x:[+past]-[$_{V_i}$ /gieß/:[+str]]						*!		

There is now no other stem left in the morphological array. Furthermore, the currently optimal stem /goss/ is specified only as [+past], and therefore compatible with either a [−fin] specification or a [+fin] specification. Consequently, whatever feature is added next to the categorizing head ([+fin] or [−fin]), /goss/ will be the optimal stem, and the ABB pattern is derived: A shows up in [−past,−fin] and [−past,+fin] environments, and B shows up in [+past,−fin] and [+past,+fin] environments.

Summing up so far, AAA, ABC, AAC and ABB patterns can be derived in the present system by postulating lexical entries for the respective stems that correspond more or less exactly to those suggested by Wiese (2008) (with privative features replaced by +-valued features). It remains to be shown that ABA patterns cannot be derived.

2.2.7. *ABA Patterns*

Recall that in a symmetric system of contextual feature specifications relying on cross-classifications of binary features, the problem of accounting for the prohibition against ABA patterns with stems for strong verbs in German results from the option of having exponent specifications as in (62) (see (37)); here, *ting* is a phonologically well-formed pseudo-verb that does not actually occur in the language.

(62) a.   /ting/ ↔ /__{[ ]}
      b.   /tung/ ↔ /__{[+past,−fin]}

The task thus is to show that a lexical entry like (62-b) cannot lead to a pattern where /tung/ is confined to past participle environments, whereas /ting/ is optimal in non-finite contexts *and* in past finite contexts – i.e., that

a verb like *tingen* ('to tring') – *getungen* ('tringed') – *ting* ('(s)he tringed')
cannot exist.[44]

As before, we can basically disregard [–past] contexts since ID-F will
always block the stem /tung/ here. Let us therefore assume that [+past]
has been instantiated on the categorizing head, as in (63).

(63) *Stem allomorphy: *A⟨BA⟩* (harmonic serialism, step 1):

I_0: x:[+past], [•V•] {[v_i /ting/:[+str] ↔[–]], [v_i /tung/:[+str] ↔[+past,–fin]], [v_j, …] … }	MIN SAT	RC	MC	ID F	DEP [+F]	MAX PAST	MAX FIN	*STR
O_1: x:[+past], [•V•]			*!			*		
☞O_2: x:[+past]-[v_i /ting/:[+str]]						*		*
O_3: x:[+past]-[v_i /tung/:[+str]]	*!							*

In the competition in (63), O_2 (which employs the underspecified stem
/ting/) is optimal because O_3 (which employs the highly specified stem
/tung/) violates MINSAT. This is basically as in the first step of the derivation of AAC patterns in [+past] contexts; cf. (54). However, one crucial
difference can already be noted: In (54), the more specific stem /gab/:[+str]
↔[+past,+fin] of suboptimal (MINSAT-violating) output O_3 also violates
DEP([+F]) (because of [+fin]); in (63), the more specific stem /tung/:[+str]
↔[+past,–fin] does not (due to [–fin]). As a consequence, this latter stem
is added to the output in the next optimization step, *even before [±fin] is
added* to the categorizing head. This is illustrated in (64).

(64) *Stem allomorphy: *A⟨BA⟩* (harmonic serialism, step 2):

I_2: x:[+past]-[v_i /ting/:[+str]] {[v_i /tung/:[+str] ↔[+past,–fin]], [v_j, …] … }	MIN SAT	RC	MC	ID F	DEP [+F]	MAX PAST	MAX FIN	*STR
O_{21}: x:[+past]-[v_i /ting/:[+str]]						*!		
☞O_{22}: x:[+past]-[v_i /ting/:[+str]]-[v_i /tung/:[+str]]								*

Here, /tung/ can be added (so as to satisfy MAX(PAST)) without violating
DEP([+F]) – [–fin] on /tung/ is too weak (or not informative enough) to
incur a DEP violation; this is where the scenario in (55) is radically different.

Next, structure removal takes place; cf. (65).

---

[44] A minimally different English 'translation' of *ting* is used here because, unlike in
German, *ting* exists as a verb in English (whereas *tring* does not).

(65) *Stem allomorphy: *A BA* (harmonic serialism, step 3):

I_{22}: x:[+past]-[$_{V_i}$ /ting/:[+str]]-[$_{V_i}$ /tung/:[+str]] {–, [$_{V_j}$, …] … }	Min Sat	RC	MC	Id F	Dep [+F]	Max Past	Max Fin	*Str
O_{221}: x:[+past]-[$_{V_i}$ /ting/:[+str]]-[$_{V_i}$ /tung/:[+str]]		*!						
☞O_{222}: x:[+past]-[$_{V_i}$ /tung/:[+str]]								
O_{221}: x:[+past]-[$_{V_i}$ /ting/:[+str]]						*!		

What is important is that all of this has taken place before further enrichment of the syntactic context domain with [±fin] occurs. If [–fin] is now added in the next step, the result is not surprising: Without any further operations, the sole remaining stem candidate stays optimal; what is more, it satisfies both Max(Past) and Max(Fin) perfectly. See (66), whose optimal output is identical to the input, and which thus serves as the source of subsequent inflectional exponence.

(66) *Stem allomorphy: *A BA* (harmonic serialism, step 4a):

I_{222}: x:[+past,–fin]-[$_{V_i}$ /tung/:[+str]] {–, [$_{V_j}$, …] … }	Min Sat	RC	MC	Id F	Dep [+F]	Max Past	Max Fin	*Str
☞O_{2221}: x:[+past,–fin]-[$_{V_i}$ /tung/:[+str]]								

The alternative is that [+fin] is added to the categorizing head of O_{222}, yielding a matrix [+past,+fin] for morphological realization by stem selection. As shown in (67), the result will have to be identical: Now the sole remaining candidate violates Id-F, but it still qualifies as optimal since there is no alternative candidate left that might block it.

(67) *Stem allomorphy: *A BA* (harmonic serialism, step 4b):

I_{222}: x:[+past,+fin]-[$_{V_i}$ /tung/:[+str]] {–, [$_{V_j}$, …] … }	Min Sat	RC	MC	Id F	Dep [+F]	Max Past	Max Fin	*Str
☞$O_{2221'}$: x:[+past,+fin]-[$_{V_i}$ /tung/:[+str]]				*				

This, in a nutshell, is the reason for the non-existence of ABA patterns with stem selection in German verbs: Any attempt to generate such a pattern will result in an (unfaithful) ABB pattern (with the latter B form violating Id-F).[45]

---

[45] So we end up with the result that there are two possible derivational sources for the optimal final stem B in [+past,+fin] contexts with an ABB pattern: B can be specified as [+past] to begin with, or it can emerge as optimal here via a non-faithful realization of [+past,–fin]. This consequence of neutralization of an input difference could in principle be addressed by postulating an additional meta-optimization procedure

To sum up, the crucial properties of the present account of *ABA are (i)
that the only stem that could evade the ID-F violation at this point – viz.,
A – has already been used up earlier in the derivation, and is irrevocably
gone; and (ii) that there is an early stage of the derivation where merging
B is optimal, and does not give rise to what would be a fatal ID-F violation
because the context feature that would trigger it is not yet present.

2.2.8. Discussion

In showing how AAA, ABC, AAC, and ABB patterns can be derived
whereas ABA patterns cannot be, I have focussed on binary versions of
the privative underspecified stem entries as they were suggested by Wiese
(and, essentially, also by Bobaljik for adjective gradation) – plus the "dangerous" entry [+past,–fin] that would permit an ABA pattern in standard
approaches to morphology (including standard parallel optimality-theoretic
ones) but could successfully be precluded from doing so in the present approach based on harmonic serialism. However, given the two binary features
[±past] and [±fin], we end up with four different feature/value combinations for stems: [–past], [+past], [–fin], and [+fin]. Accordingly, the set of
possible feature specifications characterizing stems is the powerset of this
four-member set, which has 16 members, *minus* the 7 combinations where
there are conflicting values for a given morpho-syntactic feature; see (68).

(68) a. *Possible stem exponent entries*:
          { [–], [–past], [+past], [–fin], [+fin],
          [–past,–fin], [–past,+fin], [+past,–fin], [+past,+fin] }
      b. *Impossible stem exponent entries*:
          { [–past,+past], [–fin,+fin], [–fin,+fin,–past], [–fin,+fin,+past],
          [–past,+past,–fin], [–past,+past,+fin], [–past,+past,–fin,+fin] }

The question thus arises of whether some combinations of some of the
specifications in (68-a) could give rise to patterns that do not exist for
systematic reasons. This does not seem to be the case. Typically, other
feature specifications than the ones investigated so far will give rise to one
of the patterns discussed above. For instance, if there is a stem exponent A
↔ [–past] and another stem exponent B ↔ [+past,+fin], it can be verified
that an ABB pattern will arise – albeit with an unfaithful exponent B that
violates both DEP[+F] early on in the derivation, and then ID-F later in

---

("input optimization", see Prince & Smolensky (2004)); since this does not make any
different predictions empirically, I will leave the issue open.

the derivation. In cases like this one, questions of input optimization arise naturally (see footnote 45).[46]

In some other cases, other combinations of stem specifications may lead to existing, or at least potentially existing, patterns, beyond AAA, ABC, ABB, and AAC. Thus, as noted above (see (41)), patterns like ABCD and AACD exist with strong verbs in German, and need to be accounted for in the same way as, say, ABC or AAB patterns. Thus, consider *werfen* ('throw'), which was analyzed as an ABC verb in section 2.2.4. but actually employs a fourth stem for second and third person singular present tense and imperative contexts: *werfen* ('throw') – *geworfen* ('thrown') – *warf* ('threw') – *wirfst* ('throw'$_{2.sg.pres}$). Here, the stem /wirf/ must be specified as [–past,+fin] (plus [–1,–pl] since it is confined to second and third person singular and imperative contexts). Similarly, the AACD pattern in *geben* ('give') – *gegeben* ('given') – *gab* ('gave') – *gibst* ('give'$_{2.sg.pres}$) presupposes a [–past,+fin] specification of the stem /gib/. There are even verbs instantiating an AAAD pattern, where the *only* marked stem is one specified as [–past,+fin]. This holds, for instance, for varieties of German that employ the series *backen* ('bake') – *gebacken* ('baked', past participle) – *backte* ('baked', finite past singular) – *bäckt* ('bakes', third person singular present tense).[47] This requires postulating a stem /bäck/ with umlaut that is specified as [–past,+fin] (plus [–1,–pl]).[48]

Another pattern to be looked at is ABBB; here the infinitive stem has one form A, and another form B is used in past participle, finite past tense, and finite present tense contexts. Such a pattern does not occur in German, so the question arises whether it can be derived. As it turns out, under the most straightforward assumptions about stem specifications, this is not the case. Thus, suppose that there are two stems A ↔ [–past,–fin] and B ↔ [–]. In that case, A will be optimal in [–past,–fin] environments, and B will be optimal in [+past,–fin] and [+past,+fin] environments. However, it

---

[46] It is also worth noting that the stem inventory just considered presupposes that there does not have to be a radically underspecified item in such a morphological array; this assumption may well be doubted.

[47] Similar patterns can be established in some varieties for the verbs *quellen* ('swell') and *schmelzen* ('melt').

[48] As noted, the umlaut here is not phonologically predictable in synchronic grammar; and the two forms are indeed phonologically very different: [bak] vs. [bɛk]. Irrelevantly, some varieties have a designated strong ablaut stem /buk/ for finite past tense; some varieties have a simple weak conjugation AAAA pattern, with non-umlauted /back/ as the correct stem for second and third person singular present tense environments; furthermore, combinations of these patterns have also been established as options.

is A rather than B that qualifies as optimal in [–past,+fin] environments. Here is why: [–past] is added first to the categorizing head; next, because of MINSAT, B is added first; after that, A is added to B (its [–fin] feature does not give rise to a DEP[+F] violation), and subsequently A removes B. Then, once [+fin] is added to the categorizing head, A (which is [–fin]) will violate ID-F, but still the output stays optimal: There is no other competitor around anymore. Still, the outcome is slightly different if the two stem entries are A ↔ [–past,–fin] and B ↔ [+past]. Now B is not used up at the beginning of the derivation (it is not favoured by MINSAT at this step because it violates DEP[+F], due to its [+past] specification), and may consequently step in later, when [+fin] is added (because B's DEP[+F] violation is preferable to A's ID-F violation, given that the latter constraint outranks the former one). Thus, if such ABBB patterns are to be excluded systematically, this might support the assumption that in cases of suppletion, one of the competing stem allomorphs is always radically underspecified: [–].

Finally, consider the scenario where one stem exponent is specified as [+fin]. Whereas this would never suffice to derive ABBB patterns of the type just discussed, a system where, say, there are two stems A ↔ [–] and B ↔ [+fin] should make it possible to have an ABAB pattern, where all non-finite environments use one form (A) and all finite environments use the other form (B). Such a pattern of stem selection also does not seem to exist in German verb inflection; but in this case, there does not seem to exist a straightforward way to exclude it. I surmise that the prohibition against this pattern in the grammar of German, if it can be shown to be of a systematic nature, has a different source, which is not related to *ABA considerations.[49]

To end this chapter, let me briefly come back to the question of how the current analysis accounts for the *ABA restriction in suppletion without relying on asymmetric feature sets for morphological realization (i.e., without assuming that finite past tense environments properly include non-finite past tense environments, which in turn properly include all non-past tense environments). As shown above, the account as such depends on the ordering of operations in a strictly derivational approach to grammar, where both the availability of features for realization, and the available inflectional

---

[49] Also note that this challenge (if it can be substantiated) also holds for standard approaches, which ultimately also have to find some other way to exclude it, given that the conclusion cannot be avoided that [+fin] can in principle show up independently of [+past] (see above).

resources for realization may change significantly throughout the sequence of optimization procedures. However, this account also makes use of two auxiliary assumptions that, in a way, can be viewed as residues of the standard asymmetry-based analysis. First, f-seq ensures that [±past] is treated differently from [±fin]. And second, $\text{DEP}[+F]$ distinguishes between [+F] and [–F] features. As for this latter building block of the analysis, it is instructive to see what predictions would be made without it.

First, DEP was originally required to ensure that O_{23} in (47) is excluded: Without $\text{DEP}[+F]$, the stem /warf/ ↔ [+past,+fin] of O_{23} would ceteris paribus give rise to the same (optimal) constraint profile as the stem /worf/ ↔ [+past] of O_{22} in a [+past] context, and the problem arises that /warf/ then later needs to be excluded if the [+past] context eventually ends up as a [+past,–fin] context. However, as argued in footnote 41, this may be ensured by an appropriate approach to absolute ungrammaticality.

Next, the account of *ABA would go through exactly as before. In (64), adding the stem /tung/ ↔ [+past,–fin], as in candidate O_{22}, at the stage where [+past] is present and [–fin] is not yet present on the categorizing head, vacuously satisfies $\text{DEP}[+F]$; but it is this operation that is responsible for eventually removing the radically underspecified stem /ting/ ↔ [–], and thereby guaranteeing that ABA will be neutralized to ABB.

Finally, there is one context where dispensing with $\text{DEP}[+F]$ *does* make a huge difference empirically, and that involves AAC patterns. In (55), the stem /gab/ ↔ [+past,+fin] of O_{22} would block the stem /geb/ ↔ [–] of O_{21} without $\text{DEP}[+F]$, and this would imply that any attempt to generate an AAC pattern on the basis of [–] and [+past,+fin] specifications of stems would be neutralized to an ABB pattern. Interestingly, while this consequence is untenable for stem allomorphy with verb inflection in German, it corresponds exactly to what Bobaljik (2012) has observed for comparative and superlative formation with adjectives in the world's languages: Both AAC and ABA are unattested patterns here, and unlike the standard approaches to *ABA, the present approach would in principle seem to make it possible to account for the two non-existing patterns with adjective gradation in a uniform way. But of course, as just noted, abandoning $\text{DEP}[+F]$ would make wrong predictions for ablaut verbs, where AAC and ABA patterns do not show a uniform behaviour: One is attested, the other one is not. One may speculate about various ways in which $\text{DEP}[+F]$ could be made sensitive to the difference (among them a relativization of $\text{DEP}[+F]$ to certain feature classes, and/or different rankings for different kinds of $\text{DEP}[+F]$ constraints), but I will not pursue these issues any further here.

From a more general perspective, it can be noted that the single most important theoretical innovation of section 2 of the present chapter – viz., that fully specified feature matrices for morphological realization are generated incrementally, in a stepwise fashion – is fully compatible with all preceding analyses in the present monograph. On the one hand, this assumption cannot have any interesting consequences for inflectional exponents since these, by assumption, always depend on the presence of fully specified feature matrices. On the other hand, as regards the analyses of local and non-local stem allomorphy in the first section of the present chapter, postulating a stepwise generation of feature matrices on categorizing heads may minimally change the shape of some derivations, but cannot alter optimization sequences substantially; ultimately, the reason for this is that there are always at most two different stem allomorphs that need to be considered in these cases, not three (or four).

Chapter 6

Consequences

In this final chapter, I will consider four further consequences of the approach to inflectional morphology in terms of harmonic serialism laid out in the previous pages. The consequences concern impoverishment effects, deponency, paradigm gaps, and fixed vs. variable rankings, and I will address them in this order.

1. Implementing Impoverishment

1.1. *Impoverishment in Optimality Theory*

1.1.1. *Introduction*

Impoverishment operations have been proposed in Distributed Morphology mainly to account for scenarios that suggest a deep systematicity of some syncretism pattern in a given language, i.e., cases where it looks like a given morphological system is not able to express some difference between instantiations of some grammatical category for principled reasons, and not just because of an accidental absence of morphological exponents that could realize the different feature sets; see Bonet (1991), Noyer (1992; 1998), Halle & Marantz (1993; 1994), Halle (1997), Bobaljik (2002b), Frampton (2002), Harbour (2003), Harley (2004), Embick & Noyer (2007), Arregi & Nevins (2012), and much related work. A standard assumption is that impoverishment deletes features of the syntactically determined insertion context before morphological realization takes place. Thus, the morphological component does not actually see a featural distinction that is active (and independently motivated) in the syntax.

An abstract example may serve to illustrate the working of impoverishment (see Halle & Marantz (1994)). Let us assume that X is a category (an abstract functional morpheme) that is in need of post-syntactic morphological realization via vocabulary insertion in accordance with the Subset Principle (see (2) of chapter 2). Let us assume further that X contains the

features F_1, F_2, and F_3 in the syntax, as in (1-a); and that there are two
exponents (vocabulary items) /A/ and /B/ with the feature specifications
shown in (1-b). If nothing more is said, it would thus be expected that it is
/A/ that realizes X, not /B/: /A/ and /B/ are both compatible with X's
feature specification (they both realize proper subsets), and /A/ is more
specific than /B/, under any definition of specificity. However, suppose that
in addition there is a post-syntactic rule of impoverishment like (1-c), which
deletes F_2 in X if X immediately precedes Y; and that this rule applies before vocabulary insertion. This produces the modified syntactic insertion
context in (1-d) in this environment. As a consequence, /A/ turns out to
be incompatible with X in this impoverished context (since its feature F_2 is
not part of the syntactic context anymore), and only /B/ can be inserted
without a violation of the Subset Principle. Thus, impoverishment brings
about the choice of a less specific morphological exponent, something that
Halle and Marantz refer to as a "retreat to the general case".

(1)   a.   *Category X*:
             $[_X \ F_1,F_2,F_3]$
       b.   *Features of exponents*:
             (i)   /A/ $\leftrightarrow$ $[F_1,F_2]$
             (ii)   /B/ $\leftrightarrow$ $[F_1]$
       c.   *Impoverishment*:
             $F_2 \rightarrow \varnothing$ / [X[_] Y]
       d.   *Modified syntactic context for morphological realization*:
             [$[_X \ F_1,\overline{F_2},F_3]$ Y]

Throughout this book, I have touched on the concept of impoverishment
here and there, but I have not really focussed on the question of how it
could be implemented in optimality theory, and I have not at all considered
the question to what extent it is compatible with the present approach in
terms of harmonic serialism. It is not the goal of this section to remedy
this situation; I will confine myself to pointing out some basic issues arising
under an optimality-theoretic approach, and indicating some strategies for
a serialist approach.

   Given the assumptions that were made in chapter 2 (and that have then
essentially been preserved throughout the rest of the present monograph),
four different places can be identified as regards the presence of morpho-
syntactic features relevant for inflectional morphology. First, abstracting
away for the time being from the modifications introduced to cover stem
allomorphy in chapter 5, complete feature sets are associated with stems
in the input; second, complete feature sets are associated with stems in

the output; third, underspecified feature sets are associated with morphological exponents in the input; fourth, underspecified feature sets are also associated with morphological exponents in the output. The crucial role of faithfulness constraints in morphological inflection has so far been assumed to exclusively involve the relation between fully specified feature sets on stems in the output and underspecified feature sets on exponents in the output; see $\boxed{1}$ in (2); faithfulness relations between feature sets of stems in the input and stems in the output (see $\boxed{2}$), and between feature sets of exponents in the input and feature sets of exponents in the output (see $\boxed{3}$), have so far been assumed to hold maximally throughout.

(2)   *Features on stems and exponents*:

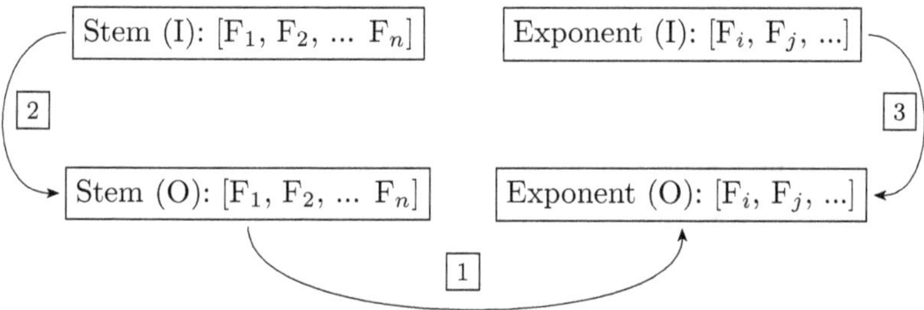

Against this background, it can be noted that what is arguably the canonical way to implement impoverishment in optimality-theoretic morphology relies on adopting special markedness constraints that preclude the realization of some feature F_i (or set of features F_i, F_j, ...) that is (or that are) part of the fully specified feature set associated with a stem in the output, by an exponent in the output, in violation of faithfulness constraints that require identity of features and feature values between a stem in the output and an exponent in the output, as in $\boxed{1}$.[1] Essentially, a markedness constraint against realizing an output stem feature by an output exponent that is ranked sufficiently high has the effect of making the feature inaccessible, as if it were absent.

In what follows, I will highlight three optimality-theoretic approaches (of the standard parallel type) that illustrate this pattern of accounting for

---

[1] Here, the role of the fully specified stem in the output is typically played by the syntactic context, or by the paradigm cell, in the analyses in question.

impoverishment: Trommer (2003), Don & Blom (2006), and Wunderlich (2004).[2]

1.1.2. Impoverishment Effects in Trommer (2003)

In his study of subject and object agreement in Ainu, Trommer (2003) assumes that there is a constraint PARTICIPANT UNIQUENESS (PU) that, despite being ranked quite low, can under certain circumstances have the effect that a number feature associated with the stem (and visible on the stem in both input and output) cannot be realized by an exponent in the output. The constraint is shown in (3).

(3)   PARTICIPANT UNIQUENESS (PU):
       For two adjacent [–3] agreement heads in the input, number should not be expressed in the output.

PU is a two-level markedness constraint, in the sense that both input and output properties must be taken into account (see page 169, and more generally the discussion of the Remove Condition in (7) of chapter 4). In transitive scenarios with two speech act participants, PU precludes the use of exponents bearing a number feature. Relevant data illustrating the effect of participant reduction with subject and object agreement in Ainu are given in (4) and (5). In 2→1 environments such as (4-a) and (4-b), both an exponent encoding the external argument and an exponent encoding the internal argument can appear.

(4)   a.   eci-un-kore
             2-O1p-give
             'you (pl) give us'
       b.   e-en-kore
             2sg-O1s-give
             'you (sg) give me'

In contrast, in 1→2 environments, there is an effect of participant reduction: Only the single exponent /eci/ can show up here; cf. (5).

(5)   a.   *ku-e ('I-you(sg)')
       b.   *ku-eci ('I-you(pl)')
       c.   *ci-e ('we-you(sg)')
       d.   *ci-eci ('we-you(pl)')
       e.   eci (for all these contexts)

---

[2] For other optimality-theoretic applications of essentially the same concept, cf. Grimshaw (2001), Kiparsky (2001), Trommer (2001), Opitz (2008), and Lahne (2009a).

Trommer (2003) accounts for this pattern by postulating an interaction of relativized PARSE constraints (which I render as relativized MAX constraints here) on the one hand, and left-alignment constraints for [+nom] and [+2] on the other hand.[3]

The specifications for some inflectional exponents are given in (6).

(6)   *Vocabulary items*:

    a.   /en-/ ↔ [+1+acc–pl]
    b.   /ci-/ ↔ [+1+nom+pl]
    c.   /eci-/ ↔ [+2]
    d.   /e-/ ↔ [+2–pl]

On the basis of these assumptions, the tableau in (7) illustrates the a priori expected situation where there is no participant reduction effect.

(7)   *$2{\to}1$ contexts: no participant reduction* (standard parallel optimality theory):

I: $[+\text{nom}+2{-}\text{pl}]_1$, $[+\text{acc},+1{-}\text{pl}]_2$	MAX (Per)$_{[+2]/[+1]}$	L⇐ [+nom]	L⇐ [+2]	MAX (Num)$_{[+1]/[+2]}$	MAX(Num)$_{[+2+h]/[+1+l]}$	P U	MAX [F]
O_1: eci$_1$ en$_2$					*!	*	**
☞ O_2: e$_1$ en$_2$						**	*
O_3: en$_1$ eci$_2$			*!		*	*	**
O_4: en$_1$ e$_2$			*!			**	*
O_5: en$_1$	*!				*	*	***
O_6: eci$_2$				*!	*		*****
O_7: c$_2$				*!		*	****

In (7), high-ranked left-alignment constraints arc active for both the feature [+nom] and the feature [+2]. However, these two features characterize one and the same argument, viz., the external one. It is therefore unproblematic to realize them both via left-alignment of a particular exponent (/e/). The

---

[3] The relativized PARSE/MAX constraints are assumed to be instantiations of the more general constraint schema in (i).

(i)   *Relativized Parse constraints schema*:
    If $A_1 \ldots A_n$ are distinct from $B_1 \ldots B_n$, and $A \geq B_i$ on a scale S_i ($1{\leq}i{\leq}n$), then there is a constraint PARSE[Agr]$_{[A_1\ldots\,A_n]/[B_1\ldots\,B_n]}$.

Also, [+h] in (7) and (8) stands for an external argument of a transitive V or an internal argument of an intransitive (unaccusative) V, whereas [+l] stands for an external argument of an intransitive (unergative) V or an internal argument of a transitive V (see Trommer (2003, 103)).

exponent faithfully encoding the remaining argument (/en/) can fail to be left-aligned without problems.

The competition in the more interesting scenario of participant reduction in $1{\rightarrow}2$ environments is shown in (8).

(8) *$1{\rightarrow}2$ contexts: participant reduction* (standard parallel optimality theory):

I: $[+\text{nom}+1+\text{pl}]_1$, $[+\text{acc},+2{-}\text{pl}]_2$	Max (Per)$_{[+2]/[+1]}$	L$\Leftarrow$ [+nom]	L$\Leftarrow$ [+2]	Max (Num)$_{[+1]/[+2]}$	Max(Num) $_{[+2+h]/[+1+l]}$	PU	Max [F]
O_1: e_2 ci_1		*!				**	**
O_2: eci_2 ci_1		*!				*	**
O_3: ci_1 eci_2			*!			*	**
O_4: ci_1 e_2			*!			*	**
O_5: ci_1	*!					*	**
☞O_6: eci_2				*			**
O_7: e_2				*		*!	**

In (8), the features [+nom] and [+2] characterize two different arguments in the input; and consequently (since there is no suitable portmanteau exponent) they are located on two different exponents. It is therefore impossible to satisfy both these constraints in an output; and since the requirement that second person information is realized in the presence of a first person argument is highest-ranked, the optimal output will be /eci/, which realizes [+2] at the cost of violating lower-ranked Max(Num)$_{[+1]/[+2]}$, which demands realization of the number of a first person argument in the presence of a second person argument. In this competition, PU plays a minor but important role: It blocks the use of the more specific exponent /e/ (that emerged as optimal in (7)) because here the PU violation automatically incurred by /e/ (and all other exponents bearing a number feature in the presence of two speech act participants) is fatal (since /eci/ can avoid it and the two exponents otherwise give rise to the same constraint profile). As noted by Trommer (2003), the effect that PU has is entirely analogous to impoverishment in Distributed Morphology: A number feature is not available for morphological realization by exponents, and exponents doing this nevertheless are blocked.

Of course, there are differences between this approach and one in terms of standard impoverishment rules. For one thing, PU is ranked quite low, so it can be violated by optimal outputs in principle (and is violated by the optimal output in (7)). For another, closer inspection reveals that an impoverishment-like effect also shows up in (8) that can be traced back not to a single constraint, but rather to the interaction of the left-alignment constraints for [+nom] and [+2] and the highest-ranked Max(Per)$_{[+2]/[+1]}$:

By working together, these three constraints ensure that [+nom] cannot be realized by an exponent in an optimal output in this context.

1.1.3. *Impoverishment Effects in Don & Blom (2006)*

Don & Blom (2006) set out to derive the generalization that person differences can never be marked morphologically by exponents in the plural in Dutch, and can also never be marked morphologically by exponents in past tense contexts in this language, irrespective of which conjugation (weak, strong, or *zijn* ('to be')) the verb stem belongs to. This is a scenario for which impoverishment has been postulated (see, e.g., Frampton (2002) and Müller (2006b) for an analogous effect in German, involving only first and third person in past tense environments). The present tense paradigm for verb inflection in Dutch is shown in (9); the past tense paradigm is illustrated in (10).

(9) *Verb inflection in Dutch* (present tense):

present tense	noem ('call')	loop ('walk')	zijn ('be')
1.sg	noem	loop	ben
2.sg.	noem-t	loop-t	ben-t
3.sg.	noem-t	loop-t	is
1.pl.	noem-en	loop-en	zijn
2.pl.	noem-en	loop-en	zijn
3.pl.	noem-en	loop-en	zijn

(10) *Verb inflection in Dutch* (past tense):

past tense	noem ('call')	loop ('walk')	zijn ('be')
1.sg	noem-de	liep	was
2.sg	noem-de	liep	was
3.sg	noem-de	liep	was
1.pl.	noem-de-en	liep-en	war-en
2.pl.	noem-de-en	liep-en	war-en
3.pl.	noem-de-en	liep-en	war-en

The constraints that Don and Blom adopt are given in (11). As concerns the MAX constraints, the only new thing to observe here is that the features [plural] and [past] are taken to be privative. *COMPLEX is a constraint that bans exponents which are associated with more than one morpho-syntactic feature.[4] Finally, the constraint *AF-TO-AF is supposed to ensure that

---

[4] Recall from chapter 3 that *COMPLEX to some extent may have similar effects to MINSAT in this respect.

there is disjunctive blocking in Dutch verb inflection – i.e., only one exponent can be attached to the verb stem as a suffix. The ranking of the constraints corresponds to the order in which they are presented in (11).

(11) a. MAX([PLURAL]):
          Realize a [plural] feature in the input by a [plural] exponent in the output.
      b. MAX([PAST]):
          Realize a [past] feature in the input by a [past] exponent in the output.
      c. *COMPLEX:
          Avoid complex affixes.
      d. MAX([αPERSON]):
          Realize an [αperson] feature in the input by an [αperson] exponent in the output.
      e. *AF-TO-AF:
          Do not add affixes to affixed stems.

Furthermore, the list of available morphological exponents is shown in (12). The exponents /en/, /t(de)/, /Ø/, and /t/ all exist, and can become optimal in certain contexts. In contrast, /st/, /ot/, and /um/ are made-up exponents that do not actually exist.

(12) a. /en/ ↔ [plur]
      b. /t(de)/ ↔ [past]
      c. /Ø/ ↔ [1]
      d. /t/ ↔ [ ]
      e. | /st/ ↔ [plur,2]   (hypothetical) |
      f. | /ot/ ↔ [2]   (hypothetical) |
      g. | /um/ ↔ [past,2]   (hypothetical) |

Importantly, it follows from Don & Blom's (2006) analysis that the hypothetical exponents /st/, /ot/, and /um/ in (12), even if they were to exist in the lexicon, could never become optimal in Dutch. This is an effect that can easily be derived by impoverishment. This effect can also be derived under the assumptions made by Don and Blom. Consider first a second person plural present tense environment. The competition is shown in (13).

(13) *Person neutralization in the plural (present tense)* (standard parallel
      optimality theory):

I: noem-[plur,2]	Max([PLUR])	Max([PAST])	*Compl	*Af-to-Af	Max([PERS])
☞O_1: noem-en					*
O_2: noem-st			*!		
O_3: noem	*!				
O_4: noem-t	*!				*
O_5: noem-ot	*!				
O_6: noem-en-ot				*!	

Since, by assumption, [past] is privative and thus does not occur in present
contexts, we can ignore this feature here. The relevant ranking is then
that of Max([PLUR]), *Complex, and Max([PERS]). The high ranking of
Max([PLUR]) vs. the low ranking of Max([PERS]) ensures that the optimal
exponent bears a plural feature rather than a person feature, given that
only one of the two features can be realized, and *Complex derives just
this latter state of affairs. In this sense, *Complex can be said to bring
about an impoverishment-like effect: Person is not accessible for morphological realization if plural needs to be realized. Furthermore, *Af-to-Af
guarantees that this restriction cannot be circumvented by providing an
additional exponent.

The category of person can also not be distinguished in past contexts
even if the number is singular. The reasoning is completely analogous
here. A maximally faithful exponent /um/ that would realize both past
tense and person fatally violates *Complex: Person is not realizable by
morphological exponence in this environment. This is illustrated by the
competition in (14).

(14) *Person neutralization in the past (singular)* (standard parallel
      optimality theory):

I: noem-[2,past]	Max([PLUR])	Max([PAST])	*Compl	*Af-to-Af	Max([PERS])
O_1: noem-en		*!			*
O_2: noem-st		*!	*		
O_3: noem		*!			
☞O_4: noem-de					*
O_5: noem-ot		*!			
O_6: noem-de-ot		*!		*	
O_7: noem-um			*!		

Finally, it is clear that the same impoverishment effect is obtained if [past]
and [plural] co-occur: Again, an exponent realizing person can never become

optimal; this feature is not available for inflectional exponence in this environment; see (15).[5]

(15) *Person neutralization in the plural (past tense))* (standard parallel optimality theory):

I: noem-[plur,2,past]	MAX([PLUR])	MAX([PAST])	*COMPL	*AF-TO-AF	MAX([PERS])
☞O_1: noem-de-en				*	*
O_2: noem-st		*	*		
O_3: noem	*!	*			*
O_4: noem-de	*!				*
O_5: noem-ot	*!	*			
O_6: noem-de-ot	*!			*	
O_7: noem-de-en-ot				**!*	
O_8: noem-um	*!		*		
O_9: noem-en		*!			*

1.1.4. *Impoverishment Effects in Wunderlich (2004)*

Russian noun declension exhibits a systematic syncretism of genitive and accusative with the first (masculine) inflection class if the stem is [+animate]; in both contexts the exponent /a/ is chosen (the exponent may then be realized as either [a] or [ja], depending on whether or not the stem ends in a palatalized consonant). In contrast, if the stem is [–animate], the accusative exponent exhibits systematic syncretism with the nominative: /Ø/. This is shown for singular contexts in (16).

(16) *Inflection class I (Masc.) in Russian, Sg.:*

| | | [–anim] | [+anim] | |
		$zavod_m$ ('factory')	$student_m$ ('student')	$žitel_m$ ('inhabitant')
nom/sg		zavod-Ø	student-Ø	žitel'-Ø
acc/sg		zavod-Ø	student-a	žitel-ja
dat/sg		zavod-u	student-u	žitel-ju
gen/sg		zavod-a	student-a	žitel-ja
inst/sg		zavod-om	student-om	žitel-em
loc/sg		zavod-e	student-e	žitel-e

In contrast to what is the case with most other approaches to nominal inflection in Russian (see Jakobson (1962a;b), Neidle (1988), Corbett &

---

[5] In principle, one might also need to consider an even more complex exponent like hypothetical /at/ ↔ [plur,past,2] here. This marker would satisfy MAX([PLUR]) and MAX([PAST]), but its satisfaction of MAX([PERS]) would again imply a fatal violation of *COMPLEX.

Fraser (1993), Fraser & Corbett (1994), Halle (1994), Franks (1995), Müller (2004), and Halle & Matushansky (2006) for some proposals), in Wunderlich's approach the genitive/accusative syncretism with animate masculine noun stems is addressed by postulating that accusative and genitive can indeed form a natural class in this language. For present purposes, we may assume that the shared features are [+gov(erned),–obl(ique)], and that the additional feature distinguishing genitive and accusative is [±verbal] (where the accusative is identified as [+v(erbal)], and the genitive as [–v(erbal)] because it also shows up in the nominal domain).[6] The accusative/genitive exponent /a/ can then be assumed to bear the features [+gov,–obl,class I].

(17) lists some of the constraints that play a role in the analysis.[7]

(17)   a.   *[+gov,–obl]/[–anim],[+v]
      b.   MAX([gov,obl])
      c.   *[+gov,–obl],[+v]

(17-a) blocks the maximally faithful exponent /a/ in inanimate accusative environments; consequently, the less specific exponent /Ø/, which we can take to be a radically underspecified elsewhere marker, must be chosen here, in violation of MAX([gov,obl]). This qualifies as a retreat to the general case, as it is standardly associated with the concept of impoverishment in Distributed Morphology (see above). The competition in inanimate accusative class I contexts is illustrated in (18) (which is simplified in various respects).

(18) *Accusative contexts, inanimate nouns, class I* (standard parallel optimality theory):

I: zavod: [+gov,–obl], [+v], [–anim], [class I]	*[+gov,–obl]/[–anim],[+v]	MAX([gov,obl])	*[+gov,–obl],[+v]
O₁: zavod-a[+gov,–obl,clI]	*!		*
☞O₂: zavod-Ø[ ]		*	

---

[6] Wunderlich (2004) actually uses the case feature [+hr] ('there is a higher role') rather than [+gov(erned),–obl(ique)], on the basis of a dependent case approach, but this difference plays no role in the present context, and I have chosen [+gov(erned),–obl(ique)] instead for reasons of overall coherence and perspicuity.

[7] As before, I tacitly adjust some of Wunderlich's assumptions to the present system here; recall, for instance, from chapter 2 (footnote 8) that Wunderlich (2004) still has designated constraints requiring compatibility and specificity, whereas I have assumed throughout that such constraints can be dispensed with completely, given IDENT-F and MAX constraints.

292   Chapter 6. Consequences

In contrast, in accusative contexts with animate nouns of class I, no impoverishment effect is present; [+gov,–obl] can and must be faithfully realized by the exponent /a/; this is shown in (19).

(19) *Accusative contexts, animate nouns, class I* (standard parallel optimality theory):

I: student: [+gov,–obl], [+v], [+anim], [class I]	*[+gov,–obl]/[–anim],[+v]	Max([gov,obl])	*[+gov,–obl],[+v]
☞O$_1$: student-a$_{[+gov,-obl,clI]}$			*
O$_2$: student-Ø$_{[\ ]}$		*!	

Since the markedness constraint *[+gov,–obl]/[–anim],[+v] is only active in accusative contexts, it is clear that inanimate nouns of class I will regularly take /a/ in genitive ([–v]) contexts. Finally, it must be ensured that the impoverishment effect does not occur with inanimate nouns in the singular of one of the two declension classes of Russian that are predominantly feminine (the old a-declension, but not the old i-declension). Here, e.g., the accusative singular form of an inanimate noun like *kart-a* ('map') is not *kart-a* or *kart-Ø*, but *kart-u*, where the nominative exponent /a/ can be assumed to bear conflicting features ([–gov,–obl]), and there is a designated accusative exponent /u/ ([–gov,–obl,+v]) that is incompatible with a genitive specification (in that context, /y/ is used). Wunderlich's (2004) account of this state of affairs relies on a high-ranked relativized (or contextual) faithfulness (Max) constraint that requires realization of [+gov,–obl] with this declension class (here referred to as [clII]) and thus blocks the otherwise expected retreat to the general case (i.e., the radically underspecified exponent /Ø/); see (20).

(20) *Accusative contexts, inanimate nouns, class II* (standard parallel optimality theory):

I: kart: [+gov,–obl], [+v], [–anim], [class II]	Id-F	Max([gov,obl])/[clII]	*[+gov,–obl]/[–anim],[+v]	Max([gov,obl])	*[+gov,–obl],[+v]
☞O$_1$: kart-u$_{[+gov,-obl,+v,clI]}$			*		*
O$_2$: kart-Ø$_{[\ ]}$		*!		*	
O$_3$: kart-a$_{[-gov,-obl,clII]}$	*!				

To sum up, against the background of the core assumptions about the place of morphology in the grammar made in the present book, all three optimality-theoretic approaches to impoverishment effects introduced so far can be conceived of as relying on the idea that markedness constraints can force unfaithful mappings from (features on) output stems to (features on) output exponents, in violation of faithfulness constraints of type ⬚1 in (2).

Things are different with the optimality-theoretic approach to impoverishment developed in Keine & Müller (2011; 2014), which, again on the basis of general assumptions as they have been adopted in the current book, can be viewed as employing markedness constraints that induce unfaithful mappings between a stem in the input and a stem in the output, i.e., violations of faithfulness constraints of type $\boxed{2}$ in (2).[8]

1.1.5. Impoverishment Effects in Keine & Müller (2011; 2014)

In Keine & Müller (2011; 2014) (also cf. Keine (2010a) and Müller & Thomas (2017)), the basic premise of Distributed Morphology concerning impoverishment – viz., that impoverishment involves a deletion of morpho-syntactic features – is preserved. Viewed again from the current perspective, a core assumption is that the fully specified feature structure associated with a stem in the input can be reduced by feature deletion in the presence of markedness constraints that outrank the counteracting faithfulness (MAX) constraints militating against deletion *before* a morphological exponent is attached. Consequently, the exponents find a reduced feature matrix, with some syntactic distinctions being neutralized for morphology, and invariant patterns of syncretism can be derived as system-wide generalizations.

More specifically, the assumption in Keine & Müller (2011; 2014) is that the MAX constraints that try to prevent deletion of morpho-syntactic features are relativized to specific syntactic environments; and the markedness constraints that bring about deletion, and thus impoverishment effects, are ususaly quite simple, often referring to no more than a single feature.

Consider, as a case study, the analysis of differential encoding of objects in the Tacanan language Cavineña spoken in Bolivia (based on Guillaume (2008)). In Cavineña, two suffixal dative/genitive markers can appear: /kwe/ and /ja/. The choice depends on person and number features of the stem – /kwe/ can only be attached to local person (i.e., first or second person) pronouns in the singular. All other combinations require /ja/. This constitutes a case of differential object marking since singular first or second person objects are highly marked. The other combinations are less

---

[8] Needless to say, the general assumptions about the organization of the grammar, and the place assigned to (inflectional) morphology in it, that are made in all four approaches are different from what is assumed in the present monograph, sometimes radically so. For instance, Trommer's (2003) approach presupposes a post-syntactic morphology realizing features on abstract syntactic heads. Similarly, in Keine & Müller (2011; 2014) an organization of the grammar along the lines of Distributed Morphology is adopted. Don & Blom (2006) and Wunderlich (2004) also rely on different assumptions as regards the general place and role of morphology in the grammar. Still, from the current perspective, and at least for current purposes, their analyses can be adjusted to present assumptions without problems.

marked in terms of Hale/Silverstein scales (see Hale (1972) and Silverstein (1976)). The distribution of morphological exponents is illustrated in (21).

(21)　*Dative/genitive exponents in Cavineña:*

Number *Person*	SINGULAR	DUAL	PLURAL
1	e-∅-kwe	ya-tse-ja	e-kwana-ja
2	mi-∅-kwe	me-tse-ja	mi-kwana-ja
3	tu-∅-ja	ta-tse-ja	tu-na-ja
3.PROXIMATE	riya-∅-ja	re-tse-ja	re-na-ja

According to the analysis in Keine & Müller (2011), there is massive impoverishment in dative/genitive contexts (which are assumed to be characterized by the features [+obl,+gov]), with the feature [+obl] removed in all contexts except the most marked ones (viz., local person singular object environments). Therefore, given the exponent specifications in (22), only /ja/ can satisfy ID-F and MAX constraints in the non-marked environments; and /kwe/ shows up only where [+obl] is protected by the highest-ranked relativized faithfulness constraint.

(22)　a.　/kwe/ ↔ [+obl,+gov]
　　　b.　/ja/ ↔ [+gov]

The constraints that underlie the analyis are given in (23); the order of presentation corresponds to their ranking.

(23)　a.　*OBJ/LOC/SG & MAX-C:
　　　　　A case feature on a stem in the input must be preserved on a stem in the output in object contexts with singular local (first or second) person.
　　　b.　*[+OBL]:
　　　　　A [+obl] feature must not show up on a stem in the output.
　　　c.　*OBJ/LOC/NON-SG & MAX-C:
　　　　　A case feature on a stem in the input must be preserved on a stem in the output in object contexts with non-singular local (first or second) person.
　　　d.　*OBJ/NLOC/SG & MAX-C:
　　　　　A case feature on a stem in the input must be preserved on a stem in the output in object contexts with singular non-local (third) person.
　　　e.　*OBJ/NLOC/NON-SG & MAX-C:
　　　　　A case feature on a stem in the input must be preserved on a

stem in the output in object contexts with non-singular non-local (third) person.

Given these constraints, subsequent realization of the feature matrices associated with output stems by morphological exponents often finds an impoverished feature structure.[9]

1.2. *Impoverishment in Harmonic Serialism*

As noted at the outset, it is not my goal here to implement full-fledged accounts of impoverishment effects in harmonic serialism. However, generally it would seem to be possible to transfer both types of approaches to impoverishment effects to harmonic serialism. As regards the more widespread approach pursued by Trommer, Wunderlich, and Don & Blom, where markedness constraints preclude the realization of contextual features (i.e., features present on the stem in the output, under present assumptions), it would seem to be transferrable in principle without any further assumptions to a harmonic serialist account, independently of whether the simple approach of chapter 2 is adopted without the subsequent extensions in chapters 3–5, or whether MINSAT-based derivations accompanied by structure removal are entertained.

A central assumption underlying the alternative approach to impoverishment effects in Keine & Müller (2011; 2014) is that there is a sequential interaction of (i) feature deletion and (ii) morphological realization of features by exponents. While such an interaction would perhaps also be statable without too much ado in standard parallel optimality-theoretic

---

[9] It should be noted that the relativized faithfulness constraints in (23) do not have to be stipulated but follow from the application of the optimality-theoretic operations of *harmonic alignment* of the prominence scales in (i), and *local conjunction* of the results with the general MAX-C constraints.

(i)   a.   *Person scale*
              Loc(al) (1/2) $\succ$ N(on)loc(al)
        b.   *Number scale*
              Sg $\succ$ Non-sg
        c.   *GF scale*
              Subj $\succ$ Obj

This means of accounting for prominence scale effects in differential argument encoding is adopted from Aissen (1999b; 2003). The main difference is that whereas Aissen's approach is purely syntactic and merely predicts the presence or absence of case as such, the approach in Keine & Müller (2011; 2014) locates differential argument encoding in the morphological component, and is compatible with two (or more) alternating morphological exponents that are non-zero (like /kwe/ and /ja/, in the case at hand).

approaches, it would seem to a priori lend itself more to an implementation in terms of harmonic serialism, with its built-in sequential order of operations. The important thing that needs to be guaranteed is that the constraint that brings about the deletion of a feature on a stem is either higher ranked than, or becomes active before, the constraints that introduce morphological exponents (the second option would arise if all stem optimization must precede all exponent optimization; see chapter 5). On this view, the morphological exponents find a truly impoverished morpho-syntactic feature structure on the stem when it comes to affixal inflection; and DEP constraints (see chapter 5) would then block their use. Thus, all in all it seems that the harmonic serialist approach can also accomodate this second type of account of impoverishment effects.

There is one qualification, though, which is not so much related to harmonic serialism as a model of inflectional morphology as such, but rather to the decision (made in chapter 1, and maintained throughout the remaining chapters) that the operations of inflectional morphology apply *pre-syntactically*, not *post-syntactically*. This gives rise to the conundrum that morpho-syntactic features which can (or, in stronger terms, and assuming that there is a strong individual motivation for impoverishment-like operations: should) be assumed to be unavailable for morphological realization are also unavailable for syntactic operations throughout; i.e., they would be expected not to be able to participate in syntactic operations involving agreement, case assignment, case transfer, etc. This would be an untenable consequence. However, this problem is not a new one.

As noted by Bobaljik (2002a), the widespread idea that properties of the morphological inventory can be held responsible for the presence or absence of an operation like V-to-T movement in the syntax (with "strong" inflection triggering the movement, and "weak" inflection blocking it) simply cannot be maintained if inflectional morphology is post-syntactic: If morphological exponence is post-syntactic, the relevant information (strength of T) is not yet available at the point where it is needed. Similar considerations apply in the case of pro-drop: The hypothesis that "strong" inflection permits pro-drop in the syntax whereas "weak" inflection does not cannot be implemented if strength of inflection can only be determined by inspecting the nature and inventory of morphological exponents that are inserted post-syntactically.

In view of this challenge, and given some independent arguments against naive classifications of T as "strong" or "weak", it is argued in Müller (2006a) that the empirically correct generalization might be that only those languages that do not show impoverishment of morpho-syntactic features relevant for verb inflection permit pro-drop. Thus, impoverishment *must* be a pre-syntactic operation on this view. However, this then gives rise to the problem encountered in the previous paragraph: Pre-syntactic impoverishment cannot actually delete features if these features are needed for subsequent syntactic operations. The solution advanced in Müller (2006a) is the following: Impoverishment *marks* features as morphologically inaccessible, but it does not actually *delete* them, and they remain accessible in the syntax. (This is fully parallel to Chomsky's (1995) distinction between deletion and erasure.) Given this proviso, the second optimality-theoretic account of impoverishment effects also emerges as fully compatible with the present approach to inflectional morphology in terms of harmonic serialism.[10]

All that said, it seems that harmonic serialism might also offer yet another option to implement impoverishment, one that cannot be adopted in standard optimality theory for very deep reasons, and that is thus practically unique to the present approach. Given that the morpho-syntactic context features of the stem are added successively (as argued in chapter 5), the hypothesis seems worth pursuing that morphological realization may have to work with incomplete realization contexts not *after*, but *before* they are complete; so impoverishment effects would be derived as instances of counter-feeding (i.e., a feature is available too late to permit morphological realization by some exponent that bears it) rather than bleeding, as is standardly assumed (where a feature is not available anymore for morpholgical realization by some exponent that bears it). Technically, this idea could be executed by postulating that an 'impoverished' feature is one that can only be added to a stem (in a given context, i.e., in the presence of other features) if inflectional exponents have been merged with it. I will leave a proper development of such an approach for future work.

2. Deriving Deponency

2.1. The Phenomenon

The (generalized) concept of deponency characterizes morpho-syntactic scenarios in the world's languages that resemble deponent verbs in Latin,

---

[10] Also recall the issue that was mentioned in footnote 9 of the previous chapter in the context of the "fully articulated feature matrix" that is required by inflectional exponents. There, I concluded that a deviation from the simplest possible conception of this concept might be required if it is assumed that contextual features on the stem can be deleted. Assuming that 'deletion' of morpho-syntactic features on stems is really to be understood as a marking of inaccessibility for morphological operations, this potential problem vanishes.

Classical Greek, and Sanskrit (where passive morphology accompanies active syntax) in that what looks like a 'wrong form' is obligatorily used. In (24), the phenomenon is illustrated for deponent verbs in Latin.

(24) *Regular and deponent verbs*:

| | regere ('rule') | | hortārī ('urge') | |
	ACTIVE	PASSIVE	ACTIVE	PASSIVE
PRES IND	regit	regitur	hortātur	—
PRES INF	regere	regī	hortārī	—
PRF IND	rēxit	rēctus est	hortātus est	—
PTCP PERF	—	rēctus	hortātus	—
SUPINE	rēctum	—	hortātum	—
PART PRES	regēns	—	hortāns	—

With the deponent verb *hortārī* ('urge'), it looks as though passive forms are used with active syntactic functions; passive contexts cannnot be realized at all (i.e., the paradigm becomes defective).

Many more phenomena fall under the generalized concept of deponency (see, e.g., the contributions in Baerman et al. (2007)). Let me just give one further example here, from noun inflection in Archi. Consider first the regular paradigms in (25) (cf. Kibrik (1991; 2003), Mel'čuk (1999), Corbett (2007), Hippisley (2007), and Keine (2013), among others).

(25) *Partial paradigm of some regular nouns in Archi*:

| | aInš ('apple') | | qIin ('bridge') | | áʕrum ('sickle') | |
	SG	PL	SG	PL	SG	PL
ABS	aInš-Ø	aInš-um	qIin-Ø	qionn-or	áʕrum-Ø	áʕrum-mul
ERG	aInš-li	aInš-um-čaj	qIin-i	qionn-or-čaj	áʕrum-li	áʕrum-mul-čaj
GEN	aInš-li-n	aInš-um-če-n	qIin-i-n	qionn-or-če-n	áʕrum-li-n	áʕrum-mul-če-n
DAT	aInš-li-s	aInš-um-če-s	qIin-i-s	qionn-or-če-s	áʕrum-li-s	áʕrum-mul-če-s
COMIT	aInš-li-ɫ:u	aInš-um-če-ɫ:u	qIin-i-ɫ:u	qionn-or-če-ɫ:u	áʕrum-li-ɫ:u	áʕrum-mul-če-ɫ:u
. . .						

The system features *parasitic* (or *'Priscianic'*) formations (see Matthews (1972)), in the sense that all oblique case forms are derived on the basis of the ergative form (and not the bare stem). In addition, as discussed in chapter 3 already, there is extended exponence: /li/ is an ergative singular exponent; /čaj/ is an ergative plural exponent; and /um/, /or/, /mul/ are plural exponents sensitive to noun class.

Interestingly, some noun stems systematically combine with what looks like a wrong number exponent in certain contexts. For instance, as shown in (26), the nouns *haʕtəra* ('river') and *c'aj* ('female goat') systematically employ plural exponents in singular environments.[11]

(26) *Partial paradigm of deponent nouns; plural markers in the singular:*

	haʕtəra ('river')		c'aj ('female goat')	
	SG	PL	SG	PL
ABS	haʕtəra-Ø	haʕtər-mul	c'aj-Ø	c'ohor-Ø
ERG	haʕtər-*čaj*	haʕtər-mul-čaj	c'ej-*ṫaj*	c'ohor-čaj
...				

It is also worth pointing out that unlike Latin deponent verbs, deponency with noun inflection in Archi, like arguably the vast majority of deponency phenomena, does not in fact exhibit defectivity: Use of the ergative plural marker *ṫaj/čaj* in singular contexts with deponent noun stems does not preclude the use of the same marker in plural contexts.

2.2. *Deponency in Optimality Theory*

There are various kinds of approaches to deponency in the more recent literature (see Müller (2013a) and Grestenberger (2017) for overviews).

In some approaches it is held that there is no mismatch after all upon closer scrutiny. In one version of this position, the morphological exponent involved in deponency faithfully realizes a morpho-syntactic property set, and the impression that something is 'wrong' can be traced back to the fact that the features involved in exponence are somewhat more abstract than one might initially have thought (see Bobaljik (2007), Keine (2010b), and Grestenberger (2014) for analyses of this type). An alternative way of denying true mismatch consists in the postulation of a faithful realization of purely morphological ('morphomic'; see Aronoff (1994)) features; there then has to be a relation between syntactic features and morphomic features, but it is indirect (see Kiparsky (2005), Brown (2006), and Hippisley (2007) for analyses of this type). Finally, sometimes the assumption is entertained that there is no true mismatch in generalized deponency because the morphological exponent in question faithfully realizes a certain more abstract semantic property; e.g., on this view, deponent verbs in Indo-European languages can form a semantically defined natural class with other, more obvious instances of non-active morphology after all (see Xu, Aronoff & Anshen (2007), Kallulli (2013), Zombolou & Alexiadou (2014),

---

[11] Note that the choice of *ṫaj* vs. *čaj* is determined by consonant-finality vs. vowel-finality of the stem.

Alexiadou (2013); but also Grestenberger (2014) for arguments against such an approach).

As yet another alternative to denying a mismatch between form and interpretation in deponency, the idea has been widely pursued that deponency involves a mismatch between the morpho-syntactic property set that a given deponent exponent realizes, and interpretation of these contextual features. Here the realization of the contextual feature matrix by the exponent is perfectly faithful; it is just the ultimate interpretation of this feature matrix that is not. These kinds of analyses (called *property deponency* in Stump (2007)) have been pursued by Stump (2007), Embick (2000), and (again) Kiparsky (2005), among others.

Finally, an account of deponency that naturally suggests itself relies on grabbing the bull by the horns: Here it is postulated that the phenomenon does indeed involve the use of a 'wrong' (i.e., unfaithful) morphological exponent for a given matrix of morpho-syntactic features. This type of analysis (which Stump (2007) refers to as *form deponency*) has been pursued in Stump (2006) and Weisser (2014) (on the basis of radically different background assumptions that nonetheless share the property of being unrelated to optimality theory); and in Müller (2013a) I argue that (standard parallel) optimality theory immediately lends itself to an implementation of such an approach to deponency.

More specifically, the gist of such an optimality-theoretic account works as follows.[12] The central assumption is that a deponent stem bears a feature co-occurrence restriction (see Gazdar et al. (1985)) stating an incompatibility with certain morpho-syntactic features provided by the context (e.g., $*[\alpha]$, where α stands for a – possibly singleton – set of features); and there is an undominated constraint LEX that demands adherence to lexically marked idiosyncrasies and thus precludes the concatenation of a morphological exponent bearing the feature(s) $[\alpha]$ with a stem characterized as $*[\alpha]$. This then basically triggers an impoverishment-like effect, but there are two core differences to standard impoverishment scenarios as they were discussed in the previous section: First, the ban on realizing certain syntactically relevant features by morphological exponents does not hold generally in the system (which can be encoded by a designated markedness constraint, as in the approaches to impoverishment effects discussed above),

---

[12] I tacitly adjust some assumptions in Müller (2013a) that diverge from the standard approaches to inflectional morphology in optimality theory as they were introduced in chapter 2 above, in particular as far as the concept of underspecification is concerned (which is not adopted in Müller (2013a)).

but shows up only with certain stems: It is encoded on these stems, and indirectly mediated via a high-ranked LEX constraint. Second, in contrast to what can be seen in the case of impoverishment, with deponency there is no retreat to the general case (i.e., to a less specific compatible exponent that violates MAX constraints more often but respects ID-F). Rather, here the optimal output must violate ID-F. Given the assumptions about the relative ranking of ID-F and MAX in inflectional morphology adopted throughout this monograph, this implies that in cases of deponency, there simply is no other compatible, MAX-satisfying exponent that would also satisfy LEX.

Based on these assumptions, consider a simplified version of the optimality-theoretic competition underlying number marker choice in deponent and regular nouns in the singular and in the plural in Archi. Suppose that deponent noun stems like *haʕtəra* ('river') and *c'aj* ('female goat') bear a feature co-occurrence restriction **[+gov,–pl]*, which is interpreted such that they cannot be combined with a morphological exponent bearing these features (and suppose that [+gov] characterizes the ergative and is present in all cases except the nominative). If such an inflection marker is attached nevertheless, LEX will be fatally violated. In ergative plural environments, choice of the maximally faithful exponent (/čaj/) is unproblematic because its use does not violate LEX; see (27).[13]

(27)   *Ergative plural, deponent noun stem* (standard parallel optimality theory):

I: haʕtər-mul-: [+gov,+pl], **[+gov,–pl]*	LEX	IDENT GOV	IDENT NUM	MAX
O$_1$: haʕtər-mul:[+gov,+pl]-li:[+gov,–pl]	*!		*	
O$_2$: haʕtər-mul:[+gov,+pl]-Ø:[–gov,–pl]		*!	*	
☞O$_3$: haʕtər-mul:[+gov,+pl]-čaj:[+gov,+pl]				

However, in ergative singular environments, where a morphological exponent /li/ would normally be expected as the optimal marker of case, LEX springs into action and forces the choice of an unfaithful plural exponent (/čaj/) again; and this time the same exponent that emerges as optimal in (27) without a faithfulness violation violates IDENT-NUM. If /Ø/ is chosen instead, this incurs a fatal violation of IDENT-GOV, given the ranking

---

[13] To simplify exposition, I here abstract away from the determination of the plural exponent /mul/, i.e., from the problem of capturing extended exponence in standard parallel optimality theory; this issue is unrelated to the account of deponency.

IDENT-GOV ≫ IDENT-NUM assumed here. All of this is illustrated in (28).

(28) *Ergative singular, deponent noun stem* (standard parallel optimality theory):

I: haʕtər-: [+gov,−pl], *[+gov,−pl]	LEX	IDENT GOV	IDENT NUM	MAX
O$_1$: haʕtər:[+gov,−pl]-li:[+gov,−pl]	*!			
O$_2$: haʕtər:[+gov,−pl]-Ø:[−gov,−pl]		*!		
☞O$_3$: haʕtər:[+gov,−pl]-čaj:[+gov,+pl]			*	

Of course, if optimization affects a regular noun stem, as in (25), where there is no feature co-occurrence restriction like *[+gov,−pl] associated with the stem as a lexical property, LEX will be vacuously fulfilled, and an output of the type O$_1$ will be optimal in ergative singular contexts (and an output of the type O$_3$ in ergative plural contexts).

2.3. *Deponency in Harmonic Serialism*

As with impoverishment, I will not attempt here to develop a comprehensive analysis of deponency in harmonic serialism. However, the first thing to note is that as it stands there do not seem to be any substantive obstacles to transferring the account just sketched from standard parallel optimality theory to harmonic serialism. As with the parallel version of the account, the core assumptions needed to cover deponency will then be (i) feature co-occurrence restrictions on stems that are then enforced by LEX, (ii) violability of IDENT constraints in optimal candidates, and (iii) an absence of radically underspecified elsewhere exponents (which could satisfy LEX without violating any IDENT constraints) in the inventories in question.

However, in addition to this straightforward transfer of the approach developed in Müller (2013a), the harmonic serialist approach might also offer another option to derive deponency. Given the analysis introduced in chapter 5, the starting point of an inflected word is not a stem but an abstract categorizing head that first selects, and then merges with, a stem; and it is successively enriched by contextual morpho-syntactic features in the course of doing so. This makes it possible in principle that there are stages of the derivation where the categorizing head has combined with the stem but is not yet equipped with a complete matrix of morpho-syntactic features that serves as the reference point for merging morphological exponents. Now, recall that the stem itself may have various kinds of inherent features that, together with the non-inherent features added to the categorizing head, may provide the context for morphological realization.

This opens up the possibility that it may be a characteristic property of deponent stems not to be associated with a prohibition against the realization of certain kinds of features on exponents (as in the approach illustrated in the previous subsection), but rather to simply bear certain kinds of morpho-syntactic features as an intrinsic property which are normally non-inherent features for this kind of stem (and thus introduced derivationally on the categorizing head). For instance, for the case of deponent nouns like *haʕtəra* ('river') and *c'aj* ('female goat') in Archi, one might assume that they are inherently specified as [+pl]. On this view, the enrichment of the categorizing head by the proper number feature ([–pl], in the relevant case), which we can take to override any prior specifications on the stem (since this is the feature that is syntactically and semantically interpreted), might come too late to block inflection via the maximally faithful plural exponent. To distinguish between [–gov] (i.e., absolutive) environments (where there is no 'wrong' exponent) and [+gov] (i.e., ergative, genitive, dative, etc.) environments (where deponency occurs), one might stipulate that [+gov] is introduced earlier on a categorizing head than [–gov], so that /čaj/ ↔ [+gov,+pl] can be faithfully merged with the categorizing head in the former context but not in the latter one. In effect, this would amount to a *property deponency* analysis (in Stump's (2007) terms), remotely related to Embick (2000), rather than qualifying as an instance of *form deponency* (like the standard parallel optimality-theoretic analysis sketched in the previous section).

Needless to say, this kind of radically derivational approach to deponency, while making maximal use of the options made available by harmonic serialism, raises many further issues and would ultimately require further assumptions, and possibly also modifications of the current system.[14] However, addressing these issues is beyond the scope of the present investigation.

----

[14] This holds, e.g., for the tenet that morphological exponents can only be merged when there is a fully specified feature structure, as with the suggestion regarding impoverishment at the end of the previous section. Also, the question arises of why the 'wrong' exponent cannot ultimately be replaced again by the expected exponent, once the proper feature structure is in place. As regards this latter issue, one might want to show that the regularly expected exponent is used up early in the derivation in the relevant contexts, and can therefore never come back again since it is not present anymore in the morphological array (as argued with respect to *ABA patterns in chapter 5; also cf. chapter 4); the technical implementation of such an account is far from obvious, though.

3. Explaining Paradigm Gaps

3.1. Buridan's Ass

Normally, all cells of an inflectional paradigm are occupied by some grammatical form. In some cases, however, there simply is no form that can successfully be used by speakers, and ineffability arises. Since the filling of what would otherwise be a gap in an inflectional paradigm is an automatic consequence of the availability of radically underspecified elsewhere exponents, paradigm gaps pose a problem for morphological theory.

A widespread intuition about the phenomenon is that speakers cannot decide between two options which both seem available in principle, but which also are both not unproblematic either. Nevins (2014) explicitly invokes the analogy to Buridan's ass in this context – i.e., the donkey that cannot decide between a trough and a stack of hay that are equally close, and ultimately dies of thirst and hunger. The phenomenon of paradigm gaps as such can be accounted for in various ways, and against the backgrounds of various morphological theories. To name just one classic approach here: In Halle (1973), it is proposed that some optimal forms determined by the morphological component may bear a feature [–lexical insertion] which simply makes them unusable in the syntax. However, I would like to contend that so far there is no systematic analysis of paradigm gaps in grammatical theory that faithfully implements the Buridan's ass intuition. It is the goal of this subsection to illustrate that things might be different in the harmonic serialist approach to morphology developed in the preceding chapters.

To begin with, recall from chapter 4 that the REMOVE CONDITION (RC) had to be understood as a two-level markedness constraint that refers both to input and output; see (7) of chapter 4, which is repeated here as (29).

(29) REMOVE CONDITION (RC):
    A removal feature [–X–] that is accessible in the input participates in (and is deleted by) a Remove operation in the output.

As argued on page 172, RC must permit a feature [–X–] for structure removal to arise in outputs if it is not yet accessible (i.e., still part of the morphological array) in the input (otherwise additional exponents bearing these features could not be merged in the first place); but as soon as [–X–] is part of the input representation, RC demands that it must be gotten rid of. Recall also that independent evidence for this constraint type has been given in the literature (see Trommer (2001; 2003; 2006a), Müller & Thomas (2017)). Still, it can at this point also be noted that McCarthy (2016, 59–60) has observed a potential problem arising with two-level markedness constraints (more specifically, anti-faithfulness constraints) in harmonic serialism: These constraints may give rise to infinite loops, and thus "undermine the convergence guarantee"; he therefore concludes that there is no room for this kind of constraint in harmonic serialism.

In view of this, I would like to point out two relevant observations. First, the two-level markedness constraint RC is in fact not prone to generating infinite loops. The reason is that (non-trivial) satisfaction of RC consumes resources that can never come back: An exponent taken from the morphological array is irrevocably gone once it has been affected by structure removal; so it can never be involved in an infinite loop. And second, assuming that there are two-level markedness constraints that do not consume resources but leave them intact for further optimization offers a new theoretical perspective on paradigm gaps that may make it possible to address all of these phenomena based on the Buridan's ass intuition. In what follows, I will tentatively pursue this latter idea, based on three preliminary case studies: In paradigm gap scenarios, a two-level markedness constraint and another, lower-ranked simple constraint conspire so as to create an infinite loop: Convergence can never be reached, and this explains the gap.

3.2. *Genitive Plural of Weak Feminines in Icelandic*

Consider first the system of weak noun declensions in Icelandic (see Kress (1982), and Baerman (2011) for the paradigm gap analysis I take as a starting point). As shown in (30), whereas there are no paradigm gaps with the weak masculines (Mw), the weak neuters (Nw), and two of the weak feminine classes (Fw_1, Fw_2), there is a gap in genitive plural of a third type of weak feminine (Fw′); this is indicated by the symbol ∘ in (30).

(30) *Weak inflection classes*:

	Mw penn ('feather')	Nw aug ('eye')	Fw_1 tung ('tongue')	Fw_2 lyg ('lie')	Fw′ hol ('hole')
NOM/SG	penn-i	aug-a	lyg-i	tung-a	hol-a
ACC/SG	penn-a	aug-a	lyg-i	tung-u	hol-u
DAT/SG	penn-a	aug-a	lyg-i	tung-u	hol-u
GEN/SG	penn-a	aug-a	lyg-i	tung-u	hol-u
NOM/PL	penn-ar	aug-u	lyg-ar	tung-ur	hol-ur
ACC/PL	penn-a	aug-u	lyg-ar	tung-ur	hol-ur
DAT/PL	penn-um	aug-um	lyg-um	tung-um	hol-um
GEN/PL	penn-a	aug-n-a	lyg-a	tung-na	∘

In Baerman's informal analysis, the source of the gap in Fw′ is that on the one hand there is a homophony avoidance requirement that demands nominative singular and genitive plural forms to be different, which is violated by an output *hol-a* (as in Fw₁; cf. *lyg-a*), and on the other hand there is an incompatibility of Fw′ with /n/, which is violated by an output *hol-n-a* (as in Fw₂; cf. *tung-na*).

Here is a sketch of a Buridan's ass reconstruction of this general analysis in terms of two-level markedness in harmonic serialism: Suppose that the system obeys the constraints in (31). MC_{Cn} triggers Merge of an exponent from the morphological array comprising case/number markers.[15] Next, NomSg≠GenPl is viewed as a two-level markedness constraint: Nominative singular forms must be different from genitive plural forms in the output, but only if they are identical in the input – if they are not, the constraint is not violated. Third, Cn⇒R is a constraint that requires case/number exponents (like genitive plural /a/) to be suffixes – more specifically, to be at the right edge of the word. Fourth, *ROOT_Fw′-/n/ is the second constraint presupposed in Baerman's original analysis: Weak feminine roots of the Fw′ declension cannot be adjacent to /n/. Finally, there are MAX and DEP constraints for this /n/; and a SHAPE CONSERVATION (SC) constraint blocking unmotivated movement (as before).

(31) a. MC_{Cn}
      b.   NomSg≠GenPl:
           NomSg ≠ GenPl in the output if NomSg = GenPl in the input.
      c.   Cn⇒R
      d.   *ROOT_Fw′-/n/:
           Weak femine roots bearing the diacritic ′ cannot be directly followed by /n/.
      e.   SHAPE CONSERVATION (SC)
      f.   MAX(/n/)
      g.   DEP(/n/)

As for the morpho-syntactic specifications of the exponents, for present purposes we may assume that /a/ is a fully specified genitive plural marker (/a/↔[gen,pl]); and /n/ is not an inflectional exponent but an epenthetic

---

[15] MAX and IDENT-F constraints that ensure that the most specific compatible exponent is chosen are not listed here. Similarly, for present purposes I abstract away from the repeated optimizations that may be necessary to select the most specific compatible exponent, via MINSAT and RC.

consonant that can be used in the morphological component, subject to
$\text{DEP}(/\text{n}/)$.

On this basis, the first optimization step for a genitive plural form of
hol ('hole') looks as in (32).

(32) *Paradigm gaps in Icelandic plural environments* (harmonic serialism,
     step 1):

I_1: $[_\text{N}$ hol$]_{\text{Fw}'}$: [•cn•], [gen,pl]	MC_{Cn}	$\text{NomSg}{\neq}\text{GenPl}$	$\text{Cn}{\Rightarrow}\text{R}$	$^*\text{Root}_{\text{Fw}'}\text{-}/\text{n}/$	SC	$\text{Max}(/\text{n}/)$	$\text{Dep}(/\text{n}/)$
O_{11}: hol-	*!						
☞O_{12}: hol-a							
O_{13}: hol-n	*!			*			*

In (32), high-ranked MC_{Cn} ensures that /a/ is merged first. As a matter
of fact, the resulting optimal output O_{12} does not violate any of the constraints in (31). In particular, $\text{NomSg}{\neq}\text{GenPl}$ is not violated because the
input form is /hol-/, not /hol-a/. However, things are different in the next
optimization round; cf. (33). Now the input form I_{12} *is* /hol-a/, which
is also the nominative singular form, so $\text{NomSg}{\neq}\text{GenPl}$ is now violated
by the output O_{121} that leaves the input unchanged (and thus qualifies an
attempt at achieving convergence). Consequently, O_{122} emerges as optimal. O_{122} adds an epenthetic /n/ that ensures distictness of nominative
singular and genitive plural forms. This violates the low-ranked constraint
$\text{DEP}(/\text{n}/)$; but it also violates the higher-ranked constraint $\text{Cn}{\Rightarrow}\text{R}$ because
/a/ is not at the right edge anymore.[16]

(33) *Paradigm gaps in Icelandic plural environments* (harmonic serialism,
     step 2):

I_{12}: $[_\text{N}$ hol$]_{\text{Fw}'}$-a: [gen,pl]	MC_{Cn}	$\text{NomSg}{\neq}\text{GenPl}$	$\text{Cn}{\Rightarrow}\text{R}$	$^*\text{Root}_{\text{Fw}'}\text{-}/\text{n}/$	SC	$\text{Max}(/\text{n}/)$	$\text{Dep}(/\text{n}/)$
O_{121}: hol-a		*!					
☞O_{122}: hol-a-n			*				*

The derivation strives to get rid of the violation of $\text{Cn}{\Rightarrow}\text{R}$ by carrying out
movement of /a/ to the right edge in the next step. This is shown in (34).

---

[16] This problem could be avoided by merging /n/ at the left edge; I presuppose here that
this option does not exist because of a high-ranked ban against inflectional prefixation
in Icelandic noun inflection (e.g., via $\text{L}{\Leftarrow}\text{N}$). Similarly, inserting the epenthetic exponent
/n/ directly between root and cn exponent would also satisfy $\text{Cn}{\Rightarrow}\text{R}$, but this option
does not exist because of the STRICT CYCLE CONDITION; cf. chapter 2.

(34) *Paradigm gaps in Icelandic plural environments* (harmonic serialism, step 3):

I_{122}: $[_N$ hol$]_{Fw'}$-a-n: [gen,pl]	MC_{Cn}	NomSg$\neq$GenPl	Cn$\Rightarrow$R	*Root$_{Fw'}$-/n/	SC	Max(/n/)	Dep(/n/)
O_{1221}: hol-a-n			*!				
☞O_{1222}: hol-n-a				*	*		

As illustrated in (34), the optimal output O_{1222} trades in O_{1221}'s Cn$\Rightarrow$R violation for a violation of the lower-ranked constraint *Root$_{Fw'}$-/n/: As a consequence of movement, /n/ is adjacent to /hol-/ which, by assumption, does not tolerate this. In reaction to this, epenthetic /n/ is deleted in the next step; see (35).

(35) *Paradigm gaps in Icelandic plural environments* (harmonic serialism, step 4):

I_{1222}: $[_N$ hol$]_{Fw'}$-n-a: [gen,pl]	MC_{Cn}	NomSg$\neq$GenPl	Cn$\Rightarrow$R	*Root$_{Fw'}$-/n/	SC	Max(/n/)	Dep(/n/)
O_{12221}: hol-n-a				*!			
O_{12222}: hol-a-n			*!				
☞O_{12223}: hol-a						*	

The optimal output O_{12223} in (35) only violates Max(/n/); so one might hope that convergence can now be reached.[17] But of course, even though O_{12223} is unproblematic vis-à-vis NomSg$\neq$GenPl in (35), the very same output O_{122231} fatally violates this constraint in the next optimization step since now the problem is already present in the input. Consequently, O_{122232}, which carries out /n/ epenthesis again, is optimal in (36).

(36) *Paradigm gaps in Icelandic plural environments* (harmonic serialism, step 5 = step 2):

I_{12223}: $[_N$ hol$]_{Fw'}$-a: [gen,pl]	MC_{Cn}	NomSg$\neq$GenPl	Cn$\Rightarrow$R	*Root$_{Fw'}$-/n/	SC	Max(/n/)	Dep(/n/)
O_{122231}: hol-a		*!					
☞O_{122232}: hol-a-n			*				*

However, the outcome of step 5 in (36) is identical to the outcome of step 2 in (33). Thus, the derivation is now caught in an infinite loop, and this accounts for the paradigm gap.

---

[17] In fact, it is presupposed here that /n/ cannot be deleted in (34) (possibly because such deletion is only possible if /n/ is directly adjacent to a root); if /n/ deletion can be optimal in (34), step 4 is skipped, and (36) is derived directly from (34).

3.3. First Person Singular Present Tense of Russian i-Conjugation Verbs

Another instance of systematic paradigm gaps is investigated by Pertsova (2016): For certain verbs of the second conjugation (i-conjugation) in Russian, speakers do not readily accept any form for first person present tense environments as grammatical. Thus, for a verb like *pylesósit'* ('to vacuum'), neither the form **pylesóšu* ('I vacuum'), nor the alternative form **pylesósju* ('I vacuum') is acceptable. As shown in (37), the former realization, with a change of the stem-final consonant before a first person singular ending, would be the one that one might expect as the grammatical outcome: The correct first person singular present tense form of *vozit'* ('to transport') is *vožu*, not **vozju*. (38) illustrates the same ineffability problem in this context with another verb, viz., *derzit'* ('to be rude'); as before, the gap is indicated by a ○ in the paradigm cell.

(37) vozit′ ('to transport'):

	sg	pl
1	vožu	vozim
2	voziš′	vozite
3	vozit	vozjat

(38) derzit′ ('to be rude'):

	sg	pl
1	○	derzim
2	derziš′	derzite
3	derzit	derzjat

Pertsova (2016) suggests that the underlying generalization relies on whether there are other well-formed output forms of the verbs in question that successfully instantiate the consonant change: Verbs of the second conjugation that have other morphologically related forms with the first person singular dental-palatal alternation are not defective, but verbs that lack such alternations in other forms are defective. On this view, the existence of past passive participles like *vož…enn-ij* ('transported') makes the first person singular present tense form *vožu* possible; and the absence of forms instantiating palatalization with *derzit'* anywhere in the paradigm is responsible for the paradigm gap arising for this verb in the environment. Two constraints that Pertsova (2016, 27–28) employs to implement this generalization are given in (39-a) and (39-b) (the latter constraint is based on earlier work by Steriade (2008)).

(39) a. $[\text{s}^j \rightarrow \text{ş}]$

    b. IDENT$_{\text{lex}}[\alpha\text{-F}]$:

        For any segment s in a subconstituent C of an expression under evaluation, if s is $[\alpha\text{F}]$ then s has an $[\alpha\text{F}]$ correspondent in a listed allomorph of C.

Pertsova's analysis relies on harmonic grammar: The constraints in (39) (and others, e.g., a ban against *sju* endings and a general faithfulness constraint for consonants) are assigned weights. Furthermore, a threshold approach is adopted: A harmony score of $\leq$–15, by stipulation, produces low confidence in outputs (i.e., it gives rise to paradigm gaps). Under these assumptions, it follows that not applying palatalization is always the worst option (–16); and applying palatalization produces a bad result if there is no other form in the paradigm that instantiates the palatal variant (–15). A peculiarity of this threshold analysis is that normally, exact numbers do not play a role in harmonic grammar; it is just the relative distances between harmony scores that count. But be this as it may; it is interesting to note that a ranking of Pertsova's two main constraints $[s^j \rightarrow \textbf{\c{s}}] \gg$ IDENT$_{\text{lex}}[\alpha$-F$]$ that corresponds to the weight assignments in her analysis (10.0 and 7.0, respectively) directly gives rise to an infinite loop in harmonic serialism. To see this, consider (39-a), which is assumed to be not a purely phonological constraint, but a morphonological constraint that is supposed to trigger palatalization more generally in a first person singular present tense environment. In the formulation that Pertsova adopts (an $[s^j]$ in the input becomes a $[\textbf{\c{s}}]$ in the output), this constraint already qualifies as a two-level markedness constraint. Together with a lower-ranked IDENT$_{\text{lex}}[\alpha$-F$]$ and a highest-ranked MC$_{\text{Agr}}$ that triggers inflection in the first place, $[s^j \rightarrow \textbf{\c{s}}]$ ensures that convergence can never be reached.

The first optimization procedure applying to an input stem *pylesósit′* in a first person singular present tense context is shown in (40). O$_{12}$ is optimal here because there is no *sju* sequence in the input yet, and use of *šu* in O$_{13}$ violates IDENT$_{\text{lex}}[\alpha$-F$]$ (there is no other form in the paradigm of *pylesósit′* that has *š*).

(40) *Paradigm gaps in 1.sg. environments* (harmonic serialism, step 1):

I$_1$: [$_V$ pylesós]$_i$: [•Agr•], [+1,–2,–pl,–past]	MC$_{\text{Agr}}$	$[s^j \rightarrow \textbf{\c{s}}]$	IDENT$_{\text{lex}}[\alpha$-F$]$
O$_{11}$: pylesós-	*!		
☞O$_{12}$: pylesósju			
O$_{13}$: pylesóšu			*!

However, as soon as O$_{12}$ is used as the input for the next optimization step, the two-level markedness constraint $[s^j \rightarrow \textbf{\c{s}}]$ becomes active, and ensures that palatalization applies; see (41).

(41) *Paradigm gaps in 1.sg. environments* (harmonic serialism, step 2):

I_{12}: [v pylesósju]$_i$: [+1,–2,–pl,–past]	MC_{Agr}	$[s^j \rightarrow \c{s}]$	$IDENT_{lex}[\alpha\text{-F}]$
O_{121}: pylesósju		*!	
☞O_{122}: pylesóšu			*

O_{122} violates $IDENT_{lex}[\alpha\text{-F}]$. Thus, in the next step in (42), where this candidate shows up as the input (I_{122}), *šu* is changed back to *sju* – since there is no *sju* in the input, this does not incur a violation of $[s^j \rightarrow \c{s}]$.

(42) *Paradigm gaps in 1.sg. environments* (harmonic serialism, step 3):

I_{122}: [v pylesóšu]$_i$: [+1,–2,–pl,–past]	MC_{Agr}	$[s^j \rightarrow \c{s}]$	$IDENT_{lex}[\alpha\text{-F}]$
O_{1221}: pylesóšu			*!
☞O_{1222}: pylesósju			

The following step instantiates the infinite loop: As shown in (43), *sju* is now changed back to *šu* again.

(43) *Paradigm gaps in 1.sg. environments* (harmonic serialism, step 4 = step 2):

I_{1222}: [v pylesósju]$_i$: [+1,–2,–pl,–past]	MC_{Agr}	$[s^j \rightarrow \c{s}]$	$IDENT_{lex}[\alpha\text{-F}]$
O_{12221}: pylesósju		*!	
☞O_{12222}: pylesóšu			*

And so on. It is clear that convergence will never be reached in this derivation, and this accounts for the paradigm gap.

3.4. Genitive Zero Plurals in Russian

As a final case study, let us look at paradigm gaps in genitive plural environments in Russian where one would otherwise expect a zero exponent; these have been addressed in Sims (2006). A relevant example is given for the word *mečtá* ('dream') in (44), where the expected genitive plural form *mečt-Ø* does not occur.[18]

---

[18] As noted by Sims (2006), the majority of the relevant nouns lacking genitive plural forms would not violate phonological wellformedness conditions of the language; see, e.g., *fat-a* vs. **fat-Ø* ('veil'), or *yul-a* vs. **yul-Ø* ('spinning top'). Therefore, a purely

(44) mečtá ('dream'):

	sg	pl
nom	mečtá	mečtý
acc	mečtú	mečtý
gen	mečtý	○
dat	mečté	mečtám
loc	mečté	mečtáx
ins	mečtój	mečtámi

Intuitively, a plausible view of the dilemma underlying the gap is that stress would be expected to fall on the zero inflection marker with these nouns, which violates one constraint, and a stress shift to the root that is not supported by either a lexical specification or a regular inflectional process violates another constraint. To flesh out this hypothesis, let us assume first that the expected zero ending in genitive plural contexts of feminine nouns like *mečtá* is an abstract yer vowel /O/ (see Halle (1994)); a yer is ultimately deleted unless it precedes another yer. (Also cf. the discussion around (7) in the previous chapter.) This makes it possible to formulate the first constraint as a constraint against stressed yers; see (45-a). On the other hand, the constraint against irregular (i.e., non-inherent and non-pattern-related) stress on roots must be formulated as a two-level markedness constraint, as in (45-b).

(45)   a.   *STRESS,YER:
            A yer vowel does not bear stress.
       b.   *STRESS,ROOT$_X$:
            If there is irregular stress on root$_X$ in the input there is no stress on root$_X$ in the output.

Given a constraint like MC_{Cn} that brings about case/number inflection of nouns, and given, furthermore, a general high-ranked requirement like HAVESTRESS ensuring that word stress does not disappear from the word, the constraints in (45) suffice to create an infinite loop in the genitive plural contexts of feminine nouns that normally have stress on the ending – assuming, as before, that the two-level markedness constraint (i.e.,

---

phonological account (which might account for cases like *mzd-Ø* for *mzd-a* ('bribe', archaic)) cannot work.

*STRESS,ROOT$_X$) outranks the other constraint that forms part of the Buridan's ass couple (i.e., *STRESS,YER).[19]

In the first step, the zero (yer) exponent is merged with the root; see (46). Assuming that stress needs to be assigned (even though it can be lexically pre-specified), only the output O$_{11}$ that does not carry out inflection can satisfy HAVESTRESS; O$_{12}$, which merges the correct inflectional exponent for genitive plural contexts with feminine nouns, cannot satisfy HAVESTRESS since input and output can only be separated by maximally one operation.

(46) *Paradigm gaps in Russian plural environments* (harmonic serialism, step 1):

I$_1$: [$_N$ mečt]$_X$: [•cn•], [gen,pl]	MC$_{Cn}$	HAVESTRESS	*STRESS,ROOT$_X$	*STRESS,YER
O$_{11}$: méčt-	*!			
☞O$_{12}$: mečt-/0/		*		

In the second step, HAVESTRESS can be satisfied by placing the stress either on the yer ending, as in O$_{122}$, which violates *STRESS,YER; or on the root, as in O$_{123}$, which violates none of the constraints depicted here – in particular, *STRESS,ROOT$_X$ cannot be violated because there is no stress in the input yet. As a result, O$_{123}$ emerges as optimal.

(47) *Paradigm gaps in Russian plural environments* (harmonic serialism, step 2):

I$_{12}$: [$_N$ mečt-/0/]$_X$: [gen,pl]	MC$_{Cn}$	HAVESTRESS	*STRESS,ROOT$_X$	*STRESS,YER
O$_{121}$: mečt-/0/		*!		
O$_{122}$: mečt-/ó/				*!
☞O$_{123}$: méčt-/0/				

However, once O$_{123}$ is used as an input, *STRESS,ROOT$_X$ becomes relevant and *will* be violated if stress remains on the root in the output, as in O$_{1231}$.

---

[19] The question arises why the paradigm gap does not affect all relevant nouns, and why there is substantial variation between speakers as to which nouns instantiate the gap and which do not. For present purposes, it may suffice to assume, as I have done in (45-b), that the two-level markedness constraint is an *indexed* constraint that only holds for a subclass of the relevant items. Ultimately, it might be preferable to pursue the idea that variable *strength* of lexical items is involved; see Smolensky & Goldrick (2016).

Consequently, O_{1232}, which shifts stress back to the inflectional exponent again, is optimal even though it violates *Stress,Yer; see (48).

(48) *Paradigm gaps in Russian plural environments* (harmonic serialism, step 3):

I_{123}: [$_N$ méčt-/0/]$_X$: [gen,pl]	MC_{Cn}	HaveStress	*Stress,Root$_X$	*Stress,Yer
O_{1231}: méčt-/0/			*!	
☞O_{1232}: mečt-/0́/				*

This establishes the infinite loop: In the next step, stress will be retracted onto the root because O_{12321} – the attempt at convergence – violates *Stress,Yer whereas O_{12322} does *not* (yet) violate *Stress,Root$_X$; etc.

(49) *Paradigm gaps in Russian plural environments* (harmonic serialism, step 4):

I_{1232}: [$_N$ mečt-/0́/]$_X$: [gen,pl]	MC_{Cn}	HaveStress	*Stress,Root$_X$	*Stress,Yer
O_{12321}: mečt-/0́/				*!
☞O_{12322}: méčt-/0/				

To sum up this subsection: By combining two-level markedness constraints that do not consume initial resources with a harmonic serialist approach to inflectional morphology, a new perspective on paradigm gaps becomes possible that can straightforwardly implement a Buridan's ass intuition regarding the phenomenon, by producing infinite optimization loops. It goes without saying that much more work on various kinds of paradigm gaps is needed to prove the viability of the overall approach; however, it should be clear that the new, loop-based approach is not available in any other existing theory of inflectional morphology, whether it relies on optimality theory or not.[20]

---

[20] In this context, it is also worth comparing the present approach with the approach to allomorph selection developed in Keine (2012), which can to some extent be viewed as a predecessor; in particular, the analysis of phonologically conditioned gaps with certain cases of suffixation in Hungarian sketched there also relies on ineffability derived by a loop in harmonic serialism (but the loop comes about by applying one and the same process of Schwa insertion ad infinitum, and it thus does not capture the Buridan's ass intuition).

4. Fixed vs. Variable Rankings

In most respects, the analyses developed in the previous chapters fully adhere to basic tenets of optimality theory and, more specifically, its harmonic serialist implementation. However, there is one particular domain where I have repeatedly deviated from what would standardly be assumed in optimality theory. The relevant cases all involve the postulate of free reranking of constraints in the *H-Eval* part of the grammar, and the concept of factorial typology (according to which any permutation of a list of constraints results in a possible grammar) that comes along with it.

For a number of constraints and constraint types, I have indeed followed the standard assumption that one can and should envisage a free reranking, thereby capturing cross-linguistic variation in morphological exponence. This holds for the various MAX (and, where relevant DEP) faithfulness constraints; it holds for alignment constraints (including the few relativized precedence constraints of type "X precedes Y" that I have employed); and it holds for many other kinds of constraints, like, e.g., COHERENCE, *STRUC, etc.[21] However, for certain other constraint types, it has proved important to postulate that free rerankability is not an option.

For some of the constraints in question, this does not necessarily imply a deviation from basic tenets of optimality theory because they can be assumed to belong to *Gen* (even if the constraint violations are registered in tableaux throughout the book). This holds for the STRICT CYCLE CONDITION (cf. chapter 2).[22] The same conclusion applies with the EX-HAUST constraint family: EXHAUST NUMERATION (cf. chapters 1 and 3), EXHAUST MORPHOLOGICAL ARRAY (cf. chapter 3), and EXHAUST SUB-ARRAY (cf. chapter 4) are all undominated and not violable by optimal outputs, and it would be unproblematic to assume that these constraints are all included in *Gen*, or at least outside of the *H-Eval* system of the grammar. Finally, a similar conclusion can be drawn for the requirement according to which inflectional exponents need fully specified feature matrices if they are to be merged with a categorizing head plus stem (see chapter 5).

---

[21] Of course, it does not hold in those cases where these constraints participate in local conjunction; but here the fixed rankings are directly determined by the operation that generates the more complex constraints.

[22] Also recall that even the weaker version of the STRICT CYCLE CONDITION permitting tucking in that was envisaged in chapter 2 in the course of the early discussion of movement in morphology (which was basically abandoned in subsequent parts of the monograph) can still be assumed to be inviolable.

However, some of the core constraints figuring in the analyses in this monograph are not like that. With these constraints, there is evidence *both* for a fixed position in rankings, *and* for basic violability.

Consider MINIMIZE SATISFACTION (see chapters 3–5) first. I have concluded that this constraint must be undominated in morphology and syntax. Still, given that there can be a transparent bleeding interaction of operations in phonology (next to the opaque counter-bleeding interactions that MINSAT helps to derive), this constraint must be rerankable in principle, at least in the phonological component. What is more, whereas the evidence in chapter 3 is compatible with the view that MINSAT may belong to *H-Eval* in the phonology, but to *Gen* in morphology and syntax, it seems clear that it must in principle be violable so as to satisfy EXHAUST constraints: If a given output can be improved based on material available in the current morphological array, or the current morphological subarray, the derivation cannot carry out some operation with material from the next array (or subarray) even if that latter operation gives rise to fewer new constraint satisfactions. Thus, whereas MINSAT outranks most of the other constraints in morphology and syntax, in what looks like a cross-linguistically invariant way, it cannot do so in the case of EXMORAR and ExS.

Next, the REMOVE CONDITION may be violable in favour of MINSAT (although it is not easy to find evidence for this, given that RC typically only triggers one new constraint satisfaction in morphology); but it does not make sense to assume that it might be rerankable with the other constraints of the H-EVAL component, in any grammar, including the MERGE CONDITION.

The MERGE CONDITION, in turn, must outrank IDENT-F, MAX, and faithfulness constraints more generally. However, even if it may be the case that it can never be violated by an optimal output at the end of a derivation, it must certainly be violable in the course of a derivation; as a matter of fact, this conclusion is unavoidable in contexts where there is more than one [•X•] feature associated with a given stem (or categorizing head, under the analysis of chapter 5). In addition, MC must be violable in favour of the EXHAUST constraints.

Finally, as noted already in chapter 2, to model the crosslinguistically invariant interaction of compatibility and specificity in morphological exponence (with the former taking precedence over the latter), it has to be postulated that IDENT-F (which derives compatibility) outranks MAX constraints (which derive specificity), with no option for reranking in the world's languages. Still, IDENT-F cannot be assumed to be inviolable in general (e.g., as a consequence of belonging to *Gen*): In the neutralization account of the *ABA pattern given above (see (67) of chapter 5), IDENT-F is violated by an optimal output; similar conclusions hold for the first of the two approaches to deponency sketched in the previous section.

So, in summary, the picture arises that there are important, high-ranked constraints regulating morphological exponence that show up in a fixed order across different languages, and that outrank most of the other constraints in language after language, but that nevertheless must be assumed to be violable. One may speculate that the kinds of restrictions on reranking that are evidently in place here can at least partly be explained by resorting to special architectural properties inherent to inflectional morphology. However, for the time being, I will leave this question as a target for future research, and draw a general conclusion.

5. Conclusion

Let me reiterate that the main goal of the present monograph has been a fairly modest one: to provide a proof of concept. More specifically, I have tried to make a case that harmonic serialism, while originally motivated on the basis of evidence from phonology and syntax, can also be viewed as a viable theory of (inflectional) morphology. If so, this can arguably be viewed as a substantive step towards a unified theory of all form-based components of grammar (phonology, morphology, and syntax) – something that would seem to be out of reach for most other grammatical theories, even though it seems to me that there is no convincing conceptual or empirical argument for a non-homogeneous approach to the different form-based grammatical areas (nothwithstanding claims to the contrary in work like, e.g., Bromberger & Halle (1989)).

It is clear that for virtually all of the phenomena I have looked at, harmonic serialism as such would also have been compatible with several other analyses than the ones that I have eventually pursued. Thus, I would like to emphasize that even if one takes issue with certain individual analytical decisions that I have made (beginning, perhaps, with the decision to adopt a pre-syntactic approach to inflectional exponence), that does not per se have to imply anything about more general conclusions regarding the viability of harmonic serialism for inflectional morphology. In this context, it is also worth pointing out that whenever there was an option of either adopting some conservative approach to a given phenomenon (one that has already been given in, or would be straightforwardly compatible with, other theories of morphology, including standard parallel optimality theory), or developing a new, more radical, approach that fully exploits the analytical possibilities offered by harmonic serialism, and that highlights systematic differences to established theories of morphology, I have consistently opted for the latter strategy.

So, my general conclusion is that, by and large, the prospects of a harmonic serialist theory of inflectional morphology can be viewed as reasonably good: All the phenomena I looked at can be covered well in harmonic serialism. In addition, the theory has made a fresh look at several empirical domains possible: affix order, extended exponence, disjunctive blocking, locality of allomorphy, *ABA patterns, and, possibly, impoverishment effects, deponency, and paradigm gaps. Still, it goes without saying that only future research in many other areas of inflectional morphology, and on the basis of many more typologically diverse languages than I have been able to consider here, could eventually establish harmonic serialism on a par with existing, well-developed theories of inflectional morphology.

References

Abels, Klaus (2012): *Phases. An Essay on Cyclicity in Syntax.* Vol. 543 of *Linguistische Arbeiten,* De Gruyter, Berlin.

Ackema, Peter & Ad Neeleman (1998): Optimal Questions, *Natural Language and Linguistic Theory* 16, 443–490.

Ackema, Peter & Ad Neeleman (2003): Context-Sensitive Spell-Out, *Natural Language and Linguistic Theory* 21, 681–735.

Ackema, Peter & Ad Neeleman (2004): *Beyond Morphology.* Oxford University Press, Oxford.

Adger, David (2003): *Core Syntax.* Oxford University Press, Oxford, New York.

Aikhenvald, Alexandra (2003): *A Grammar of Tariana, from Northwest Amazonia.* Cambridge University Press, Cambridge.

Aissen, Judith (1999a): Agent Focus and Inverse in Tzotzil, *Language* 75, 451–485.

Aissen, Judith (1999b): Markedness and Subject Choice in Optimality Theory, *Natural Language and Linguistic Theory* 17, 673–711.

Aissen, Judith (2003): Differential Object Marking: Iconicity vs. Economy, *Natural Language and Linguistic Theory* 21, 435–483.

Aissen, Judith & David Perlmutter (1983): Clause Reduction in Spanish. In: D. Perlmutter, ed., *Studies in Relational Grammar 1.* University of Chicago Press, Chicago, pp. 360–403.

Alderete, John (1997): Dissimilation as Local Conjunction. In: K. Kusumoto, ed., *Proceedings of the North East Linguistic Society.* Vol. 27, GLSA, Amherst, pp. 17–32.

Alexiadou, Artemis (2013): Where Is Non-Active Morphology?. In: S. Müller, ed., *Proceedings of the 20th International Conference on Head-Driven Phrase Structure Grammar, FU Berlin.* CSLI Publications, Stanford, pp. 244–262.

Alexiadou, Artemis & Gereon Müller (2008): Class Features as Probes. In: A. Bachrach & A. Nevins, eds., *Inflectional Identity.* Oxford University Press, Oxford, pp. 101–155.

Alexiadou, Artemis, Berit Gehrke & Florian Schäfer (2014): The Argument Structure of Adjectival Passives Revisited, *Lingua* 119, 118–138.

Alexiadou, Artemis, Hagit Borer & Florian Schäfer, eds. (2015): *The Syntax of Roots and the Roots of Syntax.* Oxford University Press, Oxford.

Anderson, Stephen (1992): *A-Morphous Morphology.* Cambridge University Press, Cambridge.

Andersson, Samuel (2018): (*)ABA in Germanic Verbs, *Glossa* 3(1).

Aronoff, Mark (1994): *Morphology by Itself.* MIT Press, Cambridge, Mass.

Aronoff, Mark & Kirsten Fudeman (2005): *What is Morphology?.* Blackwell, Oxford.

Arregi, Karlos & Andrew Nevins (2012): *Morphotactics: Basque Auxiliaries and the Structure of Spellout.* Springer, Heidelberg.

Assmann, Anke, Doreen Georgi, Fabian Heck, Gereon Müller & Philipp Weisser (2015): Ergatives Move Too Early. On an Instance of Opacity in Syntax, *Syntax* 18, 343–387.

Baerman, Matthew (2011): Defectiveness and Homophony Avoidance, *Journal of Linguistics* 47, 1–29.

Baerman, Matthew, Dunstan Brown & Greville Corbett (2005): *The Syntax-Morphology Interface. A Study of Syncretism.* Cambridge University Press, Cambridge.

Baerman, Matthew, Greville Corbett, Dunstan Brown & Andrew Hippisley, eds. (2007): *Deponency and Morphological Mismatches.* Oxford University Press (for The British Academy), Oxford.

Baker, Mark (2015): *Case. Its Principles and Parameters.* Cambridge University Press, Cambridge.

Barss, Andrew (1986): Chains and Anaphoric Dependence. Ph.d. thesis, MIT, Cambridge, Mass.

Baunaz, Lena, Liliane Haegeman, Karen de Clercq & Eric Lander, eds. (2018): *Exploring Nanosyntax.* Oxford University Press, Oxford.

Bermúdez-Otero, Ricardo (2008): *Stratal Optimality Theory.* Book Ms., University of Manchester. To appear: Oxford University Press.

Bermúdez-Otero, Ricardo (2011): Cyclicity. In: M. van Oostendorp, C. Ewen, E. Hume & K. Rice, eds., *The Blackwell Companion to Phonology.* Vol. 4, Wiley-Blackwell, Malden, MA, pp. 2019–2048.

Bierwisch, Manfred (1961): Zur Morphologie des deutschen Verbalsystems. PhD thesis, Universität Leipzig.

Bierwisch, Manfred (1967): Syntactic Features in Morphology: General Problems of So-Called Pronominal Inflection in German. In: *To Honor Roman Jakobson.* Mouton, The Hague/Paris, pp. 239–270.

Blevins, James (1995): Syncretism and Paradigmatic Opposition, *Linguistics and Philosophy* 18, 113–152.

Bobaljik, Jonathan (2000): The Ins and Outs of Contextual Allomorphy. In: K. Grohmann & C. Struijke, eds., *University of Maryland Working Papers in Linguistics*. Vol. 10, University of Maryland, College Park, pp. 35–71.

Bobaljik, Jonathan (2002a): Realizing Germanic Inflection: Why Morphology Does Not Drive Syntax, *Journal of Comparative Germanic Linguistics* 6, 129–167.

Bobaljik, Jonathan (2002b): Syncretism without Paradigms: Remarks on Williams 1981, 1994. In: G. Booij & J. van Marle, eds., *Yearbook of Morphology 2001*. Kluwer, Dordrecht, pp. 53–85.

Bobaljik, Jonathan (2006): On Comparative Suppletion. Ms., University of Connecticut. (WoTM 1 Talk, Universität Leipzig).

Bobaljik, Jonathan (2007): The Limits of Deponency: A Chukotko-Centric Perspective. In: M. Baerman, G. Corbett, D. Brown & A. Hippisley, eds., *Deponency and Morphological Mismatches*. Oxford University Press (for The British Academy), Oxford, pp. 175–201.

Bobaljik, Jonathan (2012): *Universals in Comparative Morphology. Suppletion, Superlatives, and the Structure of Words*. MIT Press, Cambridge, Mass.

Bobaljik, Jonathan (2015): Some Differences between Case and Agreement. Ms., Unversity of Connecticut.

Bobaljik, Jonathan & Heidi Harley (2013): Suppletion is Local: Evidence from Hiaki. Ms., University of Connecticut and University of Arizona.

Bobaljik, Jonathan & Uli Sauerland (2018): *ABA and the Combinatorics of Morphological Features, *Glossa* 3(15), 1–34.

Boeckx, Cedric, Norbert Hornstein & Jairo Nunes (2010): *Control as Movement*. Cambridge University Press, Cambridge.

Bonami, Olivier (2015): Periphrasis as Collocation, *Morphology* 25, 63–110.

Bonet, Eulàlia (1991): Morphology after Syntax. PhD thesis, MIT, Cambridge, Mass.

Bonet, Eulàlia & Daniel Harbour (2012): Contextual Allomorphy. In: J. Trommer, ed., *The Morphology and Phonology of Exponence*. Oxford University Press, Oxford, pp. 195–235.

Bonet, Eulàlia, Maria-Rosa Lloret & Joan Mascaró (2015a): The Prenominal Allomorphy Syndrome. *In* Bonet et al. (2015b), pp. 5–44.

Bonet, Eulàlia, Maria-Rosa Lloret & Joan Mascaró, eds. (2015b): *Understanding Allomorphy. Perspectives from Optimality Theory*. Advances in Optimality Theory, Equinox, Sheffield.

Borer, Hagit (2014): Wherefore Roots?, *Theoretical Linguistics* 40, 343–359.

Božič, Jurij (2017): Non-Local Allomorphy in a Strictly Local System. Ms., McGill University.

Božič, Jurij (2019): Constraining Long-Distance Allomorphy, *The Linguistic Review* 36, 485–505.

Bowman, Samuel & Benjamin Lokshin (2014): Idiosyncratically Transparent Vowels in Kazakh. In: *Proceedings of the 2013 Annual Meeting on Phonology*. Linguistic Society of America, Washington, DC.

Branigan, Phil (2013): Cyclicity and the Approach the Probe Principle. Ms., Memorial University of Newfoundland.

Broadwell, George Aaron (1997): Binding Theory and Switch-Reference. In: H. Bennis, P. Pica & J. Rooryck, eds., *Atomism and Binding*. Foris, Dordrecht, pp. 31–49.

Broekhuis, Hans (2000): Against Feature Strength: The Case of Scandinavian Object Shift, *Natural Language and Linguistic Theory* 18, 673–721.

Broekhuis, Hans (2006): Derivations (MP) and Evaluations (OT). In: R. Vogel & H. Broekhuis, eds., *Optimality Theory and Minimalism: A Possible Convergence?*. Vol. 25, Linguistics in Potsdam, Potsdam, pp. 137–193.

Broekhuis, Hans (2008): *Derivations and Evaluations. Object Shift in the Germanic Languages*. Mouton de Gruyter, Berlin.

Broekhuis, Hans & Ellen Woolford (2013): Minimalism and Optimality Theory. In: M. Den Dikken, ed., *Cambridge Handbook of Generative Syntax*. Cambridge University Press, Cambridge, pp. 122–161.

Broekhuis, Hans & Joost Dekkers (2000): The Minimalist Program and Optimality Theory: Derivations and Evaluation. In: J. Dekkers, F. van der Leeuw & J. van de Weijer, eds., *Optimality Theory: Phonology, Syntax, and Acquisition*. Oxford University Press, Oxford, pp. 386–422.

Bromberger, Sylvain & Morris Halle (1989): Why Phonology is Different, *Linguistic Inquiry* 20, 51–70.

Brown, Dunstan (2006): Formal Analyses of Chukchi, Kayardild, Tülatulabal. Ms., Surrey Morphology Group. Available from http://www.smg.surrey.ac.uk/deponency/Deponency.

Brown, Dunstan & Andrew Hippisley (2012): *Network Morphology*. Cambridge University Press, Cambridge.

Brown, Dunstan, Marina Chumakina, Greville Corbett & Andrew Hippisley (2003): Surrey Suppletion Database. University of Surrey.

Bruening, Benjamin (2017): Consolidated Morphology. Book Ms., University of Delaware.

Bye, Patrik (2001): Virtual Phonology: Rule Sandwiching and Multiple Opacity in North Saami. PhD thesis, University of Tromsø.

Bye, Patrik (2015): The Nature of Allomorphy and Exceptionality: Evidence from Burushaski Plurals. *In* Bonet et al. (2015b), pp. 107–176.

Caballero, Gabriela & Alice Harris (2012): A Working Typology of Multiple Exponence. In: F. Kiefer et al., eds., *Current Issues in Morphological Theory: (Ir)Regularity, Analogy, and Frequency.* Benjamins, Amsterdam, pp. 163–188.

Caballero, Gabriela & Sharon Inkelas (2013): Word Construction: Tracing an Optimal Path Through the Lexicon, *Morphology* 23, 103–143.

Caha, Pavel (2009): The Nanosyntax of Case. PhD thesis, Tromsø University.

Caha, Pavel (2013): Explaining the Structure of Case Paradigms by the Mechanisms of Nanosyntax, *Natural Language and Linguistic Theory* 31, 1015–1066.

Caha, Pavel (2017): How (Not) to Derive *ABA: The Case of Blansitt's Generalisation, *Glossa* 2(84), 1–32.

Carstairs, Andrew (1983): Paradigm Economy, *Journal of Linguistics* 19, 115–125.

Carstairs, Andrew (1987): *Allomorphy in Inflexion.* Croom Helm, London.

Carstairs-McCarthy, Andrew (1986): Macroclasses and Paradigm Economy in German nouns, *Zeitschrift für Phonetik, Sprachwissenschaft und Kommunikationsforschung* 39, 3–11.

Carstairs-McCarthy, Andrew (2008): System-Congruity and Violable Constraints in German Weak Declension, *Natural Language and Linguistic Theory* 26, 775 793.

Castillo, Juan, John Drury & Kleanthes Grohmann (2009): Merge Over Move and the Extended Projection Principle: MOM and the PP Revisited, *Iberia* 1(1), 53–114.

Chomsky, Noam (1970): Remarks on Nominalization. In: R. Jacobs & P. Rosenbaum, eds., *Readings in English Transformational Grammar.* Ginn and Company, Waltham, Mass., pp. 184–221.

Chomsky, Noam (1973): Conditions on Transformations. In: S. Anderson & P. Kiparsky, eds., *A Festschrift for Morris Halle.* Academic Press, New York, pp. 232–286.

Chomsky, Noam (1975): *The Logical Structure of Linguistic Theory.* Plenum Press, New York.

Chomsky, Noam (1977): On Wh-Movement. In: P. Culicover, T. Wasow & A. Akmajian, eds., *Formal Syntax.* Academic Press, New York, pp. 71–132.

Chomsky, Noam (1981): *Lectures on Government and Binding.* Foris, Dordrecht.

Chomsky, Noam (1982): *Some Concepts and Consequences of the Theory of Government and Binding*. MIT Press, Cambridge, Mass.

Chomsky, Noam (1986): *Barriers*. MIT Press, Cambridge, Mass.

Chomsky, Noam (1991): Some Notes on Economy of Derivation and Representation. In: R. Freidin, ed., *Principles and Parameters in Comparative Grammar*. MIT Press, Cambridge, Mass., pp. 417–454.

Chomsky, Noam (1993): A Minimalist Program for Syntactic Theory. In: K. Hale & S. J. Keyser, eds., *The View from Building 20*. MIT Press, Cambridge, Mass., pp. 1–52.

Chomsky, Noam (1995): *The Minimalist Program*. MIT Press, Cambridge, Mass.

Chomsky, Noam (2000): Minimalist Inquiries: The Framework. In: R. Martin, D. Michaels & J. Uriagereka, eds., *Step by Step*. MIT Press, Cambridge, Mass., pp. 89–155.

Chomsky, Noam (2001): Derivation by Phase. In: M. Kenstowicz, ed., *Ken Hale. A Life in Language*. MIT Press, Cambridge, Mass., pp. 1–52.

Chomsky, Noam (2005): Three Factors in Language Design, *Linguistic Inquiry* 36, 1–22.

Chomsky, Noam (2008): On Phases. In: R. Freidin, C. Otero & M. L. Zubizarreta, eds., *Foundational Issues in Linguistic Theory*. MIT Press, Cambridge, Mass., pp. 133–166.

Chomsky, Noam (2013): Problems of Projection, *Lingua* 130, 33–49.

Chomsky, Noam (2014a): Lecture 2. Class Lectures, MIT, April 2, 2014 (31:00-48:00). Available from: http://whamit.mit.edu/2014/06/03/recent-linguistics-talks-by-chomsky/.

Chomsky, Noam (2014b): Lecture 4. Class Lectures, MIT, May 19, 2014 (31:00-48:00). Available from: http://whamit.mit.edu/2014/06/03/recent-linguistics-talks-by-chomsky/.

Chomsky, Noam (2015): Simple Invisibles. In: L. Veselovská & M. Vanebová, eds., *Complex Visibles Out There*. Vol. 4 of *Olomouc Modern Language Series*, Palacky University, Olomouc, pp. 17–24.

Chomsky, Noam & Morris Halle (1968): *The Sound Pattern of English*. MIT Press, Cambridge, Mass.

Clahsen, Harald (1999): Lexical Entries and Rules of Language: A Multidisciplinary Study of German Inflection, *Behavioral and Brain Sciences* 22, 991–1060.

Clements, George, James McCloskey, Joan Maling & Annie Zaenen (1983): String-Vacuous Rule Application, *Linguistic Inquiry* 14, 1–17.

Coon, Jessica (2010a): A-bar Extraction Asymmetries. Handout; talk given at the workshop *The Fine Structure of Grammatical Relations*, Leipzig University, December 2010.

Coon, Jessica (2010b): Complementation in Chol (Mayan). A Theory of Split Ergativity. PhD thesis, MIT, Cambridge, Mass.

Corbett, Greville (2007): Deponency, Syncretism, and What Lies Between. In: M. Baerman, G. Corbett, D. Brown & A. Hippisley, eds., *Deponency and Morphological Mismatches*. Oxford University Press (for The British Academy), Oxford, pp. 21–43.

Corbett, Greville & Norman Fraser (1993): Network Morphology: A DATR Account of Russian Nominal Inflection, *Journal of Linguistics* 29, 113–142.

Culicover, Peter & Ray Jackendoff (2007): Semantic Subordination Despite Syntactic Coordination, *Linguistic Inquiry* 28, 195–217.

Cysouw, Michael (2001): The Paradigmatic Structure of Person Marking. PhD thesis, Katholieke Universiteit Nijmegen. Revised version published 2003: Oxford University Press.

Cysouw, Michael (2003): *The Paradigmatic Structure of Person Marking*. Oxford University Press, Oxford and New York.

De Clercq, Karen & Guido Vanden Wyngaerd (2017): *ABA Revisited: Evidence from Czech and Latin Degree Morphology, *Glossa* 2(69), 1–32.

De Clercq, Karen & Guido Vanden Wyngaerd (2018): Unmerging Analytic Comparatives. Ms., Universiteit Gent and KU Leuven.

De Vries, Lourens & Robinia De Vries-Wiersma (1992): *The Morphology of Wambon of the Irian Jaya Upper-Digul Area*. Koninklijk Instituut voor Taal-, Land- en Volkenkunde, Leiden.

Di Sciullo, Anna Maria & Edwin Williams (1987): *On the Definition of Word*. MIT Press, Cambridge, Mass.

Don, Jan & Elma Blom (2006): A Constraint-Based Approach to Morphological Neutralization. In: *Linguistics in the Netherlands 2006*. Benjamins, Amsterdam, pp. 78–88.

Driemel, Imke (2018): Person Mismatch Agreement. In: S. Hucklebridge & M. Nelson, eds., *Proceedings of NELS 48*. GLSA, Amherst, Mass.

Driemel, Imke & Jelena Stojković (2017): Revisiting Chain Shifts with Minimize Satisfaction. Ms., Universität Leipzig.

Drummond, Alex (2011): Romance Obviation Effects and Merge over Move. Ms., Durham University.

Dschaak, Christina (2017): A Structure Removal Approach to Restructuring in Russian. BA thesis, Universität Leipzig.

Eisenberg, Peter (2000a): Das vierte Genus? Über die natürliche Kategorisation der deutschen Substantive. In: K.-M. Köpcke, A. Bittner & D. Bittner, eds., *Angemessene Strukturen: Systemorganisation in Phonologie, Morphologie und Syntax*. Olms, Hildesheim, pp. 91–105.

Eisenberg, Peter (2000b): *Grundriß der deutschen Grammatik. Band 1: Das Wort.* Metzler, Stuttgart.

Elfner, Emily (2016): Stress-Epenthesis Interactions in Harmonic Serialism. In: *Harmonic Grammar and Harmonic Serialism.* Equinox, Sheffield.

Elson, Ben (1960a): *Gramatica Popoluca de la Sierra.* Number 6 *in* 'Gramáticas de Lenguas Indígenas de México', Biblioteca de la Facultad de Filosofía y Letras, Universidad Veracruzana.

Elson, Ben (1960b): Sierra Popoluca Morphology, *International Journal of American Linguistics* 20, 206–223.

Elson, Ben & Velma Pickett (1964): *An Introduction to Morphology and Syntax.* Summer Institute of Linguistics, Santa Ana, California.

Embick, David (2000): Features, Syntax, and Categories in the Latin Perfect, *Linguistic Inquiry* 31, 185–230.

Embick, David (2003): Locality, Listedness, and Morphological Identity, *Studia Linguistica* 57, 143–169.

Embick, David (2010): *Localism vs. Globalism in Morphology and Phonology.* MIT Press, Cambridge, Mass.

Embick, David & Rolf Noyer (2001): Movement Operations after Syntax, *Linguistic Inquiry* 32, 555–595.

Embick, David & Rolf Noyer (2007): Distributed Morphology and the Syntax/Morphology Interface. In: *The Oxford Handbook of Linguistic Interfaces.* Oxford University Press, Oxford, pp. 289–324.

Erdmann, Oskar (1886): *Grundzüge der deutschen Syntax nach ihrer geschichtlichen Entwicklung.* Vol. 1, Verlag der J. G. Cotta'schen Buchhandlung, Stuttgart. Reprint, Hildesheim: Georg Olms Verlag, 1985.

Ermolaeva, Marina & Greg Kobele (2019): Agreement and Word Formation in Syntax. Ms., University of Chicago & Universität Leipzig.

Fanselow, Gisbert (1991): Minimale Syntax. Habilitation thesis, Universität Passau.

Fanselow, Gisbert & Caroline Féry (2002): Ineffability in Grammar. In: G. Fanselow & C. Féry, eds., *Resolving Conflicts in Grammars.* Buske, Hamburg, pp. 265–307.

Fanselow, Gisbert & Damir Ćavar (2001): Remarks on the Economy of Pronunciation. In: G. Müller & W. Sternefeld, eds., *Competition in Syntax.* Mouton de Gruyter, Berlin, pp. 107–150.

Fiengo, Robert (1977): On Trace Theory, *Linguistic Inquiry* 8, 35–61.

Fischer, Silke (2001): On the Integration of Cumulative Effects into Optimality Theory. In: G. Müller & W. Sternefeld, eds., *Competition in Syntax.* Mouton de Gruyter, Berlin, pp. 151–173.

Fox, Danny (2000): *Economy and Semantic Interpretation.* MIT Press, Cambridge, Mass.

Fox, Danny & David Pesetsky (2005): Cyclic Linearization of Syntactic Structure, *Theoretical Linguistics* 31, 1–45.

Frampton, John (2002): Syncretism, Impoverishment, and the Structure of Person Features. In: M. Andronis, E. Debenport, A. Pycha & K. Yoshimura, eds., *Papers from the Chicago Linguistics Society Meeting*. Vol. 38, Chicago, pp. 207–222.

Frampton, John & Sam Gutmann (1999): Cyclic Computation, *Syntax* 2, 1–27.

Franks, Steven (1995): *Parameters of Slavic Morphosyntax*. Oxford University Press, New York and Oxford.

Fraser, Norman & Greville Corbett (1994): Gender, Animacy, and Declensional Class Assignment: A Unified Account for Russian. In: G. Booij & J. van Marle, eds., *Yearbook of Morphology 1994*. Kluwer, Dordrecht, pp. 123–150.

Gazdar, Gerald (1982): Phrase Structure Grammar. In: *The Nature of Syntactic Representation*. Reidel, Dordrecht, pp. 131–186.

Gazdar, Gerald, Ewan Klein, Geoffrey Pullum & Ivan Sag (1985): *Generalized Phrase Structure Grammar*. Blackwell, Oxford.

Geilfuß-Wolfgang, Jochen (1998): Über die optimale Position von *ge*, *Linguistische Berichte* 176, 581–588.

Georgi, Doreen (2008): A Distributed Morphology Approach to Argument Encoding in Kambera, *Linguistische Berichte* 213, 45–63.

Georgi, Doreen (2012): A Local Derivation of Global Case Splits. In: A. Alexiadou, T. Kiss & G. Müller, eds., *Local Modelling of Non-Local Dependencies in Syntax*. Linguistische Arbeiten, De Gruyter, Berlin, pp. 306–336.

Georgi, Doreen (2014): Opaque Interactions of Merge and Agree. PhD thesis, Universität Leipzig.

Georgi, Doreen (2017): Patterns of Movement Reflexes as the Result of the Order of Merge and Agree, *Linguistic Inquiry* 48(4), 585–626.

Gleim, Daniel, Gereon Müller, Mariia Privizentseva & Sören Tebay (2019): Phonological Evidence for Movement in Inflectional Morphology. Ms., Universität Leipzig.

Goldrick, Matt (2000): Turbid Output Representations and the Unity of Opacity. In: M. Hirotani, A. Coetzee, N. Hall & J.-Y. Kim, eds., *Proceedings of NELS 30*. GLSA, Amherst, Mass, pp. 231–345.

Granberry, Julian (1990): A Grammatical Sketch of Timucua, *International Journal of American Linguistics* 56, 60–101.

Grestenberger, Laura (2014): Feature Mismatch: Deponency in Indo-European Languages. PhD thesis, Harvard University.

Grestenberger, Laura (2017): Deponency in Morphology. Ms., Universität Wien.

Grimshaw, Jane (1997): Projection, Heads, and Optimality, *Linguistic Inquiry* 28, 373–422.

Grimshaw, Jane (2001): Optimal Clitic Positions and the Lexicon in Romance Clitic Systems. In: G. Legendre, J. Grimshaw & S. Vikner, eds., *Optimality-Theoretic Syntax*. MIT Press, Cambridge, Mass., pp. 205–240.

Grimshaw, Jane (2006): Chains as Unfaithful Optima. Ms., Rutgers University. Also in *Wondering at the Natural Fecundity of Things: Essays in Honor of Alan Prince*; ROA 844, 97–110.

Guillaume, Antoine (2008): *A Grammar of Cavineña*. Mouton de Gruyter, Berlin.

Guseva, Elina & Philipp Weisser (2018): Postsyntactic Reordering in the Mari Nominal Domain. Evidence from Suspended Affixation, *Natural Language & Linguistic Theory* 36(4).

Haider, Hubert (1993): *Deutsche Syntax – generativ*. Narr, Tübingen.

Hale, Ken (1972): A New Perspective on American Indian Linguistics. In: A. Ortiz, ed., *New Perspectives on the Pueblos*. University of New Mexico Press, Albuquerque, pp. 87–103.

Halle, Morris (1973): Prolegomena to a Theory of Word Formation, *Linguistic Inquiry* 4, 3–16.

Halle, Morris (1992): The Latvian Declension. In: G. Booij & J. van Marle, eds., *Yearbook of Morphology 1991*. Kluwer, Dordrecht, pp. 33–47.

Halle, Morris (1994): The Russian Declension: An Illustration of the Theory of Distributed Morphology. In: J. Cole & C. Kisseberth, eds., *Perspectives in Phonology*. CSLI Publications, Stanford, pp. 29–60.

Halle, Morris (1997): Distributed Morphology: Impoverishment and Fission. In: B. Bruening, Y. Kang & M. McGinnis, eds., *Papers at the Interface*. Vol. 30, MITWPL, pp. 425–449.

Halle, Morris & Alec Marantz (1993): Distributed Morphology and the Pieces of Inflection. In: K. Hale & S. J. Keyser, eds., *The View from Building 20*. MIT Press, Cambridge, Mass., pp. 111–176.

Halle, Morris & Alec Marantz (1994): Some Key Features of Distributed Morphology. In: A. Carnie, H. Harley & T. Bures, eds., *Papers on Phonology and Morphology*. Vol. 21 of *MIT Working Papers in Linguistics*, MITWPL, Cambridge, Mass., pp. 275–288.

Halle, Morris & Ora Matushansky (2006): The Morphophonology of Russian Adjectival Inflection, *Linguistic Inquiry* 37(3), 351–404.

Hanink, Emily (2018): Super Light-Headed Relatives, Missing Preposi-
tions, and Span-Conditioned Allomorphy in German, *The Journal of
Comparative Germanic Linguistics* 21, 247–290.

Harbour, Daniel (2003): The Kiowa Case for Feature Insertion, *Natural
Language and Linguistic Theory* 21, 543–578.

Harley, Heidi (2004): The Importance of Impoverishment. Ms., University
of Arizona.

Harley, Heidi (2014): On the Identity of Roots, *Theoretical Linguistics*
40, 225–276.

Harris, Alice (2009): Exuberant Exponence in Batsbi, *Natural Language
and Linguistic Theory* 27, 267–303.

Harris, Zelig (1945): Discontinuous Morphemes, *Language* 21, 121–127.

Hauser, Iva & Coral Hughto (2018): Faithfulness-Based Opacity in Harmonic Serialism. Ms., University of Massachusetts, Amherst.

Heck, Fabian (2016): Non-Monotonic Derivations. Habilitation thesis, Universität Leipzig.

Heck, Fabian (2018): Tucking-In and Crossing Successive-Cyclicity in English. Ms., Universität Leipzig. (Presentation, CGSW 33, Göttingen).

Heck, Fabian & Gereon Müller (2000): Successive Cyclicity, Long-Distance
Superiority, and Local Optimization. In: R. Billerey & B. D. Lillehaugen,
eds., *Proceedings of WCCFL*. Vol. 19, Cascadilla Press, Somerville, MA,
pp. 218–231.

Heck, Fabian & Gereon Müller (2003): Derivational Optimization of Wh-
Movement, *Linguistic Analysis* 33, 97–148.

Heck, Fabian & Gereon Müller (2007): Extremely Local Optimization. In:
E. Brainbridge & B. Agbayani, eds., *Proceedings of the 26th WECOL*.
California State University, Fresno, pp. 170–183.

Heck, Fabian & Gereon Müller (2013): Extremely Local Optimization.
In: H. Broekhuis & R. Vogel, eds., *Linguistic Derivations and Filtering*.
Equinox, Sheffield, pp. 135–166.

Heck, Fabian & Gereon Müller (2016): On Accelerating and Decelarating
Movement: From Minimalist Preference Principles to Harmonic Serialism. In: G. Legendre, M. Putnam, H. de Swart & E. Zaroukian, eds.,
Optimality-Theoretic Syntax, Semantics, and Pragmatics. Oxford University Press, Universität Leipzig, pp. 78–110.

Heck, Fabian, Gereon Müller, Ralf Vogel, Silke Fischer, Sten Vikner &
Tanja Schmid (2002): On the Nature of the Input in Optimality Theory,
The Linguistic Review 19, 345–376.

Hein, Johannes (2008): Verbflexion im Warembori: Eine Analyse im Rahmen der Distribuierten Morphologie. In: F. Heck, G. Müller & J. Trom-

mer, eds., *Varieties of Competition*. Vol. 87 of *Linguistische Arbeits Berichte*, Universität Leipzig, pp. 49–63.

Heinz, Jeffrey (2005): Reconsidering Linearity: Evidence from CV Metathesis. In: J. Alderete, C.-H. Han & A. Kochetov, eds., *Proceedings of the 24th West Coast Conference on Formal Linguistics*. Cascadilla Proceedings Project, Somerville, Mass., pp. 200–208.

Helbig, Gerhard & Joachim Buscha (1981): *Deutsche Grammatik*. 7 edn, VEB Verlag Enzyklopädie Leipzig, Leipzig.

Heycock, Caroline & Anthony Kroch (1994): Verb Movement and Coordination in a Dynamic Theory of Licensing, *The Linguistic Review* 11, 257–283.

Hippisley, Andrew (2007): Declarative Deponency: A Network Morphology Account of Morphological Mismatches. In: M. Baerman, G. Corbett, D. Brown & A. Hippisley, eds., *Deponency and Morphological Mismatches*. Oxford University Press (for The British Academy), Oxford, pp. 145–173.

Hoberg, Ursula (2004): *Grammatik des Deutschen im europäischen Vergleich: Das Genus des Substantivs*. Vol. 3/04 of *Amades*, Institut für Deutsche Sprache, Mannheim.

Holmberg, Anders & Christer Platzack (1995): *The Role of Inflection in the Syntax of the Scandinavian Languages*. Oxford University Press, Oxford.

Hornstein, Norbert (2001): *Move. A Minimalist Theory of Construal*. Blackwell, Oxford.

Hornstein, Norbert (2009): *A Theory of Syntax: Minimal Operations and Universal Grammar*. Cambridge University Press, Cambridge.

Hornstein, Norbert (2014a): Comments on Lecture 2: First Part. Faculty of Language Blog, Thursday, June 19, 2014.

Hornstein, Norbert (2014b): Final Comments on Lecture 4. Faculty of Language Blog, Monday, August 4, 2014.

Hyman, Larry (1994): Cyclic Phonlogy and Morphology in Cibemba. In: J. Cole & C. Kisseberth, eds., *Perspectives in Phonology*. CSLI, Stanford, pp. 81–112.

Hyman, Larry (2002): Cyclicity and Base Non-Identity. In: D. Restle & D. Zaefferer, eds., *Sounds and Systems. Studies in Structure and Change. A Festschrift for Theo Vennemann*. De Gruyter, Berlin, pp. 223–239.

Hyman, Larry (2003): Suffix Ordering in Bantu: A Morphocentric Approach, *Yearbook of Morphology* 2002, 245–281.

Isačenko, Alexander (1975): *Die russische Sprache der Gegenwart*. Max Hueber Verlag, München.

Itô, Junko & Armin Mester (1998): Markedness and Word Structure: OCP Effects in Japanese. Ms., UC Santa Cruz. (ROA 255).

Jakobson, Roman (1962a): Beitrag zur allgemeinen Kasuslehre. Gesamtbedeutungen der russischen Kasus. In: *Selected Writings*. Vol. 2, Mouton, The Hague and Paris, pp. 23–71.

Jakobson, Roman (1962b): Morfologičeskije Nabljudenija. In: *Selected Writings*. Vol. 2, Mouton, The Hague and Paris, pp. 154–181.

Johnson, Kyle (1991): Object Positions, *Natural Language and Linguistic Theory* 9, 577–636.

Julien, Marit (2002): *Syntactic Heads and Word Formation: A Study of Verbal Inflection*. Oxford University Press, Oxford.

Kager, René (1996): On Affix Allomorphy and Syllable Counting. In: U. Kleinhenz, ed., *Interfaces in Phonology*. Akademie Verlag, Berlin, pp. 155–171.

Kager, René (1999): *Optimality Theory*. Cambridge University Press, Cambridge.

Kallulli, Dalina (2013): Non-Canonical Passives and Reflexives. Deponents and Their Like. In: A. Alexiadou & F. Schäfer, eds., *Non-Canonical Passives*. Benjamins, Amsterdam, pp. 337–358.

Kastner, Itamar & Beata Moskal, eds. (2018): *Non-Local Contextual Allomorphy*. Vol. 34 of *Snippets*, Ledonline. Special Issue.

Keine, Stefan (2010a): *Case and Agreement from Fringe to Core. Impoverishment Effects on Agree*. Linguistische Arbeiten, Mouton de Gruyter, Berlin.

Keine, Stefan (2010b): Substitute Infinitives as Non-Substitutes, *Linguistische Berichte* 223, 331–341.

Keine, Stefan (2012): Accessibility and Output-Driven Vocabulary Insertion. Ms., University of Massachusetts (term paper for Ling 606).

Keine, Stefan (2013): Syntagmatic Constraints on Insertion, *Morphology* 23(2), 201–226.

Keine, Stefan & Gereon Müller (2011): Non-Zero/Non-Zero Alternations in Differential Object Marking. In: S. Lima, K. Mullin & B. Smith, eds., *Proceedings of the 39th Meeting of the North East Linguistics Society*. GLSA, Amherst, Mass., pp. 441–454.

Keine, Stefan & Gereon Müller (2014): Differential Argument Encoding by Impoverishment. In: I. Bornkessel-Schlesewsky, A. Malchukov & M. Richards, eds., *Scales and Hierarchies*. Trends in Linguistics, Mouton de Gruyter, Berlin, pp. 75–130.

Keine, Stefan & Gereon Müller (2020): Impoverishment. Ms., Universität Leipzig. To appear in Artemis Alexiadou, Ruth Kramer & Alec Marantz (eds.), *Distributed Morphology*.

Keller, Frank (2001): Gradience in Grammar: Experimental and Computational Aspects of Degrees of Grammaticality. PhD thesis, University of Edinburgh.

Kenstowicz, Michael & Charles Kisseberth (1979): *Generative Phonology.* Academic Press, San Diego.

Kenstowicz, Michael & Jerzy Rubach (1987): The Phonology of Syllabic Nuclei in Slovak, *Language* 63, 463–497.

Khan, Geoffrey (2008): *The Neo-Aramaic Dialect of Barwar. Volume One: Grammar.* Brill, Leiden, Boston.

Kibrik, Aleksandr (1991): Organising Principles for Nominal Paradigms in Daghestan Languages: Comparative and Typological Observations. In: F. Plank, ed., *Paradigms.* Mouton de Gruyter, Berlin, pp. 255–274.

Kibrik, Aleksandr (2003): Nominal Inflection Galore: Daghestanian, with Side Glances at Europe and the World. In: F. Plank, ed., *Noun Phrase Structure in the Languages of Europe.* Mouton de Gruyter, Berlin, pp. 37–112.

Kimper, Wendell (2016): Positive Constraints and Finite Goodness in Harmonic Serialism. In: J. McCarthy & J. Pater, eds., *Harmonic Grammar and Harmonic Serialism.* Equinox, London, pp. 221–235.

Kiparsky, Paul (1973a): Abstractness, Opacity and Global Rules. In: O. Fujimura, ed., *Three Dimensions in Linguistic Theory.* TEC, Tokyo, pp. 57–86.

Kiparsky, Paul (1973b): 'Elsewhere' in Phonology. In: S. Anderson & P. Kiparsky, eds., *A Festschrift for Morris Halle.* Academic Press, New York, pp. 93–106.

Kiparsky, Paul (1982a): From Cyclic Phonology to Lexical Phonology. In: H. van der Hulst & N. Smith, eds., *The Structure of Phonological Representations.* Vol. 1, Foris, Dordrecht, pp. 131–175.

Kiparsky, Paul (1982b): Lexical Morphology and Phonology. In: I.-S. Yang, ed., *Linguistics in the Morning Calm.* Hanshin Publishing Company, Seoul, pp. 3–91.

Kiparsky, Paul (2000): Opacity and Cyclicity, *The Linguistic Review* 17, 351–367.

Kiparsky, Paul (2001): Structural Case in Finnish, *Lingua* 111, 315–376.

Kiparsky, Paul (2005): Blocking and Periphrasis in Inflectional Paradigms. In: G. Booij & J. van Marle, eds., *Yearbook of Morphology 2004.* Springer, Dordrecht, pp. 113–135.

Koopman, Hilda (2006): Agreement Configurations. In: C. Boeckx, ed., *Agreement Systems.* Benjamins, Amsterdam, pp. 159–201.

Korsah, Sampson & Andrew Murphy (2018): Clausal determiners and DP shells in Kwa. Ms., Universität Leipzig. Presentation at *GLOW 41.* Research Institute for Linguistics of the Hungarian Academy of Sciences, Budapest, 11th–13th April 2018.

Kouneli, Maria (2019): The Syntax of Number and Modification: An Investigation of the Kipsigis DP. PhD thesis, New York University, New York.

Kress, Bruno (1982): *Isländische Grammatik.* 1 edn, VEB Verlag Enzyklopädie, Leipzig.

Kushnir, Yuriy (2018): Prosodic Patterns in Lithuanian Morphology. PhD thesis, Universität Leipzig.

Lahne, Antje (2008): Excluding SVO in Ergative Languages. In: F. Heck, G. Müller & J. Trommer, eds., *Varieties of Competition.* Vol. 87 of *Linguistische Arbeits Berichte*, Universität Leipzig, pp. 65–80.

Lahne, Antje (2009a): A Multiple Specifier Approach to Left Peripheral Architecture, *Linguistic Analysis* 35, 73–108.

Lahne, Antje (2009b): Where There is Fire There is Smoke. Local Modelling of Successive-Cyclic Movement. PhD thesis, Universität Leipzig.

Lechner, Winfried (2010): Criteria for Diagnosing Movement (And Some Remarks on the Duke of York). Ms., University of Athens.

Legendre, Géraldine (2009): The Neutralization Approach to Ineffability in Syntax. In: C. Rice & S. Blaho, eds., *Modeling Ungrammaticality in Optimality Theory.* Advances in Optimality Theory, Equinox Publishing, London.

Legendre, Géraldine, Colin Wilson, Paul Smolensky, Kristin Homer & William Raymond (2006): Optimality in Syntax II: Wh-Questions. In: P. Smolensky & G. Legendre, eds., *The Harmonic Mind.* Vol. II, MIT Press, Cambridge, Mass., chapter 14, pp. 183–230.

Legendre, Géraldine, Paul Smolensky & Colin Wilson (1998): When is Less More? Faithfulness and Minimal Links in Wh-Chains. In: P. Barbosa, D. Fox, P. Hagstrom, M. McGinnis & D. Pesetsky, eds., *Is the Best Good Enough?.* MIT Press and MITWPL, Cambridge, Mass., pp. 249–289.

Lehmann, Thomas (1989): *A Grammar of Modern Tamil.* Pondicherry Institute of Linguistics and Culture, Pondicherry.

Lieber, Rochelle (1992): *Deconstructing Morphology.* University of Chicago Press, Chicago.

Łubowicz, Anna (2005): Locality of Conjunction. In: J. A. et al., ed., *Proceedings of the 24th West Coast Conference on Formal Linguistics.* Cascadilla Press, Somerville, Mass., pp. 254–262.

Lumsden, John (1992): Underspecification in Grammatical and Natural Gender, *Linguistic Inquiry* 23, 469–486.

Marantz, Alec (1991): Case and Licensing. In: German Westphal, B. Ao & H.-R. Chae, eds., *Proceedings of the Eighth Eastern States Conference on Linguistics*. University of Maryland, pp. 234–253.

Marantz, Alec (1998): No Escape from Syntax: Don't Try Morphological Analysis in the Privacy of Your Own Lexicon. In: A. Dimitriadis, ed., *Proceedings of Penn Linguistics Colloquium 28*. PLC, University of Pennsylvania, Philadelphia.

Marlett, Stephen (1986): Syntactic Levels and Multiattachment in Sierra Popoluca, *International Journal of American Linguistics* 52, 359–387.

Marquardt, Christine (2018): Opacity in Mojeño Trinitario Reduplication: A Harmonic Serialism Account. Ms., Universität Leipzig. (Talk, GLOW 41, Budapest).

Mascaró, Joan (1996): External Allomorphy as Emergence of the Unmarked. In: J. Durand & B. Laks, eds., *Current Trends in Phonology: Models and Methods*. European Studies Research Institute, University of Salford, Salford, Manchester, pp. 473–483.

Matthews, Peter (1972): *Inflectional Morphology: A Theoretical Study Based on Aspects of Latin Verb Conjugation*. Cambridge University Press, Cambridge.

Matthews, Peter (1974): *Morphology*. Cambridge University Press, Cambridge.

Matthews, Peter (1991): *Morphology*. Cambridge University Press, Cambridge.

McCarthy, John (1999): Sympathy and Phonological Opacity, *Phonology* 16:3, 331–399.

McCarthy, John (2000): Harmonic Serialism and Parallelism. In: M. Hirotani, A. Coetzee, N. Hall & J.-Y. Kim, eds., *Proceedings of NELS 30*. GLSA, Amherst, Mass., pp. 501–524.

McCarthy, John (2002): *A Thematic Guide to Optimality Theory*. Cambridge University Press, Cambridge.

McCarthy, John (2003): Sympathy, Cumulativity, and the Duke-of-York Gambit. In: C. Féry & R. van de Vijver, eds., *The Syllable in Optimality Theory*. Cambridge University Press, pp. 23–76.

McCarthy, John (2007): *Hidden Generalizations. Phonological Opacity in Optimality Theory*. Equinox, London.

McCarthy, John (2008): The Serial Interaction of Stress and Syncope, *Natural Language and Linguistic Theory* 26, 499–546.

McCarthy, John (2010): An Introduction to Harmonic Serialism, *Language and Linguistics Compass* 4, 1001–1018.

McCarthy, John (2016): The Theory and Practice of Harmonic Serialism. In: J. McCarthy & J. Pater, eds., *Harmonic Grammar and Harmonic Serialism*. Equinox, Sheffield, pp. 47–87.

McCarthy, John & Alan Prince (1995): Faithfulness and Reduplicative Identity. Ms., University of Massachusetts, Amherst and Rutgers University.

McCarthy, John, Wendell Kimper & Kevin Mullin (2012): Reduplication in Harmonic Serialism, *Morphology* 22, 173–232.

McCloskey, James (1979): *Transformational Syntax and Model Theoretic Semantics. A Case Study in Modern Irish*. Reidel, Dordrecht.

McFadden, Thomas (2004): The Position of Morphological Case in the Derivation: A Study on the Syntax-Morphology Interface. PhD thesis, University of Pennsylvania.

McFadden, Thomas (2018): *ABA in Stem-Allomorphy and the Emptiness of the Nominative, *Glossa* 3(1)(8).

Meibauer, Jörg (2002): Lexikon und Morphologie. In: J. Meibauer, U. Demske, J. Geilfuß-Wolfgang, J. Pafel, K. H. Ramers, M. Rothweiler & M. Steinbach, eds., *Einführung in die germanistische Linguistik*. Metzler, Stuttgart, pp. 15–69.

Mel'čuk, Igor (1999): Zero Sign in Morphology. In: *Proceedings of the 4th Int. Tbilissi Symposium on Language, Logic, and Computation*. Batumi.

Merchant, Jason (2015): How Much Context is Enough? Two Cases of Span-Conditioned Allomorphy, *Linguistic Inquiry* 46, 273–303.

Merlan, Francesca (1994): *A Grammar of Wardaman. A Language of the Northern Territory of Australia*. Mouton de Gruyter, Berlin.

Mithun, Marianne (1999): *The Languages of Native North America*. Cambridge University Press, Cambridge.

Moskal, Beata (2015): Domains on the Border: Between Morphology and Phonology. PhD thesis, University of Connecticut, Storrs, Connecticut.

Moskal, Beata & Peter Smith (2016): Towards a Theory Without Adjacency: Hyper-Contextual VI-Rules, *Morphology* 26, 295–312.

Müller, Gereon (2000a): *Elemente der optimalitätstheoretischen Syntax*. Stauffenburg, Tübingen.

Müller, Gereon (2000b): Shape Conservation and Remnant Movement. In: M. Hirotani, A. Coetzee, N. Hall & J.-Y. Kim, eds., *Proceedings of NELS 30*. GLSA, Amherst, Mass., pp. 525–539.

Müller, Gereon (2002): Remarks on Nominal Inflection in German. In: I. Kaufmann & B. Stiebels, eds., *More than Words: A Festschrift for Dieter Wunderlich*. Akademie Verlag, Berlin, pp. 113–145.

Müller, Gereon (2004): On Decomposing Inflection Class Features: Syncretism in Russian Noun Inflection. In: G. Müller, L. Gunkel & G. Zifonun, eds., *Explorations in Nominal Inflection*. Mouton de Gruyter, Berlin, pp. 189–227.

Müller, Gereon (2005): Syncretism and Iconicity in Icelandic Noun Declensions: A Distributed Morphology Approach. In: G. Booij & J. van Marle, eds., *Yearbook of Morphology 2004*. Springer, Dordrecht, pp. 229–271.

Müller, Gereon (2006a): Pro-Drop and Impoverishment. In: P. Brandt & E. Fuß, eds., *Form, Structure, and Grammar. A Festschrift Presented to Günther Grewendorf on Occasion of his 60th Birthday*. Akademie Verlag, Berlin, pp. 93–115.

Müller, Gereon (2006b): Subanalyse verbaler Flexionsmarker. In: E. Breindl, L. Gunkel & B. Strecker, eds., *Grammatische Untersuchungen*. Narr, Tübingen, pp. 183–203.

Müller, Gereon (2007a): Extended Exponence by Enrichment. Argument Encoding in German, Archi, and Timucua. In: T. Scheffler, J. Tauberer, A. Eilam & L. Mayol, eds., *Proceedings of the 30th Annual Penn Linguistics Colloquium*. Vol. 13.1 of *Penn Working Papers in Linguistics*, University of Pennsylvania, Philadelphia, pp. 253–266.

Müller, Gereon (2007b): Notes on Paradigm Economy, *Morphology* 17, 1–38.

Müller, Gereon (2008): Some Consequences of an Impoverishment-Based Approach to Morphological Richness and Pro-Drop. In: J. Witkoś & G. Fanselow, eds., *Elements of Slavic and Germanic Grammars: A Comparative View*. Vol. 23 of *Polish Studies in English Language and Linguistics*, Lang, Frankfurt, pp. 125–145.

Müller, Gereon (2011a): *Constraints on Displacement. A Phase-Based Approach*. Vol. 7 of *Language Faculty and Beyond*, Benjamins, Amsterdam.

Müller, Gereon (2011b): Syncretism without Underspecification in Optimality Theory: The Role of Leading Forms, *Word Structure* 4(1), 53–103.

Müller, Gereon (2013a): Approaches to Deponency, *Language and Linguistics Compass* 8(6).

Müller, Gereon (2013b): On the Order of Syntactic Operations. Ms., Universität Leipzig. (Lecture Notes for a Compact Course, University of Cambridge).

Müller, Gereon (2013c): A Radically Non-Morphemic Approach to Bidirectional Syncretism, *Morphology* 23(2), 245–268.

Müller, Gereon (2014): *Syntactic Buffers*. Vol. 91, Linguistische Arbeits Berichte, Universität Leipzig.

Müller, Gereon (2015): Optimality-Theoretic Syntax. In: T. Kiss & A. Alexiadou, eds., *Syntax. An International Handbook*. Vol. 2, De Gruyter, Berlin, pp. 875–936.

Müller, Gereon (2016): The Short Life Cycle of External Arguments in German Passive Derivations. Ms., Universität Leipzig.

Müller, Gereon (2017): Structure Removal: An Argument for Feature-Driven Merge, *Glossa* 2(1). http://doi.org/10.5334/gjgl.193.

Müller, Gereon (2018a): Pseudo-Incorporation by Structure Removal. Ms., Universität Leipzig. (Talk, CGSW 33).

Müller, Gereon (2018b): Structure Removal in Complex Prefields, *Natural Language and Linguistic Theory* 36, 219–264.

Müller, Gereon (2020): Cumulative Effects in Differential Argument Encoding and Long-Distance Extraction: Local Conjunction vs. Harmonic Grammar. In: A. Bárány & L. Kalin, eds., *Case, Agreement, and Their Interactions. New Perspectives on Differential Argument Marking*. De Gruyter, Berlin.

Müller, Gereon & Daniela Thomas (2017): Three-Way Systems Do Not Exist. In: J. Coon, L. Travis & D. Massam, eds., *The Oxford Handbook of Ergativity*. Oxford University Press, Oxford, pp. 279–307.

Müller, Gereon & Wolfgang Sternefeld (2001): The Rise of Competition in Syntax: A Synopsis. In: G. Müller & W. Sternefeld, eds., *Competition in Syntax*. Mouton de Gruyter, Berlin, pp. 1–68.

Murasugi, Kumiko (1992): Crossing and Nested Paths. PhD thesis, MIT, Cambridge, Mass.

Murphy, Andrew (2017): Cumulativity in Syntactic Derivations. PhD thesis, Universität Leipzig.

Murphy, Andrew (2018): Dative Intervention is a Gang Effect, *The Linguistic Review* 35, 519–574.

Murphy, Andrew (2019): Resolving Conflicts with Violable Constraints: On the Cross-Modular Parallelism of Repairs, *Glossa* 4(1), 9. 1–39.

Murphy, Andrew & Gereon Müller (2016): The Short Life Cycle of Elided Elements: Ellipsis as Syntactic Structure Removal. Ms., Universität Leipzig. (Poster, workshop *Ellipsis Across Borders*, Sarajevo 2016).

Myler, Neil (2013): Linearization and Post-Syntactic Operations in the Quechua DP. In: T. Bieberauer & I. Roberts, eds., *Challenges to Linearization*. Mouton de Gruyter, Berlin, pp. 171–210.

Neidle, Carol (1988): *The Role of Case in Russian Syntax*. Kluwer, Dordrecht.

Nesset, Tore (1994): A Feature-Based Approach to Russian Noun Inflection, *Journal of Slavic Linguistics* 2, 214–237.

Nevins, Andrew (2007): The Representation of Third Person and Its Consequences for Person-Case Effects, *Natural Language and Linguistic Theory* 25, 273–313.

Nevins, Andrew (2014): Book review: *Defective Paradigms: Missing Forms and What They Tell Us*, *Revista Linguística / Revista do Programa de Pós-Graduação em Linguística da Universidade Federal do Rio de Janeiro* 10, 29–36.

Nikolaeva, Irina & Maria Tolskaya (2001): *A Grammar of Udihe*. Mouton de Gruyter, Berlin.

Nissenbaum, Jon (2000): Investigations of Covert Phrase Movement. PhD thesis, MIT, Cambridge, Mass.

Noyer, Rolf (1992): Features, Positions, and Affixes in Autonomous Morphological Structure. PhD thesis, MIT, Cambridge, Mass.

Noyer, Rolf (1998): Impoverishment Theory and Morphosyntactic Markedness. In: S. Lapointe, D. Brentari & P. Farrell, eds., *Morphology and its Relation to Phonology and Syntax*. CSLI, Palo Alto, pp. 264–285.

Oltra Massuet, Isabel (1999): On the Notion of Theme Vowel: A New Approach to Catalan Verbal Morphology. Master of science thesis, MIT, Cambridge, Mass.

Oostendorp, Marc van (2006): A Theory of Morphosyntactic Colours. Ms., Meertens Institute, Amsterdam.

Oostendorp, Marc van (2007): Derived Environment Effects and Consistency of Exponence. In: S. Blaho, P. Bye & M. Krämer, eds., *Freedom of Analysis?*. Mouton de Gruyter, Berlin, pp. 123–148.

Opitz, Andreas (2008): Case and Markedness in Tlapanec, *Linguistische Berichte* 214, 211–237.

Opitz, Andreas, Stefanie Regel, Gereon Müller & Angela D. Friederici (2013): Neurophysiological Evidence for Morphological Underspecification in German Strong Adjective Inflection, *Language* 89(2), 231–264.

Ortmann, Albert (2002): Economy-Based Splits, Constraints and Lexical Representations. In: I. Kaufmann & B. Stiebels, eds., *More than Words: A Festschrift for Dieter Wunderlich*. Akademie Verlag, Berlin, pp. 147–177.

Ortmann, Albert (2004): A Factorial Typology of Number Marking. In: G. Müller, L. Gunkel & G. Zifonun, eds., *Explorations in Nominal Inflection*. Mouton de Gruyter, Berlin, pp. 229–267.

Paster, Mary (2015): Phonologically Conditioned Suppletive Allomorphy: Cross-Linguistic Results and Theoretical Consequences. *In* Bonet et al. (2015b), pp. 218–253.

Pertsova, Katya (2016): Transderivational Relations and Paradigm Gaps in Russian Verbs, *Glossa* 13, 1–34.

Pesetsky, David (1998): Some Optimality Principles of Sentence Pronunciation. In: P. Barbosa, D. Fox, P. Hagstrom, M. McGinnis & D. Pesetsky, eds., *Is the Best Good Enough?*. MIT Press and MITWPL, Cambridge, Mass., pp. 337–383.

Pesetsky, David (2016): Exfoliation: Towards a Derivational Theory of Clause Size. Ms., MIT, Cambridge, Mass.

Pietraszko, Asia (2017): Clause Size and Transparency in Ndebele. Ms., University of Chicago. (LSA presentation).

Pinker, Steven (1999): *Words and Rules. The Ingredients of Language.* Basic Books, New York.

Plank, Frans (1999): Split Morphology: How Aggluatination and Flexion Mix, *Linguistic Typology* 3.

Platzack, Christer (1987): The Scandinavian Languages and the Null Subject Parameter, *Natural Language and Linguistic Theory* 5, 377–402.

Popp, Marie-Luise & Sören Tebay (2019): No Possessor Inversion in German PPs, *Glossa* 4(1)(16).

Preminger, Omer (2014): *Agreement and Its Failures.* MIT Press, Cambridge, Mass.

Prince, Alan & Paul Smolensky (1993): Optimality Theory. Constraint Interaction in Generative Grammar. Book ms., Rutgers University.

Prince, Alan & Paul Smolensky (2004): *Optimality Theory. Constraint Interaction in Generative Grammar.* Blackwell, Oxford.

Pruitt, Kathryn (2012): Stress in Harmonic Serialism. PhD thesis, University of Massachusetts, Amherst.

Pullum, Geoffrey (1976): The Duke of York Gambit, *Journal of Linguistics* 12, 83–102.

Puškar, Zorica (2016): Nominal Expressions in Languages Without Articles: Towards Resolving the NP/DP Debate by Structure Removal. Ms., Universität Leipzig.

Pyatigorskaya, Elena (2015): Subjektkongruenz im Udiheischen. Ms., Universität Leipzig.

Rasin, Ezer (2018): Stress and Vowel Length in Palestinian Arabic: Preliminary Notes. Ms., Universität Leipzig.

Ray, Sidney (1931): *A Grammar of the Kiwai Language, Fly Delta, Papua.* Edward George Baker, Government Printer, Port Moresby.

Regel, Stefanie, Andreas Opitz, Gereon Müller & Angela D. Friederici (2015): The Past Tense Debate Revisited: Electrophysiological Evidence for Subregularities of Irregular Verb Inflection, *Journal of Cognitive Neuroscience* 27(9), 1870–1885.

Regel, Stefanie, Andreas Opitz, Gereon Müller & Angela D. Friederici (2019): Processing Inflectional Morphology: ERP Evidence for Decomposition of Complex Words according to the Affix Structure, *Cortex* 116, 143–153.

Rice, Curt & Sylvia Blaho, eds. (2009): *Modeling Ungrammaticality in Optimality Theory*. Equinox Publishing, London.

Richards, Norvin (2001): *Movement in Language*. Oxford University Press, Oxford.

Riemsdijk, Henk van & Edwin Williams (1981): NP-Structure, *The Linguistic Review* 1, 171–217.

Rizzi, Luigi (1990): *Relativized Minimality*. MIT Press, Cambridge, Mass.

Ross, John (1967): Constraints on Variables in Syntax. PhD thesis, MIT, Cambridge, Mass.

Ryan, Kevin (2010): Variable Affix Order: Grammar and Learning, *Language* 86, 758–791.

Samek-Lodovici, Vieri (2013): Optimality Theory and the Minimalist Program. In: H. Broekhuis & R. Vogel, eds., *Linguistic Derivations and Filtering*. Equinox, Sheffield.

Sarma, Vaijayanthi (2003): Non-Canonical Word Order: Topic and Focus in Adult and Child Tamil. In: S. Karimi, ed., *Word Order and Scrambling*. Blackwell, Oxford, pp. 238–272.

Schiffman, Harold (1999): *A Reference Grammar of Spoken Tamil*. Cambridge University Press, Cambridge.

Schwarzer, Marie-Luise (2016): Tough: Easy. Master's thesis, Universität Leipzig.

Silverstein, Michael (1976): Hierarchy of Features and Ergativity. In: R. Dixon, ed., *Grammatical Categories in Australian Languages*. Australian Institute of Aboriginal Studies, Canberra, pp. 112–171.

Sims, Andrea (2006): Minding the Gaps: Inflectional Defectiveness in a Paradigmatic Theory. PhD thesis, Ohio State University.

Smolensky, Paul (1995): On the Internal Structure of Con, the Constraint Component of UG. Ms., Johns Hopkins University.

Smolensky, Paul (2006): Harmonic Completeness, Local Constraint Conjunction, and Feature Domain Markedness. In: P. Smolensky & G. Legendre, eds., *The Harmonic Mind*. Vol. II, MIT Press, Cambridge, Mass., chapter 14, pp. 27–160.

Smolensky, Paul & Matthew Goldrick (2016): Gradient Symbolic Representations in Grammar: The Case of French Liaison. ROA 1286.

Stabler, Edward (2013): Two Models of Minimalist, Incremental Syntactic Analysis, *Topics in Cognitive Science* 5, 611–633.

Starke, Michal (2001): Move Dissolves Into Merge: A Theory of Locality. PhD thesis, University of Geneva.

Stechow, Arnim von & Wolfgang Sternefeld (1988): *Bausteine syntaktischen Wissens*. Westdeutscher Verlag, Opladen.

Steddy, Sam & Vieri Samek-Lodovici (2011): On the Ungrammaticality of Remnant Movement in the Derivation of Greenberg's Universal 20, *Linguistic Inquiry* 42, 445–469.

Stepanov, Artur (2012): Voiding Island Effects via Head Movement, *Linguistic Inquiry* 43, 680–693.

Steriade, Donca (2008): A Pseudo-Cyclic Effect in Romanian Morphophonology. In: A. Bachrach & A. Nevins, eds., *Inflectional Identity*. Oxford University Press, Oxford, pp. 313–360.

Sternefeld, Wolfgang (1991): Chain Formation, Reanalysis, and the Economy of Levels. In: H. Haider & K. Netter, eds., *Derivation and Representation in the Theory of Grammar*. Kluwer, Dordrecht, pp. 75–143.

Stiebels, Barbara (1996): *Lexikalische Argumente und Adjunkte: zum semantischen Beitrag von verbalen Präfixen und Partikeln*. Akademieverlag, Berlin.

Stiebels, Barbara (2000): Linker Inventories, Linking Splits and Lexical Economy. In: B. Stiebels & D. Wunderlich, eds., *Lexicon in Focus*. Akademie-Verlag, Berlin, pp. 211–245.

Stiebels, Barbara (2002): *Typologie des Argumentlinkings: Ökonomie und Expressivität*. Akademie Verlag, Berlin.

Stiebels, Barbara (2006): Agent Focus in Mayan Languages, *Natural Language and Linguistic Theory* 24, 501–570.

Stiebels, Barbara (2015): Multiple Exponence: Typology, Triggering Factors, and Theoretical Modelling. Ms., Universität Leipzig.

Stojković, Jelena (2019): Exfoliation, Generalized Lowering and the Structure of DP (LBE in Bulgarian and Macedonian). Ms., Universität Leipzig.

Stump, Gregory (2001): *Inflectional Morphology*. Cambridge University Press, Cambridge.

Stump, Gregory (2006): Heteroclisis and Paradigm Linkage, *Language* 82, 279–322.

Stump, Gregory (2007): A Non-Canonical Pattern of Deponency and Its Implications. In: M. Baerman, G. Corbett, D. Brown & A. Hippisley, eds., *Deponency and Morphological Mismatches*. Oxford University Press (for The British Academy), Oxford, pp. 71–95.

Stump, Gregory (2016): *Inflectional Paradigms: Content and Form at the Syntax-Morphology Interface*. Cambridge University Press, Cambridge.

Svenonius, Peter (2016): Spans and Words. In: H. Harley & D. Siddiqi, eds., *Morphological Metatheory*. Benjamins, Amsterdam, pp. 199–220.

Torres-Tamarit, Francesc (2016): Compensatory and Opaque Vowel Lengthening in Harmonic Serialism. In: *Harmonic Grammar and Harmonic Serialism*. Equinox, Sheffield.

Trommer, Jochen (1999): Morphology Consuming Syntax' Resources. In: *Proceedings of the ESSLI Workshop on Resource Logics and Minimalist Grammars*. University of Nijmegen, pp. 37–55.

Trommer, Jochen (2001): Distributed Optimality. PhD thesis, Universität Potsdam.

Trommer, Jochen (2003): Participant Reduction and Two-Level Markedness. In: J. Spenader, A. Eriksson & Ö. Dahl, eds., *Variation within Optimality Theory. Proceedings of the Stockholm Workshop*. Stockholm University, Department of Linguistics, pp. 102–108.

Trommer, Jochen (2005): Markiertheit und Verarmung. Ms., Universität Leipzig. Presented at the Honorary Doctorate Colloquium for Manfred Bierwisch, Leipzig 2005.

Trommer, Jochen (2006a): Person and Number Agreement in Dumi, *Linguistics* 44, 1011–1057.

Trommer, Jochen (2006b): Plural Insertion is Constructed Plural. In: G. Müller & J. Trommer, eds., *Subanalysis of Argument Encoding in Distributed Morphology*. Vol. 84 of *Linguistische Arbeits Berichte*, Universität Leipzig, pp. 197–228.

Trommer, Jochen (2006c): Third-Person Marking in Menominee. Ms., Universität Leipzig.

Trommer, Jochen (2008a): Coherence in Affix Order, *Zeitschrift für Sprachwissenschaft* 27(1).

Trommer, Jochen (2008b): A Feature-Geometric Approach to Amharic Verb Classes. In: A. Bachrach & A. Nevins, eds., *The Bases of Inflectional Identity*. Oxford University Press, Oxford, pp. 206–236.

Trommer, Jochen (2011): Phonological Aspects of Western Nilotic Mutation Morphology. Habilitation thesis, Universität Leipzig.

Trommer, Jochen (2015a): Moraic Affixes and Morphological Colors in Dinka, *Linguistic Inquiry* 46, 77–112.

Trommer, Jochen (2015b): Syllable-Counting Allomorphy by Prosodic Templates. *In* Bonet et al. (2015b), pp. 315–360.

Urk, Coppe van (2015): A Uniform Syntax for Phrasal Movement: A Dinka Bor Case Study. PhD thesis, MIT, Cambridge, Mass.

Vogel, Ralf (2009): Wh-Islands: A View from Correspondence Theory. In: C. Rice & S. Blaho, eds., *Modeling Ungrammaticality in Optimality Theory*. Advances in Optimality Theory, Equinox Publishing, London.

Wasow, Tom (1972): Anaphoric Relations in English. PhD thesis, MIT, Cambridge, Mass.

Wegener, Heide (1999): Die Pluralbildung im Deutschen – ein Versuch im Rahmen der Optimalitätstheorie, *Linguistik Online* 4. (www.linguistik-online.de/3_99).

Weisser, Philipp (2014): Mismatch Verbs: A Unified Account of Unaccusatives and Deponents. In: F. Rainer, F. Gardani, H.-C. Luschützky & W. Dressler, eds., *Morphology and Meaning.* Benjamins, Amsterdam, pp. 315–330.

Weisser, Philipp (2015): *Derived Coordination. A Minimalist Perspective on Clause Chains, Converbs, and Asymmetric Coordination.* De Gruyter, Berlin.

Weisser, Philipp (2017a): Allomorphy Tracks Selection. Ms., Universität Leipzig.

Weisser, Philipp (2017b): Morphology III: Harmonc Serialism. Ms., Universität Leipzig. (Lectures Notes, IGRA 02).

Wiese, Bernd (1999): Unterspezifizierte Paradigmen. Form und Funktion in der pronominalen Deklination, *Linguistik Online* 4. (www.linguistik-online.de/3_99).

Wiese, Bernd (2000): Warum Flexionsklassen? Über die deutsche Substantivdeklination. In: R. Thieroff, M. Tamrat, N. Fuhrhop & O. Teuber, eds., *Deutsche Grammatik in Theorie und Praxis.* Niemeyer, Tübingen, pp. 139–153.

Wiese, Bernd (2005): Unterspezifizierte Stammparadigmen: Zur Systematik des Verbalablauts im Gegenwartsdeutschen. Ms., IDS Mannheim. www.ids-mannheim.de/gra/personal/wiese.html.

Wiese, Bernd (2008): Form and Function of Verbal Ablaut in Contemporary Standard German. In: R. Sackmann, ed., *Explorations in Integrational Linguistics.* Benjamins, Amsterdam, pp. 97–151.

Wiese, Richard (1996): *The Phonology of German.* Clarendon Press, Oxford.

Williams, Edwin (1981): Argument Structure and Morphology, *The Linguistic Review* 1, 81–114.

Williams, Edwin (1994): Remarks on Lexical Knowledge, *Lingua* 92, 7–34.

Williams, Edwin (1997): Blocking and Anaphora, *Linguistic Inquiry* 28, 577–628.

Williams, Edwin (2003): *Representation Theory.* MIT Press, Cambridge, Mass.

Witkoś, Jacek (2013): Parametrizing Subject and Object Control. Talk, Cambridge Comparative Syntax Conference 2.

Wolf, Matthew (2008): Optimal Interleaving. PhD thesis, University of Massachusetts, Amherst.

Wunderlich, Dieter (1996): Minimalist Morphology: The Role of Paradigms. In: G. Booij & J. van Marle, eds., *Yearbook of Morphology 1995.* Kluwer, Dordrecht, pp. 93–114.

Wunderlich, Dieter (1997a): Cause and the Structure of Verbs, *Linguistic Inquiry* 27, 27–68.

Wunderlich, Dieter (1997b): Der unterspezifizierte Artikel. In: C. Dürscheid, K. H. Ramers & M. Schwarz, eds., *Sprache im Fokus*. Niemeyer, Tübingen, pp. 47–55.

Wunderlich, Dieter (1997c): A Minimalist Model of Inflectional Morphology. In: C. Wilder, H.-M. Gärtner & M. Bierwisch, eds., *The Role of Economy Principles in Linguistic Theory*. Akademie Verlag, Berlin, pp. 267–298.

Wunderlich, Dieter (1999): German Noun Plural Reconsidered. Ms., Universität Düsseldorf.

Wunderlich, Dieter (2001a): A Correspondence-Theoretic Analysis of Dalabon Transitive Paradigms. In: G. Booij & J. van Marle, eds., *Yearbook of Morphology 2000*. Kluwer, Dordrecht, pp. 233–252.

Wunderlich, Dieter (2001b): How Gaps and Substitutions Can Become Optimal, *Transactions of the Philological Society* 99, 315–366.

Wunderlich, Dieter (2004): Is There Any Need for the Concept of Directional Syncretism?. In: G. Müller, L. Gunkel & G. Zifonun, eds., *Explorations in Nominal Inflection*. Mouton de Gruyter, Berlin, pp. 373–395.

Wurm, Stephen Adolphe (1975): The Trans-Fly (Sub-Phylum Level) Stock. In: S. Wurm, ed., *New Guinea Area Languages and Language Study, Vol. 1. Papuan Languages and the New Guinea Linguistic Scene*. Australian National University, Canberra, pp. 323–344.

Wurzel, Wolfgang Ullrich (1998): Drei Ebenen der Struktur von Flexionsparadigmen. In: R. Fabri, A. Ortmann & T. Parodi, eds., *Models of Inflection*. Niemeyer, Tübingen.

Xu, Zheng (2007): Inflectional Morphology in Optimality Theory. PhD thesis, Stony Brook University.

Xu, Zheng (2011): Optimality Theory and Morphology, *Language and Linguistics Compass* 5, 466–484.

Xu, Zheng & Mark Aronoff (2008): A Realization OT Approach to Blocking and Extended Morphological Exponence. Ms., SUNY, Stony Brook.

Xu, Zheng, Mark Aronoff & Frank Anshen (2007): Deponency in Latin. In: M. Baerman, G. Corbett, D. Brown & A. Hippisley, eds., *Deponency and Morphological Mismatches*. Oxford University Press (for The British Academy), Oxford, pp. 127–143.

Zifonun, Gisela, Ludger Hoffmann, Bruno Strecker et al. (1997): *Grammatik der deutschen Sprache*. de Gruyter, Berlin.

Zimmermann, Eva (2017a): *Morphological Length and Prosodically Defective Morphemes*. Oxford University Press, Oxford.

Zimmermann, Eva (2017b): Phonology III: Harmonic Serialism. Course Notes, Universität Leipzig.

Zombolou, Katerina & Artemis Alexiadou (2014): The Canonical Function of the Deponent Verbs in Modern Greek. In: F. Rainer, F. Gardani, H. Luschützky & W. Wurzel, eds., *Morphology and Meaning. Selected Papers from the 15th International Morphology Meeting, Vienna 2012.* Benjamins, Amsterdam, pp. 331–344.

Index

CPSIA information can be obtained
at www.ICGtesting.com
Printed in the USA
BVHW091955211220
596170BV00007B/58